D0305614

Sn∟

652 4

b

Eighteenth-Century Europe

THE NORTON HISTORY OF MODERN EUROPE

Eighteenth-Century Europe
Tradition and Progress
1715-1789

ISSER WOLOCH
Columbia University

W·W·NORTON & COMPANY
NEW YORK · LONDON

For Alex

Published simultaneously in Canada
by George J. McLeod Limited, Toronto.

Printed in the United States of America

All rights Reserved

FIRST EDITION

Library of Congress Cataloging in Publication Data

Woloch, Isser, 1937–
  Eighteenth-century Europe, tradition and
progress, 1715–1789.

  (Norton history of modern Europe)
  Includes index.
  1. Europe—Civilization—18th century. I. Title.
II. Series.
CB411.W64   1982   940.2′53   81–11226
ISBN 0-393-01506-8
ISBN 0-393-95214-2 pa.

W.W. Norton & Company, Inc. 500 Fifth Avenue, New York,
N.Y. 10110
W.W. Norton & Company Ltd. 37 Great Russell Street, London
W C 1 3NU

1 2 3 4 5 6 7 8 9 0

Contents

Illustrations

Maps and Charts

Acknowledgements

A BOOK of this kind depends heavily on other people's research. These debts are implicitly acknowledged in the Suggestions for Further Reading at the end, as well as by occasional citations in the text. Extremely useful comments were made on an earlier draft by several readers whose anonymity it is a convention to maintain and who have my deepest appreciation. Colleagues at Columbia likewise offered suggestions, and it is a pleasure to thank Marc Raeff, Sheila Biddle, and Peter Winn for giving generously of their time. I have also profited over the years from my participation in the university's faculty seminar on eighteenth-century European culture.

Donald Lamm of W. W. Norton was not only instrumental in getting this book started, but has been an editor whose unremitting interest and tangible contributions far exceed ordinary bounds. In this he has been ably seconded by Jennifer Sutherland at Norton and by my wife Nancy Spelman Woloch, who is an obliging and incisive critic in matters of style and clarity. For facilitating the preparation of the manuscript I wish to thank Miriam Levy and Eric Rustad as well as the Dunning Fund of the Columbia History Department.

July 1980   I.W.

Introduction

UNTIL RECENTLY, in a simpler historiographical universe, political and intellectual themes dominated our conceptualization of the eighteenth century. For one thing, its historical cohesiveness has always seemed most tangible on a political plane. The formal dates that define the period, 1715 to 1789, are political (as such dates usually are), marking great wars, peace treaties, or changes in regime: 1713–1715 brought the Peace of Utrecht and Louis XIV's demise, while 1789 saw the beginning of the French Revolution. The coherence of the eighteenth century politically is matched by its well-defined place in Europe's intellectual and cultural history as the Age of the Enlightenment. In the study of thought, literature, and the arts, the eighteenth century—like the ensuing Age of Romanticism—is a major area of disciplinary specialization in university literature and arts departments, and of interdisciplinary discussion in such forums as the Society for Eighteenth-Century Studies. The impact of this humanistic scholarship could not help but contribute to the historian's vision of the period's character.

With the relentless advance of contemporary scholarship, however, the texture of European history has taken on an increasingly complex appearance. Changes in the focus and methods of historical research have brought a shift of emphasis from the political history of states to the social history of local groups or regions; from the history of formal thought to the history of attitudes; from narrative history punctuated by dramatic episodes to analytic history without heroes. Population patterns, rural communities, the family economy of the poor, the circulation of books, the artifacts of popular culture, the social history of military and religious institutions—these and other topics must now take their place alongside the classic core of historical discussion. Cumulatively, they oblige us to broaden our view of the subject as a whole.

Recent scholarship has not merely multiplied the number of compelling topics and increased the complexity of regional variation within European history. It has also suggested that a major chronological dividing line is concealed within the confines of the eighteenth century. Particularly, but not exclusively, in England and France, it appears that demographic, economic, and even social patterns began to change significantly sometime around mid-century, initiating a period of transition toward modernity. Here, then, is a real problem. Taken from several points of view, the eighteenth century remains a cohesive period, the last phase of Europe's old order. Its boundary can be reasonably situated at 1789 when the political and social orders of France were dramatically ruptured with profound consequences for Europe's consciousness and history. But this same Europe of the eighteenth century was already generating certain changes well before 1789 that would gradually coalesce into a full-scale transition to another kind of society—one that would be almost unrecognizable when the process was completed at various points in the nineteenth century or even the twentieth, depending on the country or region in question.

To accommodate both these aspects of the eighteenth century I have resorted to the title, "Tradition and Progress." It is not my intention to belabor the theme of modernity, however, since much of the old order persisted more or less intact long beyond 1789. While this book will amply evoke the quickening pace of change and the dynamic elements in European society, it remains a book primarily about Europe's old order.

Since a work of synthesis inherently involves questions of emphasis and choice, the reader will find here a good deal about France. While in part a matter of personal interest, this choice can be defended objectively. In the first place, to contemporaries France was the dominant state and civilization. Despite government censorship, Paris was the acknowledged center of European intellectual life and arguably of its culture. With its formidable bureaucratic administration and large standing army at the beginning of the period, France was also at the center of the state system and a model, for better or worse, to other states. While it lost military supremacy around mid-century, it was destined to regain it more forcefully than ever in the era of the French Revolution. All told, this was in many ways the French century in Europe, much as the nineteenth century would be dominated by Britain and later by Germany, and the contemporary era by the Soviet Union and the United States.

A different kind of reason for emphasizing France is the commanding position of the French in post-World War II historiography. Inspired by the *Annales* school and its journal devoted to the history of societies, economies, and civilizations—to the ideal of ceaselessly expanding the frontiers of historical research and attaining a view of "history in its totality"—the French have been the pacesetters in new areas of research. While their objectives and methods are universal, however, they have tended to be parochial in their choice of subject matter; that is, they write mainly about France itself, no doubt for the practical reason of easy access to source material and linguistic predilection. French historians have helped to revitalize the entire discipline of history with their masterful local research on the history of social groups, economic structures, collective behavior, and "mentalities," but the bulk of their work tells us about France rather than other countries.

While the British and Americans have not been far behind with innovative research on eighteenth-century Europe, a real imbalance stems from the fate of German historiography. In the nineteenth century German historians, starting with Leopold von Ranke, dominated the profession and molded our conception of eighteenth-century states and the state system. But German intellectual life was brutally disrupted by Nazism and the resultant devastation of World War II. Since then the Germans have slowly resumed historical research, but their best minds have understandably concentrated on the period since 1870, preoccupied with tracing the origins of "the German catastrophe." The French, on the contrary, have been less absorbed with the immediate past and have instead done their most fruitful work in the history of early modern France. Thus, anyone seeking to write an up-to-date interpretive history of eighteenth-century Europe must perforce digest and do justice to an output on French history that might seem disproportionate. I have accordingly given heavy emphasis to innovative scholarship, particularly French historiography, though I have not embraced its occasionally strident dismissal of the traditional historiography that has accumulated for roughly a century. Perhaps this book bears the mark of its author's academic generation: one largely trained in traditional history, but subsequently attracted to new modes of scholarship, and thus a generation able to see the virtues of each.

CHAPTER 1

The State

By 1700 European aggressiveness had reduced the western hemisphere to colonial status, and had subjugated Africa's tribal peoples to form a reservoir of slave labor for those colonies. Much of the world, however, remained free from the direct exercise of Europe's power. Great empires still presided over highly developed civilizations: the decaying Mogul Empire on the Indian subcontinent; the vast Ottoman Empire stretching across the Moslem world from North Africa through the Middle East and into the disputed borderlands of the Balkans; and above all, the incomparably cohesive Manchu Empire in China that could still dismiss Europeans as "barbarians."

The time had long since passed when Europe too had been organized as a vast empire, or more accurately two empires, the Western or Roman Empire and the Eastern or Byzantine. Instead, one of Europe's most notable characteristics was its division into a multiplicity of states linked together in a pattern of rivalry and mutual recognition. The eventual decline of the Mogul, Ottoman, and Manchu empires would produce chaos into which Europeans would extend their political and economic domination. The decline of Europe's old empires, having occurred much earlier and in relative isolation, resulted in the emergence of competing sovereign states.

The rulers of these states—absolute monarchs in all the major countries except Poland, Britain, and the Dutch Netherlands—strove to promote their sovereignty by amassing power over policy and resources within the state, and by competing with other states for influence and territory. These two dimensions of Europe's political life—state building and international rivalry—will be treated successively in the first two chapters. It should be clear from the outset, however, that the two occurred in tandem, being two aspects of a single development.

STATE BUILDING IN THE AGE OF ABSOLUTISM

Princes, Provinces, and States

The development of Europe's sovereign states was a long, complex process. Around 1500 there were perhaps five hundred entities claiming authority over the people residing within their borders, and it was not clear which would endure and which would be absorbed by others. For every France, England, or Prussia there was a Burgundy, a Bohemia, a Lorraine, a Scotland, or a Lucca that would not survive as an autonomous, sovereign state. Small states were relentlessly devoured by larger ones, boundaries altered by force or diplomacy, and one ruling dynasty replaced by another.

The absorption of smaller entities into larger ones suggests that provinces were the building blocks of Europe's political history. Masses and elites alike generally perceived the province as their country, since provinces had their own histories, traditions, and institutions. The creation of large, effective states usually required the subordination of these provincial identities. In Europe's first major nation-state to reach its modern boundaries, Habsburg Spain, the monarchs were certainly aware of this as they strove to weld Aragon, Castile, Catalonia, Valencia and other Spanish provinces into the "New Monarchy" of the sixteenth century. Conversely, when the Dutch successfully revolted against Spanish sovereignty in the seventeenth century, they chose to form not a new unified state but rather a federated state of seven provinces (Holland being the largest) called the United Provinces—the original name for the Netherlands. But that was an exception to the norm of political development. The typical pattern lay in the other direction, best exemplified by Richelieu and Louis XIV chipping away at the political autonomy of France's various provinces. Yet even the achievements of Spanish and French state builders were deceptive, since provincial institutions and interests merely lay dormant under absolutism and would revive with vigor later on.

While France, Spain, and Britain were relatively far advanced in breaking down provincial independence and forming unified realms by the early eighteenth century, elsewhere the situation was different. On the early eighteenth-century map of Europe there was as yet neither a "Germany" nor an "Italy." Instead, some three-hundred-odd principalities were located within the boundaries of the Holy Roman Empire (see map on p. 3), a confederation of Germanic states generally dominated by the Habsburgs, who provided its elected emperor. Though its power and authority steadily waned after 1648, the confederation did serve as an umbrella for the survival of many small entities. The latter included fifty-one free cities, the domains of sovereign knights with half a million subjects, and thirty-three ecclesiastical principalities with about three million subjects. Among the more substantial German states were the Electorates of

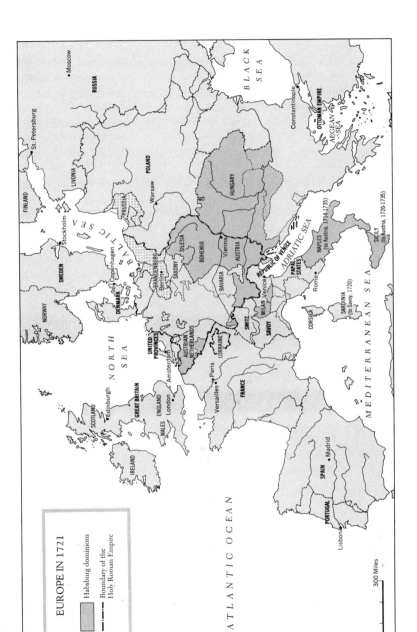

EUROPE IN 1721

Habsburg dominions

Boundary of the
Holy Roman Empire

Saxony and Bavaria. Saxony stood in the strategic center of the empire, boasted a splendid capital city in Dresden, and enjoyed prestige from the fact that its royal house frequently provided the elected kings of Poland. Bavaria in the south was an undermatched but dogged adversary of Habsburg domination, and an area that would retain its regional particularity into the twentieth century. The largest principality in northern Germany was the Electorate of Brandenburg, or, as it would become known, Prussia—a state whose meteoric rise in the eighteenth century probably has more to tell us about Europe's political order than any other example. There was no such success story, however, among the principalities of Italy. In the old regime the peninsula was fragmented into about a dozen independent states and dependencies, whose weakness served as a magnet for dynastic ambitions.

Europe's stronger states included the Habsburg Monarchy and Russia, two large-scale attempts to forge vast and ethnically diverse territories into relatively centralized realms. Starting from their core provinces of Germanic Austria, the Habsburgs operated as a kind of dynastic holding company, gathering together by marriage, conquest, and diplomacy such realms as the Kingdoms of Bohemia and Hungary. While never able to unify their possessions, the Habsburgs could tap their resources to produce formidable political power. The problem of ethnic diversity was even greater for the Muscovite rulers, who spread their claims over the Eurasian landmass of Russia southward and eastward, trying to assimilate Tatar, Cossack, and other nomadic tribes as well as Slavic populations, all of whom had their own traditions and institutions.

Whatever their form of government—absolute monarchy, constitutional monarchy, oligarchic republic—all states claimed sovereignty, or supreme legitimate power, over the people residing within their borders. Abstract definitions of sovereignty mattered little. It was the rulers' success in developing monopolies over the following four powers that brought them effective sovereignty:

Coercion: the legal disposition of armed force
Taxation: the collection and expenditure of taxes
Administration: the control of public life, especially through bureaucracy
Lawmaking: the setting of public policy and the enactment of laws
governing civil society

In trying to fashion these instruments of sovereignty, Europe's rulers faced several obstacles in addition to the provincial and ethnic diversity of their realms. First, the church in most states remained a quasi-autonomous power center with potentially great influence. The more independent the church (and in Catholic Europe, the more subordinate it was to Rome), the less complete would be the state's sovereignty. Second, there were still powerful noble families—"overmighty subjects" they have been called—whose pretensions rivaled those of their princes or kings. While this had been a more serious problem in the sixteenth and seventeenth centuries, certain families still believed in their inherent right to share in the governing process, or at least to be left alone by the state. A third form of resistance to royal sovereignty occasionally arose from the once self-governing oligarchies of the chartered towns, who used their ancient privileges and traditions to fend off the state's claims. Finally, the so-called representative institutions of early modern Europe—the assemblies, estates, and diets, as they were variously called—claimed a share of legislative and administrative power.

These bodies reflected the prevailing theory of social organization in which the state had to deal not with individuals but with "corporate" groups. There were three or four such orders or corporations: the clergy; the nobility (divided in some German and Austrian provinces into two groups, the upper nobility and the *Ritterschaft* or lesser nobility); and the commoners, that is, the rest of the population. (In Scandinavia peasants and townsmen or burghers were represented separately, while in Hungary there was a single deputy to represent all the towns combined and no representative at all for the peasantry!) Corporate groups were "represented" in deliberative bodies which existed at the national level in some states (e.g., the British Parliament, the Polish Diet, the Spanish *Cortes*, the French Estates-General), and at the local or provincial level in all major states except Britain. Not really representative in any modern sense, these diets and estates were oligarchies, usually dominated by prominent nobles. Defenders of traditional privileges and interests, the diets could be coopted by absolutism but they could also serve as a check to absolutism. Either by intimidation or agreement, the rulers had to achieve a working relationship with these bodies. For, especially in central Europe, they represented the landlord class that controlled the peasantry, the ultimate source of the state's manpower and tax revenue.

The fragility of centralized states in old-regime Europe can be illustrated by the case of France, which on the surface appeared to be the strongest and most integrated. Unlike their long-time rivals, the Habsburgs, the Bourbon kings of France essentially wore only one crown; they governed a relatively compact territory with no disconnected parts, thus making it easier to define the nation's borders and organize its territories. But what formidable obstacles remained to centralization! Within this realm there were three tariff zones; two different systems of law (Roman law in some areas, common law in others) with numerous local customs; varied systems of weights and measures; and varied systems of tax assessment. Even territorial consolidation was incomplete, since the crucial northeastern frontier was insecure until 1715, and remained irregular even after that date.

The French monarchy consisted of a central core of fairly well-integrated, French-speaking provinces, as well as an outer ring of large provinces that had come into the realm at different points historically, with Brittany and the easternmost provinces not firmly under control until the end of Louis XIV's reign. These outer provinces, called *pays d'état*, had active provincial estates, strong local nobilities, and "unwritten constitutions" for their governance. In the sprawling southern province of Languedoc, for example, where a local dialect (the langue d'oc) persisted as the spoken language of the common people, the provincial estates met annually to apportion its quota of taxes among the dioceses of the province. Historically the estates had insisted that these taxes must be used within the province for public expenditures. Only the "free gift" that it would also proffer could go to the royal coffers in Paris. For periods in which the provincial estates were not in session, syndics were elected to act in an executive capacity, and at times the estates would send delegates to Paris to negotiate with the royal council directly. For absolutism to advance, this type of arrangement had to be eliminated or reduced to empty formalities. Paris had to pull the strings and control the money, while co-opting the local elites.

Besides having to master the provincial estates in the *pays d'état*, the French monarchy had to deal with the self-governing oligarchies of the leading towns such as Bordeaux and Marseilles, whose ancient charters granted them extensive privileges and powers over their own affairs. Until brought under control, these oligarchies formed a barrier between the monarch and his urban subjects; in extreme cases they were capable of leading rebellions against the crown. Likewise the French Church remained a formidable self-governing corporation. Exempt from taxes on its vast property and income, it had its own governing body, a quasi-elective General Assembly of the Clergy, and its own executive agents who dealt with the crown almost like ambassadors. In place of taxes it negotiated a "free gift" with the crown, which it could withhold or diminish at will. Also, while the king had won the power to appoint bishops, most other matters of personnel were regulated autonomously. All told, unless the crown took vigorous countervailing measures, provincial estates, town oligarchies, and church bodies formed "intermediary corps" that stood between the monarchy and its subjects. If handled with an astute combination of firmness and flattery, however, these bodies could conceivably be converted into auxiliaries of absolutism.

Against the claims of local elites who sought to retain power for themselves at the crown's expense, kings and queens had by the eighteenth century not one but two bodies of theory to support their pretensions to

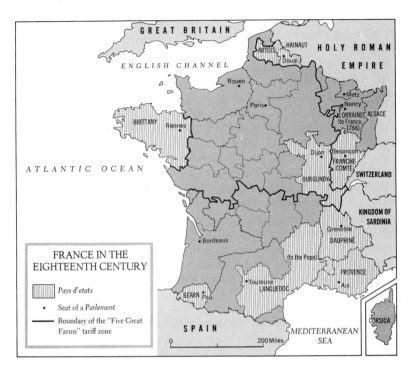

FRANCE IN THE
EIGHTEENTH CENTURY

Pays d'etats

• Seat of a *Parlement*

—— Boundary of the "Five Great
Farms" tariff zone

sovereignty. In the first place the monarchs claimed and the clergy preached a "divine right" theory of kingship according to which rulers were responsible only to God. This mandate was embodied in the ritual ceremony of the royal coronation, in which the king was set apart from even the mightiest of his aristocratic brethren. The tradition was given its definitive formulation in Bishop Bossuet's *Politics Drawn from the Words of Holy Scripture*. Written at the height of Louis XIV's reign, the book was published posthumously in 1708. As a validation of royal power, however, divine-right theory was doubtless losing its grip among the educated elites by that time.

Among the common people, kings and queens were still held in awe. In France, the Bourbon kings of the eighteenth century drew prestige from their association with a long line of popular figures such as Louis IX (Saint Louis) and Henry IV. Moreover, rulers were believed to possess the power of the "magic touch," the ability to effect cures of dread diseases and disabilities. As late as the 1770's Louis XVI "exercised" this power in public ceremonies to enhance his reputation as a good father to his people. In general, the European masses seem to have attributed their misery and oppression to evil advisors and aristocrats who deceived the ruler, for rarely did they turn against monarchy itself. Of course, force was the ultimate support of absolutism, but monarchy generally remained popular as a vague, remote image. Any alternative to monarchy in most European states was unthinkable, both among the elites and the masses. Even at the time of the French Revolution it was only when the king proved utterly unwilling to cooperate with the new regime, and indeed sought to destroy it, that its leaders embraced the concept of a republic.

Meanwhile a second body of theory merged gradually into the foundations of continental absolutism. This secular justification of strong monarchy had developed during the chaos of the sixteenth-century wars of religion. Combining Roman imperial precedents with pragmatic considerations, it defended absolute monarchy as an institution that held society together. Massive rebellions and civil wars in seventeenth-century Europe served to underscore this argument. The figure of a strong king held out hope of stability, despite the fact that in certain cases rebellions had begun as reactions against the advance of royal power. By the eighteenth century absolutism was being justified because it got the job done. Frederick II of Prussia immortalized this notion in his comment that, despite his virtually absolute power, he was merely "the first servant of the state." That in turn points up that the state was taking on an identity, a life of its own, independent of the monarch's person, though this process was far from complete.

The French Model of State Building

France under Louis XIV (ruled 1660–1715) had set the pace in establishing monarchy's authority. Continuing the work of Richelieu, the young sovereign extended the crown's control over the basic areas of sovereignty: armed force, lawmaking, taxation, and bureaucracy. In the process he subdued (for the time being) the "intermediary corps" that had always opposed the extension of absolutism. Certain great nobles who had claimed rights in the formulation of state policy were now excluded from the royal councils. Other "overmighty subjects" who had maintained private armies in the countryside were tracked down, brought to heel, and a few even executed. The *Parlements* (the realm's chief law courts), which had previously exercised an effective veto power over legislation they deemed objectionable by refusing to register and by protesting against such edicts, were summarily forbidden to do this under pain of immediate exile. The powers of the provincial estates, and of royal officials who had purchased their positions (as did the magistrates of the *Parlements*) were undercut by the creation of a new bureaucracy that gradually took over administrative tasks. The principal agents of royal absolutism in the provinces were the intendants, one stationed in each of the thirty-six *généralités* into which the realm was divided for purposes of taxation and ad-

MAJOR RULERS OF THE GREAT POWERS

BRITAIN	FRANCE	AUSTRIA	PRUSSIA	RUSSIA
	Louis XIV 1660–1715	Leopold I 1658–1705	Frederick I 1688–1713	Peter I 1682–1725
Anne 1702–1714				
George I 1714–1727	Regency 1715–1723	Charles VI 1711–1740	Frederick William I 1713–1740	
George II 1727–1760	Louis XV 1723–1774			
				Anna 1730–1740
		Maria Theresa 1740–1780	Frederick II 1740–1786	Elizabeth 1741–1762
George III 1760–1820				Peter III 1762
				Catherine II 1762–1796
	Louis XVI 1774–1792	Joseph II 1780–1790 (Holy Roman Emperor and Coregent 1765)	Frederick William II 1786–1797	
	First Republic 1792–1804	Leopold II 1790–1792		

ministration. Chosen specifically from outside the areas they served, and removable at the king's pleasure, they were in every respect the king's men, and could at least rival if not altogether displace the local elites. The intendants were in turn assisted by deputies, called "subdelegates," on the district level. Together they were responsible for the collection of land taxes, surveillance of economic activity, public order, and the implementation of royal decrees.

At the center in Paris or Versailles, Louis XIV dispensed with the advice of high aristocrats or of a prime minister. Instead he gathered around him an array of talented administrators, generally from families recently ennobled specifically for their administrative service. Among these loyal, dedicated, and energetic servitors were the controller-general or finance minister Jean Baptiste Colbert, and the members of the Le Tellier-Louvois family who helped create France's new professional army. To aid them, a corps of administrative trainees was created (the "masters of requests") who served on a rotating basis in various councils and ministries, doing clerical work, study projects, and field investigations; eventually some were elevated to the intendancies. Louis continued to sell venal offices to raise revenue, but these were merely prestigious sinecures without power. Indeed in certain cities he forced the municipal oligarchs to purchase their posts from the crown, while at the same time he stripped the offices of important functions.

At the heart of Louis' efforts was the development of a new standing army—a subject that will receive special consideration below. Largely to pay for that army, new taxes were levied without the consent of the constituted bodies that had formerly been involved in allocating taxes. Kings had once been expected to live off the revenues of their own extensive property, supplemented by whatever the diets, the cities, or the church might grant them from time to time for limited objectives and periods. Louis' predecessors had already worn away that restraint, making the *taille* (the royal land tax) into a permanent tax as early as the fifteenth century. During the seventeenth century the *taille* crept steadily upward, although most nobles and cities were privileged with exemptions. Louis introduced a new kind of head tax (the *capitation*), payable by everyone, and later a temporary income tax that in effect became a surtax on the *taille* and was borne primarily by the peasantry. In addition, the government drew vast revenues from indirect taxes that kept mounting, such as the salt tax (*gabelle*), and excise taxes on consumer items such as wine and tobacco. Peasant revolts and urban tax protests did little to stop this fiscal assault since Louis controlled enough armed force to suppress them.

Disgruntled aristocrats like the Duke of St. Simon claimed to see in Louis' entourage of newcomers like Colbert the reign of the "vile bourgeoisie." This was a gross exaggeration, though it did point to Louis' ability to associate elements of the middle class with the monarchy as a counterweight to the old aristocracy. As part of this strategy commoners were elevated to the ranks of nobility by the purchase of expensive, usually functionless venal offices. While the upper strata of government were still filled by nobles, many officials were indeed new nobles (*anoblis*). Not that Louis simply warred against or neglected the old aristocracy; on the contrary, the Sun King conceived of himself as the first aristocrat of the realm, the apex of a social pyramid in which the great nobles and peers of the realm held pride of place, not politically but socially. By organizing the routines of court life in a spectacular public fashion, Louis assured that the aristocracy's private ambition could be manipulated to his advantage. It was an environment, as one chronicler described it, "where all nobles were honored, but no one was powerful." Court life— first in Paris, and then at the new palace of Versailles—was ritualized to create an elaborate system of recognition and rewards for the courtiers, as in the moring *levée* or awakening ceremony, in which the greatest aristocrats of the realm vied for the honor of handing Louis his robe. Individuals were encouraged to compete for the king's considerable favors: sinecures, dowries, pensions, military commissions, and church appointments. Court nobles in turn acted as patrons for lesser nobles who did not have direct access to the king. Thus did Louis continue the effort begun by Richelieu to tame or "domesticate" the nobility by banning dueling and destroying the fortifications on their castles. Louis converted the high nobility (at least for the time being) into loyal servitors instead of "overmighty subjects," alternating their energies between an extravagant life at court and military service in his wars.

Further to reflect his own eminence and glory, Louis XIV supported and organized the nation's cultural life in an unprecedented fashion, helping to nurture a golden age of French culture. By establishing national academies to confer recognition and rewards on certain writers, scientists, artists, and architects, the crown aimed to uphold standards of excellence in these fields. In addition, the king was the direct patron of playwrights Racine and Molière, composer Lully, artist Lebrun, and architect Mansard, among others. Like the rulers of Renaissance Italy's city-states, the French crown moved into the business of high culture. By sponsoring opera and drama—costly forms of culture requiring subsidy—the monarchy increased its own prestige. All these social and cultural strategies were consummated in the halls of the great Versailles palace. Legendary for its overwhelming grandeur (as well as its physical discomfort, such as the lack of adequate sanitary facilities), Versailles was built to Louis' specifications and embodied his personality. It was a setting designed to overawe the French elites and the princes of Europe. Court life as shaped by the Sun King was a curious mixture of impressive high culture and wasteful pastimes such as hunting

Versailles. *Built on swampland at a prodigious cost in money and lives (for hundreds of workers succumbed to malaria), Versailles boasted seventeen acres of buildings as well as fourteen hundred fountains, and altogether created a scene of unprecedented physical splendor. It was in some ways a world cut off from reality, however, and in 1789 the royal family was forcibly returned to Paris by a revolutionary crowd. Painting by Jean-Baptiste Martin. Musée de Versailles.*

and gambling. In all, it doubtless had a civilizing influence on Europe's elites. Yet those princes who imitated only the courtly side of Louis' kingship were missing the main point. For he was truly a full-time professional king, a tireless administrator as well as a consummate socializer. To Louis XIV, ritual and recreation were merely two elements of the serious business of kingship.

The Rise of Brandenburg-Prussia

Within the fragmented territories of Germany, early modern Brandenburg was an undistinguished minor state, its capital Berlin a sleepy provincial town. The ruling House of Hohenzollern was saved from complete obscurity only by the vote it held in the electoral college of the Holy Roman Empire. In the seventeenth century, however, the margrave or prince of Brandenburg fell heir to the Duchy of Prussia, a fertile Baltic territory later known as East Prussia. This territory had been nominally ruled by a duke who was cousin to the Brandenburg Hohenzollerns and who died without male heirs, eventually causing his title to pass to his cousin in Berlin. Between Brandenburg and Prussia (which lay outside the Holy Roman Empire altogether) there was absolutely no organic relationship. Each territory had its own traditions and social structure, with Prussia dominated by nobles known as *Junkers* who possessed enormous estates worked by serfs of Slavic or Germanic origin. Moreover, the two areas were separated geographically by a vast expanse including parts of Poland and Swedish Pomerania. To make matters even more complicated, the Hohenzollerns had also fallen heir to a third set of territories far to the west of Brandenburg near the Rhine, again totally distinct from their other domains.

During the Thirty Years' War, which ended in 1648, Brandenburg had become a hapless cockpit of battle, overrun and devastated by several successive armies. Only a combination of skillful diplomacy and state building could shield Brandenburg from continued exposure to such attacks, and this was the task undertaken by Frederick William (ruled 1640–1688), soon to be known as the Great Elector for his success. By pursuing a supple diplomacy, the prince struck bargains that afforded his small army the most advantageous positions possible. In the First Northern War that raged from 1655 to 1660, for instance, he shifted from neutrality to an alliance with Sweden, and then abruptly to the side of Sweden's enemy Poland. As a reward, the Polish king gave up his nominal overlordship in East Prussia, thus permitting a Hohenzollern effort to exploit that province's resources. In 1675 the Great Elector's army won a significant battle against Sweden and cleared the Swedes out of the strategic territory of Swedish Pomerania. But at the peace table great-power politics took over. Backing his Swedish ally, Louis XIV ordered Brandenburg to return Swedish Pomerania or risk the loss of its Rhineland provinces. In the final reckoning, a state's interests could be assured only by overwhelming strength. More than skillful diplomacy, statebuilding was the key to survival: armies, taxes to support the armies, and bureaucrats to collect the taxes.

The Great Elector gave Brandenburg-Prussia a running start in this process by imposing major administrative changes from above. His objec-

PRUSSIA AND THE
HABSBURG MONARCHY

Prussian territory in 1740
Acquired to 1745
Austrian territory in 1745
------ Boundary of the Holy Roman Empire

tives were to be able to collect taxes as needed without having to plead annually with the nobles in their local diets, and to use the revenues as he saw fit regardless of where they originated. In an ordinance of 1653 the Elector struck a crucial bargain with the nobility. In return for his agreement to strengthen their control over the peasantry, he was granted substantial powers to tax without the need for further consent. This opened the way for both an intensified exploitation of the peasants by the landlords and an unprecedented growth of absolutism. For, in order to collect and disburse their revenues, the Hohenzollerns (like the Bourbons in France) gradually took over the functions of local government from provincial diets and vested them in royal officials. At first this was done on an emergency wartime basis, but ultimately it became permanent. These local royal officials (nominated from the ranks of the local nobility and soon to be known as the *Landräte*) became the chief instrument for the extension of royal power in the provinces, where once the local nobles had ruled directly through their diets. Meanwhile, town government was taken over by the monarchy's new tax commissioners appointed to collect an excise tax on the sale of most consumer goods in the towns. The commissioners were placed under the control of the war department, and the total yield of the excise tax was earmarked for the army, which reveals the army's central place in the whole effort.

State building languished during the reign of Frederick I (ruled 1688–1713), who did, however, secure the prestige of a royal crown in 1701 by consent of the Holy Roman Emperor in return for Prussian assistance during the War of Spanish Succession. The Hohenzollerns were henceforth kings in Prussia rather than mere margraves and dukes. To sustain this prestige Frederick I concentrated on promoting culture and social elegance in Berlin. But kingship would be a hollow honor if the treasury remained depleted and the army small. Fortunately for Prussian power, the next heir to the throne was a different personality entirely, and an enthusiast for the rigors of state building.

Frederick William I (ruled 1713–1740) has in fact been called "the father of Prussian militarism" and "the Sergeant King." An austere Protestant with a gruff manner who disdained all things French and cultural, he resumed the work of the Great Elector, building up the army and filling the treasury. Centralization advanced in Prussia as the Sergeant King created a superagency of government called the General Directory of War, Finance, and Domains. As the title suggests, this placed under one roof the collection and administration of both royal revenues (from the approximately one-quarter of Brandenburg's land owned by the Hohenzollerns) and state revenues (land taxes, excises, postal fees and the like). Centralization was even more apparent in the monarch's personal style, as it would also be under his more famous successor, Frederick the Great (ruled 1740–1786). Each involved himself in every aspect of government and made almost all decisions himself. Closeted in his office the king received from his officials a stream of memoranda setting forth the problems needing attention. Father and son alike insisted on absolute obedience from their officials. Dour and distrustful of human nature, they allowed bureaucrats only a minimum of discretion, yet at the same time held them responsible for any inefficiency. Most functions were accordingly carried out by collective boards rather than by individuals, so that there would be mutual surveillance among the officials. But even that did not allay Frederick William's suspiciousness. He therefore created a system of inspectors, called fiscals, to report privately to the king on the behavior of his officials. Meanwhile the two kings disdained the routines and etiquette of court life, paring the expenses of court to the bone. This austerity extended to the royal kitchens, and it was said that when Frederick

William wished a really good meal he invited himself to one of his minister's homes. Money was instead spent on the armed forces. Frederick William symbolized this commitment by dressing regularly in a military uniform and by maintaining a private regiment of grenadiers who each stood six to seven feet tall.

Frederick William's work habits, fiscal austerity, administrative reforms, and military orientation bore spectacular fruit. By the time he died in 1740 his army had grown from thirty thousand to about eighty-three thousand making it the fourth largest in Europe behind those of France, Russia, and Austria. Yet his reign was a peaceful one. For he recognized that Prussian independence and power depended on patient preparation and on choosing the right time and objective for expansion. Throughout his own reign he resisted the temptation to squander his army. Instead he left it for the use of his heir.

One of the king's most impressive accomplishments was in fact the grooming of his successor. It was a difficult task, since his son Frederick was, as a young man, the complete opposite of his father. Highly intellectual, a fervent admirer of French culture, a poet by temperament, and a deist who disdained traditional Christianity, young Frederick was more interested in flute-playing and Voltaire's writings than in armies or taxes. But his father insisted that he train himself for the job, and gradually broke the young man's will. In 1730, at the age of eighteen, Frederick tried to run away, but he was caught with a companion, and was made to

Frederick the Great. *Shown here in a characteristic pose atop his horse, the Prussian king earned his title "the Great" by virtue of his military prowess. Frederick was not only one of the century's leading military theoreticians, but was an outstanding commander in the field.*

witness the execution of his young friend. This was a traumatic event; thereafter Frederick gradually accepted his fate and began to show both zeal and talent for the affairs of state and for military leadership.

While Frederick's intellectual bent caused him to agonize over his role and theorize about it, he never flinched from exercising his power. In fact Frederick in both word and deed became a leading apologist for absolutism and state sovereignty. At a time when loyalties tended to lie elsewhere (one's village or province, one's church, one's dynasty) Frederick redirected the notion of loyalty to the state and to the fatherland. He expected the allegiance of his subjects not simply to himself but to the state, the vehicle of human destiny. Pessimistic about human nature's base qualities, Frederick believed that a well-governed state could nonetheless promote progress. His statement that he was "the first servant of the state," however, could be considered true in a tragic personal way. For his biography can be read as the story of a man forced to sacrifice his personal inclinations to his higher duty to the state. Unlike his youthful intellectual friends, he could not live on the basis of a vague idealism or a disembodied set of ethical values. His personal milieu was the competitive state system. Progress for the state could only come, in his pragmatic view, as a by-product of power.[1]

In order for the state to nurture progress and happiness, it must be forcefully organized and invulnerable to outside threats. Yet the exercise of power is notoriously difficult to reconcile with morality, and this posed a painful conundrum for the young king. A short time before he became king in 1740, Frederick had written an idealistic treatise on international relations called *Anti-Machiavel*, which, as its title suggests, argued against immorality in international relations. Still, upon assuming the throne at a dramatic moment in European history, when a crisis in the Habsburg monarchy created an inviting target for aggression, Frederick unhesitatingly launched his impressive army in an unprovoked attack to seize the rich Habsburg province of Silesia. This was the decisive act of his entire reign. He spent years consolidating that bold stroke and defending Silesia from Habsburg revenge in three Silesian wars—an effort that lasted until 1763 and left his country drained and devastated. Frederick had to devote the remainder of his reign to rebuilding. But the crucial change held: with the addition of Silesia, Prussia was now geographically and politically a great power.

Just as Frederick's moral ideals had to be suspended in the conduct of international relations, so too in the formation of domestic policy his humanitarian impulses yielded to a harsh, pragmatic appraisal of Prussian society. His social policy, as we shall see, was consequently extremely

[1] See Gerhard Ritter, *Frederick the Great* (Berkeley, Calif., 1968).

conservative. While French absolutism had in some ways promoted the position of the middle classes, Prussia under Frederick became more thoroughly aristocratic than ever. Even in his attempts to rebuild the Prussian economy, Frederick resorted exclusively to intervention by the state and did little to advance the ideologically progressive notion of individual initiative.

Modernization in the Habsburg Monarchy

The multinational Habsburg Monarchy comprised a group of territories (*Länder*) brought under the dynasty's control by strategic marriages and military conquest. At its core were the hereditary German provinces that approximate the area of present-day Austria. In 1526 the Habsburgs extended their rule to the Bohemian lands, with their large Czech populations: the Kingdom of Bohemia, the Margravate of Moravia, and the Duchies of Upper and Lower Silesia. The third major component was the Crown of St. Stephen, whose lands included the Kingdom of Hungary, its dependency Croatia-Slavonia, and the Principality of Transylvania. After a number of rebellions led by its Magyar nobility, and a determined Ottoman invasion at the end of the seventeeenth century, Hungary seemed securely locked into the Habsburg orbit in the early eighteenth century. Other territories fell to the Austrian Habsburgs when the Spanish Habsburgs' possessions were parcelled out under the Treaty of Rastatt in 1714, including the Kingdom of Naples (later lost in 1735), the Duchy of Milan or Lombardy, and the Austrian Netherlands (approximately present-day Belgium). The Grand Duchy of Tuscany was in turn acquired in 1737 when it fell to Francis Stephen, husband of the Austrian Archduchess and heir, Maria Theresa.

At the very least, three kinds of diversity had to be dealt with to administer this realm effectively. First, there were religious differences, to which the Habsburgs responded by seeking to subdue Protestants with an aggressive counter-reformation led by the Jesuits. Secondly, there was ethnic diversity. The dominant, though by no means majority, ethnic group was German, which sought to impose its hegemony on sizeable populations of Magyars, Rumanians, and several types of Slavs (Croats, Czechs, Ruthenes, Serbs, Slovaks, and Slovenes). Thirdly, there were political traditions in the various provinces, embodied in provincial and even national Diets. The Habsburgs' strategy here was similar to that of all absolute monarchs: they attempted both to win over the local elites and to bypass or co-opt provincial institutions whenever possible.

Hungary was the most important non-German Habsburg holding, and the one that proved most difficult to integrate. Three times the size of the German hereditary provinces, Hungary was a rich agricultural area and the eastern gateway to the Danubian basin. Nowhere was there a stronger local elite. The upper segment of the Magyar nobility comprised several hundred magnates with enormous estates and considerable political power, for each one sat individually in the national Diet. The Crown of St. Stephen had originally been elective with the Diet doing the choosing. In the sixteenth century one party of the divided Diet had chosen the Habsburg Archduke Ferdinand as king of Hungary so that his aid could be enlisted against the menacing Ottoman Turks. Ferdinand was unable to prevent the Turks from conquering four-fifths of the kingdom, however, and it was not too long before even the Magyars in what was left of Hungary had reason to regret their decision. For Ferdinand's successors pursued an aggressive policy in Hungary involving the suspension of constitutional liberties, the subordination of the Magyar nobility, and the imposition of Catholicism. Then, in 1683, the Turks, who had never given up their dreams of European conquest, attacked again, reaching the outskirts of Vienna itself. There they were stymied and, in one of Europe's more dramatic moments, gradually driven back until almost all of Hungary was liberated. But the country had been devastated by the long conflict and few Hungarians rejoiced at the emperor's victories. A large part of the ill-disciplined imperial army was now permanently quartered in Hungary, at a terrible cost to the peasants and townspeople; the persecution of Protestants was resumed with perhaps even greater vigor; the administration of Hungary was placed in the hands of hostile, non-Hungarian officials in Vienna; and the Diet, after being forced to accept the hereditary monarchy in 1687, was not summoned at all for the rest of Emperor Leopold's reign. Even the Magyar nobles, who had hoped to recover long-lost family estates in the liberated counties, were disappointed, since an imperial commission set up to examine their claims threw most of them out and required a large indemnity payment from those whose rights it did recognize. Eventually the various disaffected groups came together in a great national uprising led by the Magyar Francis Rákóczi II. The Habsburg dynasty was temporarily dethroned, but the revolt was ultimately crushed. The Peace of Szatmar (1711), however, did restore Hungarian institutions, in particular promising that the Diet in Pressburg would be convoked regularly, and reaffirmed the cherished immunity of the Hungarian nobility from direct taxation. Thus was Hungary bound to the Habsburgs, a pivotal but relatively independent part of their vast imperial holdings. Absolutism, for the moment, ostensibly stopped at Hungary's border.

The relationship between the Habsburgs and Hungary soon came into question again. For Emperor Charles VI (ruled 1711–1740) was faced with a possible disaster from the fact that he had not been able to produce a male heir to his throne. For several decades his prime objective was therefore to negotiate diplomatic accords with various European powers to recognize the succession of his female heir, Maria Theresa. This document, known as the Pragmatic Sanction, had first to be accepted by the estates and diets of all the Habsburg lands including Hungary, whose traditions did not provide for a woman wearing the Crown of St. Stephen. The negotiations underscored the unusual relationship between Vienna and Pressburg. Each Habsburg ruler had a written contract with the Hungarian Diet and took an oath of loyalty to it at his coronation. There was a separate administration or chancellery for Hungary, but it was located in Vienna. Land taxes had to be voted by the Hungarian Diet, but once collected they were spent by Vienna. In 1723 Hungary's Diet accepted the Pragmatic Sanction, with most European powers eventually following suit.

When Charles died in 1740, however, the Pragmatic Sanction proved to be a worthless piece of paper among Europe's statesmen. In the first place (as we have seen) Frederick II came to the throne at the same time and deemed the Habsburg succession crisis an optimal moment to grab Silesia and consolidate Prussian power. Austria's inveterate south German rival Bavaria reasoned in the same way and sought to enhance its position. Finally, dissident Bohemian elites seized this moment of Austrian weakness to rebel. Unlike the Magyars, the Czechs had been subdued but not appeased. Their diets had been bypassed; German nobles had been imported and given confiscated estates; the Catholic Reformation had been vigorously pressed on the Protestant population; and taxes had been levied harshly. What remained of the old Czech nobility therefore chose the succession crisis to rebel, and four hundred of them proclaimed Charles Albert of Bavaria as king of Bohemia. With her back against the wall, Maria Theresa personally appealed to the honor of the Magyar nobility. Resisting the opportunity to capitalize on her distress, they resolved to stand by their commitment to supply her with vital troops. This support allowed Austria to prevail against its swelling list of enemies (which was soon headed by a France unable to resist the opportunity for advantage). Though Silesia was not regained, Bohemia was retained and most Habsburg possessions emerged intact.

Survival was followed by defensive modernization, a necessary prelude to the moment when Austria would open a return engagement against Prussia. Now centralization began in earnest. While Hungary would retain its Magyar identity and institutions, Maria Theresa sought to domesticate its nobility by flattery and persuasion, luring them to Vienna and integrating them into court life as much as possible. Bohemia, on the other hand, was destined to become simply one of several German-dominated territories with few distinguishing institutions. Following the French and Prussian experience, the Habsburgs now reorganized the administration of their realm with the aim of eclipsing provincial interests and centralizing power as much as possible. Like the process of reapportionment in electoral republics, administrative reorganization involved fundamental allocations of power. The Habsburgs redrew the administrative map, creating ten newly defined units and subdividing these into districts or circles. In each new district a royal official (the *Kreishauptmann*) was appointed, replacing former employees or delegates of the diets. In essence the Habsburg *Kreishauptmann* took his place alongside the French intendant and the Prussian *Landrat* as the key instrument of absolutism. The monarchy also cajoled and persuaded the weakened diets to consent to a ten-year property-tax levy on all subjects, to be collected by a salaried bureaucracy rather than the diets themselves. Finally, there was military reform and modernization of the armed forces: the training of officers in newly established academies, the enlargement of the standing forces, and the establishment for the first time of a professional standing army in Hungary.

The rebuilding of absolutism in the Habsburg Monarchy extended through three reigns: Maria Theresa's (1740–1765); the coregency of Maria Theresa and her son Joseph II (1765–1780); and the period of Joseph's sole rule (1780–1790). While administrative reform proceeded continuously in the same direction, the passage from one phase to another of this succession brought alterations in style and policies.[2] Maria Theresa's style seemed most traditional. She was the antithesis of her arch-enemy Frederick II. The Prussian king was a deist who had a low estimation of his dynastic relatives and a secular conception of kingship. The empress, on the contrary, was still rooted in dynastic and religious loyalties. Her duty was not to some abstract conception of the state but to God and family. Yet she could rally the patriotism of her people as effectively as Frederick on his horse. Living a life of exemplary piety and domestic affection, her image as the "mother of her people" aroused considerable sentiment among her subjects. Her traditional attitudes included a resistance to the increasingly fashionable and pragmatic idea of religious toleration. While it has been said of Frederick that he "despised and protected most sects equally," for Maria Theresa toleration was mere indifference to religion, though eventually her son and other advisers prevailed on her to accept the notion that "true faith is the gift of God and cannot be imposed by force." Under the coregency the beginnings of toleration began to be felt only tentatively in the Habsburg domains of this most Catholic ruler.

While pursuing the same basic objectives of enhancing Habsburg power within the Monarchy and in Europe, her son Joseph had a decidedly different temperament. Like Frederick II he was strictly utilitarian, justifying policies by their results. Joseph brought to the throne a reforming zeal in which few traditions went unquestioned. He was both more enlightened

---

[2] For a balanced assessment see Adam Wandruszka, *The House of Habsburg: six hundred years of a European dynasty* (New York, 1964), chaps. 12–13.

The Habsburg Imperial Family. *Though she was a tireless worker, Maria Theresa always had time for her children, ten of whom survived to adulthood. Included here are her eldest son, coregent, and successor, Joseph; his intelligent brother Leopold, who briefly succeeded him; and Marie Antoinette, bride-to-be of France's King Louis XVI. Painting by Martin van Meytens, II. Schloss Schönbrunn, Vienna.*

than his predecessor, and more authoritarian. Above all he was decisive. His short reign saw a profusion of reforms that gave the cutting edge of modernization a far sharper blade than mere reforms in administration, taxation, or military life. An edict of toleration; a virtual nationalization of the parochial clergy; an assault on monasticism; a substantial loosening of the censorship; reforms in court procedure and criminal law; educational reforms which called for (though did not everywhere implement) compulsory primary schooling; a serious attempt at agrarian reform—all marked the culmination of eighteenth-century absolutism in its "enlightened" phase under Joseph. Much of this will be considered topically in due course. On the other hand, the continuities between mother and son were also notable and perhaps more durable. Both functioned within the traditions of absolutism and the state system. The exigencies of administrative reform and of making war were always the highest priorities, whether under the traditional and pious Maria Theresa or the innovative and impetuous Joseph. Moreover, most of Joseph's reforms expired with the monarch himself. After a brief holding action by Joseph's enlightened brother, Leopold II, the reactionary Emperor Francis II (ruled 1792–1835) saw to it that Joseph's policies were largely undone. Meanwhile, the monarchy's chief concern remained, as always, the struggle to hold its place in Europe, whether against Louis XIV, Frederick the Great, or Napoleon.

Russia from Peter the Great to Catherine the Great

While Bourbon and Habsburg armies fought to a standstill in the late seventeenth and early eighteenth centuries, an equally determined struggle was taking place in northern Europe, pitting Sweden against Russia. Sweden had been a dominant power in the Baltic region, and under the fervid leadership of Charles XII (ruled 1697–1718) had conquered parts of Poland and Russia. At the decisive battle of Poltava in the Ukraine (1709), however, Charles was defeated by a Russian army under Tsar Peter I. Swedish power rapidly evaporated, never to reemerge, while Russia began its inexorable drive to great-power status.

Russia had known periods of strong rule and dominance over its neighbors before, but there had been no institutionalized basis for absolutism until Peter created it during his long reign (1682–1725). Though no diets or representative institutions stood in his way—in which respect Russia differed from most other states—he certainly had been confronted by "overmighty subjects," the great aristocratic boyar families clustered around the court at Moscow. Only by brute force and terror was Peter able to intimidate them into submission. Prison, torture, and execution awaited those who challenged his authority. In the place of these scorned courtiers, Peter initially relied on new men to serve him; but where Louis XIV had promoted new men from the ranks of non-aristocratic Frenchmen, Peter frequently imported officials from abroad. In fact Peter was the first Russian ruler to travel in Western Europe, where he avidly studied military and manufacturing techniques. Back home he initiated a crash program of "Westernization," including the symbolic demand that his courtiers shave off their Russian-style beards. Soon French and German became the languages heard at court. And like Louis XIV, Peter created a physical reflection of his authority in the new administrative capital that he erected, the city of St. Petersburg.

Peter the Great's reign exemplified the process of state building as much as the Hohenzollerns' regime had in Brandenburg. Like his Prussian counterparts, Peter's first priority was to create a large standing army, whose support required that he tax and administer his vast realm with more determination than seemed possible. This army was fashioned through a new form of conscription that demanded lifetime service from one out of every twenty adult male peasants. Revenue was raised by extending the state's grip on church revenues, by squeezing more income from the state's monpolies on salt and tobacco, and by increasing the head tax on each male peasant, effectively tripling the burden of direct taxation. In exchange for conscripting and taxing their serfs, Peter (like the Great Elector in Brandenburg) tried to placate the landed nobility by otherwise increasing their control over these serfs. To equip the army, as well as a newborn navy that was one of his pet projects, Peter not only imported Western technology but helped launch Russian iron and munitions industries, the labor for which was provided by over twenty-five thousand peasants who were forcibly "ascribed" to the mines and foundries of the Ural mountains. To command his army and administer his edicts, foreigners and new men scarcely sufficed. Peter was therefore obliged to conscript his nobility into state service, much as Frederick William I had forced the sons of Prussia's nobility into military schools. Russian nobles could meet their obligatory

St. Petersburg. *Peter's new city was both an administrative capital, rivaling though by no means eclipsing Moscow, and Russia's "window on the West" —a Baltic port that facilitated trade and contact with the rest of Europe.*

state service in civilian posts or in military commands for which they were trained in special schools. Much of the nobility was thus uprooted from its estates into garrison life or into the government bureaus of Moscow and St. Petersburg.

For all the personal idiosyncrasies of his reign, Peter was laying the groundwork for an enduring, impersonal bureaucratic state. Like other rulers later in the century, he held that the state existed, over and above all its subjects, for their common good. While still claiming that his power was unlimited and came directly from God, Peter took an oath of loyalty to the state. But would his embryonic bureaucracy survive his demise? There were two reasons to be doubtful. First, much of the Russian nobility bitterly resented Peter's heavy-handed autocracy. Second, there was a serious succession problem, and no matter how it was resolved, it seemed unlikely that his innovations would be sustained forcefully. Paradoxically, the emergence of bureaucratically administered states depended historically on strong individual rulers with long reigns who, preferably, had strong successors to consolidate their gains. Peter's failure to provide for an orderly succession halted the process of state building for a number of years.

Peter's son Alexis hated him, but unlike Frederick William I who had a similar problem, the father could not overcome the son's hostility. On the contrary Alexis actively plotted with certain boyars against Peter, and after the exposure of their conspiracy, Alexis died under torture in 1721. This left no obvious successor. Boyars, guard regiments, some of the influential new nobles of foreign origin, and even certain foreign ambassadors stood ready to intrigue over the succession and to impose various conditions on the person whom they assisted to the throne. No fewer than six individuals wore the Russian crown before a successor worthy of Peter's ambitions emerged:

Catherine I	1725	(Peter's wife)
Peter II	1727	(Peter's grandson)
Anna	1730	(Peter's great-niece)
Elizabeth	1741	(Peter's daughter)
Peter III	1762	(a German nephew of Elizabeth's)
Catherine II	1762	(Peter III's German-born wife)

Each change was the product of intrigue and bargains, sometimes accompanied by the jailing of bested factions, and by various concessions to the nobility. Catherine I, for example, came to power allied with a self-constituted council of boyars, comparable to the council of peers which sought to reverse the gains of absolutism in France after Louis XIV's demise. This reaction—symbolized by the brief transfer of the capital back to Moscow—failed when Anna threw in her lot with proponents of autocracy rather than of boyar power. All in all, as one historian has put it, between

1725 and 1762 "a see-saw struggle had taken place between personal regimes of favorites and an orderly administrative system resting on regulations and laws."[3] The result was that, while many reforms of Peter I's regime were undone, the basic principle of noble service was retained, and the most extreme forms of oligarchy and rule by small cliques and foreigners were avoided.

For a moment even these gains were threatened. During his brief reign, Peter III dramatically freed the nobility from the obligation to state service, and seemed about to create a non-bureaucratic regime of favorites, which would follow a slavishly pro-Prussian foreign policy. The tsar was quickly overthrown and murdered by a faction that put his wife on the throne. But Catherine II (ruled 1762–1796), like many a would-be instrument of political plotters, took the reins of power firmly in hand and became the heir that Peter I had thus far lacked.

Determined to prevent authority from dissipating in the hands of noble factions, Catherine nonetheless recognized that autocracy depended on the nobility's support and good will. She sought to enlist the nobles by persuasion rather than by the force that Peter had used. Under her leadership the Russian social order came to reflect the nobility's dominance more explicitly than ever (see Chapter 3). Allowing the principle of obligatory service to lapse, and permitting nobles who so wished to return to their estates, she proceeded in 1775 to establish a system of local administrative bodies chosen and staffed by the provincial nobility. With authority firmly in her own hands, she sought to delegate responsibility at the local level in the countryside. While ultimate power was retained by the provincial governors who were direct appointees of the empress, the day-to-day business of governing would henceforth be handled by the local nobility. With the support of this gentry, the tsarist regime could sink deeper roots in the distant countryside, making ruler and nobility alike more secure.

In addition to her fostering of bureaucratic mechanisms, her dynamic personal style of ruling, and her interest in Western ideas, Catherine was a worthy successor to Peter in another fundamental way. Under her leadership, Russia resumed Peter's policy of territorial expansion southward to the Black Sea and westward into Poland.

THE NON-ABSOLUTIST STATES

The Decline of Sweden and Poland

As Russian power waxed, that of her immediate rivals steadily waned. It seems no coincidence that the weakness of Sweden and Poland in the eighteenth century corresponded to the absence of absolutism. In the

---

[3] Marc Raeff, "The Domestic Policies of Peter III and his Overthrow," *American Historical Review*, Vol. LXXV (June 1970), p. 1309.

Swedish case this represented a dramatic reversal. Just as Sweden's international pretensions collapsed with the defeat of Charles XII at Poltava, so too did his authoritarian rule. Absolutism could not easily survive decisive military defeat. By the time Charles died, in 1718, his plans in ruins, Sweden had been ousted almost entirely from its footholds on the European mainland, and had also to abandon any hope of reconquering Norway from Denmark. At the same time Swedish absolutism gave way to a determined assault by the Swedish nobility, inaugurating the so-called "Freedom Era" in the nation's history. Working through the Swedish Diet, the nobility reduced successive monarchs to mere figureheads, and effectively controlled public life. The Diet had four chambers, however, including one for the urban burgher class and one for the peasants, which heightened the potential for social and political conflict. Rival factions in the Diet (an aristocratic Hat party, and a more heterogeneous Cap party) wrangled for influence, supported by foreign interests that bribed and manipulated them. The Freedom Era, in other words, served as a cloak for aristocratic interests, which had the effect of undermining Sweden's independence in European affairs. Yet because of Sweden's complex social structure, privilege was likely to be more keenly resented there than in states such as Russia or Prussia. When nobles gradually erected barriers to the commissioning of non-nobles in the army, for example, the excluded social groups had the means and the will to protest. Professional and mercantile groups, as well as a peasantry with its tradition of village assemblies and its own chamber in the Diet, were a potential counterweight to the aristocratic liberties of the Freedom Era.

The ludicrous political factionalism that resulted was finally overcome by King Gustavus III in 1772. With the support of the French, he rallied Stockholm's population behind a bloodless coup d'état meant to end "the insufferable aristocratic despotism" of the Diet. It was a kind of revolution from above, a reassertion of strong monarchy. Sweden's Diet retained a certain amount of power, though it now operated under the king's leadership. As Gustavus' reign developed, however, his absolutist pretensions grew side by side with the extension of greater civil equality to non-noble groups. Disgruntled nobles eventually assassinated the king in 1792, though they did not succeed in fully restoring the oligarchic practices of the Freedom Era.

Poland and Sweden were regarded similarly by the surrounding great powers. As R. R. Palmer points out in his overview of Europe's eighteenth-century political order, "a secret treaty of 1764 between Catherine and Frederick mentioned Sweden along with Poland as likely for partition." [4]

[4] R. R. Palmer, *The Age of the Democratic Revolution: a political history of Europe and America, 1760–1800*, Vol. I (Princeton, N.J., 1959), p. 100.

Such an eventuality was possible because of the aristocratic liberties and consequent absence of strong monarchy in both countries, which gave foreign powers the opportunity for intervention in their affairs. Poland's aristocratic liberties were even more pronounced than Sweden's. They reached an extreme, just as Poland ultimately suffered the extreme fate of dismemberment by foreign powers and extinction as a sovereign state. Poland is thus the prime counter-example to eighteenth-century absolutism and state building among the leading continental powers. While Poland's social order was akin to Russia's, its political development was totally different.

In the sixteenth century Poland, or the Polish-Lithuanian Commonwealth as it was formally known, had been a major power in Eastern Europe, a rival for supremacy of its Muscovite neighbor. When feudal power relations could be invoked for military purposes, Poland still carried weight. But by the end of the seventeenth century that situation had long since changed. While Peter I was mobilizing Russian power, Poland was declining into vulnerability, a pawn and object of great power statecraft. The fundamental explanation for Polish weakness was the position of its nobility. The Polish kingdom was actually a "gentry republic" unique in European history. Its enormous nobility (one-tenth of the population) dominated all other social classes completely. The peasantry was reduced to serfdom, as we shall see, while the indigenous middle class was deprived of self-government in its towns and was so weak that much of the nation's trade fell into the hands of Germans, Greeks, and Jews.

On paper Poland had a complete set of representative institutions starting locally and moving up to the national level. The chief governing organs were the fifty-odd provincial assemblies or dietines in the countryside, whose members were chosen exclusively by the local nobility. The nobility in turn was dominated by a small group of extremely wealthy and prestigious families called the magnates, veritable princes in their own right, with hordes of lesser, and often impoverished, nobles as their dependents. The provincial dietines elected delegates to the lower house of the national parliament (called the *Sejm* or Diet), and were strongly influenced in their choices by the magnates, who themselves sat by right in the upper house or Senate. On the other hand—and wholly different from Sweden—peasants and townsmen had no representation. The Polish Diet functioned under unique rules that maximized the rights and privileges of its individual noble representatives. Any measure proposed in the Diet had to be approved by the provincial delegations unanimously. The deputies of one province alone could veto proposed legislation, a practice called the "free veto" (*liberum veto*). Polish nobles considered this the bulwark of their freedom from despotism; foreign observers regarded it as an in-

The election of King Stanislaus II of Poland. *The election of a Polish king, a unique event in Europe's political life, was theoretically an exercise of direct democracy by Poland's numerous nobles. In practice, however, it was a charade whose outcome was determined by the maneuverings of foreign powers and a handful of Polish magnates behind the scenes.*

vitation to weak government and anarchy. True, under certain emergency circumstances the Diet could be "confederated" instead of meeting routinely, in which case decisions could be made by plurality rather than unanimity. But that was unusual, and in fact of fifty-five Diets that met between 1652 and 1764, forty-eight had to be dissolved in the face of the *liberum veto*. To complete the circle of their power, Polish nobles elected the king, and obliged him to agree to stringent limitations on his authority before taking office. The election was held in a mass meeting at which each noble had the right to participate personally. Tens of thousands usually did, most being under the influence of various magnates. Influence and bribery were also exercised by foreign powers, who had a keen interest in maintaining a weak government in Poland. Playing off particular magnates and their clienteles against each other, Prussia and Russia in particular intervened in Poland's affairs. Once elected, the Polish king found himself without the instruments of effective sovereignty. His revenues were severely limited, he had no substantial bureaucracy at his disposal, and his standing army numbered no more than twenty thousand troops. For the nobles this insured that no Louis XIV, Charles XII, or Peter I would arise to tyrannize over them. For Prussia, Russia, and Austria it meant that Poland, like Sweden, would pose no challenge to their ambitions.

The English Political System

The major exception to the prevalence of absolutism in the eighteenth century was of course Britain. As in Poland, the British political system reflected the social predominance of the landed upper class, but the nature of that upper class differed dramatically (as we shall see in chapter 3), while Britain's strategic position was infinitely more favorable to its prosperity. In the Glorious Revolution of 1688 the English monarchy had been stripped of its pretensions to unchecked or "prerogative" powers. Parliament was now the supreme element in England's mixed government, and the landed ruling class was supreme in Parliament. The supremacy of Parliament and the constitutional basis of monarchy affirmed in 1688 were reaffirmed in the Hanoverian succession of 1714, which placed the British crown in the Protestant family that had been ruling the principality of Hanover in Germany. Moderate Anglicanism, as opposed to a more doctrinaire, "high church" Anglicanism, became the official religion, while Catholicism (politically suspect because of its link to the exiled Stuarts) was barely tolerated. Non-conformist Protestant dissent was granted somewhat broader toleration, but was also excluded from the "establishment." The ruling class, no longer actively fighting over fundamental religious or constitutional issues, enjoyed a relatively harmonious and tranquil existence in the eighteenth century. As J. H. Plumb has put it, the rage of party was replaced by the pursuit of place or influence, and that produced an unusual stability in British public life.

Though Britain was a constitutional rather than an absolute monarchy, the king was no mere figurehead. He still appointed his ministers who set policy, and they remained responsible to him rather than to Parliament. Yet Parliament, with power to make laws, raise taxes, and pass the budget, could exercise leverage over the king's choices. Most political controversy in the eighteenth century stemmed from this ambiguity in the balance of powers between the crown and Parliament. Yet there seemed to be agreement on the basic outline of the system, and the leadership of Robert Walpole (1676–1745) set a basic pattern. Though a commoner, Walpole enjoyed the support of influential Whig peers and the king, and led the cabinet or held office from 1721 to 1742. The king's man, he was also the effective leader of the House of Commons. William Pitt, later ennobled as Lord Chatham, (1708–1778) and his son William Pitt the Younger (1759–1806) would play similar roles in the 1750's and the 1780's and 1790's, respectively. Trying to build their governments around such talented men, or around less talented favorites, the Hanoverian kings used "influence" to support them. "Influence" meant patronage, pensions, sinecures, and favors, which helped to produce working majorities in Parliament. The Duke of Newcastle was famous in the eighteenth century as George II's chief dispenser of patronage, the man whose calculations and contacts stood at the heart of British politics.

Politicians like the Duke of Newcastle could wheel and deal because of the way Parliament was structured. Today, parliamentary government is based on popular voting and party organization. In the eighteenth century there were no parties to speak of, and there was assuredly no system of popular voting to elect the members. In most cases the right to vote was a kind of corporate or group privilege, almost a form of property, whose exercise was expected to bring some direct benefit. Of the 489 English members of the House of Commons, all but eighty represented corporate boroughs. Two or three centuries earlier these boroughs had corresponded to centers of population, to the main chartered towns or settlements, but

Walpole and the Cabinet. *Though the term "prime minister" was not yet in use, Sir Robert Walpole's long tenure as first lord of the treasury and leader of the government was a period of unusual equilibrium in English political life. Many of the king's other ministers came from the peerage. Gouache by Joseph Goupy.*

The House of Commons in session, 1793. *Without question, the British Parliament was Europe's premier deliberative body, meeting continuously and virtually without change in form throughout the eighteenth century. Its history is a complex saga of lofty ideals, special interests, and personal rivalries. Painting by K. A. Hickel.*

this apportionment was never subsequently modified to take account of shifts in population. Therefore, by the eighteenth century, many boroughs were sparsely populated and in a few instances virtually deserted, while elsewhere new cities had developed, such as Manchester and Birmingham, that had no representation at all. In general the north of England was severely underrepresented, while the south and west were overrepresented.

The franchise in the boroughs varied according to customs that had originated in the distant past, but property and patronage were the controlling factors in most. Only a detailed listing of the various franchises can convey the sense of how parliamentary voting was conducted. In descending order of liberality, there were four types of borough franchise: (1) boroughs where all primary residents or homeowners voted (those who paid the household tax called "scot and lot"); (2) boroughs where only so-called freemen, members of the various guilds, voted; (3) boroughs where only members of the town council voted; and (4) "burgage boroughs" where the franchise was attached to a small number of specific plots of land or dwellings. In general the depopulated boroughs and the boroughs with a very narrow franchise were considered by reformers toward the end of the century to be "rotten boroughs." Many were controlled by a single person in whose "pocket" they lay and were accordingly called "pocket boroughs." The Duke of Newcastle, for example, directly controlled seven boroughs. In all, there were about one hundred such boroughs, which returned about two hundred members of Parliament. Looking at it another way: out of 405 borough deputies, only 112 were ever chosen by more than five hundred voters. The few boroughs with wide franchises, such as Westminster, where nine thousand householders voted, or London, where eight thousand freemen of the guilds voted, were therefore of unusual symbolic importance in the British political system. They formed an entering wedge for broad participation and an element of democracy. The eighty remaining English members were chosen by the forty counties, two from each. They were the most independent members since they were elected by all proprietors with a freehold worth an income of at least forty shillings annually. This produced as many as fifteen thousand voters in Yorkshire, though as few as six hundred in the least populous county. Yet the hand of oligarchy was heavy in the counties too. The leading family in the county usually nominated a candidate for at least one of the seats, and a significant number of these seats seemed almost hereditary with sons replacing their fathers as the generations passed. In the Parliament of 1761 over half of the members of the House of Commons were related to baronets or peers, and threequarters had had ancestors in the House.

The oligarchic quality of the unreformed Parliament stemmed not only from its archaic apportionment or the narrow franchise in most boroughs. In addition, since 1716 Parliaments were reelected only once every seven years, and the great majority of seats were not even contested. The one hundred or so borough patrons in the rotten boroughs controlled their candidates, while the crown itself (through men like Newcastle) might have over thirty seats at its disposal. Yet it should be noted that the rotten boroughs performed a useful function as well, since they made it possible to bring talented men into Parliament where their services could be enlisted by the government. The elder William Pitt, for example, was returned from a rotten borough. In general, self-made men, as opposed to men with prominent family connections, entered politics in this way with the assistance of borough patrons.

Under the first two Georges (who reigned between 1714 and 1760) there was a period of what could be called one-party government dominated by the Whig peers in the House of Lords, and by such leaders as Walpole and Pitt in the House of Commons. Of course there was considerable personal and factional rivalry among that minority of Parliament's members who were genuine politicians, ambitious for further prominence or power, but it is difficult to follow their maneuvers since the relatively clear-cut alignments of Whig and Tory in the late seventeenth century had collapsed after 1714. It was said in the 1740's that in English politics there were only Whigs or fools. The hundred or so remaining Tories were excluded from any participation in the ministries, and were generally regarded as covert subversives or Jacobites, waiting for a chance to restore the ousted Stuarts by force. The last Jacobite uprising was put down in 1746, but even when the question of subversion was no longer pertinent, the Tories remained anathema to the mainstream politicians, whatever else they may have disagreed about. Still, the Tory viewpoint survived among certain members from the rural counties who despised the Whig oligarchs, distrusted the monied interests in London, and scorned the crown's patronage machine. Such outsiders were known as the country faction, while those who steadfastly supported the crown's ministers (often because they were indebted to them in some fashion) were known as the court faction. The politically ambitious maneuvered between these two groups, with a politician like William Pitt the Elder being the rare exception who, though ostensibly in the Whig camp, found support among the country members. This confidence he amply justified by leading the country brilliantly in the Seven Years' War (see Chapter 2). The main point about English politics remains that during much of the eighteenth century party labels were meaningless. There were no significant ideologies, party programs, or party organizations to bind individual members of Parliament together. Instead there was a loose network of interests and "connections" based on individual ties and individual ambitions.[5]

Into this extremely fluid situation stepped George III in 1760. The new king resented the pretensions of the Whig oligarchs. Asserting what he considered his prerogative to choose his own ministers regardless of their standing in Parliament, he ousted the popular Pitt and in 1762 installed his personal favorite, Lord Bute. While soon obliged to abandon that exceedingly unpopular Scotsman, he thereafter sought to navigate a relatively independent path through the various political factions, and to appoint ministers whose first loyalty was to the crown. Some of the Whig families were deeply offended by this show of independence and their consequent exclusion from power. They therefore attacked George III as a would-be tyrant seeking to upset the balance of power in the British constitution and to subject England to a continental style of monarchical despotism. The "Whig interpretation" of English history was later echoed by certain

[5] See Lewis Namier, *The Structure of Politics at the Accession of George III* (London, 1939).

nineteenth-century historians, who were judging the eighteenth century by the standards of their own times, in which Parliament had been reformed and the crown's power almost totally reduced. Recent scholarship has tended towards a more favorable view of the monarch, based on an unsentimental and realistic estimate of eighteenth-century politics. In any case, George III was destined to reign over a political establishment far less tranquil than under his two Hanoverian predecessors. The growth of "outside" political agitation in such places as London and Westminster, as well as the eruption of colonial rebellion, would place substantial strain on Britain's traditional political system.

CHAPTER 2

International Rivalry

ABSOLUTIST or non-absolutist, large or small, powerful or weak, Europe's states were linked together in a tangle of rivalries. Few borders or alliances were immutable, few thrones entirely secure from challenge. There were periods in which one ruler might show such pretensions and strength as to challenge the interests and even the survival of several states. More commonly, states vied with each other in a relatively well-matched, if intricate, fashion. This pattern of rivalry—the state system, as it is called—both influenced and was affected by the internal development of each state, above all by the ability of a state to muster effective armed force. If one tangible development cast its shadow across eighteenth century politics, it was the creation by the absolute monarchs of large standing armies. While the composition and cost of these armies were not calculated to promote their heedless use, it is clear that they were not created to preserve the peace. When opportunity for aggrandizement presented itself, these armies would march.

RELATIONS BETWEEN STATES

The State System

Our view of Europe's past has been much influenced by the nineteenth-century Prussian historian Leopold von Ranke. A pioneer of modern historical scholarship based on archival sources, Ranke and his numerous students argued for "the primacy of foreign policy" in historical development. The essence of European history for Ranke was not class struggle, or technological change, or the transformation of values, but rather the emergence of the modern state within the framework of international rivalry. In the endless succession of European wars and disputes Ranke discerned a divine design for the gradual emergence of "the great powers" that would embody Western Christendom's civilizing mission. "The positive prevalence of one [state]," he wrote, "would bring ruin to the others; a mixture of them all would destroy the essence of each. Out of separation and independent development emerges the true harmony." To be sure, Ranke mythicized this happy historical destiny: "In great danger one can safely trust in the guardian spirit which always protects Europe from domination by any one-sided and violent tendency, which always meets pressure on the one side with resistance on the other, and, through a union of the whole which grows firmer from decade to decade, has happily preserved the freedom and separate existence of each state." [1] Despite such fanciful imagery, Ranke did grasp correctly how European civilization was developing through a number of diverse states rather than one encompassing empire, each state forging its identity and power through struggle and war. The framework for this destiny, the almost metaphysical state system of Ranke's vision, seemed to work as he described it. Periodic bids for hegemony or domination of the continent—by a Charles V, a Louis XIV, or a Napoleon—were all ultimately defeated. Moreover, there was assuredly a close relationship between the pressures of international rivalry and the development of coherent centralized states in Europe.

In practical terms, however, the only principle at work in this system of international relations was the self-interest of the individual states. Though the Holy Roman Emperor still exercised moral leadership over various German principalities, most sovereign states of Europe recognized no authority above their own. International law was based on power and practical considerations. The mutual opposition of interests constituted whatever equilibrium could be found in the state system. The "balance of power" was essentially the counterbalancing of one state's ambition by another's. Yet if sheer opportunism was the dominant characteristic of international relations in this period, it was not without its advantages. For the absence of religious or ideological fervor as motive forces of international conflict meant an absence of the fanaticism that had proven so devastating in the past and would prove so destructive in the future.

The state system could appear amoral and anarchic, since the only guarantee of security in the eighteenth century was the ability to assure it by force. A commonplace corollary held that the best defense is frequently an offense or, as the renowned French jurist Montesquieu put it, "with states the right of natural defense carries along with it sometimes the necessity of attacking." States were generally eager to expand their borders. Indeed, according to Frederick the Great, "the fundamental rule of governments is the principle of extending their territories." European interna-

---

[1] See T. von Laue, *Leopold Ranke: The Formative Years* (Princeton, N.J., 1950), which prints Ranke's essay "The Great Powers" as an appendix.

tional politics exemplified the dictum that the end (security and prosperity) justified the means (the exercise of power). War, as Clausewitz
later wrote, was simply the extension of politics by other means. The "balance of power" signified a situation in which no single power dominated
Europe, but it did not imply a commitment to peace or to moral standards in international relations. If force was the usual arbiter of international disputes, however, it was force tempered by practical restraints: by a
pragmatic willingness to compromise with one's rival, and by the technical
limitations of eighteenth-century armies that we shall explore shortly.
The objectives of statecraft did not necessarily have to be pursued through
armed force. Diplomatic maneuvering or bullying could often achieve the
desired result without resort to war. For alongside their standing armies,
Europe's rulers had also created a quasi-professional diplomatic corps.

Like the state itself in this period, the craft of diplomacy was becoming
increasingly rationalized. Foreign ministries now existed in the various
capitals, employing experts, clerks, and archives, while increasing numbers
of ambassadors were stationed abroad in what amounted to permanent
embassies. Together these two developments made it possible to manage
foreign relations more systematically. They also helped foster a sense of
collective identity among European states, despite their interminable contention. Chief diplomats of all countries came from the same aristocratic
milieu. Whatever ruler they might be serving, these ambassadors regarded themselves as members of the same social fraternity. The working
language of the fraternity was now French. In this language negotiations
were conducted and treaties signed—from the Treaty of Rastatt between
France and Austria in 1714 to the Treaty of Kuchuk Kainarji between
Russia and the Ottoman Empire in 1774. Yet these diplomats were not
high-minded innocents, unaware of the underlying brutality of international relations. On the contrary, craftiness was required for success in the
game of diplomacy. Ambassadors were occasionally obliged to fabricate or
embellish ludicrous claims by their rulers to this province or that princely
title, and were routinely expected to dispense the bribes that underlay
diplomacy in places like Poland, Sweden, and the Diet of the Holy Roman
Empire. Old-regime diplomacy could be used to avoid war, but it was also
the necessary prelude to launching a war. For while limited conflicts between two states punctuated the international history of the old regime,
the most important wars were wars of coalitions, the lining up of which
was the work of diplomats.

On paper these coalitions could look formidable if not overwhelming.
Yet their very extensiveness often limited their effectiveness, for dishar-
mony was likely to develop either on the battlefield or in the treaty-
negotiating process. A sudden change of ruler, the rise or fall of a key
advisor, or a change in circumstances could prompt an abrupt reassess-

ment of a state's commitments. States were quick to go to war, but also quick to make peace. Apropos of either situation, Frederick the Great candidly remarked: "the safety and greater good of the state demands that treaties should be broken under certain circumstances." For every large coalition, there was usually a betrayal in the offing for some of its members.

The Interests of the States

The Age of Louis XIV had been a period of almost continuous warfare, culminating in the exhausting War of the Spanish Succession of 1701–1714. In the eyes of his contemporaries the Sun King wished to dominate the continent, not necessarily in the sense of establishing direct territorial control, but of being Europe's arbiter. What drove Louis to his aggressive behavior is a matter of speculation. Clearly his own self-image was crucial, his wish "to accomplish singular actions," as he put it, and his desire to be supreme among all mortals, including his fellow princes. Perhaps an added and hidden motive for launching his many wars was the need to placate and occupy his nobility. As Joseph Schumpeter has suggested, warfare remained the one politically permissible outlet for the nobility's pride, ambition, and energy. Yet Louis was far from being the only ambitious ruler. His Habsburg rival Charles VI entertained his own visions of grandeur, though they were directed eastward and southward, into Hungary and the Balkans, as well as toward Spain and Italy. Also, in 1688 the thrones of England and the United Provinces were temporarily joined in the person of William of Orange, creating a great sense of power in the two maritime nations. The major arena for these conflicting drives was the Spanish Netherlands and other German and Flemish territories to the east of France. All such ambitions exploded in 1701 when the lack of an heir to the Spanish Habsburg domains created a vacuum of power and overwhelming temptations on all sides. At the same time Russia, under the leadership of Peter the Great, was embarking on its relentless drive for territorial expansion. Its triangular rivalry with Poland and Sweden was played out in a parallel series of wars in northern Europe.

The peace treaties of Utrecht in 1713 and Rastatt and Baden in 1714 marked the end of the Spanish Succession War. The disputed Spanish crown as well as Spain's New World empire passed to a separate branch of the Bourbons, thus falling neither to Austria nor France. The Spanish Netherlands, Milan, and Naples went to the Austrian Habsburgs, while Britain gained several colonial footholds including Newfoundland and the strategic Mediterranean fortress of Gibraltar. A few years later the Treaty of Nystad (1721) brought the Great Northern War to an end, ratifying Russia's new-won dominance in the area.

Europe needed a respite. Its resources were depleted, its populations war-weary. For a few years its statesmen were anxious to settle disputes without recourse to war, and the great powers actually concerted to settle their disputes by negotiation at the international congresses of Cambrai and Soissons in the 1720's. This brief appearance of "covenant diplomacy," however, did not foretoken a move toward a new international order. Even during this interlude the interests of minor states were, as usual, ignored. In any event the congress system soon gave way to more conventional methods of conflict resolution.

Between the general peace of 1713–1714 and the outbreak of the revolutionary wars in the 1790's, there was no real threat of hegemony in Europe. Instead, a number of powerful states nurtured territorial ambitions and mutual suspicions, while lesser states pursued their own dynastic or territorial interests as best they could. There were some notable changes in the cast of characters inherited from the seventeenth century, with the decline in power of Spain, the Dutch Netherlands, and Sweden; the rise of the two great "flanking powers" at Europe's extremities, Britain and Russia; and the emergence of that spectacular upstart, Prussia.

The zones of conflict remained numerous. With its access to trade routes and naval stores, the Baltic area was always of great strategic interest, despite Russia's increasing authority in that region. In Europe's center there was still a power vacuum in which the Bourbons and Habsburgs vied for influence, along with such German states as Saxony, Bavaria, and Prussia. Britain too was involved in what might have otherwise seemed a remote area, since the accession of the Hanoverian prince George I to the British throne in 1714 made his north-German homeland of Hanover a British client state. The Italian peninsula continued to be a marketplace for kingdoms and duchies, as Spain and Austria sought to satisfy their dynastic ambitions or to compensate themselves for other losses in places like Naples, Sicily, Sardinia, and Tuscany. In the southeast, the fringes of Ottoman-controlled Europe constituted a prime battleground, as Russians and Habsburgs struggled against the Turks in a spirit of mutual distrust. There was also increasing colonial rivalry in the New World, where Portugal, Spain, Britain, and France had perhaps their most important interests. As early as the 1680's, European wars had begun to reverberate in the West Indies, on the North American mainland, and of course on the high seas of the Atlantic. In 1739, for the first time, a brief war broke out between Britain and Spain as a result of a dispute in the New World. In the course of repressing British smuggling in their empire, the Spanish had severed the ear of a British sea captain, lending to this skirmish the exotic appellation of "the War of Jenkins' Ear." Thereafter colonial issues would increasingly impinge on European diplomatic relations. As the French foreign minister Choiseul complained in the 1750's, the English "while pretending to protect the balance on land which no one threatens . . . are entirely destroying the balance at sea which no one defends."

Diplomacy in the eighteenth century still reflected traditional dynastic interests, with rulers attempting to claim new crowns or client states for themselves by inheritance, conquest, or marriage. The new line of Bourbon rulers placed on the Spanish throne by the Peace of Utrecht exemplified this tradition. Having lost Spain's former Italian dependencies of Naples and Milan in the same treaty, and new ruling house (more specifically, its ambitious Italian-born queen, Elizabeth Farnese) was eager to recoup lost prestige and provide thrones for its princes. Spain therefore provoked a series of wars in Italy and was ultimately placated by a reshuffling of Italian principalities in which Naples received a Spanish Bourbon king, and Austria was compensated by control of Parma. This protracted episode eventually merged with a dispute among the great powers over the Polish succession in 1733. Unable to agree on a candidate for that elective throne, the powers fought a brief war. After protracted negotiations, France's candidates (Louis XV's father-in-law) bowed out, being compensated in 1738 with the Duchy of Lorraine, which passed directly to France upon the duke's death in 1766. The incumbent duke of Lorraine, Francis Stephen, who married the Austrian heiress Maria Theresa in 1736, was forced to accept the Grand Duchy of Tuscany in exchange.

On the whole, however, such dynastic interests were giving way to more impersonal, abstract conceptions of statecraft. Men such as Frederick II, Count Wenzel Anton Kaunitz of Austria (1711–1794), and William Pitt the Elder of Britain saw past traditional commitments and superficially attractive opportunities for aggrandizement to shape their diplomacy to the long-term interests of their states. Less and less did the state system reflect the unrestrained egoism of princes; more and more it functioned in response to "reason of state." This basic trend can be seen in the century's major international development: the diplomatic revolution of the 1750's and the ensuing Seven Years' War.

The Seven Years' War

With at least five great powers competing for position by the 1750's, the number of possible alignments had multiplied. As Austria rebuilt its army and administration, under the leadership of Kaunitz it also reappraised its diplomacy. Until then the Bourbon-Habsburg rivalry had been the cornerstone of both French and Austrian foreign policy. By the 1750's the old enmity had been superseded by at least two other sets of fundamental antagonisms: France's competition with Britain in the New World, and Austria's vendetta against Prussia over the loss of Silesia. For Habsburg Austria the rivalry with Bourbon France no longer seemed important. Its position of leadership in Germany depended now on humbling Prussia.

While France as yet shared no such concern over Prussian power, its hostility to Austria was likewise waning. Kaunitz therefore set about to instigate a diplomatic revolution in which an anti-Prussian coalition could be forged. First, he persuaded the French to abandon their hostility to Austria, which was sensible since France had few vital interests at stake. Then, in May 1756, he convinced them to enter an alliance against their former ally Prussia, which was scarcely to France's real advantage. Finally, Russia was enticed into the coalition in December. Aside from her long-standing personal loathing of Frederick II, Empress Elizabeth perceived Prussia as an obstacle to Russian ambitions in central Europe, while Prussia's geographical vulnerability made it an inviting target.

Frederick II had understandably been active on the diplomatic front in the hope of compensating for that vulnerability, but his panicky countermoves only succeeded in alienating the other powers. Hoping to prevent the undeclared war which had broken out between Britain and France in North America in 1755 from widening into a general European conflict, Frederick had tried to stay on good terms with both sides. Having been France's ally in the past, he had sought to negotiate a treaty with Britain as well. Britain's chief interest in central Europe was to protect its client state, the Electorate of Hanover from the French, and it willingly signed a neutrality accord with Prussia (the Convention of Westminster) in January 1756. Frederick had had no intention of repudiating his relationship with France, but to Paris, which had not been informed in advance of the negotiations, the Convention of Westminster appeared as an affront if not an actual betrayal, and stigmatized Prussia as an untrustworthy ally. Hence France turned definitively against Prussia and at last fell into Kaunitz's design. On its side Russia was also pushed into a more militant position, since it considered the Convention of Westminster a betrayal by its supposed ally, Britain. British bribes and diplomacy could no longer keep Russia from actively joining Austria in an alliance against Prussia.

Out of this diplomatic revolution came a war of almost worldwide dimensions that raged from 1756 to 1763. This mid-century conflagration had two distinct theaters. The continental phase, known as the Seven Years' War, with the Austro-Prussian struggle at its core, saw the clash of two coalitions: Britain-Prussia on one side, Austria-France-Russia on the other. The second phase revolved around Anglo-French competition for empire in North America, the West Indies, and India. Colonial historians have called it the Great War for Empire, and under any label it was this phase of the Seven Years' War that produced the most striking results when the battles were over.

Fighting in Europe began in August, when Frederick II, fearing encirclement, gambled on a preventive strike through Saxony to break apart the hostile coalition. Though he quickly conquered that country—the gateway to Habsburg Bohemia—his plan backfired since it activated the offensive coalition that he dreaded. Both Russia and France met their commitments to Austria, and a grand offensive design against Prussia took final shape. Poorly led, France in effect put its army at Austria's disposal for Austrian objectives. Initially Frederick dazzled Europe by his military genius, leading a spectacular victory over a much larger combined Franco-Austrian army at Rossbach in Saxony (November 5, 1757). Skillful tactics and daring surprise movements would bring other victories, but strategically the Prussian position was poor. Frederick had to dash in several directions across his provinces to repel a variety of invading armies whose combined resources far outweighed his own. Each successive year of the war he faced the prospect of Russian attacks on Brandenburg in the north,

The Battle of Rossbach, 1757. *Frederick's splendid victory over the numerically superior French and Austrians involved skillful maneuvers designed to roll up and break through the enemy's flank. (Source: Christopher Duffy,* The Army of Frederick the Great, *New York, 1974).*

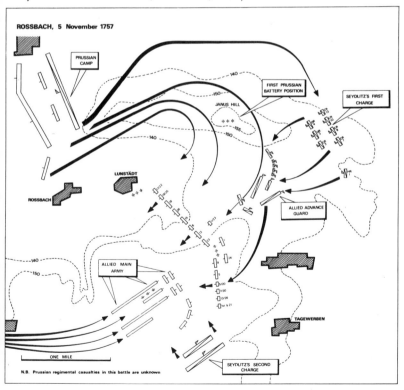

and Austrian thrusts from the south through Silesia and Saxony. Disaster was avoided mainly because of Russia's policy of evacuating for winter quarters regardless of its gains, but even so the Russians briefly occupied Berlin. At best, Frederick seemed to face a stalemate with a considerable loss of territory; at worst, continued war could bring about a total Prussian collapse. On the other hand, all the powers were war-weary, and his enemies were growing extremely distrustful of each other.

Frederick was saved from utter defeat by one of those sudden changes of reign that commonly caused dramatic reversals of policy in old-regime Europe. In January 1762 his nemesis Empress Elizabeth died, and was replaced temporarily by Tsar Peter III, a fanatic admirer of Frederick. Peter quickly pulled Russia out of the war and returned Frederick's conquered eastern provinces of Prussia and Pomerania. Kaunitz's and Maria Theresa's dream collapsed. At the same time, in Britain the belligerent Pitt had been replaced by the more pacific Bute, which cleared the way for an Anglo-French settlement that did not insist on punishment of Prussia. The peace treaty of Hubertusburg, which settled the Seven Years' War, was therefore surprisingly favorable to Prussia in view of all that had transpired. Frederick could return to Berlin, his dominions preserved. Saxony was returned to its elector, but he received no compensation from Prussia for the devastation it had inflicted. Silesia was recognized as Prussian by the Austrians. In short the status quo was restored, leaving the belligerents exhausted and burdened by war debts.

The Great War for Empire

The results of the Anglo-French colonial phase of the war were more decisive. Rival French and British colonial empires had been prospering in different patterns. The thirteen British colonies on the North American continent had reached a population of about one and a half million by mid-century, thanks to continuous immigration and natural increase. While some colonists pushed the frontier westward, others clustered around such ports as Boston, New York, Philadelphia, and Charleston, which were on their way to becoming veritable cities. In contrast, there was little enthusiasm for emigration to French Louisiana or Canada, and the French remained thinly spread in these substantial territories. Yet their North American colonies were well organized and profitable centers of fishing and fur trading. In addition, both Britain and France controlled prosperous sugar-producing islands in the West Indies, and supported rival trading companies on the Indian subcontinent.

French military support for its North American colonies seemed formidable. The greatest bastion of military strength on the continent was the French fortress of Louisbourg at the head of the Gulf of St. Lawrence. In addition, the French established a string of forts near the Great

Lakes and Lake Champlain, which served as bridgeheads for French traders and as a security buffer for French Quebec. At the other end of the continent in Louisiana, New Orleans was founded as a terminal point for trade on the Mississippi River. During the War of the Austrian Succession skirmishes were fought in the New World, but both sides were agreeable to a restitution of their conquests in the Treaty of Aix-la-Chapelle (1748). Obviously this was a truce, not a peace.

The fishing grounds and waterways of the Gulf of St. Lawrence would be a major scene of contention in any future war. A second area that now loomed into prominence was the unsettled Ohio valley. Pushing south from their Great Lakes trading forts and north from their posts on the Mississippi, the French began to assume control over that crucial wilderness. A new string of forts formed pivots for potential French domination of the whole area between the Appalachians and the Mississippi River, territory claimed and coveted by British subjects in the thirteen colonies. There was a growing threat that the French might completely cut off the westward expansion of these colonies. For their part, the French feared that British domination in the Ohio valley would bring encroachments on Canadian territory. In this jockeying for position the allegiance of the various Indian tribes was vital, and the French gradually gained the upper hand. Being traders only, and not settlers, the French did not forcibly remove Indians from their native hunting grounds as the British had repeatedly done. Hence the Indians were willing to cooperate with the French in sealing off the Ohio valley. A large British land investment company, the Ohio Company of Virginia, which was most directly affected by this development, attempted to break this monopoly by sending an expedition against Fort Duquesne in 1754. Led by a young militiaman named George Washington, the expedition failed. Thus, contrary to British traditions of letting settled colonies pay for themselves, the home government was compelled to shoulder the burden of defense. An expedition of regulars under General Braddock was sent the following year to do the job that Washington could not. But Braddock too met defeat in an ambush by experienced French and Indian skirmishers. Limited engagements were now giving way to a full state of war, as each side began to reinforce its garrisons and naval squadrons. By May 1756 a formal war was declared between Britain and France. This war (called the French and Indian War in the colonies) originated as a contest to decide the balance of power in the colonial world. Though European developments impinged on it and served to widen the theater of operations for France and England immensely, the war never lost its quality as a struggle for empire.

The Great War for Empire was one of Britain's glorious moments in history, but it started in quite another fashion. Jumping to the initiative on several fronts, the more highly coordinated French forces struck the first blows. Calcutta fell in India, Minorca in the Mediterranean, several key British forts on the Great Lakes, while in Europe the British expeditionary force suffered defeat and humiliation. Yet the French had certain inherent disadvantages that were likely to show in the long run. Spread so thinly in North America, France depended on naval support to reinforce, supply, and move its troops; unfortunately what had been a fairly even match in the 1740's turned into clear British naval superiority in the 1750's, with Britain enjoying an almost two to one advantage in ships of the line. Equally important, Britain had waiting in the wings a bold and energetic statesman. When William Pitt became first minister in 1758, he brought a single-mindedness and clarity of focus to his task. Though he honored his commitments to Prussia on the continent, Pitt attached the highest priority to defeating France in the New World. His strategy involved an immediate series of offensives and an imaginative use of the British navy. With perfect insight, he directed the largest segment of the British fleet to cover the French home fleet, and then he waited.

The Battle of Quebec, 1759. *This battle is often remembered for the clash of infantry forces on the Plains of Abraham, in which the opposing commanders were both fatally wounded. It was perhaps more notable, however, for Britain's successful use of amphibious tactics, which in turn depended on its naval superiority.*

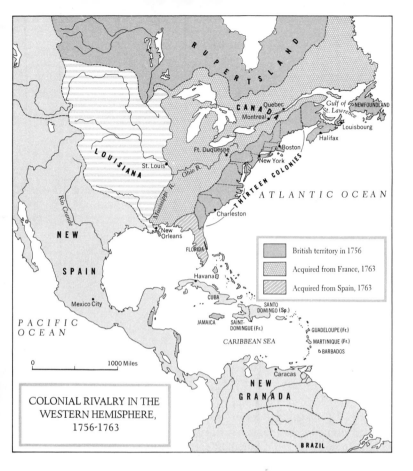

COLONIAL RIVALRY IN THE
WESTERN HEMISPHERE,
1756-1763

British territory in 1756
Acquired from France, 1763
Acquired from Spain, 1763

The French minister, Choiseul, equally aggressive in strategy, hoped to invade the British Isles as the surest method of bringing the enemy to the peace table. The French fleet was ordered to prepare the way. In 1759 major battles were joined between French squadrons from Brest and Toulon and the British squadrons assigned to cover them. At Lagos in August and Quiberon Bay in November, the French squadrons were decimated and the fate of empires decided. Henceforth the British had an almost free hand at sea. Not only were they now immune from French invasion, but they could prevent France from utilizing her superior military forces in the colonial world. Unable to transport men and supplies, the French could no longer reinforce their garrisons. Unable to match the tactical assaults of British ships, they were unable to repel amphibious landings. In every theater of war French colonial possessions were now conquered. In Canada, for example, General Wolfe defeated General Montcalm at Quebec, where their deaths on the battlefield became a widely celebrated event in the mythology of war. The French still held the strongpoint of

Montreal, and if they could have reinforced it, they could have launched a counterattack against Britain's overextended lines. Here is where Pitt's strategy triumphed, since it was now precisely impossible for the French to reinforce garrisons like Montreal. In September 1760 this last outpost of French power in North America fell to the British, who had already ousted the French from the Ohio valley and Great Lakes area. The same pattern of defeat unfolded in Africa and India. Finally, in the West Indies the long-standing duel between the two powers turned into a rout. One by one the French islands were seized, even Martinique. Meanwhile Bourbon Spain had honored its "family compact" with France and had entered the war against Britain, only to suffer the same round of defeats. Two of its key colonial strongholds—Manila in the Pacific and Havana in the Caribbean—were seized by British forces.

Not all of these conquests were preserved at the peace table, however. In exchange for peace, a war-weary Britain was prepared to return certain colonies in the Treaty of Paris (1763). France was willing to surrender Canada with its lucrative fishing and fur trading; Britain, perhaps mistakenly, chose to retain it. This removed the threat of French power on the mainland which, it turned out, had been a major factor in the loyalty of the British colonists to the mother country. On the other hand, since the planters of the British West Indies feared added competition from the inclusion of captured French islands in the British system, the British government decided to return Martinique and Guadeloupe. Likewise Manila and Havana were returned (though not before the British occupation had dramatically affected Cuban society, as we shall see in Chapter 4). In exchange, Spain ceded its claims to Florida, with France compensating Spain by turning over its claims to the Louisiana territory. In the long run India proved to be Britain's most important colonial sphere. The Treaty of Paris excluded French troops from the subcontinent, permitting British commercial influence to grow into political domination.

The First Partition of Poland

One year after the end of the Seven Years' War, the electoral throne of Poland fell vacant—always an occasion for intense diplomatic maneuvering and saber rattling among the powers. In this case Russia showed more determination than her rivals and actively intervened to effect the election of its candidate, Stanislaus Poniatowski, an astute Polish noble who had been an intimate of Empress Catherine. Stanislaus (ruled 1764–1795) would ultimately prove to be less of a cipher and more of a reformer and patriot than the Russians had expected, but that lay in the future. Meanwhile, Russia had things its way. Russia's objective was not to conquer Polish territory but to dominate Polish affairs, to reduce Poland to a kind of vassalage, if needs be by introducing troops onto Polish soil, but preferably by working through various factions of the Polish aristocracy.

What prevented the smooth operation of this strategy was the religious issue. Poland was a Catholic country, and a fierce brand of Catholicism was a hallmark of the nobility's traditional culture. Consequently Protestants and Greek Orthodox Catholics suffered severe discrimination, and they looked to Russia for assistance. Determined to provide that protection, Catherine coerced the Polish Diet into guaranteeing the rights and liberties of religious dissenters. When groups of traditionalist nobles opposed Russian policy by force in 1768, armed conflict spilled over the border into Ottoman territory and precipitated a Russo-Turkish war.

Russia's stunning victories in the Balkans could not help but alarm Austria, which seemed about to enter the war on the Turkish side. Since Prussia would have been drawn into any Austro-Russian conflict because of its alliance with St. Petersburg, Frederick desperately sought a way to reconcile the two powers. In the general confusion of the Polish revolt, Austria had annexed a few small Polish enclaves in Hungary in 1769, and this action proved to be a precedent for the "equitable" arrangement that satisfied all sides. Instead of fighting each other, the monarchs, prodded by certain advisors, sat down and negotiated the partition of Poland. The spirit of these negotiations, though not their precise out-

The Cake of Kings. Or, *more appropriately, of empresses and kings. This contemporary print captures the hypocrisy of the perpetrators, who cannot bear to look at what they are about to do to a helpless Poland.*

come, is conveyed in this remarkable secret memorandum from Austria to the two other powers:

> His Majesty the King of Prussia and Her Majesty the Empress of All the Russias have rights and pretensions to certain districts in Poland, as we [Austria], have; in order to prevent any difficulties that might arise in this connection, we declare . . . that whatever the extent of our respective pretensions, the acquisitions . . . should be perfectly equal; that the portion of one should not exceed that of another, and that . . . we should, in the case of need, mutually and in good faith aid each other, in order to facilitate our success.[2]

Thus would the balance of power in the region be maintained, not by one or two powers going to the assistance of a beleaguered Polish Commonwealth, but by all three of its powerful neighbors negotiating to apportion those parts of Poland that each coveted.

The net result (approved, it must be added, by the hapless Polish Diet and its king) was the loss by Poland in 1772 of about 30 percent of its territory and almost half of its population. Austria gained the richest share, including over 2,500,000 subjects and fertile agricultural land. Russia received the largest slice of territory, with 1,800,000 inhabitants, and pushed its border deeper into Central Europe. Prussia's gain was particularly advantageous, although smaller by half than either of the others, for Prussia gained the territory of West Prussia that had previously separated the two main portions of its realm. If the great powers had been satisfied with this brigandage by diplomacy, the Poles might have had some consolation; but the partition did not mean that what remained of Poland would now enjoy veritable independence. On the contrary, the Russians tightened their grip on Poland's internal affairs, and maintained troops on Polish soil. With the precedent of partition having been set, any pretensions by Poland to independence could and in fact did set off the process again.

The moral of this story is painfully clear. Polish vulnerability was attributable primarily to the aristocratic liberties of its constitution, which crippled effective central government. One critical result of this weakness was the absence in Poland of a large standing army, which left the kingdom's destiny in the hands of its powerful, absolutist neighbors. The story is a particularly appropriate introduction to the question of the mobilization of power under absolutism, to the subject of absolutism and armies.

---

[2] Quoted in Herbert Kaplan, *The First Partition of Poland* (New York, 1962), p. 167

THE FIRST PARTITION
OF POLAND, 1772

Boundary of Poland before 1772

To Russia

To Austria

To Prussia

0   300 Miles

ABSOLUTISM AND ARMIES

Recruitment and Leadership

The rise of professional standing armies was the most graphic dimension of eighteenth-century absolutism. Until the mid-seventeenth century the typical army was relatively small, *ad hoc*, and quasiprivate. As late as the Thirty Years' War (which ended in 1648), much of Europe's armed force was being raised by private military contractors who leased their regiments to the warring states. It had seemed sensible to raise an army only when it was needed, even if that obliged a government suddenly to borrow large sums of money at high interest. These troops were not always reliable, however. Since their supplies were uncertain they were prone to wanton pillaging and desertion; on occasion an entire army would change sides for higher rewards. None of this suited the ambitions of the absolute monarchs. A century later the typical army had become larger, permanent, and subject to the state's direct control. The French army at the accession of Louis XIV in 1661, for example, stood at only 20,000 men. By 1688, on the eve of his first European-wide war, it numbered 290,000 and would never fall below 200,000 in peace or war. At the height of the Seven Years' War, France had 500,000 men under arms. A com-

parable growth occurred in Prussia, where the foundations of the modern
state were created to support its army:

1660	6,000 men		1740	83,000 men
1688	30,000 men		1786	200,000 men
1713	39,000 men			

These numbers reflect the trend among almost all the great powers. If
absolutism involved tapping and controlling the state's resources, then
standing armies were its cutting edge.

The recruitment and composition of Europe's armies were not uniform.
Several states such as Russia, Sweden, and Prussia adopted some form of
conscription: the forcible enrollment of able-bodied peasants, ideally in
units led by their noble lords. The Prussian army, however, has been described as an amalgam of a territorial army and a foreign legion. Well over
half the troops were foreigners, and these were generally the first to see
combat and the most likely to be killed. They could be used as cannon
fodder since their loss would not deplete Prussia's agricultural manpower
or its capacity to produce children. At the same time, these foreign mercenaries were expensive to enroll and often unreliable. Therefore, the Sergeant King, Frederick William I, created the canton system. Each regiment
was allotted a rural district of Prussia as a recruiting ground. All young
males were obliged to register, though skilled artisans were largely exempt.
In their late adolescence the draftees were called up for training and thereafter became a part of the permanent reserve force. Able to work on the
farms and raise families for ten months, they were mobilized annually
for two months of summer training in peacetime. At the outbreak of war
all regiments mobilized their Prussian troops at full strength for the
duration.[3]

In France, Spain, and the Habsburg domains, on the other hand,
armies consisted primarily of volunteers enrolled for long-term service.
Some of the volunteers were foreign mercenaries drawn from the Swiss
cantons or small German states such as Hesse, which did not maintain
armies of their own but were in the business of providing units of mercenaries to other armies. Britain, it should be noted, was the one great
power that did not create a large standing army of its own. The French
army also recruited heavily among foreigners and several regiments bore
foreign names. In the eighteenth century, however, their ranks increasingly
consisted of French rather than foreign recruits. France also had a militia system of sorts to supplement its regular units, but it operated far less
effectively and provoked far more discontent than Prussia's canton sys-

---

[3] Christopher Duffy, *The Army of Frederick the Great* (London, 1974).

tem. It was in effect a draft lottery, imposed exclusively on rural communities. Peasants who had the misfortune of drawing an unlucky lot resented this service; sometimes they fled or bribed someone else to take their place, though this was illegal. Producing between sixty and eighty thousand poorly motivated troops, the militia's importance diminished as the army grew larger, yet it remained as an extreme irritant in the nation's public life, and its unfairness was universally denounced in 1789.

The majority of troops in the French, Habsburg, Spanish, and other standing armies were neither foreigners nor militia conscripts but native subjects enrolled "voluntarily" for six-year terms. Recruited by company commanders or recruiting sergeants, these men were sometimes tricked or cajoled into joining by high-pressure tactics. More commonly they were attracted by the engagement bounty (a sizable lump-sum bonus to supplement their meager pay), and perhaps by the vision of a refuge from personal troubles or hard times. The pull of example was also at work, since recruitment was invariably heavier in regions where there were large military camps. Even though a recruit's motivation for joining was often a desire to escape his lot, soldiers did not necessarily come from the very lowest social strata. In an exhaustive study of troops in the French army between 1685 and 1763 (based on an analysis of regimental troop rosters), André Corvisier has found that most came from families of small peasants and artisans. The typical French soldier was not a criminal or vagabond, though if he subsequently deserted he might well end up in that category on the wrong side of the law. Nor, incidentally, were recruits as young as one might suppose; although the minimum enrollment age was set at sixteen, the average age of soldiers was between twenty-five and thirty. Likewise French soldiers came disproportionately from cities and small towns rather than from the countryside, whose inhabitants seemed more hostile to military service. In any case, while certainly not drawn from the crown's more prosperous subjects, French soldiers were ordinary subjects of the monarchy rather than the dregs of society.[4]

For the minority of soldiers that decided to stay on for the full six years and reenlist thereafter, the army was becoming a career. Its attractions included the prospect of promotion to corporal or sergeant; transfer to elite regiments; and, in France, a small veterans' pension or sanctuary in the *Hôtel des Invalides* upon retirement or disability. On the other hand this was still a career out of the mainstream. Rank-and-file soldiers (as opposed to officers) were held in the lowest esteem by society. Military life still had the reputation of being legalized brigandage, and the element of unruly men that armies certainly harbored gave the whole institu-

---

[4] André Corvisier, *Armies and Society in Europe, 1494–1789* (Bloomington, Ind., 1978).

The Hôtel des Invalides. *Possibly the most imposing edifice in eighteenth-century Paris, this institution could comfortably accommodate over three thousand aged and disabled veterans. Here they received uniforms, linen, medical care, two meals a day (which included bread, meat, vegetables, and wine), and, by mid-century, a pocket-money allowance as well.*

tion a poor reputation. Either the army lived a life apart, physically isolated in barracks and garrisons, or it was billeted on the civilian population, disrupting its routines and devouring its resources. There was generally a reciprocal scorn between soldiers and civilians. In other words, while the composition of armies increasingly reflected the main social strata of peasants, artisans, and workers, and while military service was becoming an attractive career to some, armies were still regarded as alien, oppressive institutions by most civilians.

In the next chapter we shall explore the vast gulf in European society between its elites and its masses. Here it must be said that armies fully reflected that chasm. The officer corps and the rank-and-file troops were from wholly separate worlds. The former came almost exclusively from the elites, while the latter were conscripted or recruited solely from the laboring masses. In Eastern Europe the officers were drawn from the landed aristocracy, their men from the ranks of serfs and peasants. Yet the recruitment of officers was not without its problems. In Prussia, just as the Sergeant King conscripted peasants through the canton system, so too he compelled his nobles to serve in the officer corps. Several radical innovations were introduced. First, Prussians were forbidden to serve in foreign armies, though the Prussian army continued to welcome large numbers of foreign nobles into its own officer corps. (Prussia, it must be remembered, was a medium-sized state of five million population seeking to build an army that could match that of Austria, France or Russia.) More important, Prussian nobles were dragooned into service; teenagers were virtually forced to attend the new Prussian military academy at Berlin, or to enroll as apprentices in various regiments or the royal corps of military pages. Similar systems for training officers were employed in France and Austria, but without the element of constraint that was an essential part of the Prussian system. In times of war, when casualties caused the supply of officers to dwindle, Prussia recruited officers from the middle classes, but these were usually shunted into less prestigious branches of the service such as the artillery or engineers. For Frederick II, having bourgeois officers was "the first step towards the decline and fall of the army," and his policies embodied that attitude. By 1786 only one-tenth of the Prussian officer corps were commoners, and among the higher officers only 22 out of 711.

In France Louis XIV had opened the door to middle-class officers by selling commissions to wealthy commoners at a time when he desperately needed large numbers of officers as well as money. The practice continued into the eighteenth century but was increasingly resented by the nobility. Yet it was difficult to stop, since in France, unlike Prussia, the key ranks of captain and colonel remained venal—a form of property which their owners bought, and presumably sold at a profit when they retired. This opened the door to wealthy commoners, while sometimes closing it to impoverished nobles. Still, there was prejudice against commoners in the officer corps, and the king saw to it that the higher posts in the army went exclusively to the upper nobility—those who combined notable birth with great wealth. The lower nobility meanwhile built up seniority in the lower, non-venal ranks.[5] As a result of the conflicting ambitions and the crown's tendency to try to satisfy all comers, the French army was top-heavy with officers, including double complements of regimental officers and extremely high numbers of staff officers. Moreover, since money and favoritism talked so loudly in the French officer corps, many officers were dilettantes, not professionally adept. There was altogether a marked contrast between the tough professionalism and dedication of Prussian officers, and the bloated, costly, and ineffective French officer corps.

[5] In addition, up to 10 percent of the officer corps were so-called "officers of fortune," promoted up from the ranks for their military talent and dedication, though they rarely rose higher than lieutenant. A very small number of non-noble officers were also ennobled as a reward for continuous and distinguished military service over three generations.

Technology, Tactics, and Strategy

Though essential to the ambitions of the absolutist state, large standing armies were difficult to recruit, costly, and cumbersome to operate. Consequently they were employed on the battlefield in a restrained fashion. The tactics and strategies of old-regime armies had a distinctive cast that was only in part a result of the prevailing technology of war. For under the impact of the French Revolution, virtually the same technology was transformed into an entirely different, more aggressive form of warfare.

The eighteenth-century army was the product of the "military revolution" of 1560–1650, in which firepower had become the standard instrument of battle. The days of bowmen and mounted knights in armor were gone. Armies were now intricate combinations of massed infantry, cavalry, and artillery. The standard infantry weapon was the flintlock musket, which could be loaded more rapidly than earlier weapons but which was extremely inaccurate. Flintlocks were most effective when they could be used to produce a continuous volley of fire that would compensate for their inaccuracy. For this reason, infantry was deployed in extremely elongated lines, usually three ranks deep, with each line alternately loading and firing upon command. Three rounds a minute per man was considered an excellent rate. This tactic required incessant drilling to perfect

The Battle of Culloden, 1746. *The final battle of Scotland's last nationalist rebellion against England proved to be the last battle on British soil to this day. The engraving gives an unusually clear picture of formal line-infantry tactics at work.*

and coordinate the loading and firing tempo. Infantrymen had to become machinelike in their motions, and instinctively obedient to orders. The more they were drilled, the faster they could fire and the greater the edge they could achieve over their opponents. The perfection in the late seventeenth century of the socket bayonet—which could easily slip over a musket—allowed the infantry to alternate between firepower and steel. At its best, a bayonet charge might be the most effective use of manpower; Frederick II remarked that "you decide battles more quickly by marching straight at the enemy [with fixed bayonets] than by popping off with your musket." Old-regime armies did sometimes form into thick assault columns in order to be hurled en masse at the enemy, but it was difficult to maneuver troops from a rigid line formation into a massed column. Such maneuvering required yet further extensive drilling, as did even the simpler maneuver of moving an infantry line forward.

These technical considerations help to explain the extreme emphasis on drill that characterized the training of eighteenth-century armies, but they were not the only reasons. Volunteers and conscripts alike were often discontented sojourners in these armies, especially under wartime conditions which brought endless days of privation. Desertion was therefore a constant threat, and incessant drilling was designed to reduce the individual to a cog in a machine. As part of this process the officers maintained a rigid discipline over their men, meting out corporal punishment routinely and brutally. The troops were supposed to fear their officers more than the enemy. In battle, officers and non-commissioned officers were positioned behind their men as well as ahead of them, and elite light cavalry units were deployed in riding herd on their own infantry as well as harrassing or scouting the enemy. Prussian non-commissioned officers were equipped with spontoons, long implements designed less to wound the enemy than to prod their own men. It was this kind of consideration, as much as technological requirements, that produced the classic line-infantry formations of the old regime. Frederick II already glimpsed the possibility of a different type of warfare, with greater tactical flexibility and mobility. He in fact experimented (as did other generals) with light infantry units formed in loose order, where each individual soldier was more or less on his own as a skirmisher. Of course, only reliable men could be trusted in such units, for there was little to prevent them from fleeing the battle or deserting altogether. Likewise the use of massed columns depended on the motivation of the troops, since once they were set loose on a charge the men were beyond their officers' control. In sum, light infantry skirmishing and massed columns were known in the old regime, but that type of deployment was not widely adopted. Only with the creation of national armies in the French Revolution would mass and mobility find their full application.

The composition, costliness, technology, and tactical orthodoxies of old-regime armies combined to produce a strategy of limited warfare. Strategy was cautious, calculating, and formal, rather than bold and aggressive. It was implemented through rulebook tactics involving elaborate maneuvers in which opposing armies sought small advantages in position and avoided pitched battles if possible. Generals in the field sought to avoid engaging their troops altogether unless their state of readiness and favorable position offered a definite advantage. Each side followed conventional formalities, allowing the withdrawal of bested opponents without attempting to pursue or annihilate them. Total destruction or unconditional surrender of the enemy was rarely sought. In keeping with this strategic mentality there was an emphasis on building strongholds that could protect the

Siege warfare. *The tactics in the Battle of Landau (1704) were replicated in dozens of other engagements in the course of late seventeenth- and eighteenth-century warfare, especially in the Low Countries, northeastern France, and western Germany. Note the geometric design of the walls, calculated to reduce the city's vulnerability to assault, and the besiegers' technique of digging trenches progressively closer to the walls.*

main roads and supply depots on which armies depended as they moved toward the front. In Louis XIV's day, Vauban had raised the science of fortification to new heights and had supervised the building of dozens of forts in France's north-eastern frontier zone. The practice was emulated widely in Europe and siege warfare consequently became a key element of strategy, further contributing to its formalistic style. Indeed, the siege warfare of the old regime seemed to one French revolutionary strategist little more "than the art of surrendering strongholds honorably after certain conventional formalities." More than one revolutionary general would be court-martialed and even executed for appearing to follow such unaggressive practices in 1793.

In siege warfare, as well as infantry battles, artillery played a prominent role. It was, however, an unglamorous branch of the armed forces as well as a more scientific specialty calling for a mastery of mathematics and ballistics. Since nobles tended to disdain its low prestige, commoners played a substantial role in the artillery service, which perhaps helps to explain its relative neglect despite important technical innovations. Eighteenth-century artillery experts were challenged by the fact that heavy weight limited the usefulness of their cannons. Eventually they developed techniques for manufacturing shorter, lighter barrels that at the same time increased the weapons' firing range. The production of more mobile and accurate field artillery touched off an arms race among the great powers. Yet military strategists were reluctant to increase their reliance on artillery or to integrate the new weapons into effective new tactics. Their plausible excuse was that a large artillery force slowed down an army, and required too many horses for transporting the pieces. Like the column assault and light-infantry skirmishing, mobile field artillery would have to await the revolutionary-Napoleonic era for its most dramatic and devastating applications. Then it would add increased firepower to the mass and mobility of the new French armies.

Even less glamorous than the calculation of artillery ballistics was the mundane job of moving and supplying armies in the field. Still, as Frederick II observed, "Flour and fodder are the masters in wartime." Neither armies nor their horses could function on empty stomachs, and auxiliary services in charge of food and transport provided the lifeblood for the fighting men and their animals. The eighteenth century produced several other innovations in army life: standardized uniforms were introduced for the first time; barracks were built for peacetime quarters; and rudimentary army medical services were created, though this always held a low priority and was generally of abysmal quality. All in all, the forging of these new armies was absolutism's most striking and tangible achievement, which is not surprising. Armies alone supplied the power both at home and abroad that was the very core of the emerging sovereign state.

CHAPTER 3

The Social Order

In europe's medieval past, social organization had been simple in theory. Society was divided into orders (*Stände* or estates), each with a specific function and preordained place in its hierarchy. The clergy was nominally at its head, exercising spiritual guidance and consoling a populace that had little joy in this world with the prospect of salvation in the next. Then came the nobility who served as landlords and military protectors. Town dwellers, whose liberties and privileges were usually defined in charters, engaged in trade and manufacturing. Finally there was the mass of the population, the peasantry. Bound to the land in a servile condition, peasants were destined to live out their lives submissively while producing food for the entire society under the lord's supervision.

Over the centuries this model had begun to break down in Western Europe, though in the East it seemed as strong as ever in the eighteenth century. Several agrarian zones must therefore be distinguished and their contrasts examined. Urban society will of course be given its due in this discussion, but the focus will be on the control of land, which remained the fundamental source of wealth and status. Above all it will be clear that European society was composed of groups whose position was still largely determined by birth. For some, their birthright brought privilege and opportunity; for most, it meant a life of burdens and constraints.

RURAL SOCIETY

Lords and Serfs in Eastern and Central Europe

In Central and Eastern Europe a rule of thumb held that "there is no land without a lord." This meant that land could be legally owned only by a lord, which is to say a noble, the crown, or the church. Peasants almost never owned their own land in the modern sense of being free to dispose of it as they wished. Though the restriction of land ownership to nobles was beginning to weaken in Prussia and certain Habsburg domains, legally the monopoly endured. In Hungary, Poland, and several German states the restriction continued to hold with full force in law and in fact, while in Russia (where in theory the tsar held residual ownership of the land) Catherine introduced this proviso in 1762. As a result, in Poland, for example, the land was divided roughly as follows in 1772: the nobility owned 78 percent; the royal house 13 percent; and the church 9 percent. Moreover, in most of Central and Eastern Europe peasants were still serfs, their personal freedom severely restricted by the lords' supervision. They could not marry, move away, or enter another trade without the lord's permission—such permission usually entailing payment of a substantial fee when granted. This dependence on the lord, this personal servitude, made it certain that the peasant would be available to provide the labor or income which the lord required for his own prosperity. In theory the peasant received a modicum of security return: access to a plot of land (which he did not actually own); provision of rudimentary capital like seed (at a price, to be sure); and, in hard times, relief and charity to stave off starvation.

The great estates of Eastern Europe were divided into two parts. The primary one (known as the demesne, which is pronounced "dimain") consisted of the tracts reserved by the lord for his direct exploitation. Naturally he did not farm this land himself. To work this land he required laborers, and most commonly he obtained this labor by demanding unpaid labor services from his peasants (*robot* in the Habsburg Monarchy, *barshchina* in Russia). These labor services were the bedrock of Eastern European serfdom, and were the bane of the peasants' existence. They were extremely demanding both on a routine basis and on special occasions. The amount of labor service was determined by custom and tradition, but even in those states where it was ostensibly regulated by public law, there was no effective way the lord could be prevented from demanding additional service from his peasants. This service generally amounted to three days a week, even more during harvest time. In Russia it was said that the peasant worked "half the year for his master and half for himself." The peasants were also required to provide their own draught animals for work in the lord's fields, horses and carts to transport his produce, and even their children to perform domestic service in his household.

Apart from the demesne, the rest of the lord's estate was divided into plots that went to individual peasant households. Generally they were leased out for payments in money or kind (apart from the labor services and other dues owed or payable by the peasants). Sometimes the tenure was in the form of sharecropping. Peasants enjoyed customary rights to the use of these parcels of land, rights which in theory protected them against eviction. Some had achieved what was recognized in customary practice as a kind of hereditary right to use of the land, but this crucial security of tenure could be forfeited "for cause." That is, the lord could remove his peasant to less desirable land, or could expel him from the estate altogether, because of criminal behavior, alleged poor husbandry, or excessive indebtedness. Transfers of peasants to different holdings could also be by agreement, which the peasant would accept, even in the likely case that it involved displacement and hardship, because he had no choice. In effect the lord controlled his destiny.

This control had a number of dimensions, for the lord stood as a buffer between the peasant and the state. While the peasant paid the land tax on the plots that he cultivated—or the tax on "souls" in Russia—as well as contributions for the upkeep of the parish church, the lord was responsible for seeing to it that these taxes were paid. (The lord, meanwhile, was exempt in most states from paying taxes on his demesne land). While the onus was on the lord to provide this payment to the state, he had thereby yet another kind of control over his peasants and could perhaps turn a profit from the difference between the sum advanced to the state and the amount actually collected from the peasants. In a few states, particularly in Russia and Denmark, the lord was also responsible for providing conscripts to the army, and thus exercised a further power over his peasants. Perhaps most important of all, the lord stood between the peasant and the state in the administration of justice. In Eastern Europe the lords dispensed justice in manorial courts, either sitting personally, or more commonly hiring people for this function. The lord, in other words, was in a position to determine the outcome of disputes on the estate even when he himself was a party to them. Since most seigneurial relations were a matter of custom and interpretation, this was an immense power, and explains why the peasant was at the lord's mercy. Only if the state established a more direct control over the peasantry, undercutting the enormous power of the lord, could the peasant hope for an improvement in his status.

The power of the lords in Eastern and Central Europe extended to the point of their controlling even so-called free peasants. One must recall that these regions were relatively sparsely populated and underdeveloped in the early-modern period. Many peasants migrated to areas where they were not initially subject to a manorial lord and where they were therefore not enserfed. This was especially true in Siberia and other frontier areas of Russia that were gradually opened to cultivation by adventurous peasants to whom the tsar offered freedom or the status of state peasants. In Poland perhaps 20 or 30 percent of the peasantry was free—having emigrated from neighboring lands, having fled from masters far away, or having come from towns where they had had the standing of freemen. Gradually, however, nobles claimed jurisdiction in these areas, and were able to subject the free peasants to many of the burdens of manorialism, even if they retained personal freedom. The status of free peasants in Poland, Prussia, and elsewhere in fact deteriorated in the seventeenth and eighteenth centuries under the expanding domination of the noble lords.

There were, of course, degrees of exploitation and dependence in Eastern European serfdom and one can speak of two types or zones of serfdom. In Russia, Poland, Hungary, and certain small German states serfdom had revived in its classic medieval form and in some instances was worsening in the course of the century. In these lands the status of the serf was scarcely different from that of a slave, though he did in theory retain a "legal personality" that slaves lacked. Polish and Russian serfs were effectively chattels—a form of property—and could be sold or traded at the lords' discretion even independently of the land they lived on or their family ties. Moreover, in European Russia, where perhaps half the land was owned by the state, peasants were often assigned to work (as paid forced labor) in mines and factories. Though their status on the land was more favorable than that of the private serfs, state peasants could in fact be given away to private owners—something that happened to tens of thousands of state serfs during the reign of Catherine II. Similarly, there were few limits on the lord's powers in the administration of justice in Poland, Hungary, Russia, and certain German states. For example, Polish seigneurs could sentence peasants on their estates to death, until capital cases were finally ordered transferred to royal or city courts in 1768. Even after that date both Russian and Polish manorial courts had awesome powers. They could sentence serfs to severe corporal punishment of up to forty lashes, six months in prison, and, in Russia, to exile in Siberia. Peasants had no right of appeal against such sentences.

The situation varied considerably in particular Prussian and Habsburg provinces but was generally not as severe. Serfs could not be sold without their land, and they were free to dispose of whatever wealth they had acquired to their children without interference. But they could not leave their land, or sell or trade it without permission. In theory they could not be expelled from their land so long as they paid their dues and obligations, but in practice they could be removed. More important, while there were usually customary and sometimes legal limits on dues, charges, and labor service, in practice the lords could ignore either with impunity. Corporal punishment could be imposed for discipline, though during the eighteenth century the peasants were gradually brought under a system of more professional royal courts which served as courts of appeal.

Common to both the Russian-Polish zone of serfdom and the Habs-

Flogging a serf in Russia. *Corporal punishment was one feature of Eastern European serfdom that set it apart from manorialism in the West, not only economically but psychologically.*

burg-Prussian zone in the eighteenth century was the increasing profitability of direct farming of the demesne by the lord. Lords therefore had an incentive to bring more land under their control by ousting peasants from their tenures, and increasing peasant labor services. In Russia, for example, the obligation of labor service (*barshchina*) had been by no means universal. Especially in more developed areas, lords who were anxious to increase their supply of ready cash had commuted their serfs' labor obligations into money payments (*obrok*). This in turn had given the serfs more opportunity to work their own land or a chance to leave the village to earn livelihoods in non-agricultural pursuits. There was great variety across the breadth of Russia as between payments of *obrok* or the obligation of *barshchina*. In the later eighteenth century, however, it seems that many a lord reappraised his situation and decided that the opportunities for income were greater in the direct exploitation of his land for the market. In any case, many lords exercised their right to terminate their peasants' privilege of paying *obrok* and forced them back into rendering labor service on the demesne.[1] It was by thus curtailing the peasants' latitude that a virtual plantation style of agricultural production would be developed in the Ukraine, Russia's emerging breadbasket.

Seigneurs and Peasants in Western Europe

While the ownership of land and the status of peasants was fairly clear-cut in the zones of serfdom, Western Europe's agrarian order was more

[1] Jerome Blum, *Lord and Peasant in Russia, from the Ninth to the Nineteenth Century* (Princeton, N.J., 1961), pp. 394, 444–52.

complex and varied. In most areas west of the Elbe River—France, the
Low Countries, northern Italy, Spain, western Germany, England, and
Sweden—serfdom had more or less disappeared by the sixteenth century.
In its place there had arisen a mixed system of land ownership, a coexistence of noble landlords, urban landowners, free peasant proprietors,
peasant tenants, and landless laborers. Whereas "noble land" was restricted to the possession of nobles in Eastern Europe, that restriction had
long since disappeared in the west. In Sweden, the last Western European
country to see this change, the restriction still existed legally but did not
stop the sale of land from the nobility to the peasantry; in 1789 the
restriction was abolished altogether.

Though personally free and able to buy land in Western Europe, the
peasantry was not necessarily secure or prosperous. The quality of village
life may have been less oppressive, but insecurity still pervaded peasant
society. While personal servitude and heavy labor obligations to the lord
had generally ended, other residues of manorialism survived. Outside of
England and the Dutch Netherlands, most peasants still lived under the
jurisdiction of a seigneur—usually but not necessarily a noble, since both
church institutions and wealthy commoners could lawfully exercise that
function. Sometimes a seigneury was identical to an entire village (as it
was likely to be in Eastern Europe as well); more commonly it was
smaller and more scattered. Some of the seigneur's land would usually
be rented out under various kinds of arrangements to peasant tenants or
sharecroppers; the rest was likely to be controlled on a hereditary basis
by peasant families. Nonetheless, the seigneur retained a jurisdiction over
such land that entailed certain rights and privileges. This was the historical residue of the time when the seigneurs for various economic reasons
(shortages of labor, or the need for ready cash) had negotiated a transfer
of some of their land to various peasants, while still retaining ultimate
jurisdiction over it. While peasants in Western Europe usually did not
owe substantial labor services to their seigneurs, they were obliged to
pay various dues and fees, in addition to rent for any land they farmed
but did not own. The incidence of these dues and obligations varied
considerably from region to region, both as a percentage of the seigneur's
income and as a proportion of the peasant's total obligations. In certain
parts of France, such as Burgundy, it could be a substantial and burdensome proportion. By contrast, in the South of France where seigneurialism was weaker, seigneurial rights were more important symbolically than
economically.

The system can be best understood by enumerating the dues and
obligations owed by an otherwise free and even landowning west German,
French, north Italian, or Belgian peasant, or, putting it the other way
around, by enumerating the privileges and prerogatives still enjoyed by

the seigneurial lords despite the weakening of manorialism. There was, first of all, the *cens* or quitrent. This annual due was paid by peasants who enjoyed ownership of their land in other respects. (Technically such qualified ownership is referred to as "non-allodial" ownership: in essence the peasant owned the use or produce of the land on a hereditary basis, rather than the land itself.) The *cens* was either a fixed money charge or a small portion of the harvest paid in kind. If the former, as was often the case, it had diminished markedly over the decades because of inflation, and had remained important mainly as a symbol of the peasant's subordination to the seigneur—a psychological limitation on real ownership and freedom. In certain areas there was also an annual obligation payable on land that had been cleared in relatively recent times. The *champart* (as it was sometimes called) ran much higher than the *cens*, from 5 to 15 percent of the gross harvest, and sometimes higher. A second type of seigneurial dues were the fees owed by peasants whenever a transaction in land occurred. The *lods et ventes* had to be paid when a peasant traded, sold, or bought a piece of land, which—given the prevalence of small parcels in European agriculture—was necessarily often. This too was a basic restriction on ownership, and unlike the *cens* it was usually substantial—rarely less than 7 percent of the land's value and sometimes running as high as one-sixth. It was an affront to both the peasant's dignity and his purse. A different kind of seigneurial privilege were the monopolies the lord held in his jurisdiction over food-processing operations: flour mills, bread ovens, and wine and oil presses. Originally the lord had provided these needed services of milling, baking, and winemaking as a convenience for his peasants. By the eighteenth century, however, these hereditary monopolies had become oppressive. They prevented competition from developing and kept prices artificially high. Seigneurialism also perpetuated another kind of monopoly whose social and economic importance cannot be overemphasized: the lord's monopoly on hunting within his jurisdiction, which deprived the peasants of meat and recreation, while conferring a crucial mark of privileged social status on the lord. As we shall see in Chapter 5, the peasants resisted the monopoly by the practice of illegal hunting, or poaching.

Seigneurial prerogatives in the West were enforced, as they were in the East, by manorial courts that many lords maintained on their estates. Even in England the institution of manorial courts endured through the end of the eighteenth century. In France there were perhaps as many as sixty thousand such courts, whose fees and commissions were yet another vexation to the peasantry. More fundamental was the injustice of having the lord's employees sit in judgement of a dispute involving seigneurial rights.

Certain seigneurs used their leverage to promote innovations such as crop diversification, livestock breeding, and new methods of land management. Taking sharp issue with the traditional view that seigneurialism was an *obstacle* to capitalist development, some historians have recently argued that capitalism was advancing *through* such seigneurial initiatives. It would seem, however, that many (most?) seigneurs were content with traditional ways, their primary concern being to extract as much income as possible under existing arrangements. In any case, a more aggressive attitude toward estate management seems to have appeared in the later eighteenth century. Increasingly profit-oriented, seigneurs were less willing to allow arrears in payments, more likely to foreclose on an unpaid obligation or loan instead of forgiving it, and more likely to increase rents beyond the capacity of their customary tenants. They seemed willing to use every form of legal pressure, if not chicanery, to find in old contracts and manorial documents claims for new rights or fees.[2] Whether he was an innovator or a traditionalist, however, the seigneur's objectives clashed directly with the peasants' desire for adequate land unencumbered by manorial dues and excessive obligations.

Rural Communities

The seigneury was one element (unwelcome though it was) that gave social cohesion to the rural landscape of the old regime. Another, more positive, focal point of peasant life and consciousness was the peasant community or commune. The rural commune of old-regime Europe was not a system for collective labor on the land, nor (in most cases) for communal ownership of arable land, nor for distributing the harvest among villagers. It was a collective form of existence only in an intangible sense—a system of economic and social relations, of obligations and rights that bound together individual residents of the village.[3]

There were three patterns of cultivation or ecosystems in eighteenth-century Europe, and peasant communities took shape somewhat differently in each. Perhaps the most widespread pattern consisted of the open and elongated fields of the Great European Plain—an agrarian system that extended from the English Midlands through the northern portions of France, Germany, and Poland, as well as to parts of Scandinavia and Russia. A second ecosystem, which predominated in Mediterranean Europe, including southern France, Spain, and much of Italy, also featured open fields, but in an irregular pattern as opposed to the north's relatively uniform pattern of long, narrow strips. Finally, in certain provinces

[2] See, for example, Robert Forster, *The House of Saulx-Tavanes: Versailles and Burgundy, 1700–1830* (Baltimore, 1971), which draws a graphic portrait of an exploitative seigneur who squeezed his peasants' income in order to sustain an aristocratic life style at Versailles.

[3] See the pioneering analysis by Marc Bloch, *French Rural History: an Essay on its Basic Characteristics* (Berkeley, Calif., 1966), chaps. 2 and 5.

of western France, in the Baltic region, and in many mountainous areas, a pattern of individually-enclosed fields had developed.

While peasant communalism existed in all three regions, it reached its most intricate form in the first, or northern ecosystem. The typical peasant village contained two kinds of land: arable land individually owned or held on some kind of tenure, and common lands owned corporately by the village. In the northern open-field ecosystem, the village's arable land was divided into several sections corresponding to local soil variation and topography. Each peasant was likely to have one or more small parcels in each of these sections. The intermingling of small, long, and narrow strips belonging to various peasants in each large field or section necessitated a common procedure among the villagers for sowing, ploughing, and harvesting the same crops at the same time. Otherwise it would have been physically impossible to carry on the work of agriculture.

EUROPE'S AGRARIAN ECOSYSTEMS

Region	Type of Field	Characteristics	Settlement Patterns
Northern	open, elongated	deep ploughing/ triennial rotation	nucleated villages
Southern	open, irregular	scratch ploughing/ biennial rotation	
Bocage and Mountain	enclosed	poor soil and much wasteland	isolated farmhouses

Ploughing was especially demanding, for the thick fertile soils of this zone generally required deep ploughing with a heavy-wheeled plough pulled by large teams of draught animals. Historians surmise that it was for this reason that the fields were patterned in long, narrow strips: such a layout saved time and space by reducing to a minimum the number of times the plough team was obliged to turn around in the course of its work. In any case, this layout made the cost of enclosing such long strips extremely expensive as well as impractical, since fences would block access to neighboring strips.[4]

Besides following a uniform style and calendar of cultivation, the vil-

---

[4] In parts of Hungary and Poland, and especially in Russia, communalism was carried one step further: the village controlled the land and allotted arable strips to its families, periodically redistributing the land in order to readjust these allocations.

lagers, lacking adequate pasturage for their livestock, followed the practice of "vacant pasture." After the harvest was in, all livestock in the village was set to graze freely across all the harvested fields, rather than each peasant restricting his animals to his own small plots. To reinforce this practice, tradition forbade the use of the more efficient long-handled scythes in harvesting grain crops, preference instead going to the more primitive sickle. The latter's virtue was that it left a larger part of the stalk standing, leaving more stubble for the "vacant pasture." In addition, villages usually owned some grazing and wasteland (common land), which not only helped to sustain livestock (a major cost for the peasant), but also provided fuel and building supplies for the villagers. All of this fits together to explain, in the words of Marc Bloch, why the peasants "thought instinctively in terms of community." Community translated into the scattering of an individual's holdings among many different strips; the fact that these strips were left unenclosed; the maintenance of "vacant pasture" and of common land to support livestock; and the common pattern of cultivation followed by all peasants. In Bloch's phrase, "it is difficult to imagine a more coherent system."

An open-field village in northern France. *This map (dating from 1738) shows how the village land was blocked out into several large fields, which were subdivided into long, narrow strips owned by a variety of proprietors. The color-keys denote the scattered but substantial holdings of two of the village's larger proprietors. (Source: Marc Bloch,* French Rural History, *Berkeley, Calif., 1966.)*

Communalism was not as elaborate in the two other European eco-systems, but it was far from absent. In Mediterranean Europe the lighter soils and limited rainfall made it possible to use a much lighter "scratch plough." Without the constraints of deep ploughing, peasants had more latitude, hence the irregular shapes of southern fields. Moreover, the region's benign climate was suitable to such market crops as olives for oil, grapes for wine, and mulberry trees for growing silkworms. In the predominant portion still given over to grains, however, the open-field regimen was followed, along with "vacant pasture" and communal calendars of cultivation, typified by a primitive system of biennial crop rotation.

The third, enclosed-field region looked very different. As in the so-called *bocage* or hedgerow country of western France, for example, peasants tended to live in isolated farmhouses among their individually-enclosed fields rather than in the nucleated villages of the two other ecosystems. Still, in these areas of typically rough terrain and poor soil, there were also stretches of communally-owned wasteland, and thus even here the ties of communalism could be found.

Apart from these specific linkages, the peasant community was bound together by common attitudes and habits that can be summed up in the word "traditionalism." For the peasants generally stood united against innovations from the outside world. In their choice of crops and methods of cultivation (such as the wasteful use of fallow to restore the soil's fertility) they clung rigidly to the customs of their ancestors—with the unhappy result that soil fertility and crop yields languished. Yet there was a positive side to this peasant traditionalism in the form of an egalitarian idealism, which held that every peasant ought to be independent and control enough land to assure the well-being of his family. Believing in the social utility of small holdings widely spread among the peasantry, peasants adamantly opposed the consolidation of large farms—whether by noble seigneurs, wealthy peasant farmers, or urban bourgeois. The peasant commune favored private ownership, but within traditional small-scale bounds. It was antiseigneurial in mentality, but also anticapitalist or individualist. As such it could thwart or inhibit its more ambitious members.

This mentality was often translated into action on a quasi-political level, for the commune was also a political entity of sorts. It met in an assembly to choose local tax collectors, hire watchmen, discuss village improvements and the upkeep of the parish church. Villages decided on how to meet obligations to the seigneur or (as was becoming more common) how to oppose his new demands. Legal battles over "vacant pasture" or over the question of common lands became particularly heated, since the seigneury and the commune clashed directly. The seigneur too had a share in the common lands, and sometimes he used his power to promote a division of these lands in which he ended up carrying off a third of the land—presumably the best third—under the seigneurial right sometimes referred to as *triage*. Nevertheless, while village politics were dominated by the seigneur, and by the wealthier peasants, the peasantry as a whole was sometimes able to unite its forces against the lord. Hiring its own lawyer, it could oppose attempts at imposing *triage*, or the renovation of manorial rolls by the lord to extract higher dues, or abuses of the lord's grain-milling or wine-pressing monopoly.

The aspirations of most European peasants were extremely modest. Their first concern was simply to assure the subsistence of their families. For this reason they were afraid to risk innovation and clung to what they considered time-tested methods of cultivation. With some exceptions they also insisted on planting grains to the exclusion of other crops since grains were the staple of their diet. Apart from feeding their families the peasants were next concerned with meeting their obligations, for if they failed to do so they would lose the use of their land. In France these obligations—which skimmed off perhaps 50 percent of the gross harvest —included the tithe to the church (about one-thirteenth of the harvest); royal land taxes of various kinds; indirect taxes such as the salt tax (*gabelle*); the seigneurial dues described above; rent or sharecropping payments on leased land; and interest on the debts that invariably encumbered a peasant. In addition, approximately one-fourth of the gross harvest had to be laid aside to provide next year's seed.

Of course there was diversity within the peasant community. A fortunate few were truly independent. They controlled enough land to assure their families' well-being regardless of circumstances. Called *laboureurs* in the north of France and *ménagers* in the south, they constituted a small portion of the peasantry but controlled a disproportionately large share of land. In the southern village of Lourmarin, for example, only one-sixth of the peasants could be considered independent. The more prosperous usually owned draught animals and ploughs that they not only used themselves but rented out to poorer peasants. They frequently required the labor of other peasants, and used their capital to lend other peasants money at interest. With enough capital, a prosperous peasant could bid for contracts to serve as the "farmer" or "collector" for a large seigneurial landowner or perhaps for a monastery. He then collected the church's land-rents and tithes or the dues and rents of the seigneur who often grew increasingly dependent on cash advances from his *fermier* or agent. Pierre Goubert has traced the activities of such ambitious peasants or "rural bourgeois" who benefited in their own way from the seigneurial system: "Participating in seigneurial perquisites, admirably placed between

A peasant family. *Humble as the cottage, furnishings, and clothing of this French family might seem, they did not denote real poverty, for this was the household of a middling peasant—a small proprietor whose condition was better than that of landless peasants in the West and serfs in the East.*

primary production and exchange, subjugating their masters to the point where they sometimes became their masters' creditors. . . . Slowly but surely they gain control of land belonging to prodigal nobles and indebted peasants, and round out personal domains (which they lease out), while remaining the *fermiers* of others." [5]

The vast majority of peasants were not so fortunate. Their fate rested on each year's harvest. Whether small proprietor, renter, sharecropper, or (as was often the case) some combination of these, most peasants did not control enough land to be assured of subsistence or of the capacity to meet their obligations. In the village of Lourmarin in 1770, for example, Barthélemy Reymond was a median peasant landowner. "He owned nine separate fields amounting to about three acres planted in grain, one

[5] *Histoire économique et sociale de la France*, Vol. II, ed. by C. E. Labrousse and F. Braudel (Paris, 1970), p. 587.

of vineyard, one of wasteland, and one-sixth of an acre of orchard. . . .
Holdings of this size could barely have provided a subsistence standard
of living to their owners; about half of the villagers owned even less.
Peasants like Reymond would have had to work on other land in order
to survive." [6] Even if Reymond could manage from year to year, what
would happen if he had two or more sons who would have the right to
inherit part of his property? From generation to generation the small
holdings of many peasants were further subdivided, producing holdings
that were even less viable than they had been in the preceding period.
The relentless pulverization of peasant property by inheritance goes a long
way to explain why most peasant owners were "micro-proprietors" whose
holdings were not large enough to insure their subsistence.

It is easy enough to understand that peasants were ill-housed and
poorly clothed, but it comes as something of a surprise to learn how
deficient their diet was, limited mainly to bread and soup, and generally
lacking in meat, dairy products, and even vegetables. In good years there
were adequate calories and nutrition in the grains they consumed, but in
bad years they went hungry for days at a time. Since their heavy obligations skimmed off so much of the harvest, peasants often had to earn
additional income or borrow in order to buy back what they had in effect
produced themselves so they could feed their families. It could be a
desperate struggle. In western France, for example, nine-year sharecropping leases were common, and had the advantage of sparing the peasant
from the initial need for seed or other capital. Yet in one locality that
has been studied, at least half the sharecroppers could not complete their
contracts, and lost their land through foreclosure.

In sum, even though they were legally free, and in a substantial number of cases owned some of their land, most peasants in Western Europe
lived an insecure and often marginal existence. Struggling to hold on to
their small holdings and feed their families, they were burdened by excessive taxation, ecclesiastical tithes, and seigneurial dues. While communalism was something of a cushion for individual peasant families, it
also reinforced their narrow outlook and age-old techniques. Against the
pervasive insecurities of peasant life, clinging to tradition seemed the best
strategy.

Agrarian Reform: Failure of an Era

While peasants under seigneurial regimes in Western Europe had much
to complain about, the plight of peasants in Eastern Europe was undeniably worse. Their degraded status and lack of personal freedom stood
in sharp contrast to the century's developing humanitarian ideals. At

[6] Thomas Sheppard, *Lourmarin in the Eighteenth Century* (Baltimore, 1971), p. 18.

least a few respected writers were beginning to portray the peasants sympathetically as human beings unjustly condemned under serfdom to an unending life of toil. Without proposing to overturn the lords' position, or to end the peasants' social and economic dependence, reformers in Central Europe known as cameralists had begun to advocate a minimum program of agrarian reform that would lessen the debilitating exploitation and guarantee the peasants some degree of security. Specifically, they recommended that limits be placed on the amount of labor service that the lord could extract from his peasants to insure that the peasant would have sufficient time to work his own land; and that the peasant's tenure on the plot of land he worked be protected against arbitrary expulsion should the lord wish to assimilate the land into his demesne.

Apart from humanitarian considerations there were reasons of policy that led certain government officials to advocate agrarian reform. They wished to bring peasants more directly under the state's control, and to enhance their productive capacity. This in turn would improve their ability both to pay taxes to the state and to produce more surviving children. At bottom, the reformers sought to give the peasant more incentive to work his land efficiently. When left to themselves, the lords maximized labor services, expelled peasants when they desired their land, maintained the burden of taxation entirely on the peasant, and skimmed off as much of the peasant's productivity as possible in the form of rents or manorial dues. The state could intervene to protect the peasants, but, as we have seen, the basis of absolutism in many states was a kind of bargain with the lords guaranteeing their social and economic position. Yet there was one way in which agrarian reform could be initiated without encroaching directly on the lords. The crown, the state itself, owned vast tracts of land, which became even larger in Catholic countries such as Austria after the dissolution of the Jesuits. These crown estates could become laboratories or models of agrarian reform. The state could demonstrate on its own estates that enlightened self-interest would be served by encouraging rather than exploiting the peasants.

In Russia, however, Catherine II was so anxious to placate the nobles and promote an harmonious relationship with them that she passed up this opportunity. Instead of mitigating serfdom on the crown estates, she sold or gave away tens of thousands of state serfs to private owners under whom their condition deteriorated. For Russian serfs, the extent of the government's involvement in their plight was its admonition that they owed their masters "silent obedience." In Prussia, Frederick the Great did regard the royal domains as laboratories for progress and he ordered a number of changes there: corporal punishment was ended, peasants were made secure in their tenure on the land, and labor services were regulated. But Frederick did not make any serious effort to promote the extension of such reforms to private estates. On the contrary, his other enactments on agrarian affairs tended to bolster the lords' position in the countryside. Thus he formally reinforced the ban on the transfer of "noble" land to commoners (though the practice continued for economic reasons), and he established credit banks exclusively for nobles to facilitate reconstruction after the devastation of the Seven Years' War.

Only in the Habsburg lands (among the major powers) was any significant agrarian reform undertaken. The case merits close examination for it underscores the nature of the agrarian problem in all of Eastern Europe, the possible lines of reform, and the obstacles which eventually led to the failure of Joseph II's determined efforts.[7] Habsburg reform occurred in two phases, with the first modest steps being taken under Maria Theresa. Responding both to peasant revolts and to a pressing need to raise taxes, the state began seeking to limit labor services (*robot*) to a maximum of three days a week. Numerous decrees to this effect were issued, though there was as yet little the state could do to enforce them rigorously. By the 1760's the district officers—appointed and controlled by the crown—were given jurisdiction in this domain. Since they were drawn mainly from the local nobility, however, they were not likely to be excessively harsh toward their fellow nobles. A second thread in this first phase of reform lay in tax equalization. Indeed, Maria Theresa succeeded in doing what no French king had managed: to subject the nobility (except for Hungary's) to payment of the regular land tax, thus easing the burden on the peasants. Maria Theresa's program, motivated by the needs of the state, was not intended to disturb the basic socioeconomic structure. Still, she authorized sweeping changes on the extensive royal domains, especially in Bohemia. The "Raab system," named after its first administrator, was designed to create an almost free, small-holding peasantry on the Western European model. The system involved two major changes that were negotiated on these estates between the peasants and the royal managers. First, *robot* was commuted into a payment in money or crops, so that henceforth the peasant could spend all his time working his own land. Secondly, the demesne was broken up and parcelled out to the peasants on leases in exchange for rents. It was hoped that eventually peasants would become hereditary leaseholders, and possibly even owners, if they could raise the capital to purchase the land. The monarchy carried out this program with the hope that private lords would see that it paid —that they would benefit from freeing their own peasants from labor

[7] See Edith M. Link, *The Emancipation of the Austrian Peasant 1740–1798* (New York, 1949), and William E. Wright, *Serf, Seigneur, and Sovereign: Agrarian Reform in Eighteenth-Century Bohemia* (Minneapolis, 1966).

service in exchange for income, and from setting up the peasants as tenants on their demesnes in exchange for rent. Few lords, however, were inclined to embrace the newfangled system. Clinging to their customary rights and dues, they bitterly resented any meddling by the state. There matters stood when Joseph II succeeded his mother in 1780.

Like all rulers of the eighteenth century, Joseph's first priority was the interest of the state. He differed from his peers, however, by having no patience with the dictates of tradition. Joseph embraced the progressive notion that peasants must be raised in status from degraded objects of exploitation to free, productive citizens. The power of the state depended on economic growth, and growth could only result from increasing the peasant's incentive. Having made up his mind on this fundamental issue, Joseph's blunt and direct style took over. He let nothing stand in his way —neither the opposition of the nobles, nor the suspiciousness of the peasants, nor the lack of an adequate bureaucratic machine to carry out his wishes. Joseph's agrarian policy was radically progressive and aroused determined opposition.

As a first step, Joseph abolished serfdom in its personal aspects in 1781, freeing the serf from restrictions on his right to move about, enter a trade, or marry. The peasant became personally free, though his economic status

Joseph II visiting a farm. *Quite likely this was one of the royal estates on which Joseph and his mother sponsored the sweeping reforms known as the Raab system, which were designed to convert the serfs into free tenants.*

was unchanged. To put teeth into this and subsequent measures, Joseph launched an attack on manorial justice and began to create an infrastructure of state-licensed judges to adjudicate agrarian disputes locally. His second reform continued Maria Theresa's policy in the area of taxation. Joseph ordered a complete resurvey of all land in his dominions. After the survey was completed, all land regardless of its user's status was to be taxed at one of nine rates, depending on the soil's quality. Consequently a larger share of the tax burden would be shifted to the lords. In no other country had absolutism proceeded so far in equalizing taxation. Joseph expected that the lords would attempt to recoup their tax losses by imposing heavier labor services or seigneurial dues on their peasants. In part to head this off, and in part to consummate the monarchy's earlier policy of reducing *robot*, Joseph added his most radical measure. Henceforth, he decreed, peasants would never be required to pay more than 30 percent of their gross income to cover obligations to their lords and to the state. The land tax was set at an average rate of about 12 percent, while the lord could collect at most 18 percent of the peasant's gross income in place of all labor services and manorial dues previously owed. (The only other claim on the peasant's income was his contribution to village and church expenses, which could be a maximum of 20 percent.) With a stroke of the pen—though with numerous exceptions affecting the poorer peasants—Joseph abolished *robot* by ordering that it be commuted into a limited money payment that would leave the peasant a substantial amount of his harvest. Every element but one in the agrarian reform program of Europe's most progressive thinkers had thus been realized. The only measure omitted was the division of the lords' demesnes into smaller plots that would pass to direct peasant use. As it stood, the peasants under Joseph's plan would be free in status, free of labor services, and thus able to devote full time to their holdings. They would now have real incentive to productivity since they could retain about 50 percent of their gross harvest. The lords, in Joseph's view, were by no means being expropriated since they would now receive a sizable income annually, and they still retained ownership of the land. Moreover, being deprived of *robot* labor, they would have incentive to convert to potentially more efficient forms of estate management.

Joseph's decrees predictably aroused a storm of protest among the nobles, especially as they were meant to apply in Hungary, which had been exempted from most of Maria Theresa's reforms. Many peasants were suspicious and even hostile. Some had held millennial expectations that the emperor would abolish all dues and obligations outright. Other peasants wrangled over particular provisions of the legislation, while some were unable to understand or meet their new monetary obligations. Peasants as well as lords were traditional in their ways and did not easily fathom Joseph's style or intentions. Moreover, both had already been offended by his brusque religious reforms (see Chapter 8). Meanwhile, at court, where Joseph needed the support of enlightened bureaucrats, some officials were repelled by his arbitrary manner, while his foreign policy toward the Ottoman Empire was producing unhappy results that further sapped his popularity. The emperor had simply not bothered to build up popular support or even win sympathy within the inner circles of government. He was already on the defensive against this wave of hostility when he died in February 1790. Faced with incipient noble rebellions and a confused peasantry, his well-intentioned brother Leopold was obliged to revoke the most radical enactments, including the uniform land-tax legislation and the *robot* conversion decrees.

The Habsburg peasantry emerged from the Josephinian decade of the 1780's with an improvement in their personal status, but in economic terms they were back where they had started. For them reform had failed. In the long run, however, Maria Theresa and Joseph had opened the door to eventual agrarian reform. They had actively involved the state on the side of the peasant, though continuing to respect the lords' basic property rights. The introduction of the "Raab system" on the royal estates, and the dramatic terms of Joseph's abortive legislation set the standard for an enlightened policy in the future.

Rulers in some of the lesser states had more leeway or were able to enlist enough support among the elites to promote agrarian reform. "Feudalism" was effectively attacked before the French Revolution in the southwest German state of Baden, in Savoy, which lay between France and Italy, and in Denmark. Whereas serfdom was generally disappearing in Western Europe, the Danish state allowed it to be strengthened at the beginning of the eighteenth century. The lords desired this for obvious socioeconomic reasons; the state complied in part because a regime of serfdom—of personal servitude—helped to assure manpower for the national militia on which Denmark depended for its armed force. Accordingly in 1701 male peasants between the age of fourteen and thirty-five were obliged to remain on the manor in which they were born unless granted permission to leave. Later this restriction was extended to include younger and older men, in effect reducing the entire population to serfdom. As in Eastern Europe, Danish peasants were obliged to provide labor services to their lords averaging three or even four days a week; corporal punishment was permitted; and leases for the plots peasants cultivated were granted on precarious terms. Improvement in the lot of the Danish peasant did come at the end of the century, however, as a result of the movement for improved agricultural productivity. With much of their land given over to cattle and dairy farming, Danes were receptive to innovation in land management. The state encouraged this by sponsoring the virtually compulsory enclosure and reconsolidation of small parcels to create compact, efficient family farms, both for peasants who were already freeholders and for dependent peasants. To facilitate this costly process the government provided loans at low interest for surveying and reorganizing the land. In addition, the crown set an example by commuting labor services into money rents on the 20 percent of the land that it controlled. Then in 1786, a royal commission recommended that the personal servitude of the peasants and their liability to corporal punishment by the lords be ended. With the peasant now personally free, it was difficult for the lord to extract excessive labor services, and some were induced to commute the services into money payments. Change did not occur overnight but it did spread. By 1820 over half of Denmark's peasants had managed to buy their own land and become freeholders. On the other hand, the less resourceful peasants tended to lose their footholds on the land and entered the growing class of landless laborers.[8]

The Danish example of agrarian reform stemmed from a consensus, based on progressive economic views, between the state and a segment of the nobility. Where the state's influence was weak and the nobles all-powerful, as in Poland, agrarian reform was out of the question. In Prussia, with its delicate balance between authoritarian sovereigns and entrenched nobilities, agrarian reform in the private sector was not even attempted. Only in the Habsburg domains did reform pass from experiments on royal estates to a compulsory transformation of the entire agrarian society, and in this one major state where reform was resolutely attempted, it failed.

AN AGE OF ARISTOCRACY
The Spectrum of Noble Elites

Continental European society was organized hierarchically, with the nobility automatically entitled to precedence. Regardless of one's personal qualities or moral character, the mere fact of being born into a noble family conferred a mark of distinction—a place at the top of the social order. With this high status came privilege. Only by looking ahead to the nineteenth century can the role of hierarchy and privilege in the old regime be appreciated. Where nineteenth-century liberalism in Western Europe would promote the ideals of civil equality, equality of opportunity, and the prospect of social mobility, none of these values as yet had a place in the social order of most eighteenth-century European states.

Toward the end of the eighteenth century there were probably three

---

[8] Jerome Blum, *The End of the Old Order in Rural Europe* (Princeton, N.J., 1978), pp. 219–20, 267–71.

and a half to four million nobles in Europe, somewhere around 3 percent of the population. About two-thirds of this number came from four states: Poland, Spain, Russia, and Hungary. Fairly accurate counts of the nobility in these states, and rough estimates of their respective share of the total populations, yield the following figures: [9]

Poland around 1770:	750,000	(10 to 15 percent of the population)
Spain in 1768:	700,000	(7 to 8 percent)
Russia in 1760:	550,000	(over 2 percent)
Hungary in 1784:	400,000	(4½ percent)

In Western Europe the proportion was between 1 and 2 percent. Germany (the Holy Roman Empire excluding the Habsburg lands) had about 300,000 nobles, while France had about 120,000. Ownership of land was the foundation of wealth in eighteenth-century society and, as we have seen, in most countries the nobility was the leading, sometimes the exclusive, landowning group. The greatest landowners were usually the royal families, who were by definition the preeminent aristocrats. Apart from ennobled officials, there were very few nobles anywhere who did not have their roots in the land. But just as there were gradations within the peasantry that ran from the prosperous *laboureur* to the landless peasants, so too in the ranks of the nobility there were distinctions and even chasms separating one type of noble from another.

At the summit of the nobility stood the great princes, magnates, peers, and grandees who controlled vast tracts of land and enormous numbers of peasants. In Poland there were about fifty leading families in this category, including the Potockis, whose properties covered seventeen thousand square kilometers and provided an annual income of three million Polish florins. The Radziwills (a name still familiar in high society) topped this with an income of perhaps five million florins. In the Habsburg domains it is estimated that perhaps one-third of the land belonged to a few hundred families, especially in Bohemia and Hungary. In Hungary, where the feudal system lasted until 1848, about 40 percent of the land was owned by 150 families, and the five richest families alone possessed about 14 percent of the entire country. The greatest Hungarian magnate, Prince Esterházy, controlled perhaps seven hundred thousand peasants. In Russia, where property was reckoned in terms of the number of adult male serfs, 3 percent of the lords owned 44 percent of the serfs in the mid-nineteenth century, reflecting a similar if not quite so pronounced

[9] Adapted from Jean Meyer, *Noblesses et pouvoirs dans l'Europe d'ancien régime* (Paris, 1973), pp. 27–34.

concentration in the preceding century. Likewise, in the Kingdom of Naples in southern Italy, eighty-four noble families controlled at least ten thousand peasant tenants each, over two million people altogether.[10]

At the other end of the spectrum were hordes of poor nobles for whom a lexicon of descriptive terms is available: *hobereaux* in France, the poorer *hidalgos* in Spain and *szlachta* in Poland, and the *bocskoros nemesek* or sandalled nobility in Hungary. In extreme cases these people's lives scarcely differed from a peasant's, since they depended for their subsistence either on the direct cultivation of a small plot of land or the largesse of a magnate. Yet even then, they were set apart from the peasants by their noble status, acquired far back in time because of the military roles their forbears had played in their respective national histories. They were privileged—even if this amounted to little more than the right to wear a sword, to sit in the front pew of the local church, to be addressed with some degree of deference, perhaps to vote for (but not serve in) local diets or estates, and in some states to be exempt from most taxes. Zealous of their prerogatives, the poor nobles had the pretensions of an elite without the requisite wealth or power. Consequently they were increasingly vulnerable in the eighteenth century, particularly in lands like Spain and Poland where they were so numerous, contentious, and unproductive. It was clearly to the state's advantage to eliminate their anomalous status, if only to shore up the idea of nobility that seemed a mockery when applied to such people. Louis XIV had set an example by ordering his officials to scrutinize claims to noble status that seemed dubious, which resulted in a diminution of the ranks of the lesser nobility; Charles VI initiated a similar policy in the Habsburg lands. The late eighteenth century brought more extensive campaigns in Spain and Poland. Under these challenges initiated by the state, the number of nobles in Spain declined substantially in the 1780's and 1790's from the previously inflated total, and a similar reduction was achieved in Polish lands after the partition of 1772. In Hungary the "sandalled" nobility (so impoverished that they supposedly could not afford shoes) had lost its proud military role with the practical abolition of the mass feudal levy in which all Hungarian nobles had once served as the nation's armed force. Now these sandalled nobles were stripped of their tax exemptions, though they could still vote in elections for the local diets.

Between the magnates and grandees, on the one hand, and the poorest *hidalgos* and *szlachta*, on the other, stood the average, or middling nobles. In such countries as Prussia, France, and Austria they often held military commissions at the rank of captain (higher ranks usually going to the

---

[10] Except for Naples these examples are drawn from Blum, *The End of the Old Order*, pp. 24–25.

wealthiest of the class). The noble lived on his country estate with a retinue of servants that was the tangible hallmark of his status. Regard for this status involved a distinct set of values, including an ostensible disdain for money-grubbing activity particularly among old-line nobles as opposed to those of more recent vintage. This attitude was reflected in many nobles' habit of running up large debts, as if this were yet another noble prerogative. The virtues of frugality and thrift were not to their taste; like their kings, they often spent money first and worried about paying their debts later. For the same reasons nobles tended to look down on tradesmen and businessmen. In Spain, France, and elsewhere this attitude toward money and status was embodied in public law, which specifically barred nobles from participation in any "ignoble" occupation, such as retail business or artisinal activity. Some considered this a bias damaging to the national interest, and around mid-century a debate raged in France and Spain over the desirability of removing the barriers between noble status and large-scale commercial activity. It was proposed that wealthy nobles be encouraged to involve themselves actively in productive commercial activity, and that the most successful wholesale merchants should routinely be elevated into the nobility. Against the demeaning image of a "commercial nobility," however, other publicists successfully defended the traditional concept of a military nobility, reaffirming that noble status involved a kind of virtue that was incompatible with mere moneymaking. For them, the noble ideal was *honor*, as in the selfless heroism of military glory. But even for those nobles (especially in Spain) who had no regard for the military life, a sense of honor could be focused on the family name, the heritage of the "house" to which each noble belonged—a line of ancestors whose prestige carried forward into the present and had to be perpetuated into the future, distinct from the mass of society. Though many nobles were of relatively recent vintage, most fancied that they belonged to a race apart.

Despite these pretensions, however, nobles were not averse to profiting from commerce. In addition to their revenue from the land, military commissions, or royal sinecures—which constituted the bulk of their wealth—some nobles invested in maritime trading ventures when such opportunities were available. Perhaps more important, as an extension of their land ownership they exploited mineral rights and were thus heavily involved in such productive activities as mining, metallurgy, and glass making. A census of French iron-forge masters in the 1770's, for example, indicates that just over 50 percent were nobles. Likewise, two of the four largest coal mines in France were noble-operated enterprises. In Eastern Europe, with its paucity of middle-class merchants, nobles were often directly involved in marketing their agricultural commodities. Similarly, much of the manufacturing necessary for the village community was carried on under their supervision.

The English Upper Class

The prototype of an upper class that did not depend on birth, privilege, or an exclusive code of honor could be found in England. The island kingdom did have a small hereditary aristocracy, but it differed significantly from those on the continent. Only about two hundred family heads belonged to the peerage or titled nobility. Below these hereditary peers there were a few thousand non-hereditary knights (referred to as Sir . . .), and baronets (a new hereditary title created by James I in 1611 and sold to wealthy commoners in order to raise revenue). Knights and baronets had no legal privileges, while the hereditary peerage had few other than the right to sit in the House of Lords (the upper house of Parliament) and to be tried there by their own peers. True, membership in the House of Lords gave them great political influence, but the real basis of their power lay in their large landed estates. Though the aristocracy or peerage was a distinct segment of British society, it ought to be seen as the upper stratum of a larger landed ruling class. The great distinction in English society was not between noble and commoner but between those who were "gentlemen" and those who were not. The term was not a legal category, but rather an informal social status, comprising peers, baronets, and knights, as well as the more numerous untitled coun-

A country estate in England. *The duke of Marlborough's palatial estate of Blenheim—the gift of a grateful nation—represented a princely style found in the homes of other members of the peerage as well.*

try gentry and the upper reaches of urban merchants and professionals. Most had in common the ownership of landed estates, and acted as local elites in their communities.

Since the landed estate was the major source of wealth and status for the English upper class, peers and gentry alike strove to keep their estates intact from one generation to the next. For if an estate was subdivided among heirs, the family might eventually lose its standing in the community. This was especially true among the peerage, for English titles were supposed to go along with great estates whose income would permit the peers to maintain an appropriately luxurious life style. To keep their estates intact, peers and gentry alike resorted to primogeniture and strict settlements. Primogeniture was an exclusive preference in inheritance for the oldest son—a practice banned in Thomas Jefferson's Virginia Bill of Rights as tending to foster aristocracy. Strict settlements were designed to lock the estate legally in the grip of the eldest male heir for at least two generations against the claims of creditors or other family members. Usually these settlements provided annuities or dowries for the other children, but the estate itself—the landed property and the principal residence or manor house—went exclusively to the eldest son. He in turn maintained the family's prestige at the manor house, employing a retinue of servants to make life comfortable and impress the neighbors. Members of the peerage commonly employed thirty or forty servants at each of their homes, who themselves formed a small social pyramid, ranging from

Servants at work. A valet helps his master to dress, while a liveried footman — usually the mark of an opulent household — serves refreshments. Watercolor by Jean Michel Moreau. Musée du Petit Palais, Paris.

the butler and housekeeper at the top to chambermaids and footmen at the bottom. The latter, in their fancy uniforms called liveries, were the true mark of prestige since they had little useful function. An average untitled country gentleman would be more likely to employ six or seven servants all of whom had hard work to perform.

Unlike the French or Prussian nobility, the English upper class was willing to tax itself. The English land tax was levied on the chief source of a gentleman's income: the rent he collected on his land. In wartime it rose temporarily to four shillings per pound of assessed valuation. Though assessed values were never revised upward later in the century as they should have been, the fact remains that the English landed class probably paid the heaviest taxes in Europe. It also shouldered a large share of the poor rates that were levied locally for public assistance. In addition, these elites exercised local government functions as unsalaried justices of the peace. Of course this was to their advantage, for it meant that there was no centralized bureaucracy ordering them about, and that they could more easily control their tenants and villagers. But it also burdened them with obligations and responsibilities. Another difference between the English and continental upper class was the fact that the English was more open to new blood. English gentlemen formed a less exclusive or caste-minded group than continental nobles. Men who had made fortunes in banking, trade, or manufacturing found it easier than on the continent to retire, purchase estates, and be accepted in the ranks of the country gentry. In some cases they were awarded knighthoods or even titles, but such preferment was not as crucial as it was on the continent. Many English gentlemen were businessmen of a sort themselves: some managed their estates with the latest methods; others exploited their mineral rights by developing mines and foundries on their property; still others built turnpikes and canals to expedite commerce. Peers and wealthy gentry generally maintained establishments in London as well as their country manors, assuring that they were not cut off from the center of business, government, and culture.

English gentlemen and their wives did not have to spend their days earning a living. Income from the land they rented to tenants or farmers afforded them a life of leisure to pursue their public and private interests, whether hunting, reading, managing their wealth, or travelling. Being a leisured gentleman was in fact an ideal to which many middle-class Englishmen aspired, and certainly one which they respected. Yet this aspiration did not turn all the children of the upper class into idle drones. Male children—except for the eldest son and heir—were usually obliged to earn their livings. Titles and privileges did not pass to them, and though they usually received some parental income they were not likely to inherit large fortunes. Therefore, there was not only movement of new men into the

The country gentry. *George Stubbs was known for his paintings of the gentry's horses. In this picture, "The Reapers," he shows an English landowner check-ing on the work of his laborers. Whatever their failings, few of the gentry were absentee landlords.*

landed upper class, but also movement out of that class into other parts of society. Younger sons entered the so-called "middle ranks"—the church, the professions, the armed forces, sometimes even trade or banking, while still retaining the status of "gentlemen."

In sum, the English upper class was a relatively open group whose position was based on landed wealth. Its ties to the rest of society de-pended on wealth, function, and status—not on mere hereditary titles or privileges. Each country gentleman had personal links with large networks of relatives, friends, and subordinates such as tenants, servants, and work-men. These ties of patronage and dependence helped integrate various social strata into a relatively stable society. The upper class maintained its position in part by fulfilling its sense of responsibility and paternalism. In exchange it demanded deference from the lower classes toward their "betters."

The Nobility and the State

In the absolutist states of the late seventeenth and the eighteenth centuries, the sovereigns faced a common problem: how to subdue the nobility without incurring their enmity and without creating severe social instability. Depending on circumstances, the nobility offered an obstacle or an opportunity for the growth of absolutism. In either case the monarchs had to reckon with noble traditions and pretensions. Louis XIV decisively terminated the higher nobility's claim to political power, while accentuating its social prestige. Excluding most French peers from his council chambers, Louis feted them in the ballrooms and dining halls of Versailles. At the same time as he brought new men into key bureaucratic posts and stepped up the sale of ennobling offices to wealthy commoners, Louis showered high-ranking nobles with honorific posts in the provinces, sinecures at court, pensions, and military commissions. Depriving them of the substance of power, Louis placated them with the trappings of eminence. Also, while the Sun King stripped the *Parlements* and the provincial estates of effective power, he refrained from attacking the nobility's basic privileges. For example, though he asked them to pay

Promenade at the Spanish Riding School, Vienna. *Few contemporary illustrations convey more vividly the pomp of eighteenth-century court life, which depended on the participation of a wealthy aristocracy. Horseback riding was one of the skills cultivated by the nobility, along with dancing and (for men) fencing and other martial arts.*

certain new tax levies enacted to meet wartime expenditures, he did not try to coerce them into paying the basic land tax in those regions where they had previously been exempt. When Louis died the French peers sought to undo almost a century of absolutism by organizing the government around councils of high aristocrats, under the leadership of the regent who held the throne during Louis XV's minority. This interlude —a complete reversal of Louis XIV's policy—came to an end in short order, a complete failure. The great nobles were simply unable to weld themselves into an effective governing instrument. When Louis XV assumed full power in 1723, the theory and practice of absolutism resumed their sway. The aristocratic constituted bodies (*Parlements* and provincial estates) would continue to contest the authority of absolute monarchy throughout the eighteenth century, and would win some skirmishes in this running battle, but they would never regain their full measure of institutional power. Louis XIV (building, of course, on the work of others before him) had put the stamp of centralized authority on France that even the French Revolution would not remove.

In Russia, neither the nobility nor the tsar was as secure as their counterparts in most other states. Russia was ostensibly an autocracy headed by the tsar, who presided over a society rigidly divided between lords, serfs, and city-dwellers who had few liberties. The nobility comprised several elements that had been ennobled in different periods and in different parts of the vast realm. Moreover, much of the nobility's land was not owned outright but had been granted by the state, making their tenures vulnerable. Since there was no system of primogeniture favoring inheritance by the eldest son over his siblings, estates tended to be subdivided and noble families depended on the tsar for further grants of land. The leading nobles—the great boyar families that clustered around Moscow—were both stronger and weaker than other prominent nobles in Europe. On the one hand, they could at times make or unmake tsars, overthrowing one and installing another in a palace coup, since the lines of succession were complicated and there were always rivals eager for the throne. On the other hand, the boyars were not an organized group, for they had no special assemblies or corporate institutions. They ruled in Moscow through informal councils of precisely the kind that Louis XIV had swept away so easily in France.

Peter the Great, as we have seen, took the nobility in hand when he began to create a modern administrative state where none had existed before. Like Louis XIV he removed the boyars from their decision-making posts and chose his close advisors from among noble and non-noble, Russian and foreigner alike. At the same time, and in the absence of any real alternative, he virtually conscripted the nobility into the service of his military and civilian administrations. To enforce this regime he decreed that noble status would henceforth depend not on bloodlines and traditions but on service to the state. This was later formalized in the Table of Ranks of 1722, which specified fourteen parallel gradations of civil and military service, more or less reserving the higher ones for members of the nobility who were obliged to move up the organizational table if they sought influential positions. (By the same token, commoners could achieve noble status by means of state service.) Provided that the family served the state—if necessary by moving to Moscow or St. Petersburg—its estates would henceforth be hereditary, while its control of its serfs was bolstered. In sum, the nobility became a secure class, both functional and aristocratic: a high-status, administrative, landowning elite, known as the *dvorianstvo*. Of course the great nobles resented what often amounted to an enforced exile in Moscow or St. Petersburg; some of the lesser country nobles, on the other hand, saw it as an opportunity for rising in the social order. In any case, compulsory service survived Peter's death and continued in somewhat mitigated form until 1762 when it was finally abolished by Tsar Peter III, who thereby allowed many nobles to return to a leisured existence on their country estates.

In exchange for its political submission and cooperation, Peter's successor Catherine II granted the Russian nobility vast landed properties and extraordinary social privileges, including the exclusive right to own serfs and exemption from personal taxes and corporal punishment. She formalized this policy in 1785 with a Charter of the Nobility that formally guaranteed the nobility's position. The Charter codified and extended the *dvorianstvo*'s prerogatives over its serfs, its exemption from compulsory state service, and its exclusive right to certain high positions as well as commercial opportunities that normally went to commoners. Never in Russian history had the nobility achieved such high status, security, or advantages. At the same time, never had any tsar or empress attained so much direct administrative and political power. It was the consummate bargain between absolutism and aristocracy.

A similar bargain had evolved in Prussia. Despite his reputation for enlightenment, Frederick the Great was socially conservative. Skeptical about the capacities of the masses, he believed them destined to remain ignorant and benighted for a long time to come. Civilization and progress therefore required their firm supervision by the noble elite, whose status had to be enhanced. Frederick's father had done battle with the nobility in order to clear the way for centralized government authority. He had been obliged to confront and threaten a self-centered, provincial nobility, and to recruit commoners for his new bureaucracy. Frederick could afford a more relaxed attitude because the battle of state building had already been won.

In the long series of wars fought during Frederick's reign, the Prussian nobility had served courageously and sustained grave losses of life and property. The nobles had shown themselves imbued with the sense of duty to the fatherland that Frederick prized. The success of the canton system seemed to demonstrate that some were born to lead, others to follow. All of this strengthened Frederick's conviction that only men raised on the traditions and values of the aristocracy would make successful army officers, and, as we have seen, he attempted to restore the officer corps as much as possible to its pristine noble status. The military, then, was essentially foreclosed as a career promising advancement and status to commoners. Would the same be true of the civil bureaucracy? Under Frederick William I a system of competitive civil service examinations and merit promotions had offered such opportunities for status to commoners. Frederick the Great reversed this policy, and allowed the civil service system to be undercut by nepotism and preference for members of the nobility. Instead of gradually evolving into an alternative power structure and channel of upward mobility, the upper bureaucracy eventually became simply another outpost of the nobility. True, it was more professional than France's bureaucracy, for the latter was riddled with overlapping jurisdictions, venal offices, and sinecures. In comparison, the Prussian bureaucracy was lean and tough. It was also far more "bureaucratized," meaning orderly and impersonal. Both Frederick the Great and his father had insisted on spelling out detailed regulations, establishing clear lines of accountability, and limiting individual discretion. Once a strong royal hand was removed with the death of Frederick II in 1786, however, the Prussian realm became a kind of "bureaucratic absolutism" rather than a royal absolutism, governed by a powerful, well-insulated aristocracy. In sum, the nobility had first been intimidated by the monarchy, then co-opted into its service. After the passing of strong royal personalities it became the tail that wagged the dog. Prussia developed into the foremost bureaucratic state of the old regime, but its nobility turned out to be the chief beneficiary of the process.[11]

As in Russia, where the nobility's prerogatives were buttressed by Catherine's Charter of the Nobility, the privileges of the Prussian nobility were enshrined in a document known as the Prussian General Code. Begun under Frederick the Great and completed in 1791, the Code was intended as a kind of legal framework that would distinguish Prussian absolutism as a system of laws rather than mere arbitrary power. It also codified the rules of a segregated, hierarchical society. Whereas the French Revolution proclaimed two years earlier that "all men are born and remain free and equal in rights," the Prussian General Code stated that "the rights of man arise from his birth and from his estate." The rights of the nobility,

[11] See Hans Rosenberg, *Bureaucracy, Aristocracy, and Autocracy: The Prussian Experience 1660–1815* (Cambridge, Mass., 1958).

needless to say, were particularly advantageous. Apart from the usual rights of special judicial status and exclusive ownership of "noble" land, the Code prescribed that "the nobleman has an especial right to places of honor in the state for which he has made himself fit." Unlike the Russian Charter, however, by which the Russian nobility was given valuable commercial prerogatives, the Code rigidly segregated the Prussian nobility from the more numerous middle class, and prohibited nobles from entering trades or being associated with the guilds—activities thereby stigmatized in traditional fashion as less honorable pursuits.

The pattern of breaking the nobility's political autonomy, then enlisting it for service in the state—while protecting its social position—was initially followed in the Habsburg Monarchy as well. But Joseph II was not as rigid as Frederick in his commitment to the nobility. In the cosmopolitan atmosphere of Vienna he in fact moved further than any major ruler in Europe toward the norm of social mobility. His edicts of the 1780's were opposite in thrust to Catherine's and Frederick's. The demarcations between nobles and commoners were blurred rather than exaggerated. In the area of justice, for example, Joseph decreed that there would be no special treatment or "peer justice" in a noble's trial or punishment. A noble might even be sentenced to sweep the streets of Vienna in the company of convicted prostitutes. Whereas Frederick and Catherine augmented the privileges of noble landlords, Joseph tried dramatically to improve the peasants' position, and pressed Maria Theresa's policy of taxing the nobility to an extreme matched only by the legislation of the French Revolution. Joseph's principal successor, Francis II, however, was wholly out of sympathy with this social policy, and the Habsburg Monarchy entered the nineteenth century resembling Frederickian Prussia more than Napoleonic France. In its more radical departures Joseph's reign proved to be a brief interlude rather than a veritable turning point. Revolution, in the sense of promoting civil equality and social mobility for commoners, did not come "from above" under absolutism.

URBAN SOCIETY

Though the vast bulk of Europe's population lived in the countryside, by the end of the eighteenth century over twenty cities in a dozen countries had populations that reached the impressive threshold of 100,000 or more. London, with close to 1,000,000 inhabitants, was the largest and fastest-growing, where one out of ten English subjects lived. Paris, the second-ranking European metropolis, had grown more slowly and its population stood somewhere between 550,000 and 600,000. Following in size were Naples, Lisbon, Moscow, St. Petersburg, Vienna, Amsterdam, Berlin, Rome, Dublin, and Madrid. Berlin and St. Petersburg were of course new cities whose growth was directly attributable to the bureaucratic and military needs of their ruling houses. To put urban size into perspective, it is important to take note of the hierarchy of cities beyond these capitals. In France, for example, where over 80 percent of the population lived in rural areas, there were two cities besides Paris which had over 100,000 inhabitants, the Mediterranean port of Marseilles (a kind of regional capital in the south), and the manufacturing city of Lyon. The Atlantic ports of Bordeaux and Nantes, as well as Rouen, Lille, Strasbourg, and Toulouse had all passed 50,000, but below these big cities (by old regime standards) the scale and complexity of urban life dropped off considerably. About one hundred French cities had populations of over 10,000, and another two hundred had between 5,000 and 10,000 inhabitants. Most were undynamic, and rather parochial places, specializing as either ports or manufacturing centers, administrative or judicial seats, or cathedral towns. Many of these towns lived parasitically off the countryside, and did not differ appreciably in atmosphere from rural villages.

Urban Elites

No dichotomy can be assumed between middle-class urban elites as against noble rural elites. True, most nobles resided on rural estates, but the wealthier ones were often to be found in the cities as well, especially in the royal capitals. Those who had direct access to Europe's major or minor crowned heads were known as "court nobles." Masters of conspicuous consumption, surrounded by swarms of retainers and lackeys, they danced, gambled, consumed large meals, and vied for precedence, not only in Versailles, Madrid, Vienna, and St. Petersburg, but in the lesser capitals of the petty principalities of Germany and Italy as well. Their lifestyle entailed large expenditures and short-term debts that ruined more than one venerable family, but which were considered as investments in the future. The more visible one was in this society, the more likely one was to be rewarded with sinecures, pensions, and favorable marriage alliances for one's children. Court nobles led a generally unproductive, even dissipated existence, in which appearances and manners counted above all else. Yet they, along with church dignitaries, could best afford the time and money for supporting the arts. They bought books and sometimes even read them; attended operas, concerts, and plays; commissioned paintings and chamber music; and built magnificent palaces or townhouses that survive as national treasures today. This world of extravagant waste, high culture, and pretension profoundly influenced the social climate in Europe's capitals.

Outside the capitals, urban civilization in Eastern Europe was decidedly underdeveloped. Large regions of Poland, Russia, and Scandinavia were virtually without towns of any size, comparable to tidewater Virginia where, in the absence of towns, the fabric of civilization was woven out of life on the individual plantations. In Western and Central Europe, however, urban society had a long and glorious past. Some cities boasted charters and traditions that stretched as far back in time as the genealogy of the most venerable aristocratic family, and which engendered a similar kind of pride. In particular, there was a species of city that was distinctive for its home-grown governing aristocracy, known as the urban patriciate. Most cities in the Dutch Netherlands and Switzerland, the Hanseatic cities of northern Germany, and the ancient Italian city-states of Genoa and Venice were dominated by urban patriciates whose roots usually lay in mercantile activity. They now formed self-governing oligarchies as closed and as haughty as the Prussian Junkers or the French *noblesse de race*. The life-style of the urban patricians, however, was different from that of the landed aristocrats. In the Netherlands, for example, members of the "regent" class—approximately two thousand families who controlled the municipal councils and through them the ruling provincial estates—have been described as *bourgeois gentilshommes*.[12] They exemplified the bourgeois values of orderliness, thrift, respectability, and quiet family life that were uncharacteristic of Europe's landed nobles.

In Spain, France, much of Germany, and nothern Italy, on the other hand, traditional nobles stood at the apex of urban society. Indeed, one hallmark of the upper nobility—the dividing line between the veritable upper segment and the remainder of that order—was the ability to maintain two large-scale residences, one in the country and one "in town." Their luxurious life-style in town contributed heavily to the support of workers in the luxury trades, food trades, and domestic service. For example, Bayeux in northern France, a cathedral town and a secondary administrative center in a rich agricultural area, counted about one hundred noble families among its population of about thirteen thousand. They included the wealthiest of its residents, filled most royal and municipal offices of any importance, and constituted an exclusive social world complete with their own Masonic lodge. Similarly, in the large city of Toulouse, the regional capital of Languedoc province in southern France, the members of the *Parlement* (the "nobility of the robe," as they were called) were by far the richest inhabitants of the city, owning an estimated 44 percent of the valuable land in the city's hinterland, and constituted an exclusive social and cultural establishment, which intermarried as a rule only with other nobles.[13] In Spain, many of the wealthier nobles did not reside on their rural estates at all, but simply collected their income as

---

[12] E. H. Kossman, *The Low Countries, 1780–1940* (Oxford, 1978), pp. 30–31.
[13] Olwen Hufton, *Bayeux in the Late Eighteenth Century* (Oxford, 1968), chap. 3, and Robert Forster, *The Nobility of Toulouse in the Eighteenth Century* (Baltimore, 1960).

rentiers. They dominated the oligarchic municipal councils of the towns in which they lived, the more aggressive among them using this power for the advantageous marketing of commodities produced on their estates.[14]

Of course in most European cities there were non-noble or bourgeois elites, the upper crust of the middle classes: non-noble office holders, high-level professionals, successful businessmen and merchants, and wealthy rentiers (people who had enough income from their property or investments to live well without an occupation). Occasionally members of these elite groups moved up into the nobility, either by exercising a prestigious function in the state which the crown rewarded by granting a noble title, or by purchasing an expensive venal office that entailed noble status. Most bourgeois obviously remained outside the ranks of the nobility or patriciate, and lent their own distinctive stamp to urban civilization, especially in Britain, France, Germany, northern Italy, and the Netherlands. Going back to the example of Toulouse—not necessarily typical but certainly not an unusual kind of city—we find that 4 percent of the households were headed by rentiers, 7 percent by professionals and officeholders, and 17 percent by members of the commercial and financial bourgeoisie. The remaining inhabitants were families of master artisans and shopkeepers, journeymen, laborers, and the indigent. In Bayeux, whose nobility has already been mentioned, the middle-class represented some 25 percent of the taxpayers, and most owned some land outside of the city. Not surprisingly, the wealthiest of these bourgeois were middlemen for the nobility, church, and state, whose money passed through their hands and sometimes stuck there: collectors of seigneurial revenues, receivers of royal taxes, law court officials, as well as a handful of cattle and dairy merchants. Resourceful urban bourgeois were adept at exploiting the countryside. As Pierre Goubert has summarized the position of such men in Beauvais (northern France): "Their system of amassing wealth from the land, based on loans and *rentes* [loans in the form of annuities], profited simultaneously from the heedless and prodigal nobility of the area and the small-holding peasants who were plagued by poor harvests, taxes, and the inadequacy of their holdings." [15]

It would be entirely misleading, however, to suggest that the non-noble elites were simply parasitic middlemen in the old regime's system of property and taxation, or members of government bureaucracies. On the contrary, one distinctive feature of Western European society were the commercial or capitalist elites, as well as the smaller professional and intellectual elites. In port cities and commercial centers, the merchants, in

---

[14] A. R. M. Carr, "Spain," *The European Nobility in the Eighteenth Century*, ed. by A. Goodwin (London, 1953).

[15] *Histoire économique et social de la France*, Vol. II, p. 584.

George Taylor's words, shared a common "culture of the countinghouse." As young men they were inculcated with the lore of bookkeeping, foreign and domestic exchange rates, weights and measures, and the customs of the business world known only to insiders. Much like the nobility, the merchants had their own outlook, values, and consciousness of common interest. Unlike the nobility, their central concern was earning profit by shrewd investment, if possible without tying up their capital for long periods at a fixed return. Their wealth was "money in motion" as opposed to the slow, steady accumulation of income from landed estates or annuities. The life-style of the merchant class likewise differed from that of the nobility: it combined the pursuit of social recognition and the outward trappings of comfort with the classic bourgeois virtue of frugality. As one historian has perfectly described it, this was a life-style "simultaneously of thriftiness and calculated luxury." Merchants did not always mix harmoniously with other non-noble elites such as officials or lawyers, but, on the contrary, were often in competition with them for precedence and power in urban society. The very wealthiest might, as already indicated, be promoted into the nobility after retiring altogether from their occupation and pointing their children toward more genteel ways, but many families persevered and carried on their trade from generation to generation. Organized in chambers of commerce and other mercantile associations, the merchant class was a distinctive component of urban civilization.[16]

With certain exceptions it can be said that eighteenth-century cities no longer resembled the proud, self-governing municipalities of medieval times, when the "freedom" of the burgher or city dweller stood in marked contrast to the servitude of rural inhabitants. The pressures of venality, absolutism, and oligarchy had combined to undermine urban government and civic pride. We have remarked, for example, how Prussian absolutism intruded itself into the governance of towns, taking over their revenues and police powers. Eighteenth-century Prussian cities were to all intents and purposes run by royal officials, and the same was true in other absolutist states. While France varied too much from province to province to permit such a bald assertion, the trend was similar. In Paris, for example, there were three key officials: the royal intendant of the Paris region; the lieutenant-general of police, a royal official; and the mayor (*prévôt des marchands*), also designated by the king. Under Louis XIV the crown had raised revenue by obliging urban officials to purchase their offices from the crown. Later, new offices were established with the threat of supersed-

[16] George Taylor, "The Bourgeoisie at the Beginning of and During the Revolution," *Die Französische Revolution: zufälliges oder notwendiges Ereignis?*, ed. by E. Schmidt (forthcoming); Pierre Léon, "Les Nouvelles élites," in *Histoire économique et sociale de la France.*

ing the old ones unless the municipalities raised the money to purchase them. Moreover, larger cities had resident subdelegates who reported directly to the royal intendant, and chief police magistrates whose office had become venal.

Within the municipalities themselves, oligarchies had established an iron grip on local offices. Some were venal, some co-optive, and some took their mandate from the town's mercantile and professional corporations. Whatever their source, municipal offices were held exclusively by small cliques of wealthy families, often allied by kinship. They distributed the spoils among themselves, sometimes acrimoniously to be sure, while coming to some sort of understanding with the royal officials who actually wielded a good deal of the power. In the cathedral and manufacturing town of Reims, for example, leading merchants, nobles, and royal officials shared power on the town council with six clerical deputies, while in the textile center of Troyes the aldermen were drawn from the ranks of wealthy judges, landowners, and merchants, several of whom were related to each other by marriage. Entirely absent from such town councils were the artisans and shopkeepers, the numerical if not the moral backbone of the urban citizenry.[17]

There were a few exceptions to the general decay of municipal self-government, the most important being Europe's premier metropolis, London, and a large number of German towns that were spared from the onslaught of absolutism. London's government was somewhat similar in structure to Parliament. The upper house, so to speak, could be found in the Court of Aldermen, presided over by the Lord Mayor, and which consisted of 25 aldermen elected for life by the city's twelve to fifteen thousand freemen ratepayers. These aldermen also served individually as local magistrates. The Court of Common Council, which became the supreme organ of administration in the eighteenth century, comprised the 25 aldermen, plus 210 councilmen elected annually by and from among the ratepayers resident in the individual wards. This assured that the councillors were closely tied by residence and often by occupation to the ordinary city voters. Finally, the freemen of London's livery companies—that is, the members of its corporate occupational and professional groups, which numbered perhaps two-thirds of the ratepayers—elected the Lord Mayor, the City's four members of Parliament, and the sheriffs of London and Middlesex County. With such an electoral system, propertied Londoners enjoyed the right of self-government.[18]

The hundreds of small and medium-sized towns outside the orbit of

---

[17] Lynn Hunt, *Revolution and Urban Politics in Provincial France: Troyes and Reims, 1786–90* (Stanford, Calif., 1978), chap. 2.
[18] George Rudé, *Hanoverian London, 1714–1808* (Berkeley, Calif., 1971), chaps. 7–8.

The Lord Mayor of London. *The city's chief magistrate was elected by London's "freemen," which included most propertied citizens. There were few such popularly elected officials anywhere in Europe. Satirical engraving by William Hogarth.*

absolutism in Germany also retained an element of self-government. Without the anonymity or the mobility of large cities, these towns, with populations running from five to fifteen thousand or so, were stable and self-sufficient. Protected to a certain extent by the statutes and traditions of the Holy Roman Empire, they were neither subject to outside control by ambitious princely houses nor dominated internally by local patriciates or closed oligarchies. Thus they enjoyed an independence denied to most European cities in this age of absolutism and aristocracy. Moreover, these cities did not have large bodies of disenfranchised workers in their midst, for the majority of adult males were usually *Bürger*, or citizens. Each town had distinctive institutions and a separate identity, being a "hometown" to its citizens, in Mack Walker's phrase. Although certain states such as Bavaria and Württemberg tried to bring some uniformity to the governance of their towns, they did not stipulate the form of local elections or governing bodies. Yet these bodies all functioned similarly. Most hometowns had an executive committee or inner council of six to twelve elected aldermen who usually served for life, and an outer council of anywhere from twenty-five to one hundred members which functioned as a watchdog body, an electoral college, and a stage to higher office. The

The free city of Augsburg. *The Bavarian city of Augsburg was typical of the German hometowns, whose citizens' loyalties scarcely extended beyond the walls to any larger political entity. These independent cities may have been a source of weakness in Germany's political history, but they ensured the survival of a functional and satisfying urban life.*

members of these councils were not a distinct governing class. Like London's councillors, they remained in direct contact with their fellow artisans and tradesmen. The *Bürgerschaft* or citizenry of the German hometowns was one of the last political bastions of Europe's urban artisans.[19]

The World of Artisans and Workers

The basic dividing lines in urban society are difficult to determine with certainty, but, following Pierre Goubert, it is probably accurate to think of a threefold division. The upper or dominant class comprised wealthy rentiers, financiers, officials, merchants, and professionals, along with the resident nobility. An intermediary class included the less prosperous elements of those groups as well as the petty bourgeois (lower-middle class) of workshop masters and shopkeepers. Shading off from this petty bourgeois were the popular or working classes. The quality that separated the petty bourgeois from the worker was the same quality that distinguished the *laboureur* from the ordinary peasant: relative independence. It goes without saying, however, that a small shopkeeper or master artisan could be plunged into the working class by adverse circumstances or business failure, a fate by no means uncommon.

[19] Mack Walker, *German Home Towns: Community, State, and General Estate, 1648–1871* (Ithaca, N.Y., 1971), Part I.

One can study the urban working classes from a horizontal or a vertical perspective. Workers were stratified horizontally by trades (food trades, clothing, wood, metal, luxury trades, building trades, etc.) and vertically by their relations to production (self-employed artisans who served others as contractors or jobbers; journeymen artisans in the direct employ of others; unskilled laborers; street vendors; domestic servants). Skilled artisans who acquired formal training through apprenticeship constituted the old regime's labor elite. Apprenticeship was in itself a socially selective process, since the better trades required a substantial investment in the fee paid by the apprentice's family to the master who took him in. For two or three years, the master provided the young man with room, board, and training in exchange for the fee and the apprentice's unpaid labor. Having acquired certified skills through his apprenticeship, the worker then passed into the ranks of skilled journeymen. What happened to him next depended on the way production was organized in his trade, and on the state of the guilds in his city.

Outside of England, and even there to a certain extent, guild or corporate structures still existed in the eighteenth century, but it is hard to know how important they were in the organization of production. Where they had full power, they functioned as monopolistic corporations, regulating the conditions of apprenticeship, labor, production, and marketing. Their ostensible purpose was to protect their members against competition from "outsiders" by trying to suppress competition in alliance with local governments. In doing so, it was argued, they also upheld quality control over production, thus benefiting the consumer. The guilds protected their members' investments in workshops and tools as well as the intangible pride of craft that came from training and experience. Guild masterships could be valuable privileges. In some of the German "hometowns" studied by Mack Walker, the guilds apparently still lived up to their old ideal, which permitted the gradual ascent of journeymen toward the rewarding perquisites of a mastership. After he completed a probationary period, submitted his *chef d'oeuvre* or "masterpiece" to demonstrate his proficiency, paid the sometimes high entrance fee, and satisfied his peers as to his morals, a journeyman was admitted into the guild. In these towns the guilds also constituted the underpinning of community life. A guild mastership was not merely an economic privilege but a badge of citizenship, and an honorable social status implying a certain level of property and respectability, as well as adherence to a strict moral code.

If stability, security, and respectability in a small town setting were virtues of the guild system, they were purchased at the expense of economic growth and individual initiative. The guilds' power was inevitably eroded in larger cities as population and markets grew. By the later eighteenth century the guilds were attacked by progressive economic thinkers as economically retrograde. Moreover guild treasuries were often in the red, for their income (from fees, dues, fines, and interest on investments) could not always keep up with their expenses, such as taxes and the expenses of litigation against other guilds over economic or political prerogatives. Especially damaging to the guilds' image in the popular mind was their growing exclusivism. Most guilds, notwithstanding exceptions such as those cited by Walker, had become oligarchies. New masterships went increasingly if not exclusively to the relatives of masters or to the man who was fortunate enough to marry a master's widow.

To pursue any of this further, one must look at particular trades. For butchers, bakers, and artisans in such luxury trades as watchmaking or jewelry, guild structures tended to remain strong. These trades had a high ratio of masters to journeymen, but the skills of journeymen were highly valued and suitably rewarded. In France, for example, such artisans averaged at least two livres a day in pay. On the other hand, masterships in these trades were extremely expensive and beyond the grasp of journeymen, as preference for new openings went to the heirs of current masters. Such trades as tailoring and shoemaking, which accounted for large numbers of urban artisans, were very different. They had far more journeymen but, since it was less costly to acquire a mastership than in the luxury or provisioning trades, journeymen had a better chance of becoming masters. Yet that prize was growing less attractive. In these expansive trades it was possible for a journeyman to take in contracted piecework in his own quarters without bothering to acquire a mastership at all. Where they could, the guilds attempted to suppress these "garret-workers" or *chambrelans*, but it was a losing struggle in the larger cities. The practice was in fact a crucial stage in the expansion of production before the introduction of factories and machines in the needle trades, shoemaking, or furniture making. In the nineteenth century it would become known as "sweated" industry, and its competitiveness would drive down piece rates (as well as the quality of production), making the lot of these artisans extremely precarious.

A different form of urban production could be found in such industries as hosiery and silk manufacturing. In these trades both journeymen and masters had been reduced to dependence on merchants who provided the raw materials and orders for finished products. Masters were still distinguished from journeymen by virtue of owning their own looms and workshops, but both were governed by piece rates set by the merchants who had come to control the guild structure. Indeed labor consciousness was nowhere keener than among the masters and journeymen of the Lyons silk industry, who waged an ongoing struggle for minimum piece rates against a merchant community that periodically sought to lower piece rates as a response to the competition it encountered in marketing silk cloth.

In less skilled occupations, artisans were effectively on their way to becoming simply workers or "proletarians." In hat-making and in many of the building trades, for example, a few masters had risen to the level of entrepreneurs, totally removed from their numerous semiskilled employees. Though the latter might still think of themselves as journeymen, they had no illusions about ever becoming masters themselves. Their wages, which averaged between twenty and thirty sous a day in France, were closer to those of unskilled labor than of skilled craftsmen.[20]

Passing further along into the world of unskilled labor, we find a vast and varied terrain. Along with the less fortunate artisans, whose excessive numbers and seasonal unemployment made it difficult to earn an adequate living, unskilled workers constituted the laboring poor of the cities. The fortunate among them found their way into the organized gangs of stevedores on the docks of port and riverine cities, or the work gangs of the large urban markets. Others were on their own: water carriers, porters, common laborers in the building trades, women who worked as seamstresses or laundresses, street vendors (male or female) who sold food or old clothes. Domestic service was another major form of employment. One in four taxpaying Parisian families, for example, employed at least one servant, though there were probably more looking for such work than could find it.[21]

The workers in the best position to defend their interests collectively were the skilled journeymen. Excluded from the guilds and with little hope of acquiring a mastership in most trades, they sometimes formed journeymen's associations. Organized along craft lines, the associations facilitated the "tramping years" in which new journeymen gained experience by making a tour of various cities where they stopped to work for several months. Certain associations also provided limited forms of mutual aid during emergencies, but more commonly they provided an outlet for fraternal sociability. In France, for example, these associations were united in three loose federations, and spent much of their energy in obscure rivalries of status that hinged on secret rites and public brawls with their rivals. Because they engaged in such harmless activity, these *compagnonages* (after the French word *compagnon* or journeyman) were tolerated by the authorities though they were actually illegal.

Officials and employers alike were sensitive to the possibility of labor unrest, considering it a potentially grave threat to the fabric of public order in the cities. Social control was essential, and in the old regime that meant

---

[20] Maurice Garden, *Lyon et les lyonnais au XVIIIe siècle* (Paris, 1975), Part II; Pierre Léon, "Morcellement et émergence du monde ouvrier," in *Histoire économique et sociale de la France*. (Twenty sous = one livre).

[21] See Jeffry Kaplow, *The Names of Kings: the Parisian Laboring Poor in the Eighteenth Century* (New York, 1972).

unquestioned subordination of workers to employers. While progressive theorists opposed the guilds as an artificial restraint on trade and productivity, government officials were inclined to support them as mechanisms for the supervision and discipline of labor. As one Parisian official put it, the corporate organization of production provided "a useful chain of orderliness by virtue of which surveillance can easily be exercised over a mass of more than one hundred thousand workers." The state did its share by requiring workers to obtain a certificate from their employer stating that everything was in order before they could lawfully leave his employ. Eventually this was expanded into a requirement that workers carry a kind of passport to be stamped by their employers. In addition, the government strictly forbade strikes and demonstrations.

Though entirely lacking class consciousness in the modern sense, workers in particular trades did not always accept such subordination. Whether through clandestine journeymen's associations or in ad hoc groups, workers were beginning to fight for minimum piece rates or wage scales. Some also struggled to control the employment of fellow artisans—a crucial area of dispute between employers and journeymen. For if hiring was controlled exclusively by the employers, it was easier for them to cut the workers' pay, to discipline them, and to fire them. It was especially galling to workers that the employer could dismiss his workers abruptly, yet complained against workers' leaving suddenly and enlisted the state's aid to prevent it.[22] Despite the prohibitions against them, strikes for higher wages occurred in Paris by bakers, carpenters, printers, hosiery workers, barrel makers, locksmiths, and ribbon makers, among others. While most were short-lived and unsuccessful, some were well-organized, with strike funds and plans for the systematic harassment of non-striking workers. Strikes or "cabals" also broke out over the hiring issue, in which masters who refused to accept the journeymen's association as a placement agency were boycotted. Agitation grew particularly intense when Controller General Turgot temporarily convinced the crown to abolish the guilds in 1775. Workers apparently took this as a signal for increased militance, and as the chronicler of Parisian life, Mercier, recorded, "the apprentices and journeymen wish to act independently; they are showing disrespect toward their masters." Nonetheless, strikes and workers' associations remained illegal for decades to come, and continued to be the exception rather than the rule. As will be suggested in another chapter, working men and women of whatever trade were more likely to take to the streets over rising bread prices than over wages.

[22] Steven Kaplan, "Réflexions sur la police du monde du travail, 1700–1815," *Revue historique*, Vol. CCLXI (1979), pp. 17–77; Garden, *Lyon et les lyonnais*, Part III, chap. 2.

CHAPTER 4

The Dynamic Eighteenth Century

DEMOGRAPHIC and economic growth constituted what might be called the dynamic eighteenth century, producing changes that would eventually alter the material basis of European life. Four developments coincided with and reinforced each other in the later eighteenth century: (1) rising population; (2) increased agricultural prosperity and productivity; (3) a vast increase in commerce, particularly in the exploitation of the colonial world by Britain and France; (4) the growth of textile manufacturing, and the beginnings of its structural transformation in England. More than changes in the role of the state, social classes, ideas, or institutions, these changes arguably set off Europe's transition toward modernity.

POPULATION GROWTH

Historical Demography

In the historian's arsenal, historical demography is the most recent specialized discipline to have attained wide recognition—indeed, some might say primacy. For it seems plausible to argue that population trends constitute the bedrock on which other changes depend, or at least that population trends reflect in the most immediate way fundamental economic or social changes.

Modern historical demography dates from the post-World War II period and was initially an extension backward of interests and techniques relating to contemporary population growth. But there is an interesting difference, for the early modern era was in many ways a prestatistical age. While numerous documents offered ingenious estimates, knowledge of population remained inexact until the beginning of the nineteenth century. Only in 1801, for example, were the first official national censuses taken in France and Britain. The demographer is therefore handicapped, and readers should be warned that general or "global" population figures for early modern times are only approximations. On the other hand, there is an invaluable source to be found in European archives, the parish registers. Keeping the records of births, deaths, and marriages was not the responsibility of the state. This routine chore was handled at the local level by the clergy, and many of their parish registers have survived, allowing historians to reconstruct in fine detail the demographic profiles of specific communities. Thus, while we have only estimates (albeit reasonably reliable ones) about national population movements, we have extremely detailed case studies of individual towns and villages to work with. Parish registers can be made to yield not only the number of baptisms, marriages, and burials —the three sacraments they systematically recorded—but also such data as the age of individuals when they died or when they married. From statistics on the life cycle, historians can then pass—with some trepidation —into qualitative questions about the family and emotional life of early modern Europeans. At the same time, this information leads outward, connecting up with changing economic patterns.

The Death Rate

Until the mid-eighteenth century, Europe's demographic history seemed to be cyclical or wavelike, comparable to the flow of the tides. Population would grow vigorously and then reach a high tide level, only to suffer subsequent reversals and declines. On a local level these declines could be so severe that the inhabitants of a village would abandon it altogether. The land would turn to waste and the village would eventually disappear physically, perhaps to be rediscovered archeologically centuries later. These periods of population loss were the result of crop failures, the ravages of contagious diseases, and the destruction of war. For medieval and early modern times, any notion of uninterrupted population growth is inappropriate. The sixteenth century, for example, was a period of impressive growth, but the following century saw a slackening of growth or stagnation in many areas, dramatic decline in others. Population losses were particularly heavy in seventeenth-century Germany, Poland, and Mediterranean Europe. In the wake of the Thirty Years' War, Germany (the Holy Roman Empire) lost perhaps a quarter of its population before the Treaty of Westphalia in 1648. Later in the century Poland was a similarly devastated battleground, and its population dropped from about ten million to around eight million. Spain seems to have become overpopulated in the sixteenth century relative to its resources, with a large urban sector living parasitically off the countryside and especially vulnerable to epidemics. Its largest and most populous province of Castile lost a quarter of its population during the hard times of the seventeenth century, while Italy and southern France suffered heavy losses as well.

The vulnerability of early modern Europeans to subsistence crises was clearly one element in such fluctuations. Bread held an importance in the European diet that is scarcely imaginable today. The supply and price of grain and flour was the crucial index to the well-being and even the survival of the mass of peasants and city dwellers. Bread supplies are an obvious focus of social history, but also of demographic history. A succession of poor harvests or crop failures (an unfavorable conjuncture, to use the current term) could produce a disastrous chain of consequences—as traced in the accompanying hypothetical diagram. Following the law of

HYPOTHETICAL MODEL OF A SUBSISTENCE CRISIS

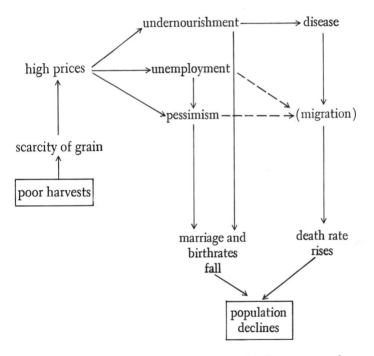

supply and demand, the price of grain would shoot up, perhaps exaggerated by the speculation of grain merchants and millers, or by the panic of peasants afraid to market their meager crops lest they go hungry themselves. This would leave the mass of small peasants and city dwellers—all purchasers of flour or bread—to face extreme privation. Hunger and undernourishment would result, while actual starvation was within the realm of possibility. Undernourishment was the likely key to the ensuing rise in mortality, since it created a favorable environment for disease. In the absence of adequate nutritional and caloric intake, people might begin to eat unwholesome and adulterated substances such as forest roots or contaminated grain, which weakened the body's resistance. Meanwhile, the unnaturally high price of grain would have an adverse effect on employment. Since there were few crops to harvest, agricultural labor would not be in demand; and since the mass of consumers were spending the bulk of their income on bread, the demand for manufactured products might also fall, thus producing industrial unemployment. One way or the other, successive crop failures set off a chain of economic side effects that reduced the income and purchasing power of the masses exactly when they needed greater income to pay higher bread prices. Despair might oblige people to take to the road in quest of food or employment, to beg, and if need be to steal. Such social dislocation might contribute further to the spread of contagious disease, though of course epidemics did not depend on subsistence crises to spread.

Soon, as the hypothetical model suggests, the demographic consequences of this might begin to appear. The cycle of privation—undernourishment, unemployment, and disease—would touch off a rise in the death rate, killing off first the most vulnerable among the very young and old, but also taking its toll on the weakened adult population that might be depriving itself to feed its children. While the death rate rose, the birthrate would likely be falling, for three reasons. First, the pessimism bred by such crises would prompt people to defer planned marriages. Second, the biological effects of undernourishment on married couples might include a temporary loss of fertility. Third, the interruption of marriages by the death of one spouse would of course cut off new conceptions. Within a short time the combination of rising death rates and falling birthrates might produce a significant drop in a region's population.[1]

Seventeenth-century France (the country in which these cycles have been most closely studied) suffered a number of such calamities, but the last major one ended in 1709–1710. At that time a famine struck several provinces coincident with Louis XIV's all-out war effort against a large European coalition, adding starvation and rising mortality to economic dislocation and excessive taxation. The Peace of Utrecht and Louis' demise coincided with the passing of this crisis, and France began the slow process of recovery along with the rest of Europe. Serious crises would recur in the future—notably in Bohemia in the 1770's, and in several regions of Europe simultaneously as late as 1816–1817. But the pattern was changing. After 1715, they became less frequent, less severe, and more local in their

---

[1] Jean Meuvret, "Demographic Crisis in France from the Sixteenth to the Eighteenth Century," in *Population in History*, ed. by D. V. Glass and D. E. C. Eversley (London, 1965).

impact. The social fear of subsistence crises remained a constant in the eighteenth century, but their demographic consequences were abating.

Toward the middle of the eighteenth century Europe's population began to grow in earnest and would never really cease growing again. It was as if some constraining barrier, some upper limit that had existed for centuries, was about to come down. Demographically, Europe's late eighteenth century was a period of sustained growth, and as such the beginning of a new historical era. Even the vast carnage of the Napoleonic wars in the early 1800's would not significantly interrupt this growth. Despite the lack of exact statistics, there are reliable estimates whose pattern is unmistakable. At the beginning of the century, Europe's population stood at about 120 million, rising by mid-century to no more than 140 million and perhaps less. At that point it began to grow rapidly, reaching 180 to 190 million by the end of the century. The growth rate of the population in the century's second half was on the average at least double that of the first half. In each state, and each region of the larger states, the scale of growth and the timing differed, but almost all states (with the exception of the Dutch Netherlands) shared in the general trends. Italy grew from 11 to 18 million, Spain from 7.5 million to about 11.5 million. Prussia and Sweden may have doubled their populations in the course of the century. The most spectacular gains were made in areas of thinly spread population and rich soil such as Russia and Hungary, which may have trebled or even quadrupled its population. In these two countries, however, there was considerable territorial expansion as well as the immigration of new subjects in this period, which makes it hard to distinguish the effect of natural population growth.[2]

England too experienced a surge in population. In the early eighteenth century the population of England and Wales stood at about 5.5 million; by the turn of the century it was just short of 9 million. A fall in the death rate seems to have been the cause of this growth. In the 1740's, just before the acceleration began, the death rate stood at 33 to 35 deaths annually per 1,000 population; by 1801 it had fallen to 26 per 1,000. It further seems likely that a decrease in the mortality of children helps explain this change. In the exhaustively studied village of Colyton, for example, about 30 percent of the children died before reaching the age of fifteen during most of the seventeenth and early eighteenth century, but after 1750 the proportion fell to about 25 percent—a small but durable increment of survival.

France was already the most populous European state and one of the most densely populated. The land could scarcely absorb the kind of

---

[2] André Armengaud, "Population in Europe, 1700–1914," in *Fontana Economic History of Europe: the Industrial Revolution* (Glasgow, 1973); M. Reinhard, A. Armengaud, and J. Dupaquier, *Histoire générale de la population mondiale* (Paris, 1968).

growth that was occurring in Hungary or even in England. Still, France shared in the expansive demographic trend of the later eighteenth century, passing from a population of about twenty million at the end of Louis XIV's reign to about twenty-six million in 1790. A few local studies have suggested that, as in England, the years of infancy and childhood were severely vulnerable, and that small increments of survival became cumulatively significant. Reconstituting the age at death of residents in the parish of Auneuil during the somber period between 1656 and 1735, Pierre Goubert has produced these revealing figures on the mortality of children: [3]

Infants (0–1 year)	28.8% of all births
Children (1–9 years)	18.3% of all births
Youths (10–19 years)	4.0% of all births

Thus, over 51 percent of all the babies born in the parish during the period under study died before reaching the age of twenty. Unfortunately we do not have age-specific figures for that particular parish in the second half of the century, but studies of comparable villages indicate that the rate of child mortality was dropping. One extensive study of several French parishes shows that in the 1780's almost 80 percent of newborns were surviving until age one, and that 58 percent survived to turn twenty.

BAPTISMS AND BURIALS IN AUNEUIL, 1660–1790

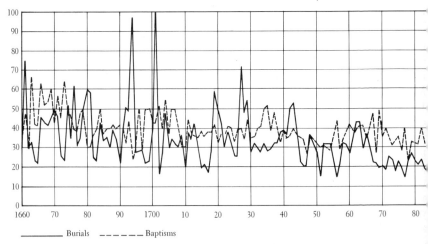

Source: Fernand Braudel and Ernest Labrousse, *Histoire économique et sociale de la France*, Vol. II, p. 40.

[3] Pierre Goubert, *Cent Mille Provinciaux au XVIIe Siècle* (Paris, 1973).

Of course these figures can and should be read the other way around as well. The mortality, by modern standards, was still extremely high even in the "expansive" eighteenth century. What Goubert has written about Louis XIV's time was still essentially true in the later eighteenth century: "Death was at the center of life, just as the graveyard was at the center of the village." Relatively few people outside of the upper classes survived to enjoy a tranquil old age. The association of death with old age is a distinctly modern notion, for in the old regime it was ubiquitous and could come in many forms. Most contemporaries were probably unaware of the extent of population growth; indeed, some intellectuals continued to worry about the problem of depopulation. The fact remains that the mortality rate was beginning to fall in a relatively uninterrupted pattern. Life expectancy rose statistically, and there was a decided net increase in population. Parts of Europe abounded with new mouths to feed and thus with potential problems. However, this added population could also be a great stimulus: a source of labor, of consumer demand, of tax revenues. Population growth could, under favorable circumstances, spur and reinforce economic development.

Health and Nutrition

A decline in the death rate could stem from improved nutrition, and from advances in hygiene or health care. The latter, however, could not have been the principal cause of the eighteenth century's population growth since there was, with few exceptions, little positive change in that area. It is true that Western Europe was now spared from the bubonic plague that had repeatedly ravaged its population. Crowded cities had been especially vulnerable to epidemics of plague that rapidly wiped out a tenth or more of their population. Seville in 1649, Amsterdam in 1664, and London in 1665, for example, experienced the dread scourge. The last outbreak in Western Europe came in 1720, when it was confined to a small area of Mediterranean France, though Moscow suffered a severe epidemic in 1771. It might also be noted that Europe had not yet begun to suffer from epidemics of cholera—a fearsomely contagious disease that would assult the world's population in the nineteenth century. With the exception of plague, however, eighteenth-century Europe still lived amidst, a formidable array of chronic and epidemic diseases. Tuberculosis, typhoid, and malaria were endemic in many areas, but probably more lethal were the periodic epidemics of dysentery, smallpox, influenza, and typhus. Dysentery, the worst of numerous digestive diseases, could destroy the alimentary canal, and some of its variants spread rapidly; in 1779, for example, over a hundred thousand people perished in a dysentery epidemic in the French province of Brittany alone. Smallpox struck particularly at children, rich and poor alike, while influenza, a respiratory disease, was especially lethal for the elderly and struck most often in winter. Finally there was typhus,

The final plague. *Scarcely distinguishable from a medieval scene, this depiction of Western Europe's last epidemic of plague in 1720 leaves no question as to the lethal effects of the disease. Plague was generally carried from the East by rats, whose infection was spread by fleas to human hosts.*

the preeminent disease of the poor, which was carried by lice that bred in the unsanitary conditions of poverty.

The habits of private hygiene as well as the practices of public hygiene seemed conspiratorially designed to propagate disease. Bathing was infrequent; water supplies often contaminated; housing extremely overcrowded and poorly ventilated; clothing rarely washed or changed. Above all, the disposal of waste was entirely haphazard, not only creating a pervasive stench in the cities, but posing a danger to health in city and countryside alike.

Against disease the eighteenth-century medical profession was undermanned, ill-equipped with knowledge or technique, and distrusted by the mass of people, who preferred folk remedies and home-brewed concoctions to its dubious treatments. There were few enough practitioners to begin with, and they were concentrated disproportionately in the cities. In any case even the most progressive practitioners understood little about the etiology or prevention of contagious diseases. Toward the end of the century a ray of progress could be discerned as some of the more enlightened doctors joined forces in the French Royal Society of Medicine, founded in 1776. This useful institution began to investigate the symptomology of disease and the conditions that seemed to promote it; in effect it tried to launch an early public health movement. At this early stage, however, it had virtually no impact on public hygiene and was able to make few inroads on the mystery of disease. The one ailment that doctors did begin to understand in the eighteenth century was smallpox, against which a form of inoculation was developed that was gradually adopted by the upper classes. Only after vaccination was developed by Edward Jenner in the 1790's, however, would this lethal disease finally begin to be conquered.

Meanwhile, the practice of medicine remained antiquated. Hospitals, in which the wealthy never set foot, were places where one was more likely to succumb to some new contagion than be cured of one's original complaint—"monstrous products of an admirable sentiment," as one critic put it. Apart from the beginnings of inoculation against smallpox, there were only two advances in health care, but these as yet had very slight impact. First, it was recognized that cemeteries were unhealthful places and that burial sites should be moved out of the village or town center. Second, since it had become apparent that ignorant midwives were killing many newborn babies, not to mention their mothers, there were some efforts to upgrade their training and refine their techniques. Still, in the face of the medical profession's ignorance and the primitive state of hygiene, none of this availed very much against morbidity.

Better health care and hygiene, then, was evidently *not* the principal explanation for demographic growth. Rather, as already implied, it seemed to lie in stabler and better food supplies. Marginal improvements in trade networks and transportation may have contributed to this, though on the whole the backwardness of road transport remained a major obstacle to effective distribution of the means of subsistence. Another factor might have been improved climate. The seventeenth century seems to have been excessively cold and wet; some historians speculate that it could be considered a "little ice age." The last decade was especially severe in northern Europe, with unusually wet summers and cold winters. In contrast, the eighteenth-century climate was, on the whole, somewhat more moderate, particularly during the summer harvests when very wet or cool weather could affect crops adversely.[4]

Europe's food supply assuredly increased in large part thanks to the eighteenth-century land clearances, notably in England during the enclosure

---

[4] E. LeRoy Ladurie, "Le Climat, Nouveau domaine de Clio," in *Territoire de l'historien* (Paris, 1973).

movement (see below); in Prussia, where colonization of the eastern provinces opened up new land to perhaps three hundred thousand settlers; in Russia and Hungary, where there was an abundance of new land; and even a bit in densely populated France, where the government offered inducements to land clearance. Likewise, improvements in livestock breeding increased the supply of meat, particularly in England, where beef found its way into the diet of all but the poorest classes. Finally, new crops had been introduced that were cheaper and hardier than the grains they replaced, and yielded more nutrition per acre as well. Maize or Indian corn, brought to Europe by the Spaniards as early as the sixteenth century, was now being used in southern France and Italy, while the potato had become a staple in Germany, the Low Countries, and Ireland. The Irish case demonstrates how an impoverished population could grow on the basis of one crucial innovation in diet. With a population in the first half of the century hovering around three million, Ireland's people, now subsisting on potatoes, increased to almost five million by 1790, and had reached almost eight million by the 1830's.

The roles of nutrition and disease can be seen in the example of Brittany, a French province where the peasants not only lived in remarkably unsanitary fashion, but where the diet was notably deficient, and the crops highly vulnerable to loss. A superstitious, poverty-stricken, and isolated peasantry grew buckwheat as its main crop, out of which biscuits and pancakes were made to provide the dietary staple. There was scant trace of meat or even dairy products in the Breton peasant's diet. A more serious problem was the vulnerability of buckwheat or "black-wheat" to damage. It was a difficult crop to cultivate, requiring a climate that was neither too humid nor too dry. Unfortunately, the Breton peasantry was not skillful in its traditional techniques, while the weather could often be harsh. Several eyewitness accounts describe the tribulations of these peasants in graphic detail. In 1774 a priest reported how his parishioners were expecting a profitable harvest of rye, which they used as a secondary cash crop to meet their obligations, when heavy rains in June and July inundated their fields and ruined the crop. Their hopes then passed to their buckwheat crop, but it too was ruined because "a dry spell succeeded the rains which had drowned the rye. It rendered the soil and to the point that the buckwheat is almost entirely deficient." Soon after, the community was struck by "a putrid and malign fever which affected mainly the poorer peasants—proving that poor nutrition is the cause of this disease." The following year, another priest recorded the situation in his parish: "A cruel dysentery and malign fever have afflicted my parishioners for the past month. Practically all our inhabitants are sick. . . . Most of our wheat is waiting to be threshed and is perishing in the fields under steady rains, while the harvesters are sick in bed." Finally, a doctor made this observation in 1769: "Last year was too rainy; there was no time to dry the wheat before gathering it and enclosing it in the large wooden boxes they use for storage. . . . It spoiled and mildewed to a large extent. The peasants had to sell the better wheat [to meet their obligations] and had to retain the poorest for themselves." It was no wonder, then, that Brittany was losing an estimated 5 percent of its population, while most of France and Europe were gaining population.[5]

Marriage Patterns and Birthrates

The statistics imbedded in parish registers tell not only of deaths but of marriages and births. These data are especially enlightening when subjected to the painstaking techniques of *family reconstitution*, pioneered by Louis Henry in France and E. A. Wrigley in England. Crulai, a village in northern France of about one thousand population, along with Colyton in England, have become for demographers what Waterloo is for military historians: exhaustively studied bench marks.[6] More important, they have inspired studies of other villages so that some degree of generalization is now possible, despite the complexity of local variation.

Family reconstitution involves taking the data from parish record books (the sacraments of baptism, marriage, and burial, entered as they occurred, chronologically), and rearranging them into family units. In essence, a detailed family tree can be pieced together for each family in the village, complete with information on age at marriage, number of births per family, survival rates of children, and even the length of intervals between births. The picture of personal life in England, France, Flanders, Germany, and northern Italy that emerges is one in which marriage was the general rule. Rates of celibacy in the villages were low—probably no more than 10 percent of the people never married. While families were frequently broken by the death of one spouse (the median duration of marriage being around twenty years), rapid remarriage was common. Illegitimacy in the countryside was apparently low, though it began to increase toward the end of the century and was especially high in some cities (see Chapter 5).

The fundamental discovery of this research is that most people in northwestern Europe married remarkably late. In the villages studied, the average age of women at marriage was at least twenty-five and often twenty-seven, and of men twenty-seven to twenty-eight. In Lyons—one

[5] Jean-Pierre Goubert, *Malades et Médecins en Bretagne 1770–1790* (Rennes, 1974), and "Le Phenomène Epidémique en Bretagne à la fin du XVIIIe Siècle," in J. P. Desaive t al., *Médecins, Climat et épidémies à la fin du XVIIIe Siècle* (The Hague, 1972).
[6] Excerpts from these two seminal studies may be found in *Popular Attitudes toward Birth Control in Pre-Industrial France and England,* (New York 1972), ed. by O. and ?. Ranum, pp. 45–99.

of the few large cities studied thus far—the average age at which men married seems to have been no less than thirty. In city and country alike, single men and women worked and saved for years in order to assemble the modest capital necessary for establishing their own household, meager as it might have been. For, with few exceptions, such as parts of southern France and Austria, most newly-married couples set up independent households and did not live in "stem" or "extended" households with their parents.[7] The most important demographic effect of late marriage was the consequent check on the birthrate. The deferral of marriage until the late twenties was a widespread, natural form of birth control. Moreover, this practice was evidently not offset by sexual relations outside of marriage, which would likely have resulted in higher illegitimacy rates.

This pattern of late marriage and low illegitimacy suggests that the population was surprisingly chaste and, perhaps by the same token, highly repressed in its sexual life. Prevailing religious injunctions, at any rate, would lead one to think so. Sex was permissible only in conjunction with procreation. Not only was premarital virginity an established community standard, and adultery considered a mortal sin, but even within marriage sexual activity was supposed to be limited and functional. The Catholic ideal of married love emphasized moral rather than sexual passion for one's spouse. Undue sexuality was considered inimical to the delicacy and consideration that a husband was supposed to show toward his wife. Among certain priests in Catholic Europe conjugal life became a matter for the confessional, and they did not hesitate to interrogate and exhort their parishioners on this subject. It would seem that in the eighteenth century the most important outlet for repressed sexuality was masturbation. There is obviously no direct evidence about this; rather we can presume it on the assumption that where there was smoke there was fire—the "smoke" being numerous exhortations against masturbation (or "sins against nature") by both the clergy and the medical profession. For, in addition to religious writings on the subject, there existed a large medico-moral literature attacking the practice and warning against its dire effects, which were presumed to range from physical degeneration to mental debility.

Once wed, most couples had their first child within a year of marriage, and additional children at fairly regular intervals thereafter. They continued having children until one partner died or until the woman's fertility came to an end, usually around the age of forty to forty-three. Thus, between marriage and the onset of infertility, women were likely either to be carrying babies or breast-feeding them. (The process of lactation for

[7] For much of what follows see: Lawrence Stone, *The Family, Sex and Marriage in England, 1500–1800* (New York, 1979 edn.); François Lebrun, *La Vie Conjugale sous l'Ancien régime* (Paris, 1975); and Jean-Louis Flandrin, *Families in Former Times: Kinship, Household, and Sexuality* (Cambridge, 1979).

breast-feeding could impede the conception of a new baby for six to eighteen months, depending on the mother's health.) The intervals between births varied from one region to another depending on biological factors and local customs of weaning. In Crulai, as well as in certain English villages, women had a child approximately every two and a half years. The average number of births per family was five, which is probably the approximate national average for France. But different patterns existed. In Brittany, conceptions were more frequent and intervals between babies shorter (three births in five years), while in the southwest of France conceptions were less frequent and the intervals between children averaged three years. The most startling variation has been found in the metropolis of Lyons. Not only did the city have a high rate of illegitimacy, but in one working-class district families had an average of eight births (despite the advanced age at which the women married) at intervals of about one year. The remarkable fecundity of these mothers, who often worked alongside their husbands in the silk-making trade, was probably attributable to the fact that they did not breast-feed. Instead they sent their babies out to nurse in the countryside with wet nurses, and hence were biologically unimpeded from conceiving again almost immediately.[8] In the countryside, however, the growth of population was held back by deferred marriage and long breast-feeding periods, as well as the taboo against extramarital sex. Population growth occurred (thanks to a decline in the death rate), but it was not explosive (since the aforementioned factors served to limit the number of new babies). Restrained as it was, however, the growth of population was not necessarily an unmixed blessing.

Indeed, according to Thomas Malthus (1766–1834), the English political economist, it was a most worrisome trend. In his *Essay on the Principle of Population* (1798), Malthus argued that whereas the food supply could be increased only arithmetically, undisturbed population growth would occur geometrically. Eventually population would outstrip the means of subsistence, and the poor would slide from misery to starvation. In this light, Malthus argued, efforts to assist the poor and relieve their misery were doomed to failure. Relief would offer a temporary margin of survival and encourage the poor to reproduce themselves. Hunger was bound to catch up and overwhelm them in the long run, according to the logic of this "dismal science," as political economy was later to be called. Furthermore, Malthus made the paradoxical contention that the great natural and man-made disasters in human history, like war and plague, were necessary evils, since they served as "natural checks" that corrected the imbalance between population and subsistence. The alternative means of keeping

[8] Pierre Goubert, "Legitimate Fecundity and Infant Mortality in France during the Eighteenth Century: a comparison," *Daedalus* (Spring 1968), pp. 593–603; Maurice Garden, *Lyon et les lyonnais au XVIIIᵉ Siècle* (Paris, 1975), part I, chap. 2.

A wet nurse at work. *The rearing of young children was routinely entrusted to a wet nurse, just as their birth was almost always attended by a midwife. Neither wet nurses nor midwives were adequately trained or supervised, and their ministrations were all too often lethal to infants and, in the case of midwives, to the mothers as well. Nonetheless, midwifery and wet nursing were among the most important and useful female occupations in the eighteenth century.*

population in check Malthus rejected as forms of "vice." While he approved of sexual abstinence as a moral way to hold down population, he disapproved of prostitution as a means of satisfying sexual urges without procreation, and likewise deplored such practices as abortion and infanticide.

The Beginnings of Contraception

Malthus projected his bleak view onto nineteenth-century Europe, believing that population would continue to rise geometrically while the food supply lagged behind. The difference would be made up either by the "natural checks" of disaster or the morally unacceptable "vices" of the poor. In fact, however, Malthus was a poor prophet of Europe's future. Better as an interpreter of a passing age (or of future prospects in the modern Third World), Malthus in effect gave a reasonable account of the old wavelike cycle of growth in population followed by contraction, with its periodic subsistence crises and demographic losses. At the very time he wrote, however, Europe stood on the eve of a new era. The productive capacity of the agrarian economy was about to increase at an unprecedented rate. Nor had Malthus reckoned with the possibility of family planning and birth control as a check on population growth. While birth control became a common practice only in the nineteenth century, it could already be found in the late eighteenth century among certain upper-class groups and even in some villages. Consequently, a brief description of what lay around the corner in Europe's demographic history is appropriate here. Otherwise we would leave our story at a point where Malthus's pessimistic and incorrect prediction would seem plausible.

The death rate (to recapitulate) had started to drop in the later eighteenth century, and the decline would accelerate in the nineteenth. This produced an upsurge in Europe's population in the last half of the eighteenth century, which was likely to continue at an even steeper rate in the nineteenth—exactly what Malthus worried over. In fact this accelerating growth of population was eventually slowed not by a catastrophe such as famine, but by an unforeseen change in behavior: the practice of family limitation. Initially this did not take the form of a married couple postponing its first child. Rather it involved spacing the children at wider intervals, or ceasing to have children at a certain point even though the wife was still fertile. Such behavior seems to have appeared first among certain English upper-class groups, the bourgeoisie in the Swiss city of Geneva, and the French aristocracy. Among the latter, for example, the average number of children declined from about six in the 1650–1670 period to less than three between 1700 and 1750, and about two from 1750 to 1800. As a consequence, since members of the aristocracy tended to marry very young (unlike the peasants and workers), the mother's age at the birth of her last child dropped from an average of thirty-one to twenty-five.

There is hard evidence that family limitation was being adopted in certain parts of France among the common people as well, during and after the French Revolution and, in a few cases, some years before. In several villages in the Paris region (Ile-de-France), for example, it has been shown by painstaking family reconstitutions that the average fecundity per couple was 6.7 children throughout most of the eighteenth century, but that after 1780 it fell to 5.3, while in the southern village of Lourmarin average family size declined from 4.9 children in the period from 1726 to 1755, to 3.9 children from 1786 to 1815. In France as a whole, a general dip in the birthrate began earlier than anywhere else in Europe. The estimated national birthrate fell from 36 or 37 per 1,000 population in 1770–1790 to about 33 per 1,000 in the Napoleonic era (1800–1815).[9] These two trends—a falling death rate, and a birthrate that was beginning to decrease—together constituted a phenomenon called the *demographic transition*. This new pattern of population growth would be nineteenth-century Europe's response to the Malthusian predicament. As

[9] See Jacques Dupaquier, "Problèmes démographiques de la France Napoléonienne," *Revue d'histoire moderne et contemporaine*, Vol. XVII (1970), pp. 339–58; E. LeRoy Ladurie, "Démographic et 'funestes secrets': le Languedoc fin XVIIIe–début XIXe Siècle," in *Le Territoire de l'historien*.

the birthrate began to fall, the natural increase in population (spurred on by improved health care and hygiene) would be restrained.

The reasons for the introduction of contraceptive practices, which involved a fundamental change of attitude and behavior, can be explained only speculatively. (There seems little question that the means employed was primarily coitus interruptus or withdrawal during intercourse before completion.) The likeliest explanation was parents' increased concern for their children, combined with an awareness that more children were surviving. Parents may have been conscious of a growing competition for land or economic advantage within their own families, and of the need to compensate by limiting the number of their children. The liberal inheritance laws of the French Revolution, requiring roughly equal shares for each child, probably reinforced this consciousness. On a more subjective level it has been argued that family fortune had always involved sexual

The Visit to the Nursery. *This painting by Jean Honoré Fragonard portrays the affectionate attitude toward young children that seemed to be developing in the eighteenth century among Europe's upper-class parents, who previously had tended to harden themselves against the likely loss of several children. Thus falling mortality rates may have resulted in a change of "mentalities" and a greater intimacy in family life.*

repression for long-term economic goals. At first this self-denial took the form of delaying marriage until the couple could establish it self financially, even at the price of deferring legitimate sexual activity. Later, as more children were likely to survive, ascetic calculation entered into conjugal life itself. Like deferred marriage, contraception involved a curbing of instinctual drives in order to promote rational economic ends, namely the life chances of family members.[10] It is also possible that women were inducing their husbands to practice contraception simply to reduce the strain of constant childbearing without requiring abstinence.

Whatever the explanation, France led the way in the demographic transition based on birth control. Its effects would be felt only in the future, however, and at the end of the eighteenth century, France remained the demographically preponderant nation in Europe, its vast pool of youthful manpower enabling it to mobilize massive armies of citizen-soldiers during the revolutionary and Napoleonic wars. This mobilization temporarily alleviated any problem of surplus population that might have existed. In the nineteenth century, however, France's precociousness in birth control would have profound effects on its fortunes, as its rate of population increase slowed earlier and more substantially than that of its neighbors. It was not long before its total population fell dangerously behind those of its chief rivals, Britain and Germany. France would enter the twentieth century with an almost zero-growth population, having resolved the Malthusian dilemma all too well.

ECONOMIC GROWTH
A Favorable Conjuncture

Demographic growth in the later eighteenth century was matched by a spurt of economic growth. Before beginning this account, however, it would be useful to pause over the patterns in which economic historians arrange their data. First there is the long-term or "secular" trend, a pattern obtained when the fluctuations that occur over a fifty- or even hundred-year period are smoothed out. It is usually fairly simple in thrust —a trend signifying expansion, stagnation, or decline—and serves to periodize economic history. For contemporaries, however, the secular trend has little meaning; it is a question of hindsight. More pertinent to them is the ebb and flow within the secular trend, the periodic cycles of inflation or contraction, of prosperity or depression—the "business cycles," which form the second level of analysis. Though the secular trend

[10] André Burguière, "From Malthus to Max Weber: Belated Marriage and the Spirit of Enterprise," in *Family and Society: Selections from the Annales,* ed. by R. Forster and O. Ranum (Baltimore, 1976); Flandrin, *Families in Former Times,* chap. IV.

may be in one direction, there are bound to be periods within its span that go the other way. Indeed a depression usually produces the very conditions that help to spur a recovery, while prosperity often creates conditions that eventually lead to temporary collapse. The mass of people are doubtless most aware of the third pattern that economic historians deal with, the short-term fluctuations of the economy. These were especially important in the eighteenth century, since the short-term conditions still depended on each year's crops. Though generally better, as noted above, harvests were still unpredictable, varying greatly from season to season, and from region to region. The seasonal crisis—a sharp drop in the amount or quality of the harvest—remained a constant danger. Even the longer business cycles seem to have been largely determined by the succession of the harvests. For in old-regime Europe the agricultural sector was dominant and probably pulled the less substantial manufacturing sector in its wake.

A key to economic growth and to the population's well-being was therefore the level of agricultural prices. If they were too high there would be hunger and suffering; if they were too low there might be economic stagnation, unemployment, and limited incentive for increased productivity in any sector. As it happens, price statistics are abundant for the eighteenth century, since governments and institutions monitored the all-important market price of grains. (Unfortunately, there are no comparable statistics for gross national product or per capita income, which economists depend on today.) These price statistics have been studied extensively, especially for France by the historian Ernest Labrousse. His conclusion is that the secular trend in the later eighteenth century was decidedly favorable. Agricultural prices *rose gently* during the century, stimulating economic activity across a wide spectrum of interests. The secular trend of gently rising prices (sometimes referred to as "profit inflation") coincided and was interdependent with demographic expansion. It began roughly between 1730 and 1750 in both France and England, where prices had been depressed until about 1740, and lasted into the second decade of the nineteenth century. Its peak came in the 1760's and 1770's. Reinforced by other trends, which we shall discuss shortly, profit inflation in agriculture stimulated economic growth.[11] While the 1780's brought a period of slump or cyclical recession, which was capped in France by a severe seasonal crisis during the politically momentous years of 1788–1789, no reservations about cyclical slumps or seasonal crises should obscure the basic secular trend—the favorable conjuncture of prices, trade, and population growth.

Obviously, large landowners were in a position to gain the most from rising agricultural prices and the ensuing rise in land values. They profited from the sale of their commodities in the market, or from the higher rents that land might command. Tenants on long-term or even nine-year leases

[11] *Histoire économique et sociale de la France, 1660–1789* (Paris, 1970), part III, especially pp. 383–416.

LONG-TERM MOVEMENT OF WHEAT PRICES, 1737–1784

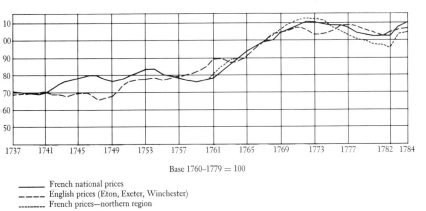

Base 1760–1779 = 100

_____ French national prices
_ _ _ _ English prices (Eton, Exeter, Winchester)
.... French prices—northern region

Source: Fernand Braudel and Ernest Labrousse, *Histoire économique et sociale de la France*, Vol. II, p. 389.

could also benefit, however, since increases in their rents were likely to lag behind the rising profits from any surplus they managed to market. Landless peasants too might enjoy the increased employment opportunities of an expansive economy, even if the purchasing power of their wages lagged behind price rises. By the same token, the healthy state of agriculture probably had a "trickle-down" or "spill-over" effect on manufacturing, stimulating production by increasing demand for inexpensive cloth items and the like. This was extremely important since manufacturing was highly elastic, and the capacity of merchants to employ workers, particularly in rural textile manufacturing, varied widely according to demand. Since rural families often depended on supplementary income from textile merchants, they had a double stake in this favorable conjuncture. Altogether, the secular trend in grain prices stimulated the growing market economy that was a prime element in Europe's transformation to modernity.

Money and Credit

Along with the push and pull of population pressures and the level of agricultural prices, the state of the money supply and of credit facilities was often an important variable in the process of economic growth. After fueling a mercantile boom in the sixteenth century, silver bullion imports from Spanish American mines fell precipitously after 1625. Historians were once inclined to attribute the seventeenth century's falling prices, trade volume, and land values almost entirely to the falling money supply; today there is considerable skepticism about this explanation, for the pattern of demand and the structure of markets seem more important. The fact remains that a new infusion of specie in the eighteenth century—both from abroad and from new European mines—almost doubled the money supply and helped to spur economic recovery. Moreover, the quality and reliability of Europe's money improved at the same time. Needy seventeenth-century governments had routinely debased and devalued their coinage by minting new coins at a certain face value while lowering the gold or silver content that such coins used to have. Eighteenth-century governments generally abandoned that practice and thereby supported monetary stability.

In the area of credit and investment, the eighteenth century did not begin so auspiciously. In 1720, ambitious promoters in both England and France offered speculators the prospect of enormous wealth by investment in new colonial trading companies. The South Sea Company in England and John Law's Company of the Indies in France both had links with the state that doubtless enhanced their appeal. (Law's plan also involved the creation of France's first national bank whose credit was tied to the Company's prospects.) In any case, the public's greed and credulity created an overheated market. Though the companies existed mainly on paper, prices of their stocks rose to ridiculously high levels. Eventually the bubbles burst, bringing ruin to many investors, disgrace to Law, and a temporary discredit to paper shares. Speculative investment was too tempting

The Island of Madhead. *One of many Dutch cartoons satirizing the folly of speculative mania in England and France in 1720. The caption reads: "Picture of the famous Island of Madhead, situated in Share Sea, and inhabited by a multitude of people who are called by the general name of Shareholders." Note the crowd of stockholders besieging the company's office.*

and rewarding to be shunned for long, however, and it soon revived without again reaching the manic proportions of 1720. Stock exchanges trading in commercial, insurance, and water companies became prominent fixtures of capital markets in Paris, London, and Amsterdam.

Meanwhile, the productive capacities of capital had been significantly enhanced by the development of banking institutions. Pioneering in that domain had occurred in the previous century. The merchant-bankers of Italy and Amsterdam had long since perfected the mechanisms whereby commercial debts (bills of exchange) could be endorsed by their holders and passed on to someone else, thus turning a sum of money owed into capital for a new venture. Bankers moved into such operations by discounting bills of exchange and taking over their collection in return for modest commissions, thereby renewing the merchants' capital and making it possible for them to initiate new ventures more quickly. Banking was especially important for Amsterdam, since Dutch commerce and manufacturing were in serious decline relative to their seventeenth-century superiority. Having ceased to be Europe's maritime middlemen, the Dutch became its financial middlemen, supplying capital both to private enterprise and foreign governments, especially in Britain. Amsterdam was joined as a banking center by London, where the Bank of England, founded in 1694, could accept deposits, effect transfers between accounts, discount bills of exchange, issue bank notes, and advance loans to the government or favored companies.

France lagged behind its maritime competitors in the area of finance and credit. Law's failure ruined the chance to create a national bank on the model of England's and doomed the French state to a dependence on private financiers for credit. Similarly, the private banking sector lagged behind the innovations of the venturesome Dutch, though certain French merchants had connections with Protestant bankers operating out of Geneva. Perhaps the chief difference between France on the one hand, and England and the Netherlands on the other, was the nature of its national debt. High interest rates paid by government bonds, notes, or annuities tended (among other adverse effects) to make it difficult for private enterprises to raise capital, since they would have to match or surpass such costly rates. The French state habitually spent far beyond its revenues and (as we shall see in Chapter 9) depended on a constant flow of loans raised through bonds and annuities. Of necessity, these ever-multiplying issues carried high interest rates ranging from 8 to 10 percent. In contrast, Dutch bonds had already fallen to 5 percent in 1640, and after 1670 fluctuated between 3 and 4 percent, while England's bonds had fallen to 5 percent by 1715.[12]

12 See Jan de Vries, *The Economy of Europe in an Age of Crisis, 1600–1750* (New York, 1978), chap. 7.

The Global Economy

The starring role in eighteenth-century economic development belonged neither to bankers nor to industrial entrepreneurs, who would dominate our image of the nineteenth century. In this era, when "the call of the market" beckoned as never before, the leading figures were the wholesale traders, especially merchants engaged in overseas trade. Admittedly this was not a very large group. Like the bulk of European agriculture, most mercantile activity was on a modest scale and very traditional. Most markets were small and localized, for on one level Europe remained extremely provincial, fragmented among other things by an inadequate network of roads and internal waterways. Moreover, few merchants of any scale were genuine innovators. They were not much concerned with originating new products, introducing new manufacturing techniques, or lowering unit costs. Their function was simply to move goods where they might be wanted, weighing costs against prices in order to profit from the transaction. Innovative or not, they did take risks investing their capital in goods of various kinds and waiting long periods for the fruition or possible failure of their ventures. The rising population and price curves of eighteenth-century Europe certainly provided opportunities for profit, but a willingness to take risks with their capital is what distinguished merchants from other wealthy people, who settled for safer if less lucrative investment in land or bonds. Among these merchants, maritime traders played for the highest stakes. Their combined enterprise assured that Western Europe would stand at the center of an expansive global economy.

While intra-European trade remained an integral and even dominant sector of total trade, overseas trade was responsible for generating much of Europe's wealth. Older patterns of trade had already waned at the century's start. The Italian and German city-states that had once been synonymous with mercantile activity had long since been reduced to a secondary position. Spain and Portugal, the original colonizing powers, whose empires had been based mainly on precious metals from America and spices from the East, were now struggling to retain their colonial resources against more aggressive newcomers. The Dutch, with a merchant fleet that surpassed the combined fleets of England, France, Spain, and Portugal around 1670, and whose advanced techniques had substantially lowered the costs of shipping, lost this supremacy in the eighteenth century to an onslaught of British and French competitors. Though Amsterdam's bankers remained indirectly involved in the eighteenth century's trade, on the high seas the Dutch gave way before the rivalry of Britain and France.

Apart from competition for European markets, that rivalry was being played out in five zones: the East Indies, the West Indies, North America,

Latin America, and western Africa. These constituted the "periphery" of the global economy that was being exploited by the "core" of European states. In India and the East Indies the principal articles of trade were still tea, spices, fine cloths, and luxury goods. The competition in this remotest of areas took place between state-supported trading companies that vied almost like armies for commercial domination. In the course of the century, this rivalry was resolved and Britain emerged as virtually the exclusive European power on the Indian subcontinent. Gradually the British extended their control until, by the mid-nineteenth century, India had become the "jewel" in the crown of the British Empire.

In the eighteenth century, however, the West Indies were the heart of both the French and British formal empires. On these small, tropical islands, staples could be grown that could not be produced in Europe's temperate climate: tobacco, cotton, coffee, the dye indigo, and, above all, the sugar that Europeans increasingly craved. Barbados, Jamaica, and Bermuda for the British, Saint Domingue, Martinique, and Guadeloupe for the French were pulsating plantation economies that fueled the pump of maritime trade, as well as serving as bases for penetrating the vast American empires of Portugal and Spain. They were excellent colonies also because they depended for almost everything else on the mother country: grain, meat, timber, manufactured products, and luxury goods. Above all, they required a ceaseless inflow of slaves, which the European powers secured in western Africa.[13]

The vast North American continent seemed less important economically than the West Indies. In certain respects the French and British ran their mainland colonies quite differently. Despite royal encouragement, there was little emigration from France to Canada. Thinly settled and autocratically governed, French North America was primarily a trading area for fur, leather, fish, and timber products. Britain, without necessarily having planned it that way, had come to possess thirteen heavily settled and prosperous colonies on the Atlantic seaboard. Though ostensibly ruled by the Board of Trade, the Royal Council, and the Parliament in London, most colonies also had relatively autonomous legislatures. Cities such as Boston and Philadelphia had thriving mercantile communities not always amenable to regulation from abroad.

Though settling and governing their colonies differently, France and Britain regulated their trade similarly. The British Navigation Acts and the French *Exclusif* were mercantilist systems designed to regulate all trade to the benefit of the mother country. By a combination of bounties, prohibitions, and high tariffs, trade was channeled into ships of the

---

[13] For a panoramic overview of this subject see J. H. Parry, *Trade and Dominion: European Overseas Empire in the Eighteenth Century* (London, 1971).

mother country; manufactured products used in the colonies were supposed to originate in the mother country; valuable colonial staples were directed toward the home market for finishing and consumption or re-export to the rest of Europe and abroad. All of this was supposed to insure a favorable balance of trade, and ultimately a flow of specie into the mother country's coffers.

The fourth zone of Anglo-French colonial rivalry was, paradoxically, the Latin American empires of Spain and Portugal. Having long since pre-empted these vast territories, the two Iberian states were clearly over-extended. Heavily dependent on their empires' resources, they defended them with rigid mercantilist regulations, but could do so only with the greatest difficulty against the voracious merchants of Britain and France. Behind the facade of Spanish and Portuguese rule, Latin American wealth was up for the taking. Portugal had long since allowed the British to become partners in the exploitation of its lucrative Brazilian empire, with its gold and silver, sugar and tobacco, cotton and cocoa, timber and hides. Lisbon's primary interest had always been gold, one-fifth of which was supposed to go straight from Brazil's mines into the royal treasury. Since the seventeenth century, English diplomacy had won concessions for the English merchant communities or "factories" operating in Lisbon and Oporto, and these privileges were strengthened by the Methuen Treaty of 1703: henceforth English woolens were allowed to enter Portugal duty-free, while in return Portuguese wine received favored treatment in the English market and indeed became the gentry's favored libation. By supplying woolens, grain, and manufactured goods to Portuguese merchants, and above all by providing them with credit, English merchants came by extension to share in the Brazilian trade.[14] Moreover with their commercial agents now allowed to operate in Brazil itself, the English gained a foothold for penetrating Spanish-American markets.

Like Portugal, Spain's principal interest in America was extracting precious metals from its mines. In good mercantilist fashion, Spain additionally wished to have its own merchants and shippers control all trade to America. The rigidity of Spain's mercantilism was unparalleled. All trade was to be in the form of official convoys from one official port—originally Seville, and in the early eighteenth century, Cadiz. Gradually the monopoly broke down, but only in 1778 did merchants in Spain's other ports gain free access to Spanish America. On paper, foreigners were at an even greater disadvantage, being altogether excluded from this commerce. But this prohibition, to put it mildly, was difficult to enforce. Among other things, the Spanish could not supply the products that

[14] Kenneth Maxwell, "Pombal and the Nationalization of the Luso-Brazilian Economy," *The Hispanic American Historical Review*, Vol. XLVIII (1968), pp. 608–17.

millions of New World inhabitants desired, while the British and French were eager to fill the void. After the Treaty of Utrecht, the French were able to penetrate Spanish-American markets indirectly as trading partners and allies of Bourbon-ruled Spain. The British had to resort to other tactics.

One wedge for British interests was the *asiento* agreement. Having conceded Portugal's rights to African dominion in the sixteenth century, Spain did not engage directly in the slave trade. To supply its Latin American colonies with slaves, Spain negotiated monopolistic supply contracts (*asientas*) with various trading companies. In the Utrecht negotiations of 1713, Britain had wrested this concession for its nationals, vesting it initially in the short-lived South Sea Company. Even in the *asiento*, however, there was a gaping distance between the letter of the agreement and its actual effects. Formally, the contract authorized Britain to import forty-five hundred adult slaves annually into Spanish America, and also permitted a single "free ship" to trade directly with the empire. Since forty-five hundred slaves scarcely satisfied the empire's needs, the limit was routinely circumvented, while the slaving ships also carried contraband goods. As for the one free ship, the strategy of repeatedly reloading it from other ships made a shambles of official restrictions. In any case, such tactics were only part of Britain's penetration of Latin America. For smuggling was rampant, whether launched from Brazil, the Caribbean entrepôt of Jamaica, or elsewhere. This illicit activity was not without its risks, for Spain tried strenuously to repress smuggling. When they happened to catch an offending ship, the freewheeling coastal patrols dealt with it harshly. Spain and Britain quarreled repeatedly over such incidents and eventually fought several naval wars, culminating in the ill-fated Franco-Spanish alliance against Britain during the Seven Years' War. The outcome (see p. 47) did nothing to halt the advancing British tide.

Global trade in the eighteenth century had numerous patterns, one of the most interesting, though by no means the most typical, being the so-called triangular trade. In this type of venture a voyage might originate in New England with a cargo of rum and head for Africa where the rum would be exchanged for consignments of slaves. The last leg of the voyage would be to one of the Caribbean islands where the slaves would be sold for either bills of exchange or molasses, the form in which sugar was usually transported. A second version of the triangular trade might involve a merchant ship sailing from Bristol in England with a cargo of pots and cloth. On the African coast these items would be exchanged for slaves, who would then be transported, say, to Virginia where payment might be in the form of tobacco. The tobacco could be carried back to England where it would be processed and reexported to Germany, with payment

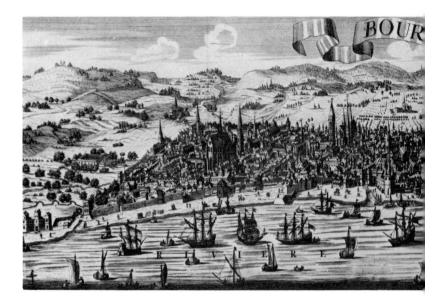

The docks of Bordeaux. *For this preeminent French Atlantic port, the eighteenth century was a golden age of prosperity and growth, fed by colonial commerce*

being made by German merchants in hard coin. More commonly, certain European merchants specialized in African slaving voyages, while others plied a two-way route between England or France and the Caribbean sugar islands, between North America and the islands, or (illicitly) between Europe and South America.

The statistics of foreign commerce dramatically reflect the extent of the global economy and the growing role of the colonial "periphery." For France the eighteenth century saw a 400 percent rise in trade, much of it attributable to the colonial sector:

	All Foreign Trade	Total Colonial Trade	(Imports of Colonial Products)
1716	122,000,000 livres	25,000,000	(16,000,000)
1789	500,000,000 livres	263,000,000	(185,000,000)

The total value of British foreign trade increased from about £10,000,000 in 1700 to about £40,000,000 in 1790, roughly the equivalent of 600,000,000 French livres.

The prosperity generated by this global trade can best be gauged by the growth of Atlantic ports such as Liverpool and Bristol in England, and Nantes and Bordeaux in France. Shipyards, factories, and refineries

—the slave trade, the reexport of sugar, and the transshipment of manufactured goods—as well as by trade in the wine produced in the hinterland.

to process colonial staples grew up alongside or not far from their crowded docks and warehouses, which were loaded with nails and pots, paper and glassware, cloth and shoes for shipment to the colonial world.

Of course, this prosperity was not evenly spread. The interests of planters, colonial merchants, and home-country merchants did not necessarily coincide. Planters, for example, were anxious to purchase slaves and supplies as cheaply as possible, which is to say, with few restrictions. Merchants, on the other hand, sought protected colonial markets where they could increase their profits. The debts that planters regularly accumulated often made them look on the merchants as their born enemies instead of their allies. There was also a distinction between privileged merchants who were partners in favored companies and outsiders or "interlopers," as well as between home-country merchants and colonial merchants, who were inhibited from pursuing profitable trade with the colonies of other powers. Then, too, as the Scottish economist Adam Smith later pointed out, mercantilist regulation undoubtedly hurt consumers in Europe by artificially raising prices as a consequence of restricting competition.

It is important to recognize, however, that colonies were exploited not simply for the benefit of Europeans who settled, invested, or traded there, but for the states that supported such activity. Colonial mercantilism involved power as well as profit. The effects of eighteenth-century imperialism can be measured not only in trade statistics, but in the naval superiority achieved by Britain and France over their Dutch, Spanish and Portuguese competitors, and by the eventual naval supremacy of Britain over France after mid-century. Navies were the guardians of these empires and the indirect beneficiaries of their growth. They were enlarged to protect trade and colonies, but they survived and flourished even after trade patterns had shifted and certain colonies had declined or were lost. Indeed, naval power was the key to a new conception of empire that was gaining currency after the Seven Years' War, the concept of "informal empire." Britain's approach to Latin America already exemplified this approach. Instead of taking on the expense and trouble of territorial jurisdiction, and to avoid losing valuable citizens through immigration to colonies, Britain wished to exploit Latin America indirectly. This became a suitable strategy in North America as well, after the thirteen colonies gained independence. At any rate, British policymakers so rationalized it: "We prefer trade to dominion," said Lord Shelburne in 1782. As one historian of empire has argued, British policy in the later eighteenth century tended toward "the concept of an 'empire' of ocean trade routes, protected by naval bases and nourished by commercial depots." [15] The concept was especially timely because of Britain's industrialization of cotton-cloth production, and the consequent need for new markets. As the tempo of British industrialization accelerated, the notion of widespread "informal empire" grew increasingly apt.

The Atlantic Slave Trade and Plantation Slavery

At the root of eighteenth-century empire and maritime commerce lay the enslavement of black Africans—a relationship widely recognized at the time. An English pamphlet of 1749 on "The Advantages of the African Trade" put it this way:

> The trade to Africa is the branch which renders our American colonies and [West Indies] plantations so advantageous to Great Britain: that traffic affording our planters a constant supply of Negroes for the culture of their lands in the produce of Sugar, Tobacco, Rice, Cotton, and all others our plantations produce. So that the extensive employment of our shipping in, to, and from America . . . are owing primarily to the labor of Negroes. . . . The Negro-trade therefore, and the natural consequences resulting from it, may justly be esteemed an inexhaustible fund of Wealth and Naval Power to this Nation.

Or, as the Nantes Chamber of Commerce (whose merchants transported

---

[15] Vincent Harlow, *The Founding of the Second British Empire, 1763–93* (2 vols.; London, 1952 and 1964), Vol. II, pp. 1 and 615–61.

over six thousand slaves from Africa annually) stated concisely: without slavery there would be no French colonial commerce to speak of at all.

The peak of the Atlantic slave trade came during the great sugar boom of the eighteenth century. Of an estimated total of 9,300,000 blacks transported from Africa in its entire history, about 6,000,000 were carried off in the eighteenth century. The geographic distribution of the slave trade's victims was as follows:

Brazil (a Portuguese colony)	38% (3,600,000 slaves)
British Caribbean	17% (1,600,000 slaves)
French Caribbean	17% (1,600,000 slaves)
Spanish America	17% (1,500,000 slaves)
Danish, Dutch, Swedish colonies	6% (about 550,000 slaves)
Thirteen North American colonies (United States after 1786)[16]	5% (about 450,000 slaves)

At the height of the slave trade, between 75,000 and 90,000 blacks were removed from Africa annually—half in British ships, a quarter in French ships, the remainder in Dutch, Portuguese, Danish, and American ships.

The slave trade had been organized originally by government-backed, chartered companies in a monopolistic fashion. By the eighteenth century the trade was open to anyone, although it was dominated by a relatively few specialized merchants operating from a handful of ports. With the exception of Portuguese Angola, slaving did not involve colonizing African territory. Instead the Europeans established strong points on the coast from which their merchants could deal with the African middlemen who actually captured members of rival tribes, and exchanged them for East Indian cloth, metal products, firearms, rum, and brandy. Periodically, competition among the slave traders drove down prices in the colonies by producing a glut on the market despite the enormous demand. When this occurred certain traders proceeded to penetrate new areas of Africa where they might secure slaves more cheaply. The result was to spread the disruption of African life and to intensify tribal warfare even further.

A slaving voyage had three legs: the trip from a European port like Liverpool or Nantes to the African coast; a period spent on the coast assembling the cargo of slaves, usually the longest phase; and the so-called "middle passage" across the Atlantic to the western hemisphere that could easily exceed a hundred days. Though lucrative for the successful

---

[16] Figures adapted from Philip Curtin, *The Atlantic Slave Trade: a Census* (Madison, Wis., 1969). The natural growth of the American slave population, rather than imports of new African slaves, accounts for the fact that the United States became a major slave power in the nineteenth century. Mortality among American slaves was low compared to most other areas.

trader, the slave trade was both highly competitive and risky. The period between investment (fitting out the ship and crew) and return was over a year, and many things could go wrong. From the perspective of the enslaved African there were a succession of physical and psychological traumas: the sudden kidnapping, confinement, and loss of freedom; the transfer to remote geographic areas and exposure to new diseases for which the person had no immunity; and, upon arrival in the totally alien New World, brutal treatment and degradation. Perhaps the most agonizing of all aspects was the nightmarish middle passage. With 300 to 450 "cargoes" jammed into medium-tonnage ships, the blacks were shackled to the decks without room to stand up, and without any sanitary facilities to relieve the stench, the heat, and the misery. Whatever the effects on their mortality, "tight packing" made for immense suffering. Under these conditions, mortality, which averaged around 11 percent per voyage at the height of the slave trade, probably increased with the length of the voyage. That factor could vary greatly, not only according to the different distances traversed from Africa to the New World but by the unpredictability of wind and ocean currents. Unforeseen delays would create disastrous shortage in the already scarce water and rations, and mortality rates could double. A severe epidemic or the repression of a shipboard rebellion could wipe out even more of the "cargo." [17]

In the New World, most eighteenth-century slaves were put to work on plantations, with the Caribbean plantations aptly described as sugar factories. The small British island of Barbados, one of the pioneering sugar producers, had initially been settled by British farmers who had brought white indentured servants with them as a labor force. In 1650, whites on Barbados outnumbered black slaves two to one, and of 25,000 whites perhaps 10,000 were indentured servants. By the end of the seventeenth century this had changed dramatically. There were now 17,000 whites (including only 2,000 indentured servants), and 37,000 black slaves who produced eight thousand tons of sugar annually. Jamaica was the leading British colony, and by the 1780's its population comprised 17,000 whites and 200,000 blacks, who produced fifty thousand tons of sugar annually. By 1808, when Parliament banned the slave trade, the island contained nearly 300,000 slaves. The largest French plantation island was Saint Domingue. With more than three thousand plantations in 1789, it had a population of 500,000 slaves and 35,000 whites, as well as about 28,000 free mulattoes and negroes. Heavy mortality among the slaves, who were worked inhumanly to produce a hundred thousand tons of sugar annually, was offset by a steady import of new slaves. Spurred on by gov-

[17] Herbert Klein, *The Middle Passage: Studies in the Atlantic Slave Trade* (Princeton, N.J., 1978).

A slaving ship. *Influential people in Britain and France seemed to prefer not to know about the horrors of the slave trade, but the evidence painstakingly assembled by the Quaker reformer Samuel Clarkson compelled them to listen. This illustration showed how every inch of the decks of a slaving ship was used in "tight packing" of the human cargo.*

A sugar plantation. *Slave labor was used not only to plant, tend, and harvest the sugar cane, but to convert it into molasses, the form in which it could be transported more easily. Engraving from A. M. Mallet,* Description de l'univers, *Vol. 5.*

ernment bounties to the merchants, the French slave trade was thriving in the 1780's.

The slave trade to Latin America, the Caribbean, and the United States lasted into the nineteenth century, and for all its humanitarianism, eighteenth-century thought had scarcely begun questioning it. Apart from the vested interests of planters and merchants, the prevalent stereotypes among educated Europeans denigrated the black race and made the continuation of black slavery acceptable. The first significant criticism arose from the Quaker church in England; in the 1770's the Quakers decided to expel anyone engaging in the slave trade or holding slaves themselves. By the turn of the century, anti-slavery sentiment had built up sufficiently to induce prohibitions of the still lucrative trade by the United States Constitutional Convention and by the British Parliament, both of which took effect in 1808. In France, on the other hand, merchants and colonial planters combined to defend the system of plantation slavery in the early years of the French Revolution. The debate on this issue among French legislators became moot, however, since the slaves on Saint Domingue acted directly in their own behalf. In a massive uprising in 1793 they wrested their freedom from the whites—the first successful slave rebellion in the New World. The radical revolutionaries who had come to power in Paris then abolished slavery throughout the French colonial world. Napoleon quietly restored it when he could, but that did not include Saint Domingue, which held off a French invasion, with the aid of a yellow-fever epidemic. The strife-torn, economically desolate island eventually emerged as the independent republic of Haiti.

When sugar production was disrupted on Saint Domingue, Cuba became the top producer for the world market. The story of how sugar came to dominate Cuba's economy draws together a number of the themes under discussion: the Spanish colonial system, the aggressiveness of the British, and the nature of sugar production with its dependence on slave labor.

Under Spanish rule, Cuba had developed a diverse economy and variegated class structure. A royal monopoly on the marketing of Cuban tobacco, the island's principal crop, had served as an umbrella protecting a class of small tobacco farmers. There was also an oligarchy of venal officeholders and self-styled nobles which, however, was being held in check by the royal government. The oligarchs looked to sugar for their fortunes, but were hampered by Spanish mercantilism, a lack of slave labor, and inadequate land. When the British captured Havana in 1762, occupying it for about a year as a tactical move in its naval war against France and Spain, the sugar-minded oligarchs were freed from all restraints. British slave traders flooded the market with slaves transported from their Jamaican depots. With this impetus, nothing could stop the planters from seizing new land to put under sugarcane or from which to cut firewood to heat the production kettles. The small holders (whose land titles had never been firm) gradually capitulated to this assault, enticed by the offer of high wages for skilled labor on the plantations. Artisans and small farmers alike were drawn from all corners of the once diverse economy to become auxiliaries of the sugar economy. Meanwhile, not only did the number of slaves in Cuba increase sharply, but work patterns were altered to increase productivity. As a leading Cuban historian has described it, "the torments of overwork reduced the slaves' useful years to an incredible extent."[18] Cuban planters were now in a position to profit from the high price levels on the world market. So extensive did their operations become that when Saint Domingue dropped out of the sugar market in 1793, Cuba was ready to assume its leadership.

THE BEGINNINGS OF STRUCTURAL CHANGE IN ENGLAND

The Agricultural Revolution

England's future as the most economically advanced major power depended on the fact that its agricultural sector modernized first and fastest. It was not until the nineteenth century that the "new agriculture" would set a model for the rest of Europe, but it was already recognized as part of the progress that educated Europeans admired in their own civilization.

Traditional forms of agriculture in Europe were designed to provide subsistence for the peasants and a steady income for landlords. It was a small-scale type of cultivation whether by serfs, sharecroppers, tenants, or petty proprietors. Villages were organized communally in the sense that similar routines were followed by all members of the rural community. Common lands and open wastelands were generally used for grazing their livestock and for fuel (see Chapter 3). The techniques were traditional, psychologically reassuring but inefficient. For example, fields were left idle or fallow every two or three years, actually a poor way to restore the soil's fertility. Under the impetus of low grain prices early in the century (when improved efficiency was needed to make the land profitable), and later under the impetus of high prices which rewarded increased production, English landlords began to innovate in large numbers. They could do so because England had a relatively good transportation network, a growing population, and an enormous market in London and its suburbs which acted as a magnet on the countryside's farms.

The techniques used to increase productivity were not invented by the English, but were adapted from practices developed in the seventeenth

---

[18] Manuel Moreno Fraginals, *The Sugarmill: the Socioeconomic Complex of Sugar in Cuba, 1760–1860* (New York, 1976), chap. 1.

century by the Dutch and Flemish in their densely populated corner of Europe. To produce more food, three major changes were introduced: (1) more land was put under cultivation by reclaiming wasteland and by dividing uncultivated common land and putting it under the plough; (2) the arable land was consolidated into larger units instead of the small, scattered parcels of traditional agriculture; and (3) the growth of crops was linked more efficiently to the raising of livestock, thereby increasing the yields of each. None of these changes involved new machines. Rather it was a question of capital investment, land management, and attitude.[19]

The twofold core of the agricultural revolution in England was convertible husbandry and the enclosure movement. Convertible or alternate husbandry was a progressive form of land use that eliminated the fallowing of land every two or three years. Instead, to restore the soil's fertility each field was planted periodically as a meadow with fodder crops such as turnips or special grasses such as clover. More livestock could then be maintained and fattened on the land. For turnips and the like provided winter fodder, whose shortage was a great obstacle to maintaining animals on the farm economically. Farmers could now diversify their livestock production, fattening cattle for market, breeding better types of cattle, and increasing their output of dairy products. The ability to maintain more and better livestock on formerly fallow fields was only half of the benefit of convertible husbandry. The other gain came from the fact that more livestock—and livestock integrated into the regular farming cycle instead of being raised separately—produced more manure. This in turn fertilized the same fields for their next period of grain planting, so that arable productivity was also raised.[20] In short, the land would always be growing something of value, its fertility constantly improving, thus increasing the yields of both livestock and grain crops. Apart from this major change in land use, English farmers also grew more adept at manipulating the texture of their soils. If the soil was light and sandy, they could resort to marling, binding the soil with claylike substances so that it would retain water and fertilizer more effectively. If, on the other hand, the soil was too heavy and claylike, they would introduce chalk and lime mixtures to break it down into a finer texture, so that it would not clot in very wet or very dry weather.

New techniques would have little effect if individual farmers were not free to use them because other members of the village community in-

<hr/>

[19] See especially J. D. Chambers and G. E. Mingay, *The Agricultural Revolution, 1750–1880* (London, 1966).

[20] This effect was heightened by two other factors. First, root crops were nitrogen-fixing, and increased the fertility of the soil more than the practice of leaving it fallow. Secondly, these crops could be "turned over" when it was time to plant the field in grain; thus turned back into the ground, the roots and grasses acted as fertilizer.

sisted on doing things the old way. Nor would these techniques avail much if the size of farms was very small to begin with. The agricultural revolution accordingly required far-reaching changes in the control of the land as well as its use. Specifically, it featured a movement to assemble large farms and to fence them off from the rest of the community. This trend was made possible in part thanks to the enclosure acts passed by Parliament. The division and enclosure of common land and the rearrangement and enclosure of arable plots within villages had been occurring sporadically for centuries by agreement. If small holders and tenant farmers opposed such changes, however, the large landowners could secure them by an individual act of Parliament. Under the spur of profit inflation caused by rising farm prices, landlords sought to enhance their holdings by absorbing as much of their villages' common land as possible, and by enclosing their farms so that new techniques could be used. Between 1760 and 1815 approximately thirty-six hundred acts of enclosure were passed, mainly in the 1760's and 1770's and again in the late 1790's and 1800's. In this period about six million acres were enclosed, roughly one-fourth of the arable land of England. Of this total, between two to three million acres was former common land that was now cleared or drained and put under cultivation. The remainder represented individual open-field plots that were reconsolidated into large, compact tracts fenced off from the other villagers, who no longer had access to them for gleaning or grazing their livestock. The resultant farms, usually between a hundred and three hundred acres in size, were worked with the new techniques by wage laborers. The crops could then almost all be sold at market rather than being consumed by the families of small farmers. Parallel to these changes in England, it might be noted, small farmers in the Scottish highlands were being dispossessed to make way for large-scale sheep grazing.

Before enclosure. *When open fields (shown here) were enclosed, propertyless villagers were deprived of free forage for their livestock, and the physical and social environment of village life was permanently altered.*

With all of these changes, the English agrarian landscape and social order began to look different not only from the regime of serfdom in Eastern Europe, but also from the Western European zone of small peasants and tenants discussed in Chapter 3. Much of the English country gentry became what is known as "improving landlords." They encouraged the use of the new techniques by the farmers to whom they leased their large farms, under terms where landlord and farmer alike could profit from increased productivity. The landlord provided the improved and enlarged tracts of land; the farmer brought working capital, livestock, and an enterprising spirit. No "feudal" or traditional constraints existed to impede the tenant's efforts. Farmer and landlord acted in a sort of partnership, sharing the costs as well as the profits of investment in the land. The actual labor was performed by salaried agricultural workers employed by the farmer. These laborers might have a small cottage and perhaps a vegetable garden, but they no longer owned or rented their own fields, nor (because of enclosure) did they routinely have access to common lands.

The agricultural revolution—a precondition for feeding the growing population of an urbanizing and industrializing society—had dramatic social consequences. According to J. L. and Barbara Hammond, the authors of several classic volumes on the dire effects of modernization in England, "enclosure was fatal to three classes: the small farmers, the cottagers, and the squatters." Further research has dulled the edge of this accusation without negating it. Enclosure was not a sudden, willful, and catastrophic expropriation of vulnerable social groups, but, in the long run, it did displace and dispossess them. The number of small owner-occupiers—the legendary independent yeomen of England—did not decline abruptly. However, their proportion of the land as well as their numbers did slip from perhaps 20 percent of the land in the mid-eighteenth century to about 12 percent by the later nineteenth century. While they were often able to raise capital to enclose their plots, it was harder for them to find other small plots to rent in order to augment the scale of their operation. Their main difficulty was the competition from large, specialized, capital-rich farms. As a result of the agricultural revolution, a farm of less than twenty-five acres or so was difficult to make profitable, and when prices slumped after 1815 small-owners were often forced to sell out.

Enclosure was particularly hard on the rights of cottagers, landless rural people whose cottages and common rights helped tide them over hard times. They received proportional allotments when village land was divided and enclosed, but they were usually forced to sell them since their plots were tiny and marginal. Squatters, whose rights on common land had been customary rather than legal, received nothing at all and were simply dispossessed. At first, cottagers and squatters enjoyed increased employment opportunities. There was work available in actually enclosing the land with fences or hedges, and in the labor-intensive methods of the new agriculture. But these laborers soon ran up against the stern challenge of rapid population growth and the consequent competition for employment in the countryside. The demand for labor simply did not keep up with the supply, and until much later when industrialization finally absorbed the surplus, there was immense suffering in the English countryside, manifested in the enormous rise in poor relief discussed below. As an authoritative study of the agricultural revolution by Chambers and Mingay concludes: "The distribution of poverty was not related to the extent of recent enclosure but to the availability of work outside farming." In much of England such work was still lacking or ill-paid. Whatever the temporary advantages of small allotments or employment opportunities for the small-holding and laboring classes, the enclosure movement and the agricultural revolution destroyed the traditional rhythms of village life.

Agricultural change on the English-Flemish model in the eighteenth century was limited to a few specialized areas outside of England. On the whole, archaic practices continued, including the wasteful method of leaving land fallow every two or three years. Accordingly, crop yields in most European agriculture remained static—whether measured by yield per amount of seed, or yield per acreage. Improvement in production came mainly from putting new land under cultivation by draining swamps or clearing wasteland, and especially by Russia's conquest of the Ukraine, which soon became one of Europe's "breadbaskets." A second source of agricultural improvement was the spread of new crops such as maize and potatoes, mentioned earlier. While they too depleted the soil's fertility in the absence of manure, they had two advantages over the grains they replaced: they yielded far more nutritional and caloric value per acre, and they were far hardier than grain, being less susceptible to bad weather and pests.

The Beginnings of Industrialization

The leading sector of Europe's industrial economy had long been textiles. Woolen cloth, for example, accounted for perhaps three-quarters of all English exports in the seventeenth and early eighteenth centuries. Emulating France, the major producer of woolens, states such as Austria, Spain, and Prussia applied mercantilist principles, nurturing their own textile manufacturers, protecting them from foreign competition, and enlisting foreign experts and techniques for their benefit. Technically and organizationally most textile manufacturing in these countries continued in timeworn fashion to the end of the century as output increased and spread geographically. In the meantime, however, dramatic innovations in

England were about to change the rules of the game completely.

Traditional textile manufacturing had several forms in the old regime, of which two were the most common. In urban textile centers, cloth was generally woven in the workshops of master artisans, and production was still subject to guild control, which tended to restrict competition as well as the supply and conditions of labor. Urban artisans tried to curb production outside their guild's jurisdiction, arguing that this was the only way to uphold standards of quality. Guild authority over the hinterland did not endure, however. In Flanders and England it had vanished long before the eighteenth century, while in France a royal edict of 1762 ratified what was already happening by opening the countryside to textile manufacturing virtually without restriction. The form of production that had developed in the countryside was known as the domestic or putting-out system, and it was here that textile output began to accelerate. Free of guild constraints, the merchant or clothier was a capitalist organizer rather than a direct producer. His principal investment was in stocks of raw materials, usually wool or flax. The material was "put out" to individual rural households, for preliminary preparation or carding in the case of wool, and for spinning on spinning wheels. The merchant then collected the yarn and passed it along to weavers, whose raw cloth he in turn sent out for finishing, perhaps to a fulling mill, bleacher, or dyer. The finished cloth was either sold by the merchant himself or taken to a centrally-located cloth factor who ultimately disposed of it, thus—at last—bringing the clothier a return on his investment.

The putting-out system was notable for the fact that spinners and weavers worked in their own cottages rather than in workshops. This domestic system of production was a classic example of the "family economy," whose implications will be discussed elsewhere. Women and even children spun, while men worked the looms. Families engaged in small-scale manufacturing without the need to secure and invest in raw materials, without worry about marketing their product, and without the imposition of external labor discipline. Perhaps most important, they could abandon their spinning wheels and looms at harvesttime, when the market for agricultural labor was favorable. They did not have to depend exclusively on either the land or the loom for their subsistence. For the merchant-clothier there were reciprocal advantages. He did not have to tie up his capital in fixed assets such as workshops or looms, and there were no restrictions on the way he engaged his workers.

Though based on an essentially unchanging technology, eighteenth-century woolen and linen production expanded rapidly in an intensely competitive environment. Heavy concentrations of cottage industry produced "a thickening of the countryside" in such mixed agricultural and textile districts as England's East Anglia and the West Riding of Yorkshire, in French Normandy, in Flanders, Westphalia, Saxony, Silesia, and Moravia. These districts may be thought of as *proto-industrial*. Free of guild restrictions, such concentrations of capital and labor turned out to be a precondition to the veritable industrialization of textiles, whose leading edge was cotton.

Calicoes or fine cotton cloths had long been one of England's prize imports from India. Indeed, the East India Company's monopolies of this product had at one time led to severe restrictions on English producers. Most European cotton manufacturing had in any case been limited to fustians, a blend of linen and cotton. For reasons involving supply, demand, and technology, however, this was beginning to change. The supply of raw cotton was rising dramatically thanks to slave-labor in plantation colonies, while the demand for cotton goods seemed almost infinitely elastic. Lightweight cotton garments were obviously suitable for clothing slaves and consumers in tropical climates, as well as being appropriate for the home market. Durable, washable, versatile, and cheaper than woolen or linen cloth, cotton had a bright future as an item of mass consumption, especially in England's expansive foreign and domestic trade.

Traditional manufacturing centers in England, however, were unable to satisfy the growing demand. Both the organization and technology of the domestic system had inherent limitations and flaws which became more apparent as the markets for cotton cloth expanded. For one thing, the clothier was limited to the labor supply in his own district; the further he went to find cottage workers, the longer and more cumbersome it became to pass the materials back and forth. Secondly, he could not adequately control his workers. Clothiers were bedeviled with embezzlement of raw materials, poor workmanship, and lateness in finishing assigned work, which slowed down the turnover of their capital. The coincidence of large potential markets and dissatisfaction with traditional labor arrangements predisposed English clothiers to technological and organizational change. Thanks to English mechanical ingenuity, such changes were becoming possible.

In 1733 John Kay designed a simple invention that simultaneously sped up the process of weaving on a loom, and permitted the construction of larger handlooms. Called the flying shuttle, it enabled the weaver to send the yarn across the loom by "throwing" it and having it return automatically, rather than passing or drawing it back and forth by hand. The device was not widely used until the 1760's, but once it was adopted, the capacity of weavers quickly outstripped the amount of yarn that traditional spinning could supply. In other words, there was now a serious imbalance between spinning and weaving, and therefore an incentive to create new spinning devices to correct the imbalance. A number of such machines were invented. Some were relatively simple hand-driven devices,

A spinning wheel and a water frame. *The first generation of British spinning machines were harnessed to water or horse power. They primarily displaced women who had worked on their own spinning wheels in their cottages or rooms.*

in effect enlarged, multiple spinning wheels; others were larger, mechanized, power-driven devices, such as the "water frame" designed by Richard Arkwright in 1769. With the adoption of such machines the imbalance shifted the other way, creating a golden age for the handloom weavers. Their skills and services were at a premium to weave the now abundant yarn, particularly for the rapidly growing market in cotton cloth.

Ultimately this imbalance was in turn corrected when a mechanized loom—originally designed by Edmund Cartwright in the 1780's—was perfected and widely adopted, starting in the 1820's. With a power loom, one small boy could run two mechanized looms, yielding an output fifteen times as great as that of a skilled weaver working a handloom. By that time it was also possible to bring power-driven spinning machines and power looms together into one large factory, dispensing almost entirely with skilled artisans, and hiring semiskilled laborers, women, and children.

Cotton production was eminently suitable to the new technology, and the statistics of British cotton manufacturing are truly spectacular, though they must be carried into the nineteenth century in order to be fully appreciated. In 1760 Britain imported 2.5 million pounds of raw cotton, which was fashioned by spinners and weavers in the traditional cottage industry; in 1787 it imported 22 million pounds, most of it now being spun by waterpower in large mills; by 1830 Britain was importing 366 million pounds of raw cotton, and cotton textiles had become the single most important industrial product in terms of output, capital investment, and number of workers. Its production was almost exclusively organized in factories using power-driven machinery at all stages. Meanwhile, the price of cotton yarn had fallen until it was about one-twentieth of what it had been in the 1770's.[21] Not only did cotton products saturate the home market and the colonial world, but British cottons were sold all over Europe—even where they were officially barred, since public demand encouraged smuggling. The full impact of technological change would be felt only in the 1830's with the widespread use of steam engines (whose prototype was invented by James Watt in 1776) and power looms, but the process was well underway with the spinning machines of the 1770's and 1780's. In the new cotton mills of Lancashire, a region endowed with abundant waterpower, the factory labor system of the future began to take shape.

While market factors, labor bottlenecks, and perhaps the ready availability of capital all contributed to the process of industrialization in textiles, the role of individual enterprise also bulked large. Mechanics and inventors provided the technical means for innovation, but it required organizational skill to apply them successfully. England was of course far from having a monopoly on mechanical ingenuity. Like other nations, England attempted to lure skilled foreign artisans to its shores; the resurgence of the woolen trade in the seventeenth century, for example, had depended heavily on the techniques of Flemish artisans. Major technical advances in such areas of textile chemistry as bleaching and dyeing,

[21] David Landes, *The Unbound Prometheus: technological change and industrial development in Western Europe from 1750 to the present* (Cambridge, 1969), chap. 2.

in shearing machines, and the ingenious Jacquard silk loom all came from France. Yet England was evidently an extremely favorable environment for successful innovation, whether of foreign or domestic origin.[22] Thousands of tinkerers and mechanics responded to the challenge of successive imbalances between spinning and weaving. Pragmatic devotees of applied science, they anticipated practical rewards for their gadgetry. While the state of English patent law was far from guaranteeing profits from effective inventions, the number of patents in England soared in the eighteenth century as a result of this activity. The same spirit of enterprise and experimentation that took hold of improving landlords and their farmers spurred on the artisans and mechanics of the Midlands textile trade.

Even more than the inventors, however, it was the organizers who created breakthroughs in productivity, by effectively combining new techniques with existing factors of production. These entrepreneurs were willing to take risks, and many failed, including some men such as John Kay who had fashioned new inventions in the first place and sought to profit from them. Edmund Cartwright, who invented a prototype of the power loom, for example, tried to set up a weaving factory using his new machines. Not only was the factory poorly managed from the start, but irate handloom weavers in the area eventually burned it to the ground, at which point Cartwright gave up. Others, however, were able to overcome the difficulties in taking innovations from the drawing board into the real world: choosing factory sites, assuring a proper power supply, recruiting and managing a labor force, finding the best markets, raising the capital and keeping off creditors until profit was coming in, and ironing out minor flaws that could keep the new machines from operating effectively. Perhaps the greatest success story was that of Richard Arkwright (1732–1792). A barber by trade, he was seized with a vision of the great wealth to be had in textiles. While not a mechanic himself he tinkered with earlier spinning devices and eventually perfected the water frame—a device that could be powered by horses or water, and later proved adaptable to steam power. Arkwright's success as an entrepreneur was formidable, as he raised capital and opened a succession of factories for spinning cotton yarn, manufacturing stockings, and cloth printing. Despite the fact that his patents were eventually voided, his entrepreneurial skill made him a millionaire, and in the Cromford Mill he created one of the largest Lancashire cotton factories, employing over two thousand workers. With Arkwright we have come to the threshold of the industrial age.

[22] A. E. Musson, "Continental Influences on the Industrial Revolution in Great Britain," in *Great Britain and her World, 1750–1914: Essays in Honor of W. O. Henderson* (Manchester, 1975).

That age, of course, cannot be depicted with reference to textiles alone. If anything, it depended even more on transformations in heavy industry, whose acceleration became breathtaking with the coming of the railroads in the nineteenth century. The precocious rise of British heavy industry, however, also had its beginnings in the eighteenth century. Because wood was scarce and expensive in England, the island kingdom made greater use than other nations of coal for domestic and industrial fuel. It is estimated that as early as 1660 British coal mines produced about five times as much coal as the combined output of continental mines. With improvements in technology—starting with Abraham Darby's iron-smelting process of 1709—iron manufacturers adopted coke (a by-product of coal combustion) as their principal fuel instead of charcoal. Responding to population growth and consumer demand for metal products, iron manufactors using the new technology began to operate on a larger scale, and sited new foundries near coal fields rather than the forests and river banks where iron forges had once been situated.

Nevertheless, until the 1780's it seemed a safe bet that England and France would continue to enjoy rough parity as Europe's two leading industrial producers. Their economic growth rates seemed to be on a par, at a healthy average of 1 or 2 percent a year, depending on which historian's figures one uses. Each country seemed to excel in certain sectors. France was still the leader in wool and linen cloth and in iron, while England outstripped France in shipbuilding, coal mining, and cotton cloth. Underlying these patterns there appeared to be a more general difference: France seemed more inclined to produce either luxury items or very cheap and low-quality goods, while England (with its possibly higher general standard of living) seemed more adept at producing standardized, mass-market goods of reasonably high quality. Ironically, France seemed to enjoy advantages that England lacked. In technical terms, it had a more favorable equilibrium of production factors. In textiles, for example, France had a larger and more stable labor supply, and while its coal deposits seemed scarcer and less accessible, it had far more abundant supplies of wood and a more developed system of internal waterways. But these very advantages served to perpetuate traditional techniques, to obviate the need for innovation. They therefore help to explain, in contrast, why England launched a series of innovative leaps that soon left its competitor far behind.[23] Only in retrospect did it become apparent that cotton, coal, and newfangled steam engines were the eighteenth-century harbingers, the advance guard, of an industrial revolution.

[23] *The Causes of the Industrial Revolution*, ed. by R. M. Hartwell (London, 1967), especially François Crouzet's superb essay, "England and France in the Eighteenth Century: a Comparative Analysis of Two Economic Growths."

CHAPTER 5

Poverty and Public Order

IN THE LATER EIGHTEENTH CENTURY, an era of demographic and economic growth, more people were surviving than in previous times—but surviving for what kind of life? In this chapter we turn from the optimistic portents of demographic and economic expansion back to the grim realities of everyday life that were yet to undergo structural transformation. Recent French and British historiography has been especially innovative in describing the life of the common people in preindustrial society, both in the countryside and the cities. We have already discussed the basic social structures. Against that background, it should not be surprising that the preponderant emphasis in this research is on poverty. While the common people struggled with poverty daily, the upper classes too were obliged to face its consequences in the realm of public order. The study of public assistance, judicial repression, and criminality of various sorts has accordingly been one of the most rewarding strategies for examining the fabric of old-regime society. While vagrancy and illegitimacy, for example, might be considered forms of deviance, they also hint at the pressures facing ordinary people who had not themselves fallen into such behavior. At the same time, the state's efforts to deal with the problems of indigence and crime tell us a great deal about the relationship of the dominant and dependent classes.

THE STRUGGLE AGAINST POVERTY

The Family Economy

Most peasants did not control enough land or income to guarantee the subsistence of their families in years of poor harvests. In Western Europe, where serfdom had waned, the typical peasant owned a small field and rented or sharecropped another few parcels of land, all of which might

146

initially produce enough food to feed his family. But his obligations—the tithe payable to the church; the land tax to the state; seigneurial dues and rents to the landlord; the interest on his loans; and the seed that had to be put aside from one year's crop in order to plant the next—ate up the major portion of the harvest before it could be used for the family's consumption. The result was that many peasants became purchasers of food, and were obliged to earn money or credit to buy back what in effect they themselves had produced. This the peasants managed by an admirable kind of resourcefulness.

In addition to farming his own plots, the peasant might hire himself out at harvesttime as an agricultural laborer on a larger farm, engage in part-time textile work like weaving, practice a handicraft like carpentry, or perhaps participate in an illegal activity such as smuggling or game poaching. Some peasants, particularly in harsh mountainous regions such as the Alps, were regular seasonal migrants. Leaving home each year for perhaps two months, they sought work as laborers in the olive and grape harvest of southern France and Italy or the grain harvests on the large farms of northern France. Other peasants might spend as many as nine months of the year away from home working as woodcutters, stone-masons, or water carriers in cities like Paris, returning home only at harvest-time. In a bad year, even these supplemental activities might not provide sufficient funds, and peasants would have little recourse but to borrow from a moneylender in town or from a wealthy peasant in the village. Indebtedness was endemic in eighteenth-century country life. Yet while often providing the margin for survival, such debts were difficult to pay off and usually insured that the peasant or laborer could not rise above his precarious station.

To speak of the head of the family, however, is to give only a partial account of the struggle against poverty. As indicated earlier, the vast majority of the working classes were married, and husband, wife, and children together developed family strategies to hold the ravages of poverty at bay. The contribution of peasant and working-class women to the "family economy" would be hard to exaggerate.[1] In both city and country, families often worked and resided in the same place. The family was both a unit of labor and a unit of consumption; except for children below the age of six or seven, all members of the family contributed to the welfare of this socioeconomic unit. As Joan Scott and Louise Tilly have explained, household composition was adjusted to production needs or to consumption capacity. That is, if labor was needed to help with the family's farming or handicraft manufacturing, the children were kept at home to work, and additional labor in the form of household servants might even

---

[1] Louise Tilly and Joan Scott, *Women, Work, and Family* (New York, 1978), Part I.

A peasant family leaves for work. *Though most land was given over to the cultivation of grain, some peasant families raised small cash crops of vegetables or dairy products. As this painting by Watteau de Lille suggests, the wife was often responsible for selling this produce, while the men headed for the fields.*

be hired. Conversely, in families where productive activity did not require the labor of all the children, and when the family income was insufficient to support them, they were usually sent out to work as servants or apprentices in other households. (Servants, meaning live-in helpers, as well as domestics such as footmen and chambermaids, constituted perhaps 15 percent of the population.) Single daughters worked to support their families, and if possible to save something for a dowry. Rarely did they live on their own before marrying. They lived either at home as farm laborers or textile spinners, or in someone else's household as a servant. The young women most likely to be drawn to the cities to work in the garment trades or as seamstresses were orphans.

Married women had a pivotal role in the family economy. On the farm they tended whatever livestock or vegetable garden there might be, perhaps selling milk, eggs, or vegetables to produce a modicum of cash. Wives of propertyless agricultural laborers worked in the fields of other farmers or as domestic textile workers (spinning, lace making, knitting), drawing pay that was perhaps half of what male workers would earn. The wives of urban artisans often helped prepare or finish their husbands' materials, or worked as embroiderers, dressmakers, or seamstresses. The wives of unskilled urban laborers and journeymen, having no income-earning work to perform in the household, were usually involved in the "economy of the makeshift" that gave urban society its bustling atmosphere.

The cities were filled with peddlers and casual laborers, many of them female. Women worked as laundresses and cleaners for the wealthy, or as food sellers and peddlers of used clothing to the laboring poor. The poor depended on such peddlers since they could not afford to buy new clothing or linen. They could not afford to buy food in quantity either, and frequently lacked the facilities or fuel to cook their own meals. Hence, to supplement the bread that was the staple of their diet, they occasionally purchased small portions of precooked food sold by peddlers. (As always the rich got richer. The affluent could afford to buy food in bulk and wine by the money-saving case or barrel; the poor could rarely afford more than a glassful of the cheapest wine at a time, which by unit cost was far more expensive.) Finally, in addition to the work they did on the land, in the shop, or on the streets, married women always managed the household. It was their responsibility to stretch whatever money was available, to procure food as economically as possible, and to preserve the clothing on which the family depended.

The family economy was extremely precarious. Illness or accident af-

Market women in Paris. *Here women are seen marketing agricultural produce. The more fortunate had permanent stalls, while others peddled their wares in the streets.*

fecting either spouse could demolish it. In the country the family economy could be wrecked by a succession of poor harvests. Crop failures might mean lack of opportunity to earn income as farm laborers, or a lack of produce to sell in order to meet one's obligations and creditors. Above all they brought high prices for bread. The country dweller's family economy could also be disrupted by the military demands of the state: the militia in France, the press-gang in England or Austria, and the canton system in Prussia. In the cities the greatest dangers were unemployment —almost inevitable from time to time in the textile, clothing, and building trades—and the vulnerability of unmarried women to seduction and pregnancy.

From Poverty to Indigence

In most regions peasant life was synonymous with poverty and insecurity. French priests who were periodically asked to supply information about the poor in their parishes developed a nuanced vocabulary for this task, being conscious of the line that separated mere poverty from destitution or indigence. "There are no poor who beg for bread from door to door," wrote a priest at Lanson. "But only two or three families at most are able to live comfortably, although obliged to work continuously like condemned criminals; as for the others, they just manage a miserable existence." [2] As his first statement implied, things could be worse. His parishioners were miserably poor but they were not yet reduced to begging. The difference between poverty and indigence was the difference between the threat of disaster and its actual occurrence. The typical peasant family lived in poverty, but with bad luck—a crop failure, a sharp rise in bread prices, a foreclosed debt, the loss of a job, a serious illness or accident, or the death of a spouse—the family might be plunged into indigence, a condition in which the routine and stability of a normal life collapsed. In both country and city the distinction between poverty and indigence was razor-thin and by definition a line extremely easy to cross. It was the line between the "respectable" working poor and those who could no longer make ends meet by normal means. The indigent fell either into dependency or into what sociologists call deviant behavior. They either became wards of charity, or lived outside the bounds of the community as beggars, vagrants, prostitutes, or criminals. The majority of the common working people in city or country (defined as those who had to live off their physical labor in order to survive) were poor. The indigent were those among the poor who for lack of employment or bad luck could not survive any longer by working.

Charity and assistance, as we shall see, were inadequate and often

[2] Quoted in Olwen Hufton's luminous *The Poor of Eighteenth Century France, 1750–1789* (Oxford, 1974), p. 21.

punitive in nature. Therefore, a large proportion of the indigent population took to the roads as wanderers or vagabonds, living a hand-to-mouth existence by begging, petty theft, odd jobs, and other desperate strategies. At their worst, vagabonds were extremely dangerous to the rest of society, preying on farmers and peasants, and harassing city dwellers. Unfortunately, dangerous vagrants were impossible to distinguish from the more harmless ones or for that matter from the bona fide seasonal migrants on the road in search of work. Where wanderers were common, rural society lived in the grip of heightened insecurity. In France and England—the two most economically developed nations in Europe and two of the least "feudal"—the number of indigent persons was estimated to be 10 percent of the population in the economically troubled years at the century's end (the late 1780's in France, the 1790's in England). That is to say, about 10 percent of the population, having passed from ordinary poverty into indigence, had either become dependent on charity and public assistance or had taken to the road as vagrants. While estimates from Spain and Italy are not so readily available, it seems likely that the problem was even worse there.

Traditionally the more fortunate citizens of Christian Europe took it as their duty to assist the needy. In God's eyes the poor were supposed to be the blessed children of Christ. The wealthy too could be blessed by assisting the poor, either by offering alms directly or by contributing to charitable foundations, confraternities, and convents dedicated to aiding the needy. This attitude began to change in the eighteenth century. The sacred character of poverty seemed increasingly dubious, while the Calvinist sense that worldly success was a sign of divine favor evidently penetrated into the Catholic world as well. For those of a secular turn of mind, the whole idea of blessed poverty and salvation through charity obviously had no power. On the contrary, the newer view held that indiscriminate almsgiving, whether to individuals or religious institutions, tended to encourage the idleness, laziness, and vice of the impoverished. In France as well as in Spain and Italy, where the habit of charity was encouraged by the large populations of priests, monks, and nuns, progressive writers began to attack the traditional forms of charity. Apparently the intellectuals were striking a responsive chord in the dominant classes generally, for there seems to have been a hardening attitude on the part of those who normally preferred charity. A readiness to give alms to beggars was replaced in some quarters by revulsion, fear, and hardheartedness.[3] Impatience with beggars was reinforced by anger toward the professionals (as Olwen Hufton has termed them), who constituted a subculture of

---

[3] Changing attitudes toward the poor are discussed by Hufton and by Jean-Pierre Gutton, *La Société et les pauvres en Europe, XVIᵉ–XVIIIᵉ siècles* (Paris, 1974).

full-time beggars. Such people were adept at feigning ugly wounds or deformities, and apprenticed many young people in their techniques. Their ploys and high-pressure tactics were designed either to win sympathy or to intimidate the citizenry into giving alms. Professional beggars made it all the harder for the haplessly indigent to tide themselves over by begging during a period of unemployment or ill-health. For they too might have ugly sores, twisted limbs, and ragged clothes, as a result not of larcenous disguises but of malnutrition and desperate circumstances. Yet such signs of need made a diminishing impression on some among the comfortable classes who were becoming fed up with the indigent and, both fearful and repelled, were turning against them.

If the indigent and disabled had trouble collecting alms in the countryside, their other traditional recourse was to head to the towns where churches, municipal governments, and charitable foundations had established institutions to aid them. These hospices or poorhouses were places of asylum and shelter for those unable to care for themselves. The "deserving poor" who were most welcomed here were the aged and infirm, the blind and disabled, the insane, and the orphaned. In France such institutions had been founded during the Catholic reformation by the order of St. Vincent de Paul and by the Sisters of Charity, among others. They used a monastic model, emphasizing strict routines, cleanliness, and moral preaching to the inmates. Royal edicts encouraged the creation of this new kind of shelter, called the *hôpital général*, thought it was not a medical hospital. No government subsidies were provided, however, nor

Beggars. *Begging was an everyday sight and one of the leading social problems of the old regime. Most beggars were old and infirm, or women with small children. In hard times as much as 10 percent of the population in England or France was said to depend on charity for subsistence.*

any authorization for local tax levies. The institutions depended instead on charitable bequests, and on selling annuities, lotteries, and other financial stratagems. On the whole they were badly underfinanced, and had a limited capacity. The typical *hôpital général*, and comparable institutions elsewhere in Europe, had perhaps 150 places, which could barely accommodate the "deserving" local poor, let alone refugees from the countryside. The attack on indiscriminate almsgiving did not spare these institutions. As the view spread that indigence was not caused by the will of God but by personal shortcomings or flaws in the socioeconomic system, these institutions appeared inadequate or even harmful. Donations began to fall off, while theorists and government officials considered the possibility of taking them over.[4]

The Indigent and the State on the Continent

All across Europe in the later eighteenth century enlightened officials and writers were beginning to argue that poverty ought to be the state's concern. In theory, if not yet in practice, the state was beginning to displace the private and religious sectors as the agency responsible for the relief of poverty and the control of its consequences. The able-bodied poor in particular were at the center of the growing debate over how to deal with the proliferation of vagrants and beggars. If they were no longer "Christ's poor," what were they? Were they a police problem? a socioeconomic problem? The response was hesitant, often inconsistent. Confronted with what appeared to be a flood of vagrants, beggars, and unemployed, European governments wavered between trying to repress and trying to assist them, in the end accomplishing neither.

Indigence was considered at least in part to be a police problem. Vagrancy and begging had been crimes in most states since the late sixteenth century, but there was now a growing determination to enforce such laws. The rationale was quite simple. In the words of a French official in 1789, "Beggary is the apprenticeship of crime; it begins by creating a love of idleness which will always be the greatest political and moral evil. In this state the beggar . . . does not long resist the temptation to steal."[5] Vagrants—people without roots in the community, and without a known source of income—were considered a particularly grave threat to an underpoliced society. As harvesttime neared, and the population waited uneasily for the grain to ripen, vagrants had an excellent means of extortion at hand: they could threaten to burn the crops if a peasant did not hand over food, clothing, or shelter. Vagrants could also coalesce into

---

[4] See Cissie Fairchilds, *Poverty and Charity in Aix-en-Provence, 1640–1789* (Baltimore, 1976).

[5] Quoted in Jeffry Kaplow, *The Names of Kings: the Parisian Laboring Poor in the Eighteenth Century* (New York, 1972), p. 134.

bands of brigands, which terrorized travelers on the highways. Ignoring the question of what caused this growing social problem—whether it was the willful immorality and sloth of the vagrant, or the lack of jobs and low level of wages—the governments of Europe adopted an increasingly punitive policy toward vagrants and beggars, stigmatizing them as the "undeserving poor." In 1724, for example, the French royal government ordered a general roundup of vagrants by the mounted constabulary (*gendarmerie*), with the aim of incarcerating them in existing poorhouses. This put a tremendous strain on the inadequate institutions, and it badly confused their mission by lumping vagrants together with disabled and dependent groups. The plan did not work, and while the *hôpital général* continued thereafter to include vagrants among its inmates, there was no possibility of an effective roundup which depended solely on those institutions.

In the 1760's the French government (among others) tried again, this time establishing a new kind of institution to receive vagrants, the *dépôt de mendicité*. In effect these were jails, in which "bad beggars"—the idle and potentially criminal—were to be incarcerated for up to eighteen months. Lip service was paid to the idea of accustoming them to work under the supervision of the *dépôt*, but in fact there was little work available. Another intention was to deter them from begging in the future by holding out the prospect of incarceration. Yet if no alternative source of steady income was provided, how could this deter anyone? It is more likely that the real objective of the *dépôt* was simply to control

A charity hospital. *The Hôtel Dieu in Paris was a vast hospital staffed by the Sisters of Charity and a small group of medical men. People with means never set foot inside eighteenth-century hospitals, for their discomfort and mortality rates were notorious.*

the population of beggars, to remove them from sight for a period of time. In fact, incarceration in a *dépôt de mendicité* was an extreme form of punishment, for the conditions were abysmal. Makeshift and over-crowded, they were filthy breeding grounds for contagious diseases, and the nourishment provided was as minimal as it could conceivably be. It was no wonder then that as many as a fifth of the persons incarcerated in the first wave of arrests died while in custody. Worse yet, there was really no way of determining who was a criminal beggar and who was on the road legitimately in search of work. Since the constables were of-fered a bounty for each vagrant arrested, their interest was in coming up with bodies rather than checking a ragged person's reason for being on the road. A study of the *dépôt* in the city of Aix-en-Provence indicates that about half of the unfortunate inmates could not really be considered criminal beggars or illegal vagrants.

The *dépôt de mendicité* treated the symptoms rather than the causes of poverty and as such was doomed to failure. There were far too many beggars, impoverished peasants, and unemployed laborers to accommo-date. Criminality and begging could not be halted by the *dépôts* unless the government was prepared to sweep up perhaps a tenth of the popula-tion and maintain it in custody, netting the potentially criminal element along with the much larger body of unemployed and desperate workers and their dependents. In any case, the true vagrant or criminal was prob-ably adept at evading the *gendarmerie*, and was less likely to wind up in a *dépôt* than an innocent migratory laborer, or a hapless widow encum-bered with a couple of young children who was on the road begging.

Though there clearly were willful vagrants, and though vagrancy some-times did lead to crime, officials were beginning to recognize that in-digence was not exclusively a moral or police problem, but a socioeco-nomic problem that had to be attacked at its roots. At the initiative of Turgot, the minister of finance, the French government swung to an al-ternative policy in the 1770's: public works projects were set up to pro-vide supplemental employment for poor peasants and agricultural laborers during the off-season in the countryside, where most of the poor resided beyond the reach of urban charitable institutions. The projects, mainly in the form of road building or textile work, were financed by small royal grants from rural tax revenues, and were usually administered by the in-tendants in concert with local elites. But the funding was meager. Indeed, the entire royal budget for public assistance in all forms was miniscule, amounting to no more than a fraction of the expenditure on royal pen-sions for court favorites. Consequently, during the terrible winter of 1788–1789—when the highways of France were swarming with destitute laborers and vagrants—the works projects were assisting only about thirty thousand people.

A similar gap between planning and implementation, as well as a perplexed shifting between repression and assistance, can be found in other European states. In Spain, where traditional almsgiving and religious hospices were still widespread, progressive thinkers such as Pablo Olavide argued for the organization of charity by the state instead of the church, and for assistance through work rather than alms. The government of Charles III made several initiatives to bring the state actively into the area of relief, for example at the national hospice of San Fernando, founded in 1766 outside of Madrid, where work was provided for the indigent in an institutional setting, with the women engaged in sewing, and the men in construction work or weaving. Joseph II in Austria, and his brother Leopold in Tuscany, both visualized a range of state-supported institutions designed to meet different types of need: hospitals, asylums, poor-relief bureaus to provide home relief to the disabled, and workhouses to provide organized work projects. For the able-bodied poor who insisted on drifting or begging, there would be punitive institutions like the *dépôts de mendicité*. Only a few such institutions were actually established, however. Frederick II also espoused a coordinated program of national assistance, but as in France, Spain, and Austria, the results were meager. A few workhouses were established, subsidized by local taxes, including one in Berlin that accommodated over a thousand inmates. But none of this made much of a dent on the need and misery of the common people, many of whom could no longer survive on the land and who drifted to the cities where an uncertain fate awaited them. As J.-P. Gutton has written of eighteenth-century Europe's approach to this issue, "secularized assistance most often consisted of drawing up plans for hospices and workhouses, which were [only] occasionally implemented, rather than attacking the roots of pauperism." [6]

The state was thus no more effective than private and religious charity had been in relieving poverty or staunching the flow of vagrants. Eighteenth-century writers on the subject were understandably caught between the two views of poverty as a police problem and a socioeconomic problem. Still, the lines of future policy were becoming clear. The French revolutionaries would adopt the view that assistance to the deserving poor should be based not on charity but on a kind of entitlement. While punitive treatment would continue for the "undeserving" poor, the revolutionaries declared a national policy of institutional or home relief for the disabled and dependent, and state-sponsored employment opportunities for the able-bodied unemployed. While these intentions were not actually carried out very far in the revolutionary decade because of unforeseen dislocations in the nation's finances and administration, the policy repre-

[6] Gutton, *La Société et les pauvres en Europe*, pp. 158–99.

sented an unprecedented commitment that would stand as an ideal for the future. The era of uncertain charity was drawing to a close, though the era of effective public assistance would be very slow in arriving.

The English Poor Laws

England's comprehensive approach to the treatment of the poor set it apart from the continent. Back in 1601 during the reign of Elizabeth, the government systematized prior legislation in order to promote three objectives: (1) "to set the poor on work"—that is, to employ the unemployed, able-bodied poor; (2) to relieve the "impotent"—the blind, disabled, aged, insane, orphaned, and chronically sick; and (3) "to correct the willfully idle"—that is, to punish or deter the vagrant who avoided work, the criminally inclined poor, in short, the "undeserving." These objectives were not to be accomplished by a centralized system of government funding and institutions, but by the local parish. As early as 1572, each of the almost fifteen thousand parishes in England had been ordered to levy a local tax, the poor rates, on all residents able to pay such a tax. Unpaid Overseers of the Poor, elected by the parish vestry (the governing council of the local church), administered the money. In addition, the local justice of the peace had a supervisory role over the parishes in his locality, to settle any disputes between parishes or between the poor and the overseers.

A second aspect of the poor laws developed in the later seventeenth century with the Act of Settlement. Parliament decreed that the parish in which a person was born would bear the responsibility for that individual's relief throughout his or her lifetime, unless the person settled in and was accepted by another parish. This policy was aimed directly at the problem of vagrancy: it was designed to curb vagrancy by insisting that the indigent remain in their parish of origin if they hoped to receive any assistance, and by stipulating that if they took to the road they could be forcibly returned to their parish of origin. The law also provided an incentive for a parish (other than the parish of origin) to expel the indigent, because once a new parish granted a settlement it became permanently responsible for that person's support should he or she need it. Obviously poor people could easily be victimized by this practice, being repatriated against their will from a place where they had hoped to settle or had found work. It was particularly hard on an unmarried woman who became pregnant, for she was routinely expelled and sent back to her parish of birth so that her parish of residence could avoid the costs of caring for her baby.

Thus the English system was a curious mixture of responsibility for and calculated cruelty toward the poor. On the one hand, it provided a "right" to public assistance under certain circumstances; on the other hand, it drastically abridged the freedom of poor people to choose their place of residence, and reduced them to pawns in a game played by the local parishes to minimize their responsibilities.

At its best the system did work effectively because it was inherently flexible, allowing each locality to deal with its particular types of dependent and poor parishioners. Parishes could provide "outdoor relief" or non-institutional assistance if they wished: small pensions to widows, orphans, and the aged; goods in kind, like food or clothing; rent subsidies; medical care; publicly financed work. At a time of economic recession the parish might even provide a supplement to the regular income of poor workers, to help them keep up with the cost of bread when wages were unusually low and bread prices high. (This became known as the Speenhamland system, when it was used in the district of that name in the 1790's.) In contrast to "outdoor" or home relief, a second way of caring for the poor was "indoor" or institutional relief. A large parish or a group of parishes (called a union) could construct a workhouse to take in various kinds of poor people. They were intended originally as a way of caring efficiently for the "impotent," using economies of scale to provide inexpensive food, lodging, and medical attention for people who could not provide for themselves. The workhouse resembled the *hôpital général* of France with the difference that it was supported by the poor rates instead of charitable donations. Like the *hôpital général*, however, the workhouse was increasingly used as a punitive means of dealing with the "undeserving poor" or the able-bodied poor who needed work and who were often given make-work by the overseers to perform in the workhouse itself. Depending on whom you asked, the workhouse was being used as a form of deterrence against vagrancy or as a form of rehabilitation and assistance, putting the poor to work. In either case, it existed as a last refuge for the poor who could not survive on their own. As the century wore on the conditions in these workhouses became more crowded and wretched, throwing orphans and the blind together with hardened beggars. The routines in the workhouses tended to fall into two extremes: very lax supervision and disorder, or severe punitive discipline. In either case workhouses were proving costly to the ratepayers. Yet the expense of outdoor relief was also soaring to unimagined heights because of the increasing numbers of paupers.[7]

By the end of the eighteenth century the poor laws were under mounting criticism for two reasons. In the first place, the local poor rates had risen dramatically to keep pace with the growing burden of relief. With the harsh combination of high prices and unemployment in the 1790's, heavily populated agricultural districts were groaning under the burden.

[7] G. W. Oxley, *Poor Relief in England and Wales, 1601–1834* (London, 1974).

In 1802 it was revealed that there were 1,000,000 "paupers" in England. One out of every nine people was on relief, including about 700,000 permanent "welfare dependents," as we would call them today. Among them were 300,000 children and 165,000 aged and disabled, but also 200,000 able-bodied adults who had simply become unable to get along on their own. Meanwhile about 3,700 workhouses had been constructed (most of them local and small), which provided for about 83,000 paupers. Between the exorbitant cost of the workhouses and the growing cost of "outdoor relief" to the underemployed and unemployed, the English rate-payers had seen their costs rise from a total of £1.5 million in 1776 to over £4 million in 1802. Under these circumstances it was being argued that the wealthy needed relief as well as the poor!

The second criticism of the poor laws was related to the same stark fact of growing "pauperism": perhaps the very existence of the poor laws was helping to create paupers. Since the poor could turn to the parish for sustenance, it was argued, their motivation to seek work was eroded, while the paying of allowances to a poor family for its children merely encouraged irresponsible procreation. In short, the argument was made that automatic assistance eventually turned into permanent dependence, sapped the morality of the poor, and perpetuated pauperism. In the light of this attitude, men like Thomas Malthus concluded that the poor laws should be abolished entirely, in favor of self-help for the poor supplemented by private charity. This extreme measure was resisted for political reasons, but eventually the poor laws were drastically reformed with the aim of coordinating their administration nationally and eliminating outdoor relief in most cases in favor of the workhouse. The workhouse, in turn, was made as unattractive as possible in order to give the poor an incentive to avoid it and thus stay off the poor rolls. This harsh attitude (adopted in 1834) marked the end of the local responsibility and paternalism that had distinguished England's treatment of the indigent.[8]

Unwanted Children

One category of the "deserving poor" that cried out for attention was the unwanted child. While there were orphans among them, most unwanted children were foundlings abandoned by their mothers; most, though not all, of them were illegitimate. We have noted earlier that illegitmacy was quite low in the countryside, though it was on the increase later in the century. In the cities it was a growing social problem, but one that reveals how permeable was the boundary between city and country. Eighteenth-century cities grew because of immigration from the country-

[8] See J. R. Poynter, *Society and Pauperism: English Ideas on Poor Relief, 1795–1834* (Toronto, 1969).

side. Without it, few could have replenished their populations let alone grown in size. Impoverished immigrants were likely to be insecure, disoriented, and vulnerable—none more so than the young single women who found employment as servants, seamstresses, and the like. A study of illegitimate births recorded in the French city of Nantes reveals two patterns of seduction, neither of which suggests unusual promiscuity on the part of the mothers. First, upper-class men seduced or raped their social inferiors, often their servants, many of whom were orphans without the familial support systems so necessary to well-being. The fathers included the cream of Nantes society, directors of the West Indian trading companies and the presiding judge of the city's highest court, for example. The second pattern that emerges from the registers of illegitimate births was the seduction of the same kinds of women by men of their own social class. In some cases these working-class couples lived together without marrying, but often the woman was deserted by her lover once she had become pregnant, despite an initial promise of marriage. Some, possibly most, of these births resulted from legitimate courtships that went sour.[9]

The sequel to many a seduction and unwanted pregnancy was the abandonment of the newborn baby. Such illegitimate babies often ended up in the foundling hospitals of Europe's major cities, institutions whose capacity was strained as the century wore on. In Aix-en-Provence, a city of thirty thousand people whose poor have been studied in depth, an average of a hundred or so infants a year were taken into the foundling hospitals in the 1720's through the 1760's. By the 1770's and 1780's the average had risen to over 250 a year. This reflected a national trend in France in the 1780's, when charitable institutions were being swamped with perhaps as many as forty thousand abandoned children annually. With an illegitimacy rate that may have reached as high as 20 percent of all births by the 1780's, Paris led the nation in this social problem. In addition to caring for its own abandoned babies, however, the foundling hospital in the capital also took in babies from the countryside. A nefarious traffic was run by carters who were paid by local officials in the provinces to remove abandoned babies in their jurisdictions to the Paris foundling hospital. Paid by "the head" at the point of origin, the drivers profited despite the fact that fewer than half their helpless passengers survived the journey. This traffic, combined with the rising rate of illegitimate births in the capital itself, resulted in an increase in the number of babies taken in

[9] Jacques Depauw, "Illicit Sexual Activity and Society in Eighteenth-Century Nantes," in *Family and Society: Selections from the Annales,* ed. by R. Forster and O. Ranum (Baltimore, 1976). See also Hufton, *The Poor of Eighteenth Century France,* chap. 12, and C. Fairchilds, "Female Sexual Attitudes and the Rise of Illegitimacy: a case study," *Journal of Interdisciplinary History,* Vol. VIII (1978), pp. 627–67.

by the foundling hospital from an average of about two thousand a year at the beginning of the century to a peak of seventy-six hundred in 1772. That year new rules limited entry to Parisian babies only and cut off the lethal traffic from the provinces. Even so, the hospital was still admitting about six thousand infants a year in the 1780's.

Illegitimate babies were not the only kind of unwanted pregnancies in the old regime. For many poor families another mouth to feed proved an insupportable burden. In desperation they sometimes turned to foundling hospitals, which not only took in abandoned illegitimate children, but accepted the legitimate offspring of poor couples unable to care for their babies themselves. True, babies were usually turned over with the ostensible intention of reclaiming them when they reached the age of seven or ten and could begin to earn their own upkeep. But this could only have been a form of self-delusion, since the foundling hospitals were notorious for their high mortality rates. The hospitals did not care for most infants directly, but arranged to farm them out to wetnurses in the countryside. (If the mother or parents were able to afford the wetnurses' fees themselves, they did not have recourse to abandonment.) But who were these wetnurses? And why were their ministrations so often deadly to the babies? The answer is that they, in turn, were impoverished country women who took on this function in order to bring some money into their households—whether or not they could supply the milk and nutrition the baby required. For while it was considered desirable to send babies out into the fresh air of the countryside, the conditions in which most wetnurses lived were generally squalid. That, at any rate, was true of the wetnurses employed by the poor and the foundling hospitals; the healthier, cleaner, and more reliable wetnurses were monopolized by wealthier families that could afford high fees.

So, to the dismay of officials and social critics, the numbers of foundlings (both illegitimate and legitimate) grew during the century, the wetnursing business prospered, and the mortality rates of the infants soared. Fewer than half survived to the age of seven to return from the country back to the hospitals. In Lyons, for example, the number of foundlings doubled, but in reaching out to more remote and impoverished villages for wetnurses, the city's two foundling hospitals insured that the mortality rate trebled. Reacting to this frightful trend, the archbishop of Lyons offered a monthly stipend to poor Lyonnais mothers who agreed to nurse their children themselves, a system which indeed lowered the mortality rate of these infants. Unfortunately, his limited funds could provide for only about a hundred women, perhaps one for every forty who could have used such a subsidy.[10]

[10] Maurice Garden, *Lyon et les lyonnais au XVIIIe Siècle* (Paris, 1975), pp. 59–84.

Intentionally or not, then, abandoning an infant to the foundling hospital and in turn to an impoverished wetnurse was in a majority of cases equivalent to killing it. Of course a large proportion of infants died from natural causes under the best of circumstances. In other cases, the death of a newborn infant in its bed—suffocated in a blanket, for example—may have been an unconsciously welcomed remedy for an unwanted child. Abortion, another possible solution, was not unknown in the old regime but does not seem to have been common because it was so hazardous to the mother.

The most extreme response to an unwanted pregnancy was infanticide. This practice, common in many civilizations such as ancient Rome or China, had by no means disappeared in the age of Enlightenment. There were enough trials for infanticide and discussions in literary works to suggest the tip of an iceberg. At least one event cited by Hufton documents that supposition: when a storm drain in the city of Rennes (France) was opened in 1721 during an excavation, the skeletons of over eighty newborn babies were discovered. Court cases allow us to reconstruct the typical pattern of eighteenth-century infanticide, always supposing that most perpetrators escaped detection and trial. A study of some sixty cases in London during the century indicates that the mothers were unmarried women of poor economic background, usually domestic serv-

A case of infanticide. *This German engraving depicts the discovery of the infant's smothered body, and the repentant mother being led from prison to execution. A third panel shows the mother after she has been decapitated before a huge crowd.*

ants. For a servant, pregnancy almost surely meant discharge, as well as social disgrace. In an age when chastity for women was still demanded, even a woman's family might turn against her in these circumstances. The combination of shame and insecurity over keeping her job could lead the girl to conceal the pregnancy by wearing loose clothing and feigning illness toward the end. She would then try to give birth in solitude, kill the infant immediately, and dispose of the corpse in a deserted place. Most of the sixty trials ended in acquittal simply because it was difficult to prove that the baby had not been stillborn, despite the incriminating impression created by the woman's attempt to conceal the pregnancy and birth. In any case, this study allows us to glimpse the desperate vulnerability of seduced servants.[11]

CRIME AND PUNISHMENT

Judicial Mechanisms

In the central and eastern zones of serfdom, social control was relatively simple. Most of the peasant masses were bound to the land and under their lord's jurisdiction, which included the administration of ordinary justice. Backed up by bailiffs, the lords doubled as local judges or employed surrogates for that purpose. Manorial justice, fundamental to the perpetuation of serfdom, also dealt with criminal behavior. But the state, as part of its efforts to assert power over its subjects in the countryside, was now attempting to enforce its jurisdiction directly over both lords and peasants. Accordingly, in Prussia and the Habsburg Monarchy, royal courts were established in the later eighteenth century to deal with serious cases and appeals. By the end of the century the two systems coexisted—manorial justice at the lower level, and a quasiprofessional state judiciary at a higher level. The expansion of the latter system would be one cornerstone of the state's growing powers.

The more complex societies of France, Italy, and England developed somewhat different patterns in the administration of justice. Manorial justice still survived, but only to settle minor civil disputes. In the area of crime, for all but the pettiest offenses, the state had asserted its jurisdiction and created layered systems of courts to hear cases. At the base of the French pyramid were the provosts courts. Though established in the towns, they were meant to control crime in the countryside. The provosts courts, in conjunction with the mounted constabulary (*gendarmerie*), an understaffed, underpaid royal police force for the countryside, dealt swiftly and harshly with rural people accused of vagrancy, theft, and

---

[11] R. W. Malcolmson, "Infanticide in the Eighteenth Century," in *Crime in England, 1550–1800*, ed. by J. S. Cockburn (Princeton, N.J., 1977).

murder. The courts were an example of class justice, since their defendants were invariably impoverished and usually illiterate peasants and workers. Townspeople and wealthier rural subjects could expect to be tried by more formal and less arbitrary French courts if they ran afoul of the law. In each district there was a royal court, whose judges purchased their offices and were irremovable. Despite this unprofessional mode of recruitment, many took their work seriously and certainly were more scrupulous than the provosts. At the top of the judicial pyramid were the august *Parlements,* whose routine business was not the great political struggles discussed elsewhere, but the trial of serious criminal cases, especially on appeal.

The contrast between summary justice in the provosts courts, and the long, protracted procedures in the district courts and *Parlements* does not complete the description of police powers in France. Several other aspects are worth noting. The policing of Paris—a metropolis regarded in Europe as far more peaceful than underpoliced London—was handled in part by several thousand royal troops, a practice quite alien to England. In addi-

The Bastille. *By no means the only royal prison in Paris, the Bastille actually contained only a handful of prisoners when it was liberated by a revolutionary crowd on July 14, 1789. The fortress was nonetheless an appropriate symbol in the Parisian rising against royal despotism.*

tion, an official called the lieutenant-general of police used spies and informers as a means of controlling crime in the capital. Then, there was the legendary weapon of French absolutism that would be universally denounced at the time of the French Revolution: the *lettre de cachet*, or general warrant, that the crown issued at its discretion in order to imprison an individual without trial. The victim was usually secreted in the Bastille or a comparable dungeon (where, it should be added, a wealthy person could purchase favored treatment from the jailers). The *lettre de cachet* was not only used against errant intellectuals and political antagonists, but was also granted as a favor to individuals who sought the incarceration of an unruly relative, such as a nobleman who had committed some form of larceny. In either case it was an arbitrary and rather sinister power that helped blacken the monarchy's reputation.

If the Bastille and *lettre de cachet* symbolized the quality of French justice (which was actually both better and worse than that would imply), English justice was known for its unique practice of trial by jury. In fact, however, juries came into play only at the second level of criminal justice. At the base—playing a comparable role to manorial or provosts justice on the continent—the local justice of the peace heard petty criminal cases without a jury. These magistrates were the quintessential members of the English ruling class. Appointed by the noble lord-lieutenants of the realm (who were in turn the king's appointees), the justices of the peace came from the ranks of the local gentry, and embodied their social and administrative power. Besides sitting individually for petty cases, they met in groups at the four-times-yearly quarter sessions, where they handled a wide variety of criminal indictments and trials. More serious crimes were tried at the assizes by professional royal judges based in London who rode circuit in the counties for most of the year. At the twice-yearly assizes and at the quarter sessions two processes took place for those accused of felonies and certain lesser crimes. First, having waited in jail or out on bail, the accused were presented privately to a grand jury which decided whether there were grounds for an indictment. In an estimated one of seven cases the grand jury dismissed the case; the remainder went to trial in public before a regular jury. The jury's function was to determine the facts of the case and decide whether under the law the indicted person was guilty. If so, the judge would do the sentencing. Until the later seventeenth century it had sometimes been the practice of judges to direct the jurors' deliberations and, in cases where they stubbornly delivered what the officials considered a false verdict, to prosecute them in turn. These practices came to an end around 1670, and the independence of the jury was then considerable. Thus, while members of the gentry wielded considerable power as local judges, they did not monopolize the administration of justice, for the last word was delivered by the lesser property owners who made up the juries. Indeed it has been estimated that between a quarter and a half of those indicted in criminal proceedings were acquitted by the jury. Sometimes jurors were expressing their objections to the capital sentences legislated by the gentry in Parliament for crimes against property. By refusing to convict defendants in certain cases despite strong evidence against them, they could effectively nullify the excessive penalties.

Torture and Punishment

English justice also differed from the continent's in its early elimination of judical torture. Practiced almost everywhere on the continent until the later part of the century, judicial torture was used as a means of gathering evidence before the trial. It was originally instituted because of the desire for certainty before convicting someone of a capital offense, that is, before passing a death sentence. Under Roman law, which remained the foundation of most European jurisprudence, circumstantial evidence, no matter how convincing, did not suffice for conviction of a capital crime. Absolute certainty was required, either in the form of two separate eyewitnesses or in the form of a confession. Since there were rarely two eyewitnesses to a capital felony, judges were obliged to seek confessions. If they had what was termed "half proof" or "probable cause" in the form of one witness or other strong evidence, they could then proceed to torture the accused in order to obtain the confession. Under this law of proof, the confession had to be more than an admission of guilt. It was supposed to involve verifiable details which only the guilty person could know, so as to protect an innocent person who might confess to avoid the pain of torture. Thus, in theory, judicial torture was designed to minimize the discretion of the judge. The use of thembscrews, the rack, and other abominable instruments would bring objectivity to the trial of capital offenses in the form of a confession!

Everywhere in use (except in Britain) in the early eighteenth century, judicial torture disappeared in its later decades. Phased out in Prussia in the 1740's and 1750's, it was abolished in Sweden in 1772, in Austria and Poland in 1776, and in France in 1780. The cruelty of the practice had come under increasing attack, notably in the writings of Christian Thomasius, Voltaire, and especially the young Milanese nobleman Cesare Beccaria (1738–1794), whose short book *On Crimes and Punishments* (1764) was a widely heralded plea for more humane jurisprudence and less extreme punishments. As a legal historian has recently suggested, however, the disappearance of judicial torture probably had more to do with change in the law of proof, which had necessitated judicial torture in the first place. Judges were beginning to move away from the need for "certainty" in favor of a more discretionary evaluation of evidence. They

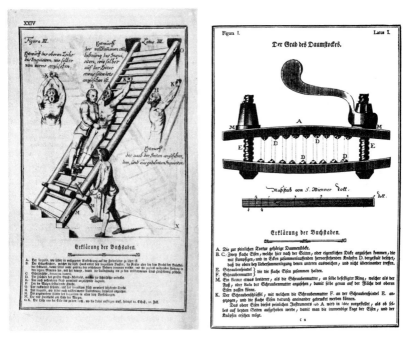

Instruments of judicial torture. *The most commonly used devices were variants of the thumbscrew and the rack. Their specifications and use were described in an official handbook issued by Maria Theresa's government.*

did this in part because greater options in punishing serious crime were open to them, short of executing the guilty.[12]

In southern Europe condemnation to the galleys became a principal form of punishment, convicts being sent to Mediterranean fleets to pull their oars. When sailing ships replaced oar-driven vessels, convicts were sent to the ports to live in stationary ships or prison hulks, sometimes being taken daily into the towns to work. In Prussia and Austria, where there was no such option, life sentences with forced labor were frequently substituted for execution in the eighteenth century, the convicts being sent to mines or forts to serve their time. England instituted transportation as a new kind of punishment. Starting in 1660, and especially in the early eighteenth century, convicts were sent to such colonies as Virginia and Maryland as indentured servants for a term of seven years, after which they were freed. Between 1717 and 1776 approximately thirty thousand British convicts were thus sentenced. After the American Revolution, the British established a new penal colony at Botany Bay in the territory of Australia.

[12] John Langbein, *Torture and the Law of Proof* (Chicago, 1977).

At the start of the eighteenth century physical brutality was still the essence of punishment. The body of the criminal was made to expiate his crime, and public infliction of painful punishment was meant to intimidate the population. It was, as Michel Foucault describes it, punishment as physical spectacle.[13] Capital punishment headed the list of punishments, and even execution had its degrees of brutality. A nobleman, for example, enjoyed a quick and dignified beheading. Ordinary citizens, if they were lucky, were hung on the gallows. For especially serious crimes various refinements were added, such as being broken on the wheel: having one's bones systematically cracked prior to execution. Likewise, drawing and quartering was still sometimes practiced, submitting, the body to additional pain before death, and to humiliation afterwards. Even in punishments short of death, physical or corporal pain was routinely inflicted. Galley rowers were branded before being sent down. Those subject to the common penalty of banishment from their community were often branded or exhibited publicly in the stocks first. When fines were imposed, they were sometimes accompanied by flogging. In short, physical pain was by no means limited to pretrial judicial torture, but was an integral part of punishment. The body of the condemned person was crucial in the ceremonial of public punishment.

Notwithstanding its progressive stance in the use of juries and abolition of judicial torture, Britain was as committed to the death penalty as any continental state. Parliament, dominated by the landowning, property-conscious gentry, made more and more crimes against property into capital offenses during the eighteenth century. By 1800 almost two hundred different crimes could bring the death penalty. While British laws grew sterner and convictions more frequent, the proportion of death sentences actually carried out was declining. The harshness of the law was balanced by scrupulous court procedures in favor of the accused and by pardons for perhaps half of those sentenced. According to Douglas Hay, the act of clemency too was a form of spectacle: a symbolic exercise of authority that combined terror and mercy. Harsh laws were meant to inspire dread, but the majesty of British criminal procedure, with its frequent acquittals on technicalities, was designed to inculcate respect for the law. Finally, the pardons, as well as the character references that prominent people frequently supplied for their accused employees, were calculated to create gratitude, and thus to uphold the whole structure of paternalism and deference.[14]

When hangings did occur they drew large crowds. Onlookers who de-

[13] Michel Foucault, *Discipline and Punish: the Birth of the Prison* (New York, 1977), Parts I and II.
[14] Douglas Hay, "Property, Authority and Criminal Law," in *Albion's Fatal Tree: Crime and Society in Eighteenth-Century England* (New York, 1975).

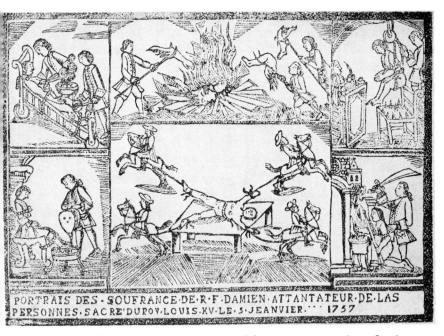

PORTRAIS DES · SOUFRANCE · DE · R · F · DAMIEN · ATTANTATEUR · DE · LAS
PERSONNES · SACRE' DU ROY · LOUIS · XV · LE · 5 · JEANVIER.··· 1757

The execution of Damiens. *After an unsuccessful attempt to assassinate Louis
XV in 1757, Damiens was subjected to virtually every form of physical punishment then in use until the coup de grace was finally administered hours later.*

sired a program could purchase penny pamphlets purporting to recount
*The Behavior, Confession, and Dying Words of the Malefactors who were
Executed.* Written by the chaplain at Newgate prison, or by other unofficial competitors, these popular pamphlets rehearsed the three rituals
of execution: the judge's death sentence, the chaplain's sermon to the
condemned person, and the hanging itself, interspersed with a biography
and the last words of the criminal. There was a great morbid interest in
all this, and people even paid to attend the preaching of the sermon to
the condemned. Did this make the condemned into a hero or an unpaid
circus performer? No one can say for sure, but public spectacle and cruelty
were fundamental aspects of traditional punishment.

In the meantime, a new orientation was developing toward the objectives and methods of punishment. The French writer Mably put it this
way: "punishment should strike the soul rather than the body." There was
a growing desire to rehabilitate and treat the criminal, rather than exact
retribution from his body. Beccaria and other reformers argued that punishment should be designed to deter and not exact vengeance; that it
should "fit the crime" and not be excessively barbarous. In some quarters
sentiment was turning against capital punishment itself. In Frederick the

A public hanging at Tyburn. *Public executions were doubtless meant to deter crime, but they were scarcely scenes of law and order. Occasionally riots broke out at Tyburn Square in London when surgeons attempted to make off with the corpses for use in their dissection lessons, while friends and relatives of the condemned sought to save the bodies for a decent burial. Engraving by Willliam Hogarth.*

Great's Prussia, for example, executions dwindled to perhaps a dozen annually in the 1770's, while in Tuscany, Europe's most enlightened ruler, Grand Duke Leopold, abolished capital punishment and maiming in his new criminal code of 1786. A few years later French legislators would advocate an abandonment of capital punishment in the early phase of the Revolution. Still, capital punishment was by no means on its way out. While it seems to have peaked in France in the 1760's, it apparently was being increasingly applied in cases of crimes against property. What can be said is that the emphasis on corporal and capital punishment was beginning to decline, along with the use of judicial torture, and a new form of punishment was appearing on the horizon. As Foucault has argued, the key change in European penal procedures was the rise of the prison.

Prisons had existed for a long time, but were designed primarily to detain the accused before trial to insure their presence, just as debtors were imprisoned to secure their persons. Prisons also housed those condemned to death and awaiting execution. At Newgate prison in London, for example, the usual period of detention was a week to three months as the defendant awaited trial. For the wealthy, prison could be something like a hotel, with fancy meals brought in. For the typical impoverished prisoner, it was a miserable experience—occasionally a lethal one, since the squalid, vermin-ridden conditions could produce a contagion known as "jail fever." In the year 1726, for example, a total of twenty-one people were hanged in London, but eighty-three died in Newgate prison from an epidemic of jail fever.[15] In sum, jails were disorderly places that reflected class differences, that could be unintentionally lethal, but that had little to do with the routines of punishment. All that began to change when penal reformers started looking to prisons as an alternative to more barbarous punishments, one which would help rehabilitate the convicted criminal by a regimen of discipline and work. Models of the new type of prison were created in a few northern European cities such as Ghent in the early seventeenth century, at Gloucester prison in England in 1779, and at the Walnut Street prison in Philadelphia, whose fame soon spread to Europe. These were early forms of what would become known as the penitentiary, and would soon be used as a major form of sentencing. By the early nineteenth century, for example, France would rapidly develop a system of district prisons that replaced the galleys, banishment, and many capital sentences. In these prisons convicts were isolated in individual cells, disciplined through sanctions like deprivation of food and the threat of solitary confinement, put to work, and given religious ministrations. The private, inexorable mechanism of prison punishment began to replace the "theater" of physical punishment at the end of the eighteenth century. Only later would the thought arise that such punishment was dehumanizing in its own way.

Criminality

The four basic types of criminality in the eighteenth century were crimes of violence including murder, assault, and rape; crimes against property such as theft, burglary, robbery, fraud, and poaching; crimes against the state such as counterfeiting, smuggling, and religious offenses; and vagrancy and begging. Although research into patterns of crime and punishment is as yet fragmentary and confined largely to France and England, there is general agreement that the eighteenth century probably saw a relative decline in crimes of violence and a rise in crimes against property. Research on the countryside in the French province of Normandy suggests such an evolution from violence to theft. It was found in two samples taken from the late sixteenth and seventeenth centuries that 75 and 83 percent of crimes were crimes of violence, whereas in the 1770's and 1780's the incidence of violent crime had declined to 33 and 47 percent, respectively. These researchers have argued that the very nature of

[15] P. Linebaugh, "The Ordinary of Newgate and his Account," and W. J. Sheehan, "Finding Solace in 18th Century Newgate," both in Cockburn, *Crime in England, 1550–1800.*

crime and criminality had changed dramatically in these rural regions. In their view, seventeenth-century criminals were undernourished, desperate people who erupted into unpremeditated violence, while the eighteenth century produced a different type of criminal, more cunning, and calculating. Seventeenth-century delinquents were usually impoverished peasants or workers; eighteenth-century criminals were more likely to be uprooted vagabonds, "possibly professional criminals unwilling to work." As a result, more crime was committed by organized groups, and theft was committed more frequently and skillfully. The notion that vagrancy and crime were linked is supported by the most ambitious local study to date of provosts justice in France. Based on almost four thousand cases between 1773 and 1790, this study found that 53 percent of those indicted for vagrancy were simultaneously charged with some other criminal act.[16]

Two other cross-sectional studies of criminality in eighteenth-century France suggest slightly different though comparable patterns. One is a survey of the major criminal court in Paris, and the other a census of approximately four thousand Frenchmen being punished as galley-rowers in the year 1748. The galleymen—women were never given this harsh sentence—included thieves (47 percent), vagrants, smugglers of illicit salt or tobacco (25 percent), and military offenders including deserters (13 percent). Crimes of violence accounted for only 8 percent of the convicts; only fifteen, for example, were rapists, which suggests that rape was either not very common, or, more likely, that it was not a vigorously prosecuted crime. On the other hand, there were as many as fifty-nine counterfeiters, for that was a crime of extreme interest to the authorities. While between 40 and 50 percent of the Frenchmen sentenced to the galleys were under thirty years of age, including young soldiers who had deserted, those convicted of smuggling were generally older, settled men, usually peasants with families. The oldest offenders were largely sentenced on vagrancy charges, indicating a group of castoffs from society who could not maintain themselves in the community.[17]

The Paris Criminal Court was of course different, not being concerned with many vagrants, smugglers or deserters, essentially rural criminals. Crimes against property loomed very large in the city, accounting for up to 93 percent of the cases. The number of homicides in the metropolis was low: only 13 out of 276 cases tried in 1755, declining to a mere 4

[16] The two case studies of Normandy by B. Boutelet and J.-C. Gégot are part of a project directed by Pierre Chaunu and were published in the *Annales de Normandie* (1962), pp. 235–62, and (1966), pp. 103–64. On the provosts courts see Nicole Castan, "Summary Justice," in *Deviants and the Abandoned in French Society: selections from the Annales*, ed. by R. Forster and O. Ranum (Baltimore, 1978).

[17] André Zysberg, "Galley Rowers in the Mid-Eighteenth Century," in *Deviants and the Abandoned in French Society.*

out of 216 cases in 1785. On the other hand, this study does not support the idea of the "professionalism" of eighteenth-century criminality that some historians have posited. Only about 6 percent of the criminals in this sample were repeaters, the most telling sign of a professional criminal class, while only 28 percent of the accused were apprehended in groups of more than one.[18] Urban crime was usually committed by relatively young, recent arrivals who had not put down roots in the community, who had few employable skills, and who were frequently thrown out of work. In Olwen Hufton's words, they often had time on their hands and an empty stomach. Theft, then as now, was the principal crime. But there were differences. In the first place, the scale of theft was generally very modest and filled an immediate need. In the countryside food and clothing were the usual objects of theft; alternately (especially in the city), linens, belt buckles, jewelry, and the like, things which could be easily disposed of through street peddlers or pawnshops. The second major difference was that theft could bring the death penalty. Hufton has speculated that the easier the theft was to commit, the steeper the penalty. For example, stealing clothes from an untended clothesline, pilfering unwatched goods in a public place, or "domestic theft" by servants from their masters—crimes which breached a form of public trust—could bring severe penalties, including execution. Breaking and entering, especially at night, could also bring the death penalty. Since collective crime was the most menacing, burglary and theft by bands of criminals, even if violence was not used, generally ended in a capital sentence.[19]

The statistical study of criminality in eighteenth-century England is still in its initial stage, but the results are already suggestive. Studying two counties, largely agricultural Sussex, and Surrey, which encompassed rural parishes as well as part of suburban London, J. M. Beattie has analyzed the indictments of criminals before the quarter sessions and assizes in sample years. He found that urban areas experienced an overall rise in indictments during the period 1660–1800, whereas crime declined in rural areas until about 1770, when it began to increase there too. More specifically, crimes against persons and the peace (crimes of violence) peaked about 1730 and declined thereafter, confirming our sense of what was happening in France, while crimes against poperty rose, especially in Surrey with its large urban sector.

Carrying his study one step further, Beattie has attempted to explain the fluctuations of crime. In rural crime patterns he has found a correlation with fluctuations in the price of grain. An increase in rural crime

[18] P. Petrovitch, "Recherches sur la criminalité à Paris dans la seconde moitié du XVIIIe siècle," in *Crimes et criminalité en France 17e–18e siècles, Cahiers des Annales*, No. 33 (Paris, 1971).
[19] Hufton, *The Poor of Eighteenth Century France*, chap. 9.

after 1770 coincided with rising wheat prices, whereas good harvests and stable population prevailed in the earlier part of the century. Poor harvests, rising population, and scarcity of employment seemed to induce higher levels of crime. This was true not only for long-term trends, but was reflected in short-term fluctuations as well. In sum, Beattie is prepared to argue that rural crime was largely a response to subsistence problems by the laboring poor. Annual fluctuations of crime in metropolitan Surrey, on the other hand, were different from those in rural areas. In charting these fluctuations, he has found that they correspond to another variable: the cycle of war and demobilization. Troughs in crime came during years of war, while peaks followed the end of hostilities. War apparently removed men in crime-prone age and social groups, providing employment in the London naval yards or as soldiers. At war's end, the armies demobilized and the war industries closed down. So in the city, crime seems ultimately to have been related to patterns of unemployment.[20]

Another dimension of these indictment statistics is the contrast between male and female criminality. In general Beattie found a strikingly lower level of crime by women, with men outnumbering women three or four to one in the largest categories of property offenses and crimes of violence. (The total number of such indictments in Surrey in sample years between 1660 and 1802 was 12,017 of which 2,616 or 22 percent were against women.) There were also qualitative differences. Most crimes of violence by women were directed either at members of their own households or arose from actions taken in defense of family interests, a pattern explicable perhaps by the narrower focus and circumscribed life of women. In the area of property offenses, women were rarely indicted for crimes which could involve the death penalty. Theirs were less direct and open forms of larceny, and on the whole less serious than crimes by men. The final point in Beattie's analysis is the suggestion that women's contribution to the crime rate was much higher in the urban setting, where their roles were less restricted and subject to less supervision, and where they were in direct contact with the harsh and uncertain conditions of the labor market. Thus, of the total crimes against property studied, 66 percent of those by men, but 82 percent of those by women were committed in urban parishes. Not only were women's crimes more heavily concentrated in the city, but their pattern and levels were closer to those of men there than in the rural parishes.[21]

[20] J. M. Beattie, "The Pattern of Crime in England, 1600–1800," *Past and Present*, No. 62 (1974), pp. 47–95.
[21] Beattie, "The Criminality of Women in Eighteenth-Century England," *Journal of Social History*, Vol. VIII (1975), pp. 80–116.

Poaching and the Game Laws

Beattie's study of criminal indictments does not include one major category of rural crime: offenses against the game laws. These were tried most often not in the regular quarter sessions but by individual justices of the peace who disposed of the cases without juries and usually without keeping records. Enough records have survived, however, to permit study of this crucial aspect of eighteenth-century rural life both in England and on the Continent, and we now have a vivid picture of the significance of these laws. Historians of criminality and justice have argued that their subject is important because it reveals the workings of the social system: the position of various groups, the bonds that unite them, and the conflicts that separate them. In the case of the game laws this is assuredly true.

Nowhere was the class structure of England more apparent than in the remarkable game laws of the seventeenth through the nineteenth centuries. The objective of the game laws, consolidated in a statute of 1670, was to ensure that the hunting of game (hares, partridges, deer, and the like) was reserved exclusively for the landed gentry, both on its own estates and on all other land as well. In order to hunt legally, one had to be "qualified" under this law, either by owning a very large freehold, or holding an equivalent type of leasehold. Only people who held large landed property could thus qualify, in all perhaps one-half of one percent of the population. To take a regional example, only eight hundred men qualified out of the population of over two hundred thousand in the county of Stratfordshire. The game laws excluded from the right to hunt not only agricultural laborers, artisans, and tenant farmers, but even wealthy farmers and merchants. The basic penalties for illegal hunting were a £5 fine (the equivalent of at least one-third of the annual wage of an agricultural laborer), or three months in jail. Killing a deer could bring as much as a £30 fine or a year in prison, and in some circumstances (such as hunting at night), the death penalty. More important, merely possessing the instruments necessary for hunting, such as guns, nets, snares, or hunting dogs, constituted a violation of the game laws. The possession of illegal game or selling game were also violations.

The way these laws were enforced was particularly resented. Qualified hunters, the owners of large estates, were empowered to employ gamekeepers who enjoyed the right to search anywhere within the estate's jurisdiction for illegal game or hunting devices, and to destroy the latter when found. This meant that he could force his way into a laborer's cottage, and, if he found a valued hunting dog there, could shoot it on the spot. The keeper would then take the offender before the local justice of the peace, who was empowered to try offenses without a jury. Thus the gen-

The right to hunt. *Whether consciously or inadvertently, Thomas Gainsborough's portrait of the Andrews unmistakably calls attention to the importance of hunting in the life of the English gentry.*

try were both the beneficiaries of the game laws and their enforcers. Despite the universal opposition to the laws among the vast bulk of the population, the gentry attempted to enforce them rigorously. Prosecutions rose as associations of qualified hunters were formed to underwrite the cost of prosecution. In one county studied, each decade between 1760 and 1790 saw the number of committals triple. Violations of the game laws, or poaching, as it was called, occurred with regularity despite the severe penalties and the will to enforce them. For the game laws deprived the English common people of traditional recreation or sport, meat for their table, and a source of extra income from selling game or skins. There was a great demand for game, which poulterers and innkeepers were anxious to meet, despite the prohibition on the sale of game by "unqualified" people. Indeed, there was an active black market in game, which poachers supplied despite the risks.

The gentry defended its enforcement of the game laws by arguing that they wanted to prevent idle pursuits by men who ought to be working, and also by the somewhat circular claim that poaching was related to general criminality and that the prosecution of poachers was thus a service to the community. In fact, there was relatively little connection between the two kinds of crime. Poaching largely depended on community solidarity—as did other tolerated forms of illegal activity such as taking fuel from former common lands, or smuggling to evade excise taxes. The community did not, however, condone common theft, and local poachers were seldom active thieves. The obsession of the gentry with the game laws is still understandable. As Douglas Hay argues, it is not to be explained "by the profits of rabbits and the wish to discipline idle rogues. Game itself and the laws used to protect it served to define and maintain class distinctions in rural society." The exclusive entitlement to game was regarded as a symbol of the power and position of the gentry, who organized much of their social life around hunting parties. "Pheasants, hares, and sides of venison were, therefore, so many tokens of social position; . . . they could be spent lavishly at dinners in order to command esteem, or given to others to mark important relationships." But if the game laws functioned as the clearest indicator of class relations in the countryside, they were also an occasion for class conflict. Poaching—for sport, for meat, or for profit—was probably the most widespread form of illegal behavior, and one point at which the deference generally shown to the gentry threatened to break down.[22]

While the game laws had an especially turbulent history in England, the same situation prevailed in other forms elsewhere. In France, for example, the nobility monopolized hunting rights in most provinces. As in England, this meant that commoners were entirely barred from hunting, while the lords could hunt anywhere, even trampling through the peasants' fields. It was no wonder that complaints against hunting rights probably led the list of grievances in the cahiers of 1789 (the grievance petitions solicited by the crown for the meeting of the Estates-General). In various German states where serfdom in some form still prevailed, the situation was even worse. Not only was all game exclusively reserved for the lords, but the peasants were not infrequently pressed into service as "beaters" for the lords' hunting parties, that is, they were obliged to scour the woods and fields to root out the game and chase it into the open where the nobles could shoot it. Almost everywhere in eighteenth-century Europe hunting was the monopoly of the landed class, and was an exceptionally important symbolic and real privilege. By the same token, poaching was an irrepressible urge among the peasants and laborers, even though it resulted in prosecutions and convictions. Along with vagrancy, poaching was a distinctive crime of the age.

Rights and Riots

As the widespread disregard for the game laws shows, one group's definition of crime was not necessarily shared by others. Many laws were made in the interest of the large landowners or the state, but they were not al-

---

[22] Hay, "Poaching and the Game Laws on Cannock Chase," in *Albion's Fatal Tree.* See also P. Munshe, "The Game Laws in Wiltshire, 1750–1800," in *Crime in England, 1550–1800.*

ways endorsed or respected by the common people. Violations of the game laws represented one chronic conflict over the legitimacy of laws. Similarly, much of the community did not regard smugglers as criminals, though it was in the government's interest to pursue them vigorously. For the state it was a matter of raising revenue; the average consumer was more likely to feel that by evading tariffs and excise taxes, smugglers helped bring down the cost of commodities such as tea and spirits.

From the point of view of the state and the ruling classes, one of the most serious crimes was riot—breakdown of public order, the violence of the mob, or, as George Rudé prefers to call it, crowd action. In both Britain and continental Europe, in city and countryside alike, the most common type of general disorder was the food riot. As with poaching, there was sharp disagreement over whether or not this was criminal behavior. What appeared as a dangerous form of disorder to the propertied classes was regarded as a legitimate defense of a basic right by others. The right in question was the right to subsistence. To place these frequent disorders in context, we must refer again to the developing market economy on the one hand, and the chronic uncertainty over subsistence on the other. When crops were short, would small consumers passively watch the price of grain or flour rise beyond their reach? Would they permit merchants to carry off local supplies in order to meet contractual obligations elsewhere? In an era of uncertain grain supplies, there was a fundamental clash between the interests of small consumers in an assured, moderately priced supply of subsistence, and the profit opportunities of larger farmers, landlords, grain merchants, and millers.

Subsistence was of great concern to all governments. Their "police" powers had traditionally been used to maintain public order by trying to assure the subsistence of the people. The king's justice involved the right of his local officials to intervene in the market as best they could to insure an adequate supply and reasonable price for grain, flour, and bread. England's Elizabethan government, for example, promulgated emergency procedures in 1580 whereby magistrates could order farmers to send "convenient quantities" of grain to market, there to be sold at "reasonable prices." Laws going back centuries similarly prohibited "forestalling and engrossing," or what we would call today "cornering the market" in grain. These laws stipulated that the poor must have the opportunity to buy grain or flour in small parcels. Farmers were not supposed to negotiate contracts in advance of the harvests, nor sell their entire crop upon presentation of a sample to a merchant. Instead, they were required to bring their grain directly to the marketplace where all consumers could presumably have direct access to it. Behind these measures there was a keen psychological insight by the government into the consumer's insecurity. Such paternalistic laws were designed to maintain a visible supply of food to reassure the masses, who were (for good reason) inclined to panic at the first hint of shortages.

These tactics gradually came into conflict with the demands of cities and armies, which required large-scale commodity transactions. Police regulation of the grain trade also clashed with the wish of landowners and large farmers to market their grain as profitably as possible. Such interests found their advocates among progressive economic theorists in the 1760's and 1770's, notably among the physiocrats in France. We shall discuss their theories in detail elsewhere, but they must be invoked here to help explain the gradual abandonment of paternalistic regulation in England and, hesitantly, in France. Physiocratic theory advocated unrestrained freedom for private property, in particular a completely free grain trade whose price structure would provide an incentive for increased productivity. "Good prices," it was argued, would eventually promote a national market in grain that could overcome regional fragmentation and bring about better distribution of grain supplies. Even if this meant higher prices, it was supposed to guarantee a steady and affordable supply of subsistence in the long run.[23] Physiocratic doctrine triumphed in France temporarily, when the government endorsed deregulation in 1763. Under this radical reform merchants were given a free hand in their conduct of the grain trade. With the exception of special police controls for the food supply of Paris, the government dug in its heels and for the remainder of the decade resisted calls for regulation and intervention. These calls were increasingly insistent, however, since the new policy coincided with a series of crop shortages, which led to widespread subsistence crises, doubled prices, and popular suffering. Eventually a new minister named Terray came to power in 1770 and reversed the deregulation policy, though ironically his efforts to stockpile large emergency reserves of "the king's grain" engendered charges of speculation and corruption against royal officials. In any case, the reversion to regulation was not permanent. Liberal doctrines of deregulation were too powerful to resist, and in 1775 Louis XVI's new administration attempted to deregulate the grain trade again, with dramatic results which we shall examine in a moment.

It should be noted, however, that this issue was not confined to England or France. Similar debates among intellectuals and officials raged in Italy and Spain, and while liberal economic thought had not yet had a sharp impact in Central Europe, the clash between large landowners and

[23] This subject is examined in detail by Steven Kaplan, *Bread, Politics and Political Economy in the Reign of Louis XV* (2 vols.: The Hague, 1976). See also Louise Tilly, "The Food Riot as a form of Political Conflict in France," *Journal of Interdisciplinary History*, Vol. II (1971), pp. 23–57. For the debate on this issue in Italy and Spain see Franco Venturi, *Italy and the Enlightenment* (New York, 1972), chaps. 8 and 11.

small consumers was just as acute. Nowhere, in fact, were the results more tragic than in Bohemia. When torrential rains in 1770–1771 ruined large portions of the crops in that region, the landlords' remaining surpluses gained in value. Despite prohibitions by the Austrian government on the export of grain, Bohemian lords continued to sell their grain to merchants in Saxony and Prussia at very high profits. They thereby contributed to the starvation that helped carry off an estimated one-tenth of the Bohemian population.

As a market economy developed in the means of subsistence, consumers looked back to the old ways in which a paternalistic government had intervened to help assure the availability of grain and flour in the local marketplace at prices people could pay. Against the "good price" advocated by theorists of economic growth, consumers argued for the medieval ideal of a "just price." Against the liberal theories of "political economy," the popular masses invoked the traditional precepts of a "moral economy," in E. P. Thompson's phrase. This concept denotes an outlook in which the customary, moral claims of consumers took precedence over the rights and interests of property. The "moral economy" of the poor, and of their allies within the magistracy, demanded that grain, flour, and bread prices be kept at reasonably affordable levels; that in times of scarcity the magistrates search out grain supplies and bring them to the open market; and that grain not be transported out of an area until local needs were satisfied.[24]

SUBSISTENCE POLICY: THE CLASH OF IDEOLOGIES			
	Advocates	*Policy*	*Desired Results*
Liberal Political Economy	Merchants and large landowners	Free market	"Good prices"
Traditional Moral Economy	Small consumers	Police regulation	"Just prices"

Since the common people had no regular channels for exerting political influence, no routine way of compelling action on their behalf, the only way that this program could be implemented was by rioting for their rights. Eighteenth-century food riots accordingly took two forms: block-

[24] George Rudé, *The Crowd in History: a Study of Popular Disturbances in France and England, 1730–1848* (New York, 1964), chaps. 1–3 and 13–16; E. P. Thompson, "The Moral Economy of the English Crowd in the Eighteenth Century," *Past and Present*, No. 50 (1971), pp. 76–136.

age of grain shipments in areas being depleted by an outflow of grain to other markets, and price riots, or *taxation populaire*, as it was known in France. A generation of research by historians such as George Rudé and E. P. Thompson has shown these disorders in a new and sympathetic light. It has demonstrated that it was not simply hunger and desperation that drove peasants, farm laborers, miners, weavers, or urban laborers of both sexes to riot. These consumers had a sense of their rights, of the just "moral economy." Thus, rather than pillaging or stealing, the crowds often forcibly set the price of grain or flour at the customary "fair" level. True, there was a threat of violence in their actions, but on the whole they showed notable restraint. Large farmers, merchants, or millers who complied with the crowds' demands, who brought out their stocks from hiding and allowed them to be distributed, were generally paid; those who resisted, who denied the "rights" of the crowd, lost their property, which would be wrecked. As an English sheriff reported of rioters in his district in 1766:

> They visited Farmers, Millers, Bakers, selling grain, flour, bread, cheese, butter, and bacon, at their own prices. They returned in general the money to the proprietors or in their absence left the money for them; and behaved with great regularity and decency where they were not opposed, [but] with outrages and violence where they were.[25]

This episode was but one of hundreds that occurred in 1766 throughout southern England and the Midlands in response to crop failures of unprecedented severity in recent memory.

A similar series of disturbances—also the worst of the later eighteenth century before 1789—swept north-central France in 1775, during the government's second ill-fated attempt at deregulation. Dubbed the "flour war," market riots began in one town and spread in a chain reaction by the combination of local initiative and the impact of rumor from other localities. As in the English riots, the main form of disturbance was popular price-fixing of commodities at "fair prices" instead of the exorbitant market prices that reflected the year's severe shortages. Barns and graneries of wealthy peasants, large farmers, and millers were broken into in the countryside, while in the market towns, cities, and even Paris, grain merchants and bakers were attacked. When the riot spread to Versailles, the city magistrates reverted to customary practices and ordered bakers "in the name of the king" to sell bread at 2 sous per pound instead of the 3½-sou level it had reached. Thereafter, word spread in many places that the king favored direct action to lower the prices. With or without the

[25] Quoted in Thompson, "The Moral Economy," p. 111.

king's alleged complicity, the people believed they were acting to restore their customary rights in the area of subsistence.

Reflecting on the many similarities of the English price riots of 1766 and the French "flour war" of 1775 (which in turn were merely the most severe of numerous episodes), Rudé observes in conclusion: "In both countries, the 'just' price [set by the rioters] was that prevailing in years of good harvests and of normal plenty; and in both, the old practice of official intervention to protect the poor against famine prices had been abandoned sufficiently recently to live on in popular memory." [26] Once the authorities were able to restore order with troops, however, they tended to view these events as a form of criminal riot. In both the English and French cases numerous prosecutions ensued, resulting in dozens of hangings. In the final reckoning, riot was a crime rather than a right.

[26] Rudé, *The Crowd in History*, p. 44.

CHAPTER 6

The Varieties of Culture

CULTURAL ANTHROPOLOGISTS studying non-European societies generally distinguish between a society's "great tradition" and its "little tradition." The former, also called high culture, refers to the official or elite culture, the written and artistic culture that is the patrimony of the priesthood or the ruling classes. The "little tradition," found among the folk, the popular masses, is unofficial and usually unwritten. As Robert Redfield puts it, "the great tradition is cultivated in schools or temples; the little tradition works itself out and keeps itself going in the lives of the unlettered in their village communities."

This twofold distinction is helpful in confronting old-regime Europe, but it is not entirely adequate. For there were really three distinctive levels of culture in eighteenth-century society, which, moreover, were not watertight compartments entirely separate from each other. The first might be called learned culture, and its essence was the knowledge of Latin. It was the culture of scientists, jurists, religious scholars, philosophers, and intellectuals, of poets and dramatists, and of their patrons among the aristocratic and the wealthy. Salons, academies, and universities were among the institutions of this cosmopolitan cultural milieu, and the structures of the legal and medical professions mirrored its influence as well. There was a growing literate public, however, that did not share in this culture because, among other reasons, it did not have a working knowledge of Latin. Middle-class culture (as it can be loosely and perhaps misleadingly described) therefore included women in large numbers, avid readers who rarely knew Latin. This public provided a market for new periodicals, for the eighteenth century's new novels, and for popularizations of scientific and philosophical writing. Its characteristic cultural institutions (limited, it is true, to men) were coffeehouses and Masonic lodges. Among the popular classes of town and country there was yet a third cultural environment. It would be simple if one could state that this was a purely oral culture and that the masses were illiterate. In fact, it was not quite so simple. Literacy was low in certain parts of Europe and among certain social groups, but illiteracy was by no means universal. Popular culture did have its print media, whose nature we shall examine. In the main, however, oral tradition in the form of songs and tales was the dominant mode of cultural transmission. Popular culture was collective in nature and revolved around festivals, partly religious, partly secular. Just as the learned elites had their salons and academies, and the middle classes their coffeehouses and Masonic lodges, the popular classes had their taverns as convivial meeting places.

HIGH AND MIDDLING CULTURE

Learned and Elite Cultures

While it is difficult to define the boundaries of high culture it is easy enough to pinpoint its two distinct constituencies: a refined and extremely wealthy public of laymen, and a learned body of intellectuals, professionals, and artists. The aristocracy was a key element in the support of high culture. A recent study of the French nobility suggests that perhaps 10 percent of that group, including elements of the court nobility and the *Parlement* magistrates, enjoyed access to high culture. True, "the mass of the nobility was alien to the world of high culture, but the elite constituted an important fraction of its creators and consumers." [1] While the average country noble had as little to do with high culture as the average workingman, elements of the upper nobility—made up of those who had superior wealth, education, and taste—were deeply involved in its propagation.

High culture was cosmopolitan, a kind of international civilization, unconfined by national or linguistic boundaries. Most of its devotees knew at least some Latin, the international language of learning. While people usually wrote in their own language they derived their sense of taste from the Latin classics, and peppered their conversation with Latin phrases. Moreover, in this century dominated in so many ways by France, French had become the international language used by the cultural elites. Ladies and gentlemen of refinement could usually read French as well as quote Latin epigrams, and translation of works from other languages into French helped to internationalize high culture. The elites were cosmopolitan too, in that they could afford to travel and did so with enthusiasm. Some made the "grand tour" of the continent, whose highlights were visits to

---

[1] Guy Chaussinand-Nogaret, *La Noblesse au XVIIIe siècle: de la féodalité aux lumières* (Paris, 1976), p. 109.

resplendent urban centers and the ruins of classical civilization. Along with a revival of the writings of pagan philosophers, there was a renewed interest in the monuments of ancient Greek and Roman architecture and sculpture. Europeans endorsed the view of the German art historian Johann Winckelmann that Greek sculpture was the ideal standard of aesthetic beauty. They flocked to Rome to see firsthand the awe-inspiring remains of that great pagan civilization, and eagerly bought up the etchings of engraver Giovanni Battista Piranesi as mementos of their visits. The most durable result of this fascination with antique ruins was Edward Gibbon's decision, on visiting the Colosseum, to undertake his great history, *The Decline and Fall of the Roman Empire* (1776–1788).

In the domain of publishing, the elites supported undertakings that were of no interest to the general reading public. Depending on their particular interests, the learned elites purchased books on law, science, medicine, theology, and philosophy, including certain pathbreaking works of the Enlightenment to be discussed in the next chapter. Many writers stood comfortably astride learned and middling culture. Rousseau's novel *The New Héloïse*, for example, was devoured by a mass audience, while his *Social Contract* was a demanding philosophic treatise that had a minimal sale before the French Revolution dramatized its argument.

The place of learned, Latin-based culture can be seen in the quantitative studies of book publishing and of the contents of private libraries that have been carried out for France.[2] Aside from indicating the growth in publishing (around 300 new legally-authorized titles in 1750 compared to about 1600 annually in the 1780's), these studies reveal that the output in traditional areas of high culture remained steady. Latin classics and books about classical subjects, such as rhetoric, remained a staple of publishing. Books on history and the arts and sciences rose proportionately during the century, and only titles in theology declined (from about 35 percent of all titles to about 10 percent). However, theological publishing involved the reprinting of many standard texts that did not require new authorization and hence did not always enter this count.

Interest in poetry was another hallmark of high culture. Poetry was still the most prized form of literary expression among the cultivated classes. Unlike fiction, poetry was not developing in new directions. Unchanging classical norms on what made good poetry still prevailed. Each type of poem had its special rules. In the neoclassical tradition, art was imitative of nature, which offered eternal standards of truth and beauty, as interpreted by authoritative critics starting with Aristotle. It was not expected that poets would unburden their souls or hold forth on their own experi-

---

[2] François Furet, "La Librairie du royaume en France au XVIIIᵉ siècle," *Livre et Société dans la France du XVIIIᵉ siècle*, Vol. I (Paris and The Hague, 1965).

ence. The raw materials of emotion were supposed to be muted and filtered through language and allusions that only the highly educated would appreciate. Thus, the audience for poetry was generally the most elitist segment of the reading public—"the wealthy few," in the phrase of William Wordsworth, who criticized eighteenth-century poets for addressing their work exclusively to that group. Yet poetry remained a prime path to literary prestige, the source of Alexander Pope's reputation in England and of Voltaire's early triumphs in France. By the end of the century, the restraints of neoclassicism, long since shattered in the domains of drama and fiction, were finally thrown off by a number of German and British poets. Writers like Friedrich von Schiller and Wordsworth defiantly celebrated individual feeling and inner passion in their poems, and in the process helped launch the movement known as romanticism. Hoping to appeal to a broader audience, they changed the nature of poetic art and made poetry, like the novel, an adaptable vehicle of expression. But that would come only at the century's end. Until then, neoclassical poetry, like the Latin classics, formed a cornerstone of high culture.

Both must certainly have been common coin in the salons, which epitomized both the achievements and limitations of high culture. The salon's chief virtue was that it brought together types of people who might otherwise not have mixed socially: authors, savants, intellectuals, and artists on the one hand, leisured aristocrats, wealthy afficionados of culture, and men of affairs, who were in a position to appreciate and assist talented writers, on the other. Women, however, held the pivotal role in salon society, for they were its organizers. They invited the guests, insured the proper atmosphere, and saw to it that the discussion flowed smoothly. The salon's reason for existence was good conversation—witty, eloquent, and original, but never ponderous, radical, or argumentative. Only gracious and eloquent people were welcomed. At its best a salon could be useful to serious-minded intellectuals. Diderot (a key figure in the French Enlightenment to be discussed in the next chapter) penned a double-edged and oft-quoted tribute to the Parisian salons: "Women accustom us to discuss with charm and clarity the driest and thorniest of subjects. We wish them to listen; we are afraid of tiring or boring them; hence we develop a particular method of explaining ourselves easily and this passes from conversation into our written style." Yet the unwritten rules of the salons could be extremely frustating. Rousseau, for one, would have nothing to do with them because they seemed pretentious, superficial, and cynical in their worldly ways. Even more conventional intellectuals found the insistence on smoothly flowing conversation and the avoidance of real controversy tiresome. Such was the case in perhaps the most renowned salon of the Enlightenment period, Mme. Geoffrin's. A wealthy bourgeois widow whose soirées had their heyday in the 1750's and 1760's, Geoffrin

Mme. Geoffrin's salon. *This painting by Anicet Charles Lemonnier shows someone reading a piece by Voltaire who was absent in exile at Ferney, but there in spirit.*

perfected the art of fostering stylish conversation. But her devout Catholicism and traditionalism ruled out any forceful discussion of religious or philosophic heterodoxy. Though she welcomed and indeed sought out the period's most advanced thinkers (and in private extended them financial support), in her salon they were, as one put it, "led about and restrained on a leash." In short, the salon was a triumph of style over substance, a tyranny of propriety over candor. For that reason a number of intellectuals in the 1770's sought refuge in the all-male gatherings at the home of the wealthy Baron d'Holbach in Paris, where they could freely discuss their sometimes scandalous ideas. If there was an exception to this characterization of the eighteenth-century salon it might have been the London salon of Lady Mary Wortley Montagu, where the literary conversation was uncommonly serious. But then Lady Mary—a productive travel writer and poet herself—was an exception to most rules.

Along with sparkling conversation, Europe's cultured elites counted music as a routine feature of the good life. Most notable musicians—who usually doubled as performers and composers—worked for a patron, princely, ecclesiastical, or aristocratic. Alessandro Scarlatti, the author of over one hundred Italian-style operas, was chief court musician (kapell-meister) in Naples early in the century, while his son Domenico, a brilliant harpsichordist and the composer of over five hundred sonatas for that instrument, held similar posts in Rome, Portugal, and Spain. Johann Sebastian Bach (1685–1750) spent the last twenty-seven years of his life as organist and music director at St. Thomas Church in Leipzig, having previously held comparable posts at Weimar and other German courts. For Franz Joseph Haydn (1732–1809), the benefactor was Prince Esterházy, for whom Haydn served as kappelmeister between 1761 and 1790, all the while enjoying great latitude for his composing. Such was not the happy fate of the child prodigy Wolfgang Amadeus Mozart (1756–1791), arguably the greatest genius of this musical golden age. Mozart too sought a patron, but his six years with the Archbishop of Salzburg were burdensome. He eventually headed for Vienna where, for the most part without a permanent employer, he was obliged to eke out an inadequate living by teaching, filling private commissions, and giving public concerts. His decidedly less talented and now largely-forgotten rival, Antonio Salieri, on the other hand, was safely ensconced as court composer to the Habsburgs. In any case, eighteenth-century composers of all kinds had to be prolific in order to meet the demands of their patrons for weekly church music or background, dancing, and concert music.

A chamber music performance. *The soloist in this ensemble at Frederick the Great's palace of Sans Souci was Frederick himself, who occasionally composed for the flute and played it whenever he had the chance.*

The multiplicity of patrons in Italy and Germany—so well endowed with bishops and princes—assured that these regions would be the font of musical life. During the early part of the century, Italy set the fashion in both opera and instrumental music, with rigid styles of composition designed to provide the listener with pleasant melodies in predictable forms. This style has come to be known as "rococo" and, though it gave and continues to give enormous pleasure, even its staunchest partisans would admit that rococo music was "light," elegantly decorative, and highly stylized, but rarely profound or original. One hesitates to push such analogies, but rococo music would seem to match perfectly the style of conversation in the salons, where so much of it was played. Yet the musical scene was beginning to change toward the end of the century in several ways. The center of gravity was shifting from Italy to Vienna, where a trio of geniuses transformed eighteenth-century forms, including the opera, concerto, and symphony. The early symphonies of Haydn and Mozart, for example, had been triumphs of rococo decorativeness, light and tuneful. Gradually they altered and then stabilized the form, moving from the three-movement Italian style to the classic four movements, and using the sonata form. Their symphonies became longer, more complex harmonically, and more venturesome melodically. They began to infuse the symphonic form with a lyricism and emotionalism scarcely comparable to the elegant trifles of their early years. Ludwig van Beethoven (1770–1827) sealed this evolution. Though outliving Mozart by many years, he produced far fewer works. Instead, each of his nine symphonies was marked by original, individualized qualities, and by the outward signs of inner artistic struggle. For some composers, the days of grinding out masses of routine music were passing.

Not coincidentally, music was increasingly moving out of churches, salons, and private chapels into public concert halls. The elderly Haydn had helped lead this change himself. Having left Esterházy's employ in 1790, he signed on with the London impresario Salomon, for whom he composed his last twelve symphonies, performed on what proved to be immensely successful public concert tours in England. Mozart had perforce made increasing, if less lucrative, use of tours and public subscription concerts, while for Beethoven the latter became a characteristic way for earning a living in the absence of a patron. As we move towards the nineteenth century, music, like poetry, was changing from the classic to the romantic style, while musical audiences were growing larger and more diverse.

Writers, Publishers, and Readers

The expansion of publishing and the growth of the reading public were even more pronounced. Together, they constituted the eighteenth century's pivotal cultural development. There were more writers, more readers, and new forms of literary communication. Spanning the spectrum from poetic geniuses to crude pornographers, authorship now embraced leisured aristocrats taking up their pens for philosophical discourse; clerics carrying on long traditions of religious argumentation; hack writers grubbing for a living; and versatile intellectuals whose literary fame has endured for two centuries. While much of the written word was still addressed to a small learned public, the bulk of literary output was increasingly aimed at the burgeoning middle levels of society. This stratum was expanding in numbers and in kinds. Women readers were becoming important in the old regime's cultural life, providing a substantial audience for certain kinds of periodicals and for the era's new novels; in Western Europe, the reading public included increasing numbers of urban artisans as well.

Between author and reader the publisher was an indispensable middleman. Also known by the term "bookseller," publishers were the businessmen who assessed the market and met the increasing demand for books. In the process, they eventually made it possible for writers to earn a living through their pens without the need for aristocratic patrons. The publishers (some of whom formed highly capitalized entrepreneurial syndicates) maintained networks of salesmen who supplied local bookdealers with both legal and prohibited books. Books and periodicals were also marketed directly by subscription.

Though there is no precise way of measuring this, Britain, along with the Dutch Netherlands, probably held the premier position in the expansion of publishing and reading. Britain assuredly pioneered in the development of magazines and newspapers. In 1700, about 25 periodicals were being published in the island kingdom; by 1760, there were 103, and by 1780, 158. Also, whereas most earlier periodicals had been addressed to particular political factions, religious viewpoints, or specialized interests, the eighteenth century saw the development of general periodicals.[3] Indeed, as a cultural era, the beginning of the eighteenth century can almost be dated from the appearance of Richard Steele's *Tatler* in 1709 and, above all, Joseph Addison's and Steele's *Spectator* in 1711. The *Spectator* was a revolution in publishing, original both in form and content, and influential far beyond its short duration and far beyond Britain's shores. Appearing daily except Sunday for a total of 555 issues through December 1712, it consisted of one long essay per issue, a form first developed experimentally in the *Tatler*. This turned out to be an ideal way both to stimulate and satisfy the reading public's taste. The essay form

[3] R. S. Crane and F. B. Kaye, "A Census of British Newspapers and Periodicals, 1620–1800," *Studies in Philology*, Vol. XXIV (1927), pp. 179–201.

afforded the authors maximum flexibility and provided the subscribers with a steady diet of edifying reading matter.

Eighteenth-century writers sought to entertain and instruct their readers simultaneously, and the *Spectator* gave this objective its classic embodiment. The authors strove "to enliven Morality with Wit, and to temper Wit with Morality. . . . To bring Philosophy out of the closets and libraries, schools and colleges, to dwell in clubs and assemblies, at tea-tables and coffeehouses." Thus the *Spectator* cultivated a general reading public which liked to read polished language that was nonetheless easily comprehensible. Benjamin Franklin noted in his *Autobiography* that he used the *Spectator* as a model when trying to teach himself to write stylishly, while Samuel Johnson declared it "a model of the middle style . . . familiar but not coarse, and elegant but not ostentatious." Mild wit, polished vocabulary, and pleasant turns of phrase were hallmarks of the *Spectator* style. Its content was serious but not too serious, thought-provoking but not too demanding. The authors attempted to make moral behavior fashionable by attacking the prevailing boorishness, prejudice, gambling, and violence of their society, while praising marriage, familial devotion, and good manners as the true ideals of a gentleman. If their essays sometimes resembled sermons, the preaching was mild and never ponderous or pointedly sectarian. In fact, the *Spectator* consciously avoided the narrow sectarian viewpoints that dominated most political and religious discourse at that time. Another feature of the *Spectator* was its authors' interest in reaching women. While displaying a somewhat patronizing attitude toward "the fair sex," Addison and Steele flattered their numerous female readers with substantial attention. Women especially appreciated the *Spectator*'s efforts to promote civil behavior in an age that was brutal even in the highest social circles. Promoting the ideals of refinement and morality, the *Spectator* and its many imitators in England and abroad helped set a new tone in social behavior, both for the established aristocracy and the aspiring middle classes. Later we will see that as one moves eastward toward the culturally undeveloped areas of Europe, the first rays of literary culture to penetrate were usually in the form of *Spectator*-type periodicals. Indeed, to be accurate about it, the same was also true moving westward to that other outpost of European society, the American colonies. For Benjamin Franklin republished several essays from the *Spectator*, though they were already over fifty years old.

Other types of periodicals flourished in England as well. Miscellanies featured extracts from other periodicals along with entertainment and reports of current affairs. The most popular was *The Gentleman's Magazine*, which began in 1731 and, a decade later, reached the impressive circulation of fifteen thousand. More important for the public's reading habit was the growth of the daily press. Newspapers, whose income came from subscriptions and advertising, combined commercial announcements and advertisements with general news and features. Then as now they were relatively inexpensive. Though daily newspapers could not continue to sell at the original rate of one penny because of rising taxes on paper, the standard three-pence price (half being a tax) was still low enough to remove them from the luxury category. Besides, many people could read newspapers without buying them thanks to the development of coffee-houses in the eighteenth century. Offering a quieter and more respectable atmosphere than taverns, coffeehouses provided racks of newspapers for the use of their patrons.

The passion for reading was not restricted to London. By 1780 no fewer than thirty-seven English towns had local newspapers of their own. These newspapers in turn lubricated the literary marketplace by advertising new books, magazines, number or subscription books (forthcoming books published in installments), used-book auctions, and circulating libraries. The latter first appeared in 1740 when booksellers, unwilling to rely on stores or subscriptions alone, sent wagons from house to house in the provinces renting out books. By the end of the century there were probably a thousand circulating libraries, which especially helped make books available to women readers.

Supplying the growing reading public was big business. Publishers met the demand for easy-to-digest fiction and nonfiction with a steady flow of melodramatic novels, potboiler histories and biographies, and scientific popularizations. All this provided a living for hack writers paid by the page. Yet while booksellers pandered to popular taste, they also backed expensive quality ventures that produced literary masterpieces. In England, for example, Samuel Johnson (1709–1784) could live an admittedly penurious but distinguished life of letters essentially independent of any aristocratic patron, though he did gratefully receive a small government pension. His publishers exploited him often, but they also provided the means for his livelihood. Two of Johnson's greatest works were produced on commission from booksellers: the *Lives of the English Poets* (1779–1781), a masterful series of short critical biographies, and his *Dictionary* (1755), which helped to purify and standardize the English language. Johnson's friend Oliver Goldsmith (c. 1730–1774) was a less distinguished and thus less unusual example of a man who lived by his pen. While he is justly remembered for his novel, *The Vicar of Wakefield* (1766), and his long poem, *The Deserted Village* (1770), these peaks came amidst a staggering output of mediocre histories, literary criticism, and scientific popularizations. At one point, for example, this would-be poet was paid £800 for producing a seven-volume scissors-and-paste *Natural History*.

Johnson and Goldsmith were always writing magazine articles and at

Samuel Johnson. *The great English man of letters was immortalized by the period's leading portrait painter, Sir Joshua Reynolds, the first president of London's Royal Academy of Art. Reynolds and Johnson were friends who frequented the same informal club, a counterpart perhaps of the Parisian salons.*

various times launched publications of their own. In the preface to one such venture, *The Literary Magazine* (1756)—ostensibly devoted to the affairs of literature, politics, and science—Johnson candidly admitted that "it will be necessary to dwell most upon things of general entertainment, the elegant trifles of literature, the pleasing amusements of harmless wits. . . ." He was trying to reassure his audience. Of course he would seek to instruct them, but they need not be frightened off, for he recognized their overriding desire to be entertained. The new reading public was thus both a liberating force and a troublesome one in the writer's destiny. Its demands created all sorts of new opportunities for writers to earn a livelihood. But the public insisted on being entertained, and in the long run this could threaten the writer's independence. From being the captive of aristocratic patrons in times past, writers might now become the captives of the mediocre tastes of their wider audience. They might be forced to violate their standards and stifle their creative inspiration in order to turn out platitudes, oversimplified nonfiction, and vulgar fictional romances. The tyranny of the mass market was first felt in the eighteenth century. From then on a struggle would persist between talent and literary creativity on the one hand, and commercialism and the demands of public taste on the other. Yet certain writers were able to bridge the gap and produce that ideal book, a popular literary master-piece.[4]

The Rise of the Novel

The great innovation of eighteenth-century literature and perhaps its most popular genre was the novel. Without getting involved in scholarly disputes over its origins and lineage, we can safely say that the modern novel was produced in the context of a vibrant English society by the 1740's. One of its acknowledged pioneers was Samuel Richardson (1689–1761), a man who personified middle-class consciousness. The son of a carpenter, Richardson was a successful printer by trade. Essentially self-made, self-righteous, and ambitious, he was fully aware of the power of the printed word. Yet it was only in his fifties that he became a writer and, in a manner of speaking, by accident. In 1739 he was asked by some bookseller friends to compose a volume of "familiar letters," model letters to be used by ordinary people in various social situations. Sharing Addison's aim of raising society's moral tone, Richardson became absorbed by this trifling venture. Realizing that people preferred moral exhortation to be packaged in interesting plots, his letters began to include fictionalized incidents. As he worked on Number 138—"A Father to a Daughter in (Domestic) Service, on hearing of her Master's attempting her virtue"—he became fixated. In the letter he advised the besieged servant girl to resist her master's attempts at seduction and to leave the household promptly. Richardson also began to ponder what might happen if she did not leave, but was instead endowed with a combative spirit and the gift of writing. He began to compose an epistolary novel—a novel in the form of exchanged letters—on these premises. *Pamela; or, Virtue Rewarded* (1740) was filled with titillating scenes of attempted seduction that came within a trice of succeeding but always failed. Pamela Andrews not only fended off her employer but explored her own emotions at great length in her letters home. Gradually her employer became obsessed with these letters, which he was eventually permitted to read. Taken with her mind as well as her body, he abandoned his effort to seduce her and married her instead. Thus was "Virtue Rewarded." However, as one commentator has recently put it, the moral of the novel could also be taken as "Writing Rewarded." Pamela's writing was rewarded with marriage; Richardson's with instant literary popularity.[5]

---

[4] See L. Lowenthal and M. Fiske, "The Debate over Art and Popular Culture in 18th Century England," in *Common Frontiers of the Social Sciences*, ed by M. Komarovsky (Glencoe, Ill., 1957); Ralph M. Wardle, *Oliver Goldsmith* (Lawrence, Kans., 1957).

[5] T. C. Duncan Eaves and B. D. Kimpel, *Samuel Richardson: a Biography* (Oxford, 1971); Ellen Moers, "Women's Liberator," *New York Review of Books*, 10 February 1972, pp. 27–31.

Pamela. *Several artists portrayed Richardson's popular fictional heroine. In this illustration by Joseph Highmore, her employer comes upon Pamela as she writes one of her famous letters. National Gallery, London.*

In his next and immensely successful novel, *Clarissa Harlowe* (1747–1748), Richardson continued his moral crusade in another context. This time his heroine was a young lady from an unsympathetic upper-class family, which insisted that Clarissa marry a suitor she found loathsome. Resisting family pressure, she ran off with a rake named Lovelace, whose intentions were strictly dishonorable. When she resisted his advances he finally drugged and raped her. For Clarissa death remained the only honorable course, and one might say that she died of a broken heart, despite pleas from many readers of the novel's installments that Richardson spare her. The fact that Lovelace subsequently died in a duel and that Clarissa's family was contrite only heightened the novel's effect. Though egregiously melodramatic, it proved irresistably moving to its readers. As Samuel Johnson remarked: "If you were to read Richardson for the story . . . you would hang yourself. But you must read him for the sentiment." Richardson's moral earnestness appealed to the period's sentimental tastes. His talent lay in his ability to dissect emotion and inner feeling, especially of women. Female readers doted on him, and a few began to write fiction themselves under his inspiration. At the same time some of Europe's most subtle intellects, such as Goethe and Rousseau, were directly influenced by his novels.

Not all readers admired Richardson. In reacting against him, however, Henry Fielding (1707–1754) in turn propelled the art of fiction in new directions. An accomplished though frustrated playwright (and unlike Richardson, a worldly and colorful individual), Fielding saw in *Pamela* a cloying hypocrisy, a stuffy moralizing, and a false prudishness that was transparently prurient. In response he dashed off a crude burlesque called *Shamela*, in which the heroine acted without scruple as a lewd temptress out to capture a rich husband by playing hard to get. Not content with that weak blast, Fielding began a second satire using Pamela's brother Joseph as the protagonist; his inspiration was to describe an attractive young man heroically struggling to perserve *his* virginity and virtue. But in the course of writing *Joseph Andrews* (1742), Fielding soon went beyond that notion and created a full-scale novel of the open road— robust, hilarious, and affecting. Fielding's success spurred him on to elaborate this form of fiction, which he called "a comic epic in prose," thus rejecting the classic rules governing the epic. The result was that masterpiece of comic fiction, *The History of Tom Jones, A Foundling* (1749). Built on an enormous canvas that ranged from the depths of London low life to the distant outposts of the rural gentry, *Tom Jones* was populated by a gallery of outsized and hilarious characters who nonetheless corresponded to real social types. Unlike Richardson, Fielding was more interested in manners and behavior than inner feeling. His characters developed through action rather than self-examination. Yet he too was ultimately concerned with moral issues, and the book is a long assault on various forms of hypocrisy, affectation, and moral shortcomings.

Together Richardson and Fielding launched the modern novel as the chief vehicle for fictional writing. Breaking with the standard forms and heroic subjects of most previous narrative fiction, they dealt with recognizable types of people in plausible social settings. The novel proved to be a supremely flexible genre, adaptable to an emphasis on setting, plot, or inner feeling. A form without fixed rules of composition or aesthetic norms, it lent itself to endless experimentation. Thus, with Laurence Sterne's *Tristram Shandy* (1760–1767) chronology and plot were dropped altogether in favor of a kind of literary free-association. The century's best novels became part of learned culture, as was the case with Goethe's *The Sorrows of Young Werther* (1774)—a *Bildungsroman* (novel of education) which told the tragic tale of the coming of age of a melancholy youth. Nevertheless, if some novels were creatively original or at least serious in artistic intent, most were inevitably little more than superficial melodramas riding the coattails of Richardson's success, and pandering to the lowest common denominator of taste.

CULTURAL INSTITUTIONS
Secondary Education and Universities
Though there was no formal system of secondary education run by either church or state in eighteenth-century Europe, secondary schools were familiar landmarks on the cultural scene. These institutions went by different names in different places: public school and grammar school in England, *collège* in France and Spain, *Gymnasium* in Germany and Austria. All were similar in their heavy emphasis on Greek and Latin. They provided a classical education that set their graduates apart from the rest of society.

France had about 350 endowed *collèges*, including institutions directly under royal patronage (the *grandes écoles* or great schools in Paris that to this day confer tremendous prestige on their graduates); municipal *collèges* supported in part by city governments; and, most common, *collèges* sponsored by religious orders. Until they were expelled in 1768 the Jesuits ran about one hundred of the largest and best, most of which were subsequently taken over by local boards or other religious orders— a change that occurred throughout Catholic Europe. Around fifty thousand students attended these 350 institutions annually, an estimated 2 percent of the young men between the ages of eight and eighteen. The establishment and recruitment of *collèges* was related to urbanization. A majority of French towns with a population over five thousand, and all but a handful of those over ten thousand could boast such institutions, most of whose students came from urban backgrounds. Most *collèges* were small, however, with three-quarters having fewer than two hundred students and, of necessity, a limited curriculum that did not include the last two years that were supposed to be devoted to philosophy.[6]

The majority of students paid tuition and fees to their teachers as well as the costs of room and board, but there was scholarship assistance available for youngsters of modest means: approximately three thousand full scholarships and a variety of partial scholarships. In some cases tuition was covered by state grants, in others by town funds, or by charitable endowments administered through religious orders. Though in certain respects this financial aid was considerable, it was also extremely localized and hap-

---

[6] R. Chartier and D. Julia, *L'Education en France du XVIe au XVIIIe siècle* (Paris, 1976), chaps. 5–7; D. Julia and P. Pressley, "La Population Scolaire en 1789," *Annales*, Vol XXX (1975), pp. 1516–47.

hazard. It permitted what sociologists call "sponsored upward mobility" as opposed to open competition. In order to benefit from the system, a boy from a poor family needed the patronage of local clerics or notables. Having satisfied such patrons of his character and morals, he might then be assisted in entering a *collège*. In any case, the dropout rate among lower-class pupils was extremely high, while most of the poorer boys who did persist ended up in the clergy. The same pattern obtained in German secondary schools, where scholarship aid was provided for similar kinds of students destined for careers in the church. On the whole, then, these schools served to reinforce elite status rather than to facilitate social mobility. As the conservative politician François Guizot would state a few decades later: "Far from secondary education being a means of social change, it should reflect social distinctions and the divisions of society."

The curriculum of Europe's endowed secondary schools was not designed with practical or vocational objectives in mind, but was almost entirely concerned with the mastery of Latin and Greek. Ancient classics were its core, as students labored wearily over exercises in Latin grammar, rhetoric, and composition. Mathematics, science, history, and modern languages were largely or totally neglected, and while philosophy and logic were included in the last two years of study, they focused mainly on Aristotle. The result was not exactly stimulating, but the schools undeniably promoted linguistic eloquence. Within this ossified system of instruction, changes did occur in the eighteenth century in respect to the age of students and the calendar of study. Where the students' ages had once covered a wide spectrum, each class or form in the seven prescribed years of study now came to be associated with a particular modal age. And where once students entered and left school at several points during the year, enrollment now began to take place specifically in October. The "lock-step" system of educational gradations was beginning.

A great deal of the old regime's secondary education, however, occurred outside the endowed institutions in privately operated schools. A university graduate might first set himself up as a tutor, then take in a number of student boarders, and finally convert his operation into a small profit-making school. These private schools taught Latin of course, but frequently added subjects such as mathematics and modern languages that might be useful in future careers. Merchants appreciated this, for they did not care to waste their children's time at *collèges* or grammar schools studying year after year of Latin if these children were destined to enter the family business. Private schools brought secondary education to locales that could not support a full-fledged endowed institution, and to families of modest means that could not afford the time or money for a classical education. Among the more successful schools of this modern, utilitarian type were the *Realschulen* of Germany, and the English academies sponsored by Dissenters. Similarly, proprietary schools of this kind, along with convents in Catholic countries, took on the entire burden of formal education for upper-class girls. Generally young women were not taught Latin, their studies centering instead on religion and domestic skills along with a smattering of music, foreign languages, and other subjects that contributed to refinement. For girls, secondary education was essentially decorous.

In Europe's venerable universities, the eighteenth century was an era of stagnation that was all the more pronounced for its contrast to an earlier period of vitality. In England, Spain, France, the Low Countries, and Germany, "the number of university students increased handsomely between the middle of the sixteenth century and the middle of the seventeenth," thereafter declining precipitously and, in most cases, persistently, until the nineteenth century.[7] This pattern was most dramatic in England and Spain. Lawrence Stone has found nothing less than an "educational revolution" in England between 1560 and 1640, one of whose effects was a huge increase in enrollments at Oxford and Cambridge in the early seventeenth century. Abruptly cut off by the English revolution, enrollments plummeted and did not recover until the nineteenth century. Similarly, in Castile (Spain's dominant province) students poured into its nineteen universities until a peak enrollment of almost twenty thousand was attained in the 1590's—an astonishing 5 percent of the age cohort. At Spain's largest university of Salamanca, as many as six thousand students were registered. But by the early 1700's this had totally changed. No more than five or six thousand students were matriculated in all of Castile's universities combined.[8] Though not as stark as in England and Spain, the trends elsewhere were similar, as the accompanying diagram suggests. Only one major exception to the trend, the University of Coimbra in Portugal, has thus far been found. In the thirty-four universities of Germany, for example, there was a predictably severe decline in enrollments during the Thirty Years' War, and while recovery occurred later, enrollments generally fluctuated below the levels of the early seventeenth century. Universities in the Low Countries also experienced a sharp falling-off of students in the later seventeenth century. In the Dutch Netherlands, the downward trend continued through the eighteenth century even more steeply than in England and Spain.

Universities were complex corporate institutions subject to varying degrees of state control. Typically they had four separate parts or faculties: theology, philosophy or letters, law, and medicine. During the great boom

---

[7] R. Chartier and J. Revel, "Université et Société dans l'Europe moderne: positions des problèmes," *Revue d'histoire moderne et contemporaine*, Vol. XXV (July 1978), pp. 353–74—an important comparative study.

[8] Lawrence Stone, "The Size and Composition of the Student Body in Oxford, 1580–1910," and Richard Kagan, "Universities in Castile, 1500–1800," in *The University in Society*, ed. by Lawrence Stone (2 vols.: Princeton, N.J., 1974).

STUDENT ENROLLMENTS IN EUROPEAN UNIVERSITIES
(Ten-Year Averages)

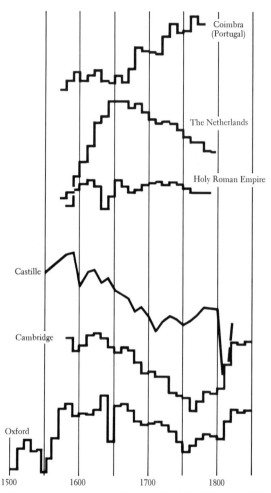

Coimbra
(Portugal)

The Netherlands

Holy Roman Empire

Castille

Cambridge

Oxford

1500　　　1600　　　1700　　　1800

Source: R. Chartier and J. Revel, "Université et Société dans l'Europe moderne:
position des problèmes," *Revue d'histoire moderne et contemporaine*, Vol. XXV (July
1978).

in university enrollments of the sixteenth and early seventeenth centuries,
law had generally overtaken theology and philosophy as the university's
most popular course of study. Law degrees had become passports to official positions in the growing bureaucracies of Western Europe. It is possible that the decline in enrollments began when the bureaucracies had
become saturated. Colbert, among others, had warned in the 1680's that
an excess of university graduates was becoming a problem in France. It

seems too that many nobles had joined the flood of university matriculants in the earlier period, at a time when there was uncertainty about their future status under the Spanish Habsburgs or the Bourbons. When the balance of social forces had clearly shifted back to traditional noble groups, there was perhaps less reason to compete with the middle classes, for whom a legal education remained a channel of social ascent. It was probably no coincidence that the eighteenth century saw the proliferation of schools specifically designed for nobles, such as the *Ritterakademien* of Germany or the French military schools, where a smattering of modern studies was added to the Latin curriculum, and where the noble arts of riding and fencing were emphasized.

In any case, law remained the faculty of choice for the more ambitious and well-heeled university students, while theology was the faculty of young men from more modest social backgrounds and the younger sons of aristocrats destined for the episcopacy. Of the total student population of France's twenty-four universities in the 1780's, about six hundred were studying medicine, while law still drew a heavy contingent of thirty-five hundred. This could be misleading, however, since only 60 percent of the law students in the University of Paris actually took degrees. About five thousand students were inscribed in the faculties of philosophy, but that too is misleading, since the number includes students in the last two years of study in the many *collèges* affiliated with the universities. Relatively few students actually took the faculty's Master of Arts degree. Finally, theology had four thousand students, some of whom simultaneously pursued studies in various seminaries.[9]

With a handful of exceptions, European universities in the eighteenth century were suffering from acute intellectual sclerosis. The Austrian reformer Josef von Sonnenfels (1733–1817) was effectively describing not only the universities of his country, but those of Spain, Italy, France, Germany, and England as well, when he complained of their backwardness. "In theology, scholasticism and casuistry dominated; philosophy was about one hundred years behind the times. . . . Critical history, natural sciences —which are supposed to make enlightenment general and combat prejudice—were neglected or wholly unknown."[10] Enlightenment ministers and rulers tried to institute reforms later in the century, especially in Austria, Spain, and Portugal. In Austria chairs were founded in public administration, with Sonnenfels appointed to one of the first in 1763. Attention was lavished on the law faculties, which would produce future bureaucrats, while the study of theology was reformed in the hope of producing better-trained and more responsible clergymen. The University of Vienna also had a superior medical faculty which made it—along with Montpellier in

[9] Chartier and Julia, *L'Education en France,* chap. 9.
[10] Quoted in Robert Kerner, *Bohemia in the Eighteenth Century* (New York, 1932), pp. 345–46.

France, Leiden in the Netherlands, and Edinburgh in Scotland—a reputable place to study. Vocationally, the University of Vienna became one of Europe's more effective institutions of higher learning. In France, meanwhile, the government bypassed the universities altogether to train the technical experts it needed in such institutions as the School of Bridges and Roads, the School of Mines, and the Royal College of Military Engineering.

Other exceptions to the unimpressive state of eighteenth-century universities were two of the newest, the University of Halle in Prussia and the University of Göttingen in Hanover. Most of Germany's thirty-odd universities were languishing, with skimpy resources, few professors, and no more than three hundred or four hundred students, if that many. The livelier students and professors were readily attracted to the new institutions, each of which had particular strong points. Founded in 1694, the University of Halle was expressly modern in emphasis. Under the leadership of Christian Thomasius (1655–1728), the faculty sought to provide a useful and stimulating education. Halle led the way in liberating philosophy and letters from the pedantry of the medieval scholasticism that Sonnenfels deplored. With Germany's leading rationalist philosopher Christian Wolff (1679–1754) on its faculty (until he was exiled by an intolerant Frederick William I), theology and philosophy were revivified, and a golden age of German philosophy was inaugurated, culminating much later in the work of Kant and Hegel. Here was one of the few cases, in other words, where university teaching influenced the development of intellectual life. Halle was no less notable in producing a steady flow of university-trained civil servants and progressive clergy. It is not surprising, then, that its approximately fifteen hundred students made Halle Germany's largest university by the 1740's.

The University of Göttingen, founded in Hanover in 1734, had other strengths. With its dynastic connection to England, Hanover and its university became something of a conduit for English ideas and enjoyed a freer intellectual environment than was typical in Germany's larger states. Moreover, Göttingen was better endowed than most institutions, and had unrivaled library and laboratory resources, in which most universities were deficient. Apart from excelling at the teaching of jurisprudence and history, Göttingen's faculty produced a revival in the realm of classicism itself. The traditional approach in secondary schools and universities had been to drill students in classical speech and composition, seeking to perpetuate the stylistic eloquence of ancient Greece or Rome, without much attention to the content of the literature. At Göttingen emphasis was placed on a critical reading of the Latin texts in order to refine the students' taste and train their intellects. This approach to learning helped renew European scholarship on ancient civilization, and attracted first-rate talent to Hanover.

If Göttingen was at the top level of university life, England's Oxford and Cambridge must certainly have ranked near the bottom. With the "educational revolution" of 1560–1640 long since a memory, these venerable institutions had become notorious for their lack of serious purpose. Structurally different from continental universities in that they did not award law degrees, Oxford and Cambridge otherwise shared the period's intellectual torpor. Endless comments about the dubious value of an Oxbridge education can be cited, none more caustic than Adam Smith's. A philosophy professor at the more vibrant University of Glasgow, Smith regarded Oxford and Cambridge as "sanctuaries in which exploded systems and obsolete prejudices found shelter and protection, after they had been hunted out of every other corner of the world."

Teaching at these universities was dysfunctional. Many faculty tutors at the university's various colleges were young clerics awaiting nomination to a parish, who were little concerned with their students. Professorships were regarded as comfortable sinecures, with no incentive to do much teaching, let alone research. Cambridge (Newton's alma mater) did establish a few new chairs in science and mathematics, but they had little impact on the university's ambience, while Oxford remained resolutely reactionary in its Tory politics, theology, and intellectual values. At both institutions the core of the average student's study remained either theology or the classics, both taught in archaic ways and tested in meaningless rote fashion, amidst a stodgy, parochial environment.[11]

Oxford and Cambridge were also outposts of religious segregation, matriculation being limited to adherents of the Church of England, and of a two-class social system. Wealthy gentlemen enrolled as "Gentlemen-commoners," which entitled them to privileged treatment. Since little was expected of them, they could live an idle existence. With cricket and football awaiting future development, these students amused themselves by drinking, gambling, and carousing. At the other end of the scale were students of modest means who earned their keep by acting as servants for the wealthy ones. While this system was perhaps most blatant at Oxford and Cambridge, institutions elsewhere were probably similar. Napoleon Bonaparte, for example, the son of an impoverished noble family from remote Corsica, smoldered in resentment against the snobbism of his rich aristocratic classmates during his student days at the French Military School.

The World of the French Academies

Apart from the few exceptional institutions such as Göttingen, Halle, Edinburgh, Vienna, and Leiden, most scholarship, research, and intel-

---

[11] For a description, see C. Mallet, "Education, Schools and Universities," in *Johnson's England*, ed. by A. S. Turberville (2 vols.: Oxford, 1933). For analysis see Brian Simon, *Studies in the History of Education, 1780–1870* (London, 1969).

lectual innovation occurred outside the universities. Free of the latter's corporate and intellectual deadweight, the great national academies of science were the veritable elite institutions of their day: The Royal Society of London, founded in 1660; the French Academy of Science, taken under the monarchy's wing by Louis XIV; the Berlin Royal Academy of Science and Letters, whose patron was Frederick the Great; and, one might add, Philadelphia's spirited American Philosophical Society. Comparable if somewhat less distinguished academies were founded in Sweden, Denmark, Spain, Russia, and various Italian and German states. Together they constituted one of the fundamental structures in Europe's "republic of letters," facilitating the flow of scientific information across national boundaries. Sponsoring and publishing research by their members, reporting on other research, and sifting research to uphold scientific standards, the national academies rather than the universities assured a central place for science in Europe's civilization.

The French Academy of Sciences was arguably the finest of these elite institutions. Its membership roster featured numerous luminaries in chemistry, astronomy, and mathematics, while its leading spirit and institutional spokesman in the later part of the century was Antoine Lavoisier, the century's greatest chemist. The French Academy of Sciences developed as an adjunct of the state, its members being paid by the government and

The French Academy of Sciences. *The patronage of Louis XIV, shown here visiting the Academy, insured that the members enjoyed suitable financial rewards and high prestige. Engraving by J. Goyton after S. Leclerc.*

its institutional identity having the cachet of a state organ. While most of its research was individually generated, the state called upon it from time to time to solve particular problems. Its official position, however, was a quality that made some outsiders uneasy. Should there be an official arbiter of what makes good science? Scientists whose work was rejected obviously had reason to argue against this. In a particularly controversial case, Franz Mesmer's extravagant therapeutic claims for his popular electromagnetic treatments were derided by the Academy as a form of charlatanism. Mesmer's supporters in turn charged that the Academy was privileged and despotic. Likewise, when the future revolutionary Jean Paul Marat submitted a book of theory and experiments claiming to have toppled Newton's sacrosanct science of optics, the Academy—after some polite exchanges—categorically denounced the book as bad science. Marat nursed his grievance and had his revenge in 1793 when he was instrumental in bringing about the abolition of France's corporate academies. While few showed Marat's animus, serious scientists outside the Academy's precincts objected to its monopolistic position and, well before the Revolution, began to develop a series of "free" or unofficial scientific societies that soon became important forums for research and discourse.[12]

France's claim to primacy in Europe's intellectual life was founded not only on its august national academies of science and literature. A more remarkable feature of learned culture in France were the academies founded in no fewer than thirty-one provincial cities. The word "provincial" is often derogatory, implying a remoteness from the excitement of the capital, a local insularity and narrow-mindedness. Quite the contrary, France's provincial academies nurtured a vigorous intellectual life in most regions of that large realm. With their sense of common purpose, and not least by their use of Parisian French instead of local dialects, they assured that French learning and culture would be national in scope. The intellectual and social evolution of these academies tell us a great deal about eighteenth-century French culture and are well worth close scrutiny.

The earliest began at the century's start as literary academies, local imitations of the august French Academy of Literature in Paris. Concerned with literary style and rhetorical skills, they naturally adhered to orthodox religious and stylistic values in their early decades. Some continued to do so down through the century. The Montauban academy—a bastion of conservatism in southwestern France—sponsored essay contests on subjects which revealed its traditional values: in 1744, "The Vanity of science without religion"; 1752, "True Philosophy is incompati-

---

[12] See Roger Hahn, *The Anatomy of a Scientific Institution: The Paris Academy of Sciences, 1666–1803* (Berkeley, Calif., 1971).

ble with irreligion"; 1759, "The Alleged philosophy of the present century"; 1777, "The Zeal of Louis XIV for religion and morality." Most of the academies, however, outgrew both their emphasis on literary style and their commitment to orthodox values. In the words of Daniel Roche, who has studied these institutions exhaustively, their ideology became "a conservatism open to change." [13]

By the 1750's most had shifted their focus to philosophical, scientific, and practical interests. Physics, chemistry, natural history, agronomy, economics, and political science began to replace oratory and poetry as the staples of their deliberations. The academies had become places for serious study, complete with libraries and laboratories. An increasingly utilitarian outlook prompted them also to involve themselves with social problems. Moreover, in the critical spirit of science, some began to discuss the controversial writings of the Enlightenment (see Chapter 7), not always endorsing their philosophy, but at least familiarizing themselves with these works and resisting attempts to suppress them. Once in a while, royal censors intervened to prevent publication of their proceedings, but on more than one occasion the academies awarded prizes for essays that were radical critiques of contemporary society, such as Dijon's award to Jean Jacques Rousseau for his scathing essay on the decadence of art and science in 1749. By the 1770's their essay contests and members' research increasingly focused on problems such as capital punishment, the effect of luxury, education, public assistance, the grain trade, and agricultural innovation. Gradually, in other words, the academies had gone beyond their original role as forums for congenial sociability and the diffusion of learning. They now promoted the ideal of civic service, both to the state and to their own communities. Loyal to the monarchy —which provided their charters and thereby helped to bolster their status —the academicians wished to be "counselors to power."

These shifts in function and ideology corresponded to a broadening of the academies' membership, to a limited expansion of their social base. The Bordeaux Academy, for example, had started as an informal group of rather aristocratic amateurs in music and literature, who won the patronage of a local duke and received a royal charter in 1712. Dues were correspondingly high at three hundred livres a year, though a series of bequests made it possible eventually to eliminate the fee. The nobility constituted the bulk of the initial membership, though commoners were admitted from the start as corresponding or associate members. Gradually the participation of the middle classes was allowed to increase. Membership in the Academy became a source of status for them, but it also raised

[13] Daniel Roche, *Le Siècle des lumières en province: académies et académiciens provinciaux, 1680–1789* (2 vols.: Paris and The Hague, 1978).

the group's intellectual standards and promoted the academicians' self-image as a genuine elite. As in the other academies, substantial contingents of members increasingly came from the medical profession, law, and public administration, as well as from the clergy, while only a few members originated in the world of trade and industry. Toward the end of the old regime the Bordeaux Academy comprised 56 nobles (including 32 magistrates of the *Parlement*), 38 clergymen, and 68 bourgeois (including 30 doctors). Each academy, of course, varied in composition. In Dijon, for example, the proportion of bourgeois was higher: 112 nobles, 48 clergymen, and 200 bourgeois. At Arras the Academy's permanent secretary was a prominent noble; one of its brightest young stars was a local lawyer named Maximilin Robespierre; and one of its corresponding members in the hinterland was the lowly seigneurial clerk François Noël Babeuf, who would end his life as the most radical figure in the French Revolution. This pattern of membership is instructive. Even the most ideologically progressive academies remained official, self-selecting, and thus "closed" institutions in which nobles commanded deference, and in which unwritten rules created a social boundary beyond which regular members would not be recruited. An obscure employee like Babeuf, with his fervent interest in ideas and reform, might be admitted to corresponding membership but would never be accepted as a regular member.

The provincial academies promoted a fusion of elites. Like the Parisian salons, they brought together men of birth and rank with men of talent and public reputation. Unlike the salons, however, their enterprise was sustained and serious. Together their members formed a "cultural class," in Roche's phrase, which aspired to influence and power in the community. Altogether the provincial academies had about sixty-four hundred members during the eighteenth century, of whom 43 percent were nobles.

Social Composition of the French Provincial Academies

	Nobles	Non-Nobles	Total
Regular Members	1,369 (49%)	1,438 (51%)	2,807
Corresponding Members	847 (29%)	2,084 (71%)	2,931
Honorary Members	562 (85%)	102 (15%)	664
Total	2,778 (43%)	3,624 (57%)	6,402

It was precisely this mix of elites that made these institutions so prestigious and so effective. Within the confines of their unwritten rules of selectivity and deference, the academies were egalitarian, as befitted a serious intellectual or cultural enterprise. They promoted social cohesion within the elite elements of a stratified social order.

Like the Academy of Science in Paris, the provincial academies had the drawbacks as well as the virtues of elitism. Most citizens were perforce left on the outside, while their official status inherently limited the academies' independence. Even thirty-one provincial academies could not come near to serving the enormous demand in France for organized intellectual activity, let alone sociability. To meet these needs, Frenchmen banded together in reading clubs, whose history is not yet well charted, and in Masonic lodges.

Freemasonry was a brotherhood dedicated to celebrating human dignity. Its lodges provided a means for socializing, nurtured a comforting commitment to philanthropic ideals, and catered to the human penchant for secrecy and ritual. Starting in England, the movement quickly spread to Germany, France, and elsewhere as the century progressed. Freemasonry spread socially as well as geographically, when prominent aristocrats were attracted to it and lent it their prestige. For example, Frederick the Great and Louis XVI's cousin, the Duke of Orléans, were the heads of Masonic federations in their respective countries. Certain lodges brought together

A Masonic lodge in Vienna. *Allegorical symbols, blindfolds, and swords were all part of eighteenth-century Masonic ritual, whose contents were one of the world's more poorly kept secrets. In Vienna a group of Freemasons called the Illuminati was especially serious in its efforts to promote universal brotherhood.*

elements of the upper and middle social ranks; usually, however, the lodges were more homogeneous, with one lodge comprising mainly nobles, and another mainly professionals or merchants. One important type of lodge was limited to military officers.

Evaluating the significance of Freemasonry has always been difficult. In one sense it cut across social barriers, but it certainly accentuated another dividing line by its thorough (if unofficial) exclusion of working people. Ideologically, Freemasonry could appear progressive and even radical in its idealism. It clearly attracted many non-believers who found in its ideals and rituals a substitute for religion. Yet clerics also joined the lodges (despite the pope's condemnation in 1738), for there was nothing explicitly antireligious in its creed. On the contrary, it pledged submission to both monarchy and church. At the least, Freemasonry satisfied the need to socialize with like-minded people, while expressing the eighteenth century's infatuation with high-toned ideals.

Law and Medicine

The training, recruitment, and organization of the legal and medical professions are instructive because these occupations too reflected prevailing social and cultural conditions. Neither law nor medicine were the relatively homogeneous vocations that they are today. Rather, they were divided into what might be called upper and lower branches. In law, barristers constituted the upper level and attorneys the lower; in medicine, physicians sat atop the hierarchy while surgeons and apothecaries filled the ranks. Barristers and physicians exemplified the relationship of learned culture to social status. While both had specific professional training, the real basis of their position was the "liberal" (i.e., classical) education they had received, a prerequisite for entry into the upper branch of either profession. Gentlemen first and professionals second, they had to be men of some means to begin with. For their education was prolonged and costly, requiring a substantial investment of capital and a long deferral of earnings. Subsequently, they clustered in the cities and fraternized with other gentlemen, with the relatively well-heeled clients who could afford their fees. Gentility was insured by shrouding the amounts of these fees in the mystique of professionalism. Finally, both physicians and barristers were organized into quasi corporate groups that were officially recognized by the state, and hence part of the "Establishment." In contrast, members of the lower branches were far more numerous, of lower social origins, distributed geographically all over the country, and likely to deal with the common people in their daily routines.

England's legal system was vital to a nation that believed it lived under the rule of laws rather than of men. Englishmen were proud of their common-law tradition—a system based on previous court decisions, or precedents, rather than statutes alone—and of trial by jury. This high regard for the law was bolstered by Sir William Blackstone (1723–1780). Appointed to the first professorship of common-law studies at Oxford, Blackstone took his work seriously (unlike most fellow professors) and developed a lively course of lectures which he subsequently published in four volumes. Blackstone's *Commentaries on the Laws of England* (1765–1769) became the basic textbook—one might say the bible—of the legal profession. Systematizing the subject in scholarly but elegant fashion, with a particular emphasis on land and property law and constitutional law, Blackstone's work was widely read by laymen as well, thereby spreading his conviction that English law was virtually perfect.

The guardians and expounders of this law were the 350 barristers. Most lived and worked at the Inns of Court in London, which was also where new barristers were trained and certified by their peers. Barristers had the exclusive right to appear in court and plead for their clients. This was the prestigious, learned, and eloquent side of the profession. The barristers governed themselves as a co-optive oligarchy of professionals. Disdaining the routine transactions and paperwork of the legal profession, they lived as scholars and gentlemen.

Not so their lesser colleagues, the attorneys. An attorney did not have a university education, nor did he study law at the Inns of Court. Instead he served a five-year apprenticeship as a clerk to an established attorney, much like the vocational training of a carpenter or printer. Then, to be admitted to practice, he had only to pass a perfunctory oral examination by a judge, who certified his fitness to serve. Attorneys obviously came from humbler social backgrounds than barristers, but a legal clerkship was usually a step up for most future attorneys, and in itself required an apprenticeship fee that averaged between £100 and £200—meaning that the laboring classes were not beating down the profession's doors even in its lower branch. As the century wore on, attorneys strove to raise their status. In 1739 a group of London attorneys founded the Society of Gentleman Practicers in the Courts of Law and Equity—a voluntary organization that sought to upgrade ethical and vocational standards. Putting the word "gentleman" in the organization's title was perhaps putting the cart before the horse, but self-regulation was a crucial first step if this lower branch was to eliminate the unqualified and unscrupulous practitioners who gave the entire group a bad reputation. Respectability was their objective: to be distinguished from those they thought beneath them, and to win recognition from those who undeniably stood above them. By the end of the century, English attorneys were beginning to gain this respectability, for their standards were rising. The regulation of apprenticeship was becoming more stringent; the voluntary associations were projecting an image of rectitude and professionalism; and attorneys were proving most useful and necessary in the complex property and financial transactions of a dynamic society.[14]

In France the structure of the legal profession was somewhat different, but barristers there held a similarly distinctive status, and for the same kinds of reasons. Unlike English attorneys, all French lawyers attended university. Students were obliged to matriculate for two years to take a law degree, and one further year of inscription was required for the *licence*, which entitled a man to qualify as a barrister (*avocat*). Legal education, incidentally, was of a piece with university education in general—Latin-based, hidebound, and perfunctory. Attendance was largely pro forma once the student registered: he had no need to attend lectures, but could simply cram for the obligatory examination at the end of his second year. Since the professors collected their fees upon passage of this examination, there was every incentive for them to make the examinations as routine and undemanding as possible.

The question remains, why would anyone spend an additional year to qualify as a barrister instead of simply becoming an attorney? The answer, of course, is that the two titles differed both in function and status. As in England, barristers enjoyed a monopoly on the right to plead in court, while attorneys handled their clients' transactions outside the courtroom. Leading avocats were known for their eloquence—one potential benefit of a classical education; a few built lucrative practices as well as scholarly reputations. Most did neither. Indeed, at the bar of Toulouse—a leading judicial city in southern France—only about 10 percent of the graduating *avocats* from the local university served the two-year internship required for formal admission to the bar. Moreover, of 215 barristers inscribed at the city's bar in 1788, only 42 (less than one-quarter) actually pled a case. In other words, far more barristers graduated than could make a living from the profession. Most had independent incomes from land and annuities which, while not great, were comfortable. In addition they were able to marry well and command handsome dowries from their brides.[15] The evidence thus converges around the surprising conclusion that to be a French barrister "was as much a social status as a career, a way of life more than a function." It was in essence the life of a leisured gentleman, enhanced by the prestige of belonging to a learned profession, even if one did not actually practice it. In England, where there were far fewer barristers and most did practice, their highly specialized, learned work lent itself to a similar life style. In sum, while most attorneys scrambled for a living, barristers and *avocats* lived as gentlemen and were so regarded.

[14] Robert Robson, *The Attorney in Eighteenth-Century England* (Cambridge, 1959).
[15] Lenard Berlanstein, *The Barristers of Toulouse in the Eighteenth Century* (Baltimore, 1975).

Medicine was the profession whose organization and methods were most remote from today's. Unlike the army, the church, or the law, eighteenth-century medicine would be virtually unrecognizable. The medical world comprised three distinct types of practitioners. At the summit stood the physicians, who had the exclusive right to regular medical consultations with patients and to substantial fees in payment thereof. Physicians were certified and their corporate privileges defended by the Royal College of Physicians in England and similar bodies in other countries. In England there were scarcely a hundred practicing physicians in the early eighteenth century as a result of this exclusive licensing practice. Only university graduates could become physicians. Their education, conducted in Latin, was entirely theoretical and depended mainly on ancient authors such as Galen. Testing was in the usual rote manner, while practical or clinical experience was absent from the curriculum of English and French universities. Medical education was somewhat more advanced at a few universities mentioned earlier, but one could arrange to purchase a medical degree at some of those institutions without pursuing the course of study. All in all the competence of most physicians was perhaps inversely proportional to their privileged position.

The backgrounds and status of surgeons were distinct from and generally inferior to those of physicians. Surgeons were originally barbers by trade and were known in England as barber-surgeons until mid-century. Their main activities were bleeding patients with leeches and performing crude kinds of surgery. Like English attorneys, surgeons were trained by apprenticeship and did not have a gentleman's classical education. Like attorneys too, their status improved as they became more competent, as well as more effectively organized in promoting their interests. A new surgeon's guild was formed in 1745, completely divorced from the barbers. Under its auspices surgery was transformed from a trade similar to butchering into a near science, as surgeons began a systematic study of anatomy through the dissection of corpses. The same sort of evolution was occurring in France, where the leading edge of change came by way of the military surgeons. With royal backing, they established a network of clinical teaching hospitals which combined on-the-job training with anatomical studies. Eventually the treatment of battle casualties was improved by the skillful amputation of limbs, which saved many wounded soldiers from lethal infections or gangrene. So effective were these surgeons that the distinction between physician and surgeon was all but eliminated during the French Revolution. The medical profession was then free to reorganize itself and create the kinds of general practitioners that were so desperately needed.

Physicians in England clung to their exclusive corporate identity longer, despite the rapid climb of surgeons toward general practice. By 1800 sur-

The medical profession. *This engraving by one of the century's greatest caricaturists, Thomas Rowlandson, depicts the crude techniques of the surgeon.*

geons had won recognition for a certifying body known as the Royal College of Surgeons, which could set licensing standards that required clinical experience in a hospital. Though physicians continued to enjoy a legal monopoly on medical consultations, most surgeons now practiced all forms of medicine because there were simply not enough physicians available to serve the population, particularly in the countryside. English physicians were almost exclusively London-based, while surgeons resided in both cities and villages.

Actually, most of the common people turned not to surgeons for routine medical assistance, but to the third type of medical practitioner, the apothecary or pharmacist. These shopkeepers dispensed the herbs and medicaments that people sought for the relief of pain and illness. Ostensibly they were "the physician's cooks," carrying out the latter's prescriptions and supplying the patient with potions and compounds. In fact, people turned directly to apothecaries for diagnoses and prescriptions as well as the actual provision of remedies. If the symptoms were unusually complicated, the apothecary might consult a physician (assuming one were available) and for a fee get his prescription, even without the physician having seen the patient. He would then sell the patient the appropriate nostrums. Yet even the licensed apothecaries could not satisfy the public's demand for miraculous potions—besides which their prices were often higher than people cared to pay. Accordingly, a large number of unlicensed practitioners flourished in this premodern era of medicine. "Empirics" who believed that they had figured out simple remedies for illness by trial and error—without training or theoretical knowledge—publicized their formulas in widely selling books, while quacks peddled patent medicines, touting their miraculous powers at fairs and street corners and advertising them in newspapers.[16]

To recapitulate this brief survey of eighteenth-century medical practitioners, we find three types: (1) the handful of university graduates and gentlemen who monopolized the title and prerogatives of the physician; (2) the surgeons whose image was just beginning to shift from that of mere tradesman to clinically-trained medical doctor; and (3) the apothecaries who—along with their rivals, the unlicensed and the quacks—constituted the most widely consulted practitioners, and met the public's crying need for medical assistance, while indulging its faith in nostrums. In taking this tour we have in fact moved through three sociocultural milieus: the learned culture and high status of the physician; the middling, incipient respectability of the surgeon; and the world of apothecaries and unlicensed practitioners, which was in the main the world of popular culture.

POPULAR CULTURE

For the great majority of Europe's people, popular culture was their only culture. Barred by their lack of education and wealth from access to the heritage of Western learning and arts, the popular classes nonetheless had ample sources of diversion and stimulation. They mounted festivals, passed on oral tales and performances from one generation to the next, sang ballads, bought and read aloud various types of brochures and almanacs, socialized in taverns, and patronized a variety of fairs and sporting events. There was a time when this "folk culture" was shared by the elites as well, who moved easily from the village festival to the more refined pursuits of high culture. By the eighteenth century, however, that bivalence was diminishing. Popular culture was attacked as retrograde and vulgar by a mounting array of elite critics. The clergy, secular moralists, and public officials alike found reasons to condemn many of its timeworn aspects.

[16] Lester King, *The Medical World of the Eighteenth Century* (Chicago, 1958), chaps. 1–2.

Festivals and Recreation

Popular culture was essentially public and collective. Group recreation and socializing were its principal attributes and the public festival was its characteristic form, both in town and country. In Catholic Europe most villages and towns had their own patron saints, who served as a focal point for local festivities. These celebrations usually combined religious elements with secular or "profane" amusements. In a pilgrimage, for example, the entire population of a village might set out for a local shrine, accompanied by its livestock, in a motley but gay procession led by an image of its patron saint or, better yet, a supposed relic of the saint. While it was an act of religious homage—perhaps, too, an attempt to enlist the saint's intervention for good weather—the pilgrimage at some point might give way to drinking, dancing, games, and who knows what else.

Carnival was the most spectacular form of festival in Mediterranean Europe (Spain, Italy, and France) as well as in Germany and Austria. In January or February prior to the start of the Lenten season, Carnival was a calculated antithesis to the austerity and self-denial of Lent. More than that, it provided a stark contrast to the greyness and deprivation of everyday life in general. For Carnival was a great binge, a massive indulgence of eating, drinking, dressing up, masquerading, and ritualistic behavior in which the taboos and restraints of daily life were lifted. At least symbolically, as a contemporary dictum stated, "everything is permitted in Carnival." [17] The central events at Carnival were performances of various kinds—plays, farces, mock presentations—in which the everyday world was turned upside down, where peasants were kings, nobles were humbled, and fools became philosophers. At this one time of year people were free to express sexual or violent drives in rituals of verbal aggression. Thus Carnival functioned as a safety valve for the resentments and pent-up feelings that people carried around. It was an occasion for "rites of reversal," a time for sassy behavior and for mocking the normal order of things. When it was over the world returned to its regular patterns, and indeed, with the arrival of Lent, life became even more austere than usual.

Other festivals were not as elaborate or as ritualized as Carnival, but they shared the same element of self-indulgence, the same brief compensation for the daily grind of labor and poverty. After spring sowing was completed, or in early autumn when the summer crops were harvested, villages often held annual festivals. The public feasts could last several days and were given over to eating, drinking, dancing, contests and games and especially to merrymaking among young men and women. Youth was

---

[17] Peter Burke, *Popular Culture in Early Modern Europe* (New York, 1978), chap. 7.

especially active in the festivals of early modern Europe. In some of the larger villages and towns young men were organized into loose associations whose leaders played an active role in Carnival and other festivals. Sometimes they armed themselves and eagerly sought a trial of strength with their counterparts from a neighboring community. Brawling was in fact the frequent and predictable climax of the high spirits that were set loose in festivals. The associations of young men simultaneously threatened community peace and channeled youthful energies into relatively harmless outlets.

While religious and secular festivals were the high points of each calendar year, recreation of other sorts was built into the fabric of daily life. Spring and summer may have brought long hours of daylight and a surfeit of hard work in the fields, but the coming of winter meant an easing of work loads if for no other reason than because the long nights made work outdoors impossible between 5:00 P.M. and 6:00 A.M. Cold, boredom, and claustrophobia could well have filled the gap, as they seem to have done in Puritan New England or on the sparsely settled frontier of western America. But in certain parts of Europe, such as the well-documented case of southern France, the long nights brought people together. At the *veillée*—a gathering around the fireplace in someone's cottage—women gossiped, sewed, and perhaps spun yarn in groups. Meanwhile the men went off to the tavern, as central a fixture in Europe's cultural landscape as the coffeehouses or reading clubs of the middle classes.

In the case of southern France (an area known for its unusual sociability), there was a remarkable number of cabarets, or taverns, some full-time places of business, others part-time enterprises. Taverns were ostensibly places where travelers could pause to refresh themselves with food and drink, but most catered to the neighborhood men who used the tavern as their gathering place. The regulars came to drink, gossip, play games of skill or chance, and settle minor business matters. The favored drinking place of town dwellers was usually located outside the city walls, where consumers did not have to pay excise taxes on alcoholic beverages. In England, incidentally, the poor person's drink was gin—a cheap and plentiful by-product of grain production. In fact, it seemed to run like water, to the extent that poor people were drinking themselves into stupors, debility, and even death. Eventually Parliament acted to stop this excess by levying a hefty excise tax on gin, even though this cut into the economic interests of the great landowners. In Russia, vodka played a similar role in the lives of the common people. There the state held a monopoly on the distilling of vodka and shared in the proceeds of its distribution in inns and taverns. Thus, though Russian peasants drank the cheap vodka to excess much the way the English poor had long consumed gin, the government did not undertake to cut off the flow.

Urban and Rural Sociability. *In the towns, workers came together in taverns or cabarets (called* guinguettes *in France), which were often located outside the city limits in order to avoid the excise taxes on wine and spirits. During long winter nights in the countryside, peasant families sometimes pooled their resources—fuel, gossip, and stories—and huddled around a single fireplace for the* veillée *between the evening meal and bedtime.*

In France taverns aroused the moralists and officials, who were ever alert to denounce popular dissipation. A police ordinance for the city of Aix-en-Provence in 1764 complained that "Disorder has reached the point where the bulk of the workers abandon their tasks, peasants leave their field work, and domestic servants neglect their duty toward their masters, in order to spend part of the day in those perpetual drinking places and taverns. . . ."[18] Apart from the time wasting, drunkenness, and disorderly behavior that this habit was alleged to promote, it was also claimed that cabarets bred gambling on their premises, and that by staying open illegally on Sunday, they induced people to absent themselves from church. Even if taverns were not yet the symbols of irreligion that they would become in the nineteenth century, they did offer an alternative to the church for sociability. Indeed, toward the end of the old regime there are signs that the regulars in some taverns were formalizing this conviviality by arranging to take over the backroom in which they could forgather with their selected companions. From such beginnings the nineteenth century would see the growth of certain working-class associations, though for the moment, there was no political dimension in this custom.

Though masses and elites generally went their own ways in recreational activities, there were forms of amusement that brought them together. At street fairs and at spectator sports one might find fashionable society rubbing shoulders with artisans, laborers, scrubwomen, and pickpockets. A trend which historians have called "the commercialization of leisure" was nourished by elements from several social classes. The urban fairs that developed in the eighteenth century combined the features of today's amusement parks and shopping malls. Three popular and quasipermanent fairs in Paris, for example, produced a lively atmosphere that attracted a wide spectrum of society to sample their food, wares, and entertainments. The fairs featured a kind of theater similar to the farces put on during Carnival, except that it was more professional. Featuring insults to social conventions, and a grotesque, often scatalogical humor (as in *Le Marchand de merde*), these spectacles appealed to "people of all kinds." Moving on from these performances, one could find an array of daring, exotic, or magical entertainments. There were acrobats, stunt performers, and tightrope walkers; exotic animals and freak shows; and *cabinets de physique*, featuring mechanical and optical devices to amaze or fool the audience with magic lanterns and other illusions. The people who flocked to these generally inexpensive diversions wished to be awed by the incredible and fantastic—a feeling that one can as easily impute to a duchess as a laborer.

In the realm of sport, the eighteenth century was notable less for de-

---

[18] Quoted in Maurice Agulhon's seminal *Pénitents et Francs-Maçons de l'ancienne Provence: essai sur la sociabilité méridionale* (Paris, 1968), p. 240.

Popular entertainment. *A travelling puppet show at a fair. Engraving by Franz Anton Maulbertsch.*

velopments in participant sports, such as lawn bowling or football, than for the rise of spectator sports. The commercialization of leisure brought a proliferation of traveling circuses, boxing matches, horse races, and bull fights, entertainments for profit which attracted both the elites and the popular classes. Part cause, part result of this trend, Europe acclaimed a new breed of sports heroes, such as favored matadors or boxers. Another feature of eighteenth-century sporting life was the growing popularity of "blood sports." In bullbaiting or bearbaiting, an innkeeper and a butcher usually collaborated, the latter providing the animal which would subsequently be slaughtered and dispensed as meat, while the former made available the yard of his inn and sold refreshments to the spectators. The "sport" involved setting loose a pack of dogs on the tethered and helpless beast. Cockfighting was similar in its gory results, and was especially popular because the spectators could wager on the outcome.[19]

[19] See Robert Isherwood's fascinating paper, "Entertainment in the Parisian Fairs in the Eighteenth Century," (to be published in the *Journal of Modern History*, 1981), and Robert Malcolmson, *Popular Recreation in English Society, 1700–1850* (Cambridge, 1973).

Cockfight. *Engraving by William Hogarth.*

Like Carnival, saints' days, drinking in taverns, or gambling, blood sports were denounced by moralists and public officials for promoting bad habits and disorder among the popular classes—though few denounced the comparable barbarity of the gentry's fox or rabbit hunting. Indeed, scarcely any form of popular recreation and pleasure escaped the censorious criticisms of the high-minded among the elites. To begin with, in the sixteenth century the clergy of the Protestant Reformation had attacked the ribaldry of popular festivals as unchristian and sinful. Seeking to separate the sacred from the profane, they hoped to end this popular mixture of religiosity and recreation, much as they sought to eliminate the grossly superstitious elements of popular religious behavior such as excessive devotion to saints, or obsession with witches and devils. Soon the spearheads of the Catholic Reformation took the same tack, and everywhere in Europe the clergy became outspoken critics of popular culture.

Meanwhile, there had long been underway a movement among the nobility to adopt more polished manners. This trend originated in the patrician circles of Renaissance Italy, peaked at Louis XIV's Versailles, and spread from there across Europe. As a result, important segments of the nobility no longer associated themselves with festivals and other types of popular recreation. Popular songs and ballads, fairs and festivals, rustic dances and games were now considered vulgar. Middle-class moralists followed suit and began to denounce the dissipation allegedly bred by taverns, the excesses of Carnival, the riotous behavior at some football matches, and the barbarity of blood sports. All in all, the recreational side of popular culture was stigmatized as sinful, vulgar, and disorderly. Such criticism was an important element in the emergence of class consciousness at the end of the century, and in the growing estrangement of classes.

Oral Tradition and Popular Literature

Without the need for literacy or print media, traditional songs and stories could be enjoyed from one generation to the next, as they were passed along by local people or wandering entertainers. It is generally impossible to trace the forms and motifs of this material back to their origins; on the contrary, such classic folktales as "Cinderella" have appeared in many different countries as seemingly authentic native tales. It is also difficult to recapture the extent to which this "oral tradition" pervaded the lives of the common people. Indeed, it is possible that it might have gradually disappeared altogether with the modernization of society in the nineteenth and twentieth centuries. Just when that process was beginning, however, individuals such as Johann Gottfried von Herder and the Grimm brothers became interested in this cultural heritage and began to collect, transcribe, and classify its sources, thus creating the new discipline of "folklore." Because of their efforts, at least certain aspects of this unwritten culture have been preserved.

Though its forms were many, we can, following Peter Burke's pioneering synthesis on early modern popular culture, point to three basic genres. First, there was the narrative song: the short ballad, or the longer epic. Then there was the comic form of popular entertainment: partly ritualized, partly improvised satires using stock characters familiar to everyone (the so-called *commedia dell'arte*), and parodies of familiar, serious occasions such as mock sermons, trials, or funerals. Finally, there were improvised forms of drama such as the mystery play, which adapted its subjects from the Bible, or the miracle play, based on saints' lives.

Certain types of figures kept turning up in oral tradition (as well as in the literature to be discussed next), the heroes, villains, and fools of popular myth. Heroes included saints or, in Protestant cultures which did not recognize canonization, religious martyrs. Also popular were heroic rulers, either military conquerors or Solomon-like figures revered for their wisdom or generosity, such as Saint Louis of France, "Good King Wenceslaus" of Bohemia, or King Olav of once-independent Norway. Warriors were often the heroes in popular tales or songs, for the romance of chivalry, with its emphasis on brave deeds—originally an upper-class cultural form—had long since passed into the popular tradition. The genres of oral as well as printed popular culture were teeming with standardized villains as well. Tyrants included biblical personages, such as Herod, and secular figures, such as the Sheriff of Nottingham (Robin Hood's nemesis), who was typical of the evil servitors who misled their kings. The middle classes too provided villains: rapacious lawyers, royal officials, and tax collectors, the "bloodsuckers" of the people. Also among the villains who populated ballads, stories, and mock performances were malevolent cultural outsiders: Turks, Jews, and witches. While the preoccupation with witches was beginning to recede by the eighteenth century, Jews were still portrayed as Christ's killers who continued their bloody ways by murdering children in the Passover ritual. Like Judas, they were also depicted as despicable usurers. The classic popular image was the "wandering Jew," condemned to that remorseless fate as the murderer of Christ.

If we ask how ordinary people saw themselves in their songs and stories, the answer is elusive. One of the most typical popular tales, found in both oral and written versions, was the story of *Bonhomme Misère*, the average fellow. This poor but kindly peasant was more or less content with his lowly lot, and despite the misfortunes that beset him, he proves to be indestructible. What seems most striking is how little he asks for. Specifically, when he is offered any wish he cares to make by a magically endowed traveler to whom he has been hospitable, *Bonhomme* simply asks that his one valued possession—a single pear tree—be made secure from theft or damage. In the same spirit was a Russian proverb cited by Peter Burke: "too much luck is dangerous." People feared not only misfortune, but also the envy of others, the evil eye that was such a pervasive image in popular superstition. Their lives were so difficult that too much good fortune might appear as a dangerous tempting of fate.[20]

A major artifact of popular culture was the chapbook, which sometimes transcribed traditional songs and stories into print. In France historians refer to chapbooks as the *bibliothèque bleue* or the blue library, since many of these short, inexpensive brochures were printed on the cheapest kind of paper that had a bluish tint. Usually twenty-four pages long, these brochures were circulating already in the seventeenth century and continued to appear in similar form well into the nineteenth century. Their interpretation poses some difficult problems. Were they authentic representations of popular culture, or were they more indicative of the notions of popular taste held by the middle-class writers and publishers who actually produced them? And how widely were the chapbooks distributed? That we cannot know. But examples of the *bibliothèque bleue*, of British and of German chapbooks (*Flugschriften*), do exist, and provide

[20] Burke, *Popular Culture*, chaps. 4–6.

a basis for inferences about the tastes and attitudes of the peasants and artisans who purchased them from traveling peddlers. Some of this popular literature merely echoed the oral tradition, while other genres such as almanacs were unique to the printed medium.

One kind of popular literature was intended strictly for entertainment, and its distinguishing feature was a mixture of the mundane and the miraculous. There was a good deal of what passes for history in this material, but it was history transformed and fictionalized. Heroes and villains alike were usually endowed with superhuman qualities. History often became fable, with a moralistic lesson in the outcome of the tale. Other brochures sought to amuse through crude satires and burlesques, written equivalents of the mock sermons or mock trials staged by street entertainers.

A second variant in the *bibliothèque bleue* was material on religious themes: popular versions of religious stories; catechisms; manuals of penitence; saints' lives. These chapbooks were not always pious, but could be broadly humorous, as when the dialogue of confessor and penitent was parodied. Their intention, however, was usually serious and in its own way reverent, even when a biblical story came out sounding like a fabulous adventure tale. Underlying the appeal of this religious material was the dread of death. As if the burdens of poverty in this world were not enough, peasants and workers had to bear the enormous uncertainty of their fate in the next. Hence this literature sought to provide solace by implying that a virtuous life would bring recompense in the hereafter and spare the reader from the torments of purgatory or hell.[21]

Consumers of popular literature were not exclusively preoccupied with the hereafter, nor in simply amusing themselves with adventure stories or satires. A third type of popular literature, the almanac, offered readers advice on how they could help themselves. It was in these volumes that the printed word took on an importance apart from the oral tradition which the other types of chapbooks reflected. In one respect popular almanacs were similar to the religious brochures and entertainments, in that they too reflected the great superstition of the popular masses. It was precisely this characteristic that set apart popular culture from the increasingly rationalized values of the elites. Yet while playing on and encouraging superstition, almanacs provided the lore that was supposed to help their readers cope with the capricious forces of nature. Originating as manuals in astrology—indeed, the symbols they used made it possible even for illiterate folk to understand their contents—almanacs taught the art of divining portents of evil or good in various natural signs such as the stars, the behavior of animals, plants, the weather, and dreams. To

[21] Geneviève Bollême, *La Bibliothèque bleue* (Paris, 1971).

be forearmed with these signs promised the chance of avoiding the menaces that hovered over everyday life. It was a frightening outlook, yet was also reassuring in its way.

Almanacs and other pamphlets offered additional kinds of advice for successful living: on medication, for example, which was the art of gathering, blending, and cooking the right herbs and nostrums; or on the rules of civilized social behavior, which extended even to describing the proper form to be used in writing certain kinds of letters. Though almanacs were largely repetitive and unchanging over the decades, there is some evidence of a slight evolution in their emphases, namely a diminution in the weight of supernaturalism, and an increase in the amount of useful information. By the end of the eighteenth century almanacs still featured elaborate astrological charts, but also real calendars and real historical accounts of the previous year's notable events. There might have been some trickle down of useful information in these almanacs, and even a slight change in the frame of reference offered for arranging one's life. Yet it remains difficult to say just how much this evolution counted against the traditional material that continued to fill them.[22]

On the whole, then, chapbooks echoed the motifs and genres of oral tradition, serving either to entertain or to cater to the superstitious religiosity of the popular masses. In this sense it was an escapist literature, which reinforced a fatalistic acceptance of the status quo. On the other hand, though almanacs and self-help brochures were still permeated by a supernatural outlook, their (arguably) slow evolution did provide practical advice on coping with everyday problems, and thus helped make the printed, secular word of some relevance to the popular masses.

Another point about the chapbooks was that most were probably written in the national languages rather than the local dialects that still prevailed in many parts of Europe. We do not know enough about their circulation to affirm how commonly they were bought or read in, say, the parts of southern France where the Occitanian dialect (the langue d'oc) was the language of the common people, and where songs and stories transmitted orally were doubtless in that dialect. If the brochures did circulate in such places, then they introduced an element of standardized French, German, or Italian into the cultural horizons of those who bought them or heard them read aloud. Perhaps the chapbooks, rather than being simple emanations of popular culture, were more like a bridge between the dialects and folk cultures of the oral tradition, and the languages and values of the national elites. Of course, more fundamental still to the process of cultural accommodation was the development of

---

[22] Bollême, Les Almanachs populaires aux XVIIe et XVIIIe siècles (Paris, 1969); and Bernard Capp, English Almanacs 1500–1800: Astrology and the Popular Press (Ithaca, N.Y., 1979).

general literacy, whose prerequisite was primary education. Chapbooks were certainly accessible to illiterate people when read aloud to them by those who could read. For the printed word to enter the mainstream of popular life, however, literacy was obviously essential.

Literacy and Primary Education

The only way of measuring literacy in the eighteenth century thus far contrived is to count the proportion of people who could sign their names on public documents, such as marriage contracts, instead of merely placing an "X". There is some disagreement over exactly what the ability to sign actually signified. It has long been assumed that signing reflected an ability to read, but not necessarily the ability to write, apart from one's own name. (Five-year-olds, in the same way, can often write their names without knowing how to write other words.) Children who received any schooling at all learned to read first. Writing was taught later, and many did not stay long enough to learn it, especially girls. On the other hand, according to recent research on the better-documented nineteenth century, the capacity of adults to sign their names usually did reflect a knowledge of both reading and writing. At the very least, then, signing one's name indicated an ability to read, which can be taken as a mark of literacy in the old regime.

For Catholic Europe, comprehensive national research on changes in literacy over time exists only in the case of France. The Maggiolo study (named after the educator who organized it in the 1870's), though containing a possible error factor of 5 to 10 percent, provides solid data. Based on the proportion of signatures versus X's on marriage contracts for the years 1686 and 1786, and the 1870's, its conclusions are striking. First, the national average reveals a dismayingly low level of literacy in the old regime, especially among women:

Estimated Literacy Rates in France

	1686	1786
Men	29%	47%
Women	14%	27%
Total	21%	37%

Second, the study shows that literacy was fairly widespread in northeastern France but less common in the south—an area also considered relatively "backward" economically. It is true that there was an acceleration of literacy in the last quarter of the eighteenth century in which the south began catching up, and in which women began their slow progress in closing the gap with men. On the whole, however, the French masses did not enjoy an impressive level of literacy.[23]

The Maggiolo figures leave important questions unanswered. What were the social and economic determinants of literacy? Who was most likely to be illiterate? Thanks to recent research, a correlation seems to have been established between one's position in the social structure and literacy, and also between the development of a market economy and literacy. Predictably, the upper-class elites were almost always literate, including nobles, who in centuries past did not always include reading and writing among their skills. Literacy was higher in the cities, which under closer examination points to the heavy concentration of artisans in urban society. Artisans seem to have been the most mobile groups economically and geographically, and literacy was evidently a crucial qualification in their search for better opportunity. In Marseilles, for example, literacy among male artisans and workers rose from an estimated 28 percent in 1710 to 85 percent in 1789, though the rate for women scarcely moved from its low level of about 15 percent. Peasants, however, constituted over 75 percent of France's population and their sector presents a depressing spectacle of illiteracy. Agricultural laborers almost always signed their documents with X's, but even among peasant proprietors, over two-thirds were probably illiterate, while female illiteracy was almost total in the peasant community.[24]

There was no absolute correlation between the size of communities, the availability of primary schools, and literacy, but there was surely some relationship among the three. In Catholic Europe in the early eighteenth century, neither the church nor the state took responsibility nationally for primary education, which remained a local matter. Few communities of under a thousand inhabitants could maintain a school on a permanent basis, and the presence of primary schools was therefore haphazard. Primary schools were sometimes run by the parish, the teachers being paid in certain cases out of small parish endowments. More commonly, either the pupils' parents payed the schoolmaster directly (with provision sometimes made for the very poor to go free of charge), or the community itself paid all or part of the teacher's salary. But when municipal finances were hard pressed, expenses for schools might be among the first to be cut. It should go without saying, incidentally, that the wealthy

---

[23] Pierre Goubert, The Ancien Régime (New York, 1973), chap. XI, and F. Furet and W. Sachs, "La Croissance de l'alphabetisation en France, XVIIIe–XIXe siècles," Annales, Vol. XXIX (1974), pp. 714–37.

[24] Michel Vovelle, "Y-a-t-il eu une révolution culturelle au XVIIIe siècle? A propos de l'éducation populaire en Provence," Revue d'histoire moderne et contemporaine, Vol. XXII (1975), pp. 89–141.

elites did not use such primary schools, but hired tutors for their young children or, in the case of daughters, sent them to exclusive convent schools. Primary teaching had not yet become a career and there was no special training or system of certification for the vast majority of schoolteachers. Since there was no national responsibility for or supervision of primary education, facilities were makeshift, financing erratic and inadequate, and attendance sporadic.

The Habsburg Monarchy was the only Catholic realm that seriously promoted primary education. Both Maria Theresa and Joseph II believed that education would not only inculcate morality and religion but would, like agrarian reform, help to make their subjects more productive. When the Pope dissolved the Jesuit order in 1773 (Chapter 8), Maria Theresa decided to use the Jesuits' resources for a national system of primary education. The General School Ordinance of 1774 was a landmark act. Going beyond mere wishful thinking, it authorized state subsidies, in combination with local funds, for the support of a school in every community. Not only was attendance supposed to be compulsory, but the state would actively supervise these local institutions. What is more, the founding of a normal school several years earlier was designed to produce at least some trained teachers. A census of school-age children in the Austrian and Bohemian provinces in 1781 indicates that out of 776,000 school-age children, 208,000 were attending the monarchy's *Volkschulen*, where, incidentally, the Czech population of Bohemia and Moravia was obliged to use German.[25] In France, by contrast, primary education was left entirely to local initiatives. While the Jacobin constitution of 1793 would declare that universal and free public education was one of the rights of man, the Jacobins fell from power before they were able to implement this principle, and subsequent regimes did not honor it.

Protestant Europe seems on the whole to have been quicker and more effective in promoting literacy and primary education. The Reformation had spurred literacy directly, since Protestant denominations had generally insisted that personal knowledge of the Bible was a requisite for salvation. In the ensuing rivalry between Catholics and Protestants, both sides sought to win converts or maintain their faithful by means of propaganda and indoctrination as well as repression, and these methods were more effective if the population could read. In any case, the first areas to experience widespread popular literacy were two of Protestantism's original strongholds: the Swiss cantons (one of the first to make primary education compulsory), and Presbyterian Scotland. Long before any other country approached such a system, Scotland had developed a linkage

---

[25] Kerner, *Bohemia in the Eighteenth Century*, p. 348.

between a higher education that produced teachers, and a system of primary schools that employed them.[26]

Scandinavia, especially Sweden, also had impressive literacy rates, but England's were less so. At the century's end, male literacy in England was probably no more than 60 percent, while the female rate was about 40 percent. Moreover, as in France, national estimates conceal wide disparities between relatively literate and illiterate regions. In Germany, a number of Protestant states such as Württemberg, Saxony, and Prussia encouraged primary education, and sought to make attendance compulsory, at least on paper. In Saxony after 1769, for example, children between the ages of five and fourteen were supposed to be in school, though whether or not this was so is another matter. Similarly, Prussia under the Sergeant King, Frederick William I, had considered primary education to be in the state's interest, and each parish was ordered to organize schools.

The English, however, rejected state control over education just as they resisted the building of a large standing army or royal bureaucracy. Sectarian religious rivalry in the seventeenth century made any centralized system of education that might enforce religious uniformity highly suspect. There were three types of primary schools in England: Church of England schools; charity schools and Sunday schools for the poor; and profit-making schools. The oldest and best were the endowed schools administered by certain parishes of the Church of England. They provided a substantial, free primary education, especially for the children of artisans. They were relatively few in number however, and could not make much of an impact on mass illiteracy. The free charity schools, financed by private contributions and usually run by laymen, were designed to produce pious, hardworking servants and laborers. Accordingly, their curriculum was extremely limited, emphasizing reading but often omitting writing and arithmetic. Reading was restricted to the Bible, the catechism, and parables of moral inspiration. Manual skills were also taught, such as sewing for girls being trained for domestic service. The free charity schools were usually mournful places, similar to the factories where some of their pupils would soon be working. Like the factory, they created an oppressively disciplined environment whose long hours, lack of playtime and tedious routines served to deaden the personality. Working-class families often avoided these schools, for although they were free, attendance entailed a loss of earnings by their children. To meet this objection, the sponsors also established Sunday schools, which the parents might more readily accept.

More numerous than these externally funded schools were the profit-

[26] Lawrence Stone, "Literacy and Education in England, 1640–1900," *Past and Present*, No. 42 (1969), pp. 69–139.

making schools. Artisans and workers who sought full-time education for their children favored these small private schools when they could afford them. Often run by a local woman who simply set herself up in business, they were the most direct and accessible form of mass education, even though fees were required and standards were erratic. A recent estimate suggests that at least two-thirds of the parents whose children attended some form of primary school in England chose to pay for this education in a kind of free marketplace, over which they therefore had an element of control. Thus the English working classes in the later eighteenth century relied less on church, state, or charity to promote their children's literacy, than on themselves.[27]

The deficiencies of primary education in most of Europe stemmed from many things, including the dearth of financial resources and trained teachers, as well as a lack of interest among the overburdened peasants. Beyond such practical matters, however, there was a fundamental ambivalence in the attitudes of the elites toward education for the masses. The best way to grasp the point is to consider the extreme case. In most slaveholding colonies, slaves were kept illiterate by law. Masters were prohibited from allowing their slaves to learn reading or writing, and slaves with such knowledge were punishable. Obviously this was done on the theory that illiterate slaves would be more docile when insulated from the attractions of the outside world, and the same attitude could easily be applied to serfs, or even to free labor. Education could be deemed inappropriate for the lower classes since it might disorient them. As Voltaire put it, "For those destined to drudgery . . . nothing but early habit can render it tolerable. Therefore to give the meanest of the people an education beyond that station which Providence has assigned them, is doing them a real injury." At the least, this kind of attitude made primary education a low priority. More important, it shaped the nature of the schooling offered to the common people, a carefully limited education designed to help them fill their fated position in the world. In Frederick the Great's view, "it is a good thing that the schoolmasters in the country teach youngsters religion and morals. . . . It is enough for the country people to learn only a little reading and writing. . . . Instruction must be planned so that they receive only that which is most essential for them but which is designed to keep them in the villages and not influence them to leave." In other words, education should be used to inculcate religion and morality, to propagate the virtues of hard work, sobriety, and deference toward one's superiors. It should help turn youngsters into good

[27] Thomas Laquer, "Working-Class Demand and the Growth of English Elementary Education, 1750–1850, in *Schooling and Society*, ed. by Lawrence Stone (Baltimore, 1976).

Christians and loyal workers or servants. Conservative evangelical Hannah More, who was active in the charity-school movement of the late eighteenth century, spoke for many when she declared: "My plan of instruction is extremely simple and limited. They learn on weekdays such coarse work as may fit them for servants. I allow of no writing for the poor. My object is to train up the lower classes in habits of industry and piety." In this spirit, clerics, government officials, and intellectuals could all support some form of education for the poor.

CHAPTER 7

An Age of Enlightenment

"WE ARE PROMOTING a revolution in men's minds to free them from prejudice," wrote Denis Diderot in 1762. Diderot spoke for the philosophes, a group of French intellectuals who stood at the center of a current in European thought known as the Enlightenment. These men and their ideas—the way they fashioned their lives and what they wrote in their books—produced a dramatic alteration in the values of many educated Europeans. Their bold and self-conscious break with deeply ingrained traditions of authority produced a new intellectual climate in which reason, experience, and utility were enthroned.

The principal figures of the Enlightenment were of varied nationalities, social origins, and talents. Their interests ranged from literature to mathematics, history to political theory, economics to formal philosophy. Many were French, but they had counterparts in Germany, Italy, Scotland, England, and even in Spain and the American colonies. Some were nobles, some of middle-class background, a few of lower-middle-class origin: the Baron de Montesquieu, for example, came from a distinguished family of noble judges, while Diderot was the son of a provincial knife-maker. These men came together into what has aptly been called a "family circle." They shared a commitment to intellectual freedom, and a belief that tradition, especially religious authority, was an obstacle to human fulfillment. It is impossible to reduce their concerns to a formula, but the German philosopher Immanuel Kant (1724–1804) came closest to doing this successfully. In an article entitled "What is Enlightenment?" he answered: "*Dare to know!* Have courage to make use of your own understanding." Man's perennial immaturity, Kant continued, had been caused by his "lack of resolution and courage to use his understanding without the guidance of someone else." To modern ears this exhortation to use reason to its full potential sounds self-evident. In its time it was a battle cry.

THE PHILOSOPHES

Reason and Religion

The philosophes owed a great deal to the achievements of Descartes, Newton, and Locke in the preceding century. Using the powers of reason, the data of observation, and the calculus (a mathematical system of his own invention), Newton had charted the basic laws governing motion both on earth and in space. His work set a new standard for what the human mind could achieve. Even for those who could not grasp its technicalities, Newton's physics created a sense of confidence about the potentialities of research and reason. This feeling was bolstered by the work of John Locke (1632–1704). Whereas Newton had looked outward toward the universe, Locke looked inward to that equally mysterious and complex subject, human nature, and seemed to demonstrate that its functioning too could be explained. While Newton's universe was unchangeable or at least stable, man's nature, according to Locke, was malleable. The essence of human understanding was its susceptibility to change, and therefore to improvement. The universe could not be improved, but human society could.

The writings of Descartes were in some respects too abstract and rationalistic to suit the philosophes. But his *Discourse on Method* (1637) inspired the Enlightenment by its insistence that ideas must be analyzed without preconceptions. The exercise of intellect must be completely free from dependence on or guidance from accepted authority, be it the Bible or the treatises of Aristotle. According to Descartes, nothing must be taken for granted or accepted on faith in science and mathematics. Everything must be rigorously demonstrated. In the philosophes' hands the legacy of seventeenth-century science and rationalistic philosophy was broadly applied in a manner that Descartes and Newton would have disapproved. Reason was given the task of shaping human values, as the critical method was extended from mathematics and science to a wide range of issues. Descartes had specifically argued that methodical doubt should not be applied to history or religion, since these domains were not susceptible of certainty, but others would not stop at such boundaries.

For his pioneering efforts in this respect the philosophes were much indebted to Pierre Bayle (1647–1706), a professor of philosophy at the University of Rotterdam whose French Huguenot family had suffered persecution under Louis XIV. Bayle insisted that nothing was too sacred to escape being examined critically. His widely read *Historical and Critical Dictionary* (1697) subjected a variety of religious claims and philosophical dogmas to a searching skeptical critique. In this light many traditional religious notions appeared to him to be myths intended to terrify infantile minds. Scripture was not reliable, according to Bayle, "if it clashes with the clear and definite conclusions of the natural understanding, especially in the domain of ethics." Bayle exposed the crimes and inhumanity of religious persecution; alleged miracles that did not square with natural laws; and certain episodes in the Bible, such as the story of King David, whose moral implications offended common sense. Yet Bayle stopped short of total skepticism. Philosophically, he seemed to imply that reason alone could not produce certain truth, and thus spoke as a "Christian skeptic," maintaining his faith in God.[1] In practical terms, Bayle's importance lay less in his elusive philosophical stance than in his uncompromising advocacy of complete religious toleration. In an almost unprecedented fashion, he espoused the individual's right to any religious belief or to none. Morality, in his view, did not depend on religion. A man's behavior rather than his creed was what counted, for even atheists could behave morally.

Owing a great deal to Bayle, the Enlightenment was a movement of intellectual liberation from the bonds of tradition. In the words of historian Ernst Cassirer, "the Enlightenment was beholden neither to a God beyond its comprehension, nor to existing arrangements which are not necessarily the best possible ones, and may even be the worst." Or, to return to Diderot's words, it promoted "a revolution in men's minds to free them from prejudice." In the eighteenth century, "prejudice" meant religion above all. The philosophes came to visualize their own position in relation to antiquity and to the medieval Christian era, finding a kinship with the first. For the philosophes, Christianity had been an historical disaster, destroying a tradition of civilization in Greece and Rome that had sought to live by reason. In their view the Middle Ages were truly "the Dark Ages." It seemed to them a time when religious myth was the chief source of authority. Medieval learning was dominated by the church and was designed to lead people toward God, while medieval science and historiography were devoted to discovering God's purpose and interventions in the universe. The philosophes felt that it was essential to revitalize these areas of learning, to extrude myth from Western thought and direct it back to reality. They sought to define the limits of knowledge and reason, and to stretch them as far as possible. To this challenge the philosophes came, in Peter Gay's words, with a modest confidence in themselves and their educated fellow men.[2]

Though the attack of reason on religion was the eighteenth century's greatest intellectual drama, it should be noted that religious authority was also loosening from within. In the seventeenth and eighteenth centuries a number of educated Christians sought to reconcile reason and religion,

[1] *Pierre Bayle: Historical and Critical Dictionary Selections*, ed. by Richard Popkin (Indianapolis, 1965), Introduction.
[2] For a comprehensive view of the philosophes see Peter Gay, *The Enlightenment: An Interpretation* (2 vols., New York, 1966–69).

to accommodate religion to the advances of science and philosophy. The superstitious beliefs and practices of their less-educated Christian brethren appalled them. Witchcraft trials, for example, with their accusations of pacts with the devil and grisly burnings at the stake, were an embarrassment to educated Christians. (The last such trial was held in England in 1710, and not much later than that in France, though they persisted in Spain and Poland.) Learned believers tried to make theology more "rational" by concentrating on God the creator, while God's subsequent interventions in an individual's life were deemphasized. They argued that nature was a form of revelation just as important as the Bible in revealing God's grandeur, and they stressed Christianity's moral code. This line of argument was encapsulated in the very title of Locke's pamphlet, *The Reasonableness of Christianity* (1695). It exemplified the notion that nature and reason could be relied on to lead to a consciousness of God. An approach stressing God the creator, nature as revelation, and the moral side of Christianity could easily shade into the essentially non-Christian spiritual attitude known as deism. Acknowledging the mystery of creation and attributing it to a supreme power, deism held that once created, the universe was endowed with its own immutable laws that were independent of the creating force. For most philosophes, deism became a convenient stopping place and refuge from Christianity. Others, however, were unwilling to accept even that minimal concession to God. For radical spirits such as Diderot and Baron d'Holbach, nothing less than atheism was philosophically acceptable.

In view of this complexity, it is important to establish the veritable dividing line between Christians and unbelievers, whether deists or atheists. Educated Christians, as indicated, could go a long way in accommodating science and scholarship. Some, for example, accepted the scientific view of the earth's development propagated by Georges Comte de Buffon (1707–1788). Buffon's *Natural History of the Earth*, a multivolume "best-seller" that appeared between 1749 and 1778, described the geological and zoological development of the planet in a manner that simply ignored the biblical account of creation. Concentrating on observable phenomena, such as the fossils that scholars had accumulated, Buffon argued for a kind of evolutionary relationship between "the most perfect creature and the most formless matter." His account depicted various stages in the earth's development which was measured not in seven days but in hundreds and thousands of centuries. Yet a leading Jesuit editor of the 1750's was able to review Buffon's work favorably, praising its empirical scientific demonstrations, and indicating that the "seven days" of creation need not be taken literally but could be regarded as seven periods.

Where good Christians drew the line was at their conviction that man required certainty on fundamental issues. On such matters as the explanation of creation, or the moral standards governing human behavior, only faith in the Bible provided that certainty. Furthermore, man "needs more lofty motives for loving his fellow men" than his own instincts can provide. Only submission to God's commandments could effectively restrain man's natural selfishness and irresponsibility. (In the Jesuits' view, atheists and deists wished to destroy the moral authority of Christianity in order to indulge their passions.) [3] Above all the Church was necessary to deal with sin. Christians, as opposed to deists, still believed in the soul and in the drama of salvation. The great obstacle to salvation was sin, and it was the Church's mission to help mortals deal with their sinful natures. In Catholicism especially, the Church claimed a direct role in absolving men and women from sin and assuring their salvation in the hereafter. In order to accomplish this, the Church was obligated to propound standards of behavior based on the Bible's moral precepts. And in order to enforce these standards for the good of the flock, the Church believed that it was necessary to suppress heretical ideas and influences. The philosophes vehemently opposed this attitude, arguing that religion should be a purely private affair. Each individual should have complete freedom to think or worship as he chose, and the only religious policy should be toleration. Here was the real battle line. No matter how "reasonable" Christianity might be in accommodating science, its mission was still to save souls, and the Church felt that it could not do this effectively if deprived of public influence. Until the eighteenth century this attitude prevailed in Europe. Now it was challenged by the philosophes, and especially by Voltaire.

Voltaire: The Eye of the Storm

Young Voltaire (the pen name of François Marie Arouet, 1694–1778) followed a classic writer's path to success. The son of a notary and recipient of an excellent secondary education at one of France's best *collèges,* Voltaire began his career by composing neoclassical poems and tragic dramas which, though scarcely remembered today, won him celebrity in his own time. His literary skill was further rewarded after he turned to writing histories, for he was granted the sinecure post of royal historiographer to Louis XV. Along the way Voltaire cultivated friends in high places and made a fortune for himself in financial speculation. He also had the humiliating experience of being beaten by the lackeys of a prominent aristocrat whom he had offended, and being thrown into the Bas-

[3]. John Pappas, Berthier's *"Journal de trévoux"* and the Philosophes, Studies on *Voltaire and the Eighteenth Century*, Vol. 3, (Geneva, 1957).

tille when he sought redress; he was finally ordered out of the country until the episode blew over. Here then was a writer who had made his way very nicely within the old regime's institutions, but who also nursed a certain resentment against privilege and injustice. If Voltaire's career had leveled off at this point, it would have been without much historical importance. But in addition to mastering the classic forms of literature, Voltaire went on to become a brilliant advocate of the Enlightenment, of its passion for reason and justice, and its conception of the intellectual-as-activist. As he withdrew from the world of Parisian high society, eventually settling on his estate at Ferney near the Swiss border, his writings became increasingly didactic and polemical—arguing for a cause, attacking some institution, or satirizing some absurdity in contemporary life. Though a number of his later books and pamphlets had to be published anonymously and were in any case banned and burned by the authorities, harassment could not stop him. Eventually he became one of the most widely read and influential writers in the history of western civilization, a man who exemplified the notion that the pen is mightier than the sword.

Voltaire at work. *This view of the great man at his desk captures the playful spirit that was an intrinsic part of Voltaire's literary genius and appeal.* Musée Carnavalet.

The work that launched Voltaire on his new course as critic and gadfly was his *Philosophical Letters on the English*, written after a long visit to England (the result of his ¬aforementioned exile), and published illegally in 1734. This book merits close attention, for it was one of the Enlightenment's first major works. As the title indicates, it was not a mere travelogue. There were serious lessons to be drawn from what he considered the exemplary character of English society. With exaggeration that was partly purposeful and partly a result his inadequate perceptions, Voltaire viewed England as an admirably open, humane society. Implicitly he urged the French to compare it to their own.

For Voltaire, England had four fundamental virtues. First, in England he found political freedom and balanced government: a supreme House of Commons, a king with enough power to do good but not enough to do harm, and an aristocracy by and large reasonable and responsible. In comparison, he was implying, the French monarchy could be too despotic, its middle class was without representation, and its aristocracy was wildly irresponsible and selfish. It was no coincidence, secondly, that there was also considerable intellectual freedom in England. Its scientists, artists, and intellectuals were honored and esteemed even though they were not nobles. In England "a man of merit always makes his fortune" and the arts are treated "with the consideration that is due them." In discussing England's great men, Voltaire wrote, "we shall begin with the Bacons, the Lockes, and the Newtons. The generals and ministers will come after them in their turn." (These three individuals were elsewhere referred to by Voltaire as his own personal trinity.) Voltaire's emphasis on culture as against politics was later developed in his great history, *The Age of Louis XIV* (1751). There he praised that reign not for its military power or the monarch's quest for glory, but for its great cultural flowering. Third, Voltiare was impressed by the multiplicity of religions in England, implicitly comparing this to France, where only Catholics were free to practice their faith unimpeded, and Protestantism had been outlawed by the revocation of the Edict of Nantes in 1685. "If there were only one religion in England, there would be fear of despotism; if there were but two, the people would cut one another's throats; but there are thirty and they all live happy and in peace." This was of course an exaggeration, since Catholics, Dissenters, and Jews still suffered certain civil disabilities. Nevertheless, all were free to practice their religion and Voltaire's basic argument was sound. There was one last thread in the fabric of English freedom, as seen by Voltaire. In addition to enjoying political, intellectual, and religious liberty, England was a country that valued commercial enterprise and initiative. "Commerce, which has enriched the citizens of England, has helped make them free, and this freedom has in turn extended commerce; hence the greatness of the state." English commercial prosperity was related to its relatively flexible social structure. In one of the passages where Voltaire explicitly compared England to France, he continued: "In England the younger son of a peer of the realm does not disdain trade. . . . In France [even] the merchant hears his profession spoken of scornfully and he is foolish enough to be ashamed because of it."

Here then was a standard of progress for continental Europeans. Though England was France's traditional rival—its Protestant nemesis and perennial diplomatic and naval adversary—Voltaire used England for his vision of modernity. There was of course no way that English society could be recreated in France, let alone central Europe, but Voltaire sensed the existence in France of a large and talented middle class waiting to be liberated by opportunity and freedom. The Enlightenment was not "middle-class" in the sense that its principal writers were bourgeois: some were, while others were nobles. However, it can plausibly be regarded as "middle-class" in its broadest implications, in the sense that its values would benefit and indeed depended on the existence of a substantial middle class. Voltaire was no doubt read admiringly by Polish nobles, professors in Naples, and the Empress Catherine in Russia, but the practical implications of his views were severely limited in such places. France, however, was fertile territory. Yet no exaggeration should be implied that would depict Voltaire as a revolutionary or a "precursor" of the French Revolution, which began fifteen years after his death. There is not the slightest suggestion in his works that the government could or should be overthrown to bring about the progress he applauded in England. The social order, while distasteful in some of its special privileges and traditions, was not alien to Voltaire, who had little concern for the popular masses. It was a question of educating the existing elites—noble and nonnoble alike—by the force of argument and literary skill. His goal was to reshape the values of the nation's elites, who could then gradually alter the nation's laws and institutions.

The linchpin in the system of outmoded tradition was organized religion, whose historical record Voltaire regarded as scandalous. This was the target of his scathing and popular *Philosophical Dictionary*, published anonymously in 1764. Of this book he observed that the authorities in Paris, Geneva, the Netherlands, and the Vatican were burning it and yearned to burn its author as well. Using every weapon in his arsenal of satire, Voltaire launched a frontal assault on the contradictions and claims of organized Christianity. He was convinced that Christianity—Catholicism and Protestantism alike—was not only false but evil, a source of fanaticism and brutality. "Everything that goes beyond the adoration of a supreme being and of submitting one's heart to his eternal orders is superstition." Voltaire was a deist, with a poetic sense of a supreme being who had created a universe with order and purpose but did not interfere with that universe. "The emblems of divinity were one of the first sources of superstition. Once we made God in our image, the divine cult was perverted." Superstition inevitably bred fanaticism, the eagerness to persecute those who believed or behaved differently. Thus, to Voltaire the historic crimes of Christianity—its indisputable record of persecution of outsiders and heretics—were not incidental but of its essence.

Voltaire did not believe that perfection would be achieved if organized religion was banished from the world. He was not overly optimistic. Considering natural disasters like the catastrophic earthquake in Lisbon of 1755, as well as the record of military pillage, rape, slavery, and other human horrors that he chronicled in his satirical tale *Candide* (1759), he was in fact bound to be demoralized. The world sometimes appeared to him as a shipwreck, and Voltaire's advice at the end of *Candide* was that the best a person could do was withdraw from the world and "cultivate his garden." His pessimism, however, alternated with a more hopeful sense that within limits progress was possible, justice could be won, absurd and cruel customs could be vanquished, and the limits of knowledge expanded. For this admirer and popularizer of Newton, the individual above all had to be free to think for himself. With his fellow philosophes, Voltaire was a tireless fighter for a limited but essential conception of freedom: the rule of law, civil liberties, freedom of expression, and religious toleration.[4]

Voltaire published hundreds of works ranging from his early poems, dramas, and histories to satirical tales, treatises, polemics, and pamphlets. Perhaps his most influential writing, however, was his correspondence. Since he lived in voluntary exile from Paris during his most productive decades, he was physically out of touch with the mainstream of intellectual life. But he more than compensated for this by his voluminous correspondence. Princes and ministers, Englishmen and Germans, philosophes and poets, mighty aristocrats and young writers wrote to Voltaire and heard from him. All literary roads led to his estate at Ferney for men and women aspiring to a place in the world of "modern" ideas and literary activity. A network of adherents and disciples felt the full impact of Voltaire's attitudes, since no censor could interfere with his expression in this form. The cumulative impact of this outspoken correspondence can only be guessed at, but it must have been enormous.[5]

Eventually, the rebellious critic was recognized for the literary genius he was. His ideas prevailed, his renown increased, and toward the end of

[4] Within the voluminous literature on Voltaire, see especially Peter Gay's admiring *Voltaire: the Poet as Realist* (Princeton, N.J., 1959).

[5] A modern admirer of Voltaire's, the Swiss scholar Theodore Besterman, has devoted decades to retrieving and publishing an exhaustive edition of this correspondence, which now runs to about thirty volumes.

his life he passed from rebel to leader of the Establishment. In 1774 he returned to Paris in triumph, greeted like a conquerer. Yet Voltaire had his critics, not only among his archenemies, the Jesuits, but among certain men of letters in France and abroad. It is important to understand these criticisms of Voltaire in order to judge his limitations. In the first place, some found that Voltaire emphasized style over substance. Elegant wit was the highest virtue in the salon society of the eighteenth century and in the correspondence that lubricated it, and no one was better at this game than Voltaire. But his witty, ironic style was considered by some people to be a sign of superficiality. Others (misreading him, this time) felt that his faith in reason and progress was naive. A more serious charge was that Voltaire was fanatical in his antifanaticism. His attack on religion, on Christianity itself rather than specific shortcomings of that faith, was seen as reckless and excessive. A different, almost contradictory, criticism of Voltaire arose in the 1770's and 1780's, at a time when he was being celebrated as France's leading man of letters. Certain young writers who were frustrated in their own aspirations viewed Voltaire from the perspective of outsiders looking in. They found him to be far too "establishment," far too immersed in success and high society. They felt (perhaps with justification) that the "ins," including Voltaire, regarded anyone who had not yet won recognition with disdain. This criticism may have simply been the price of fame or the fate that befalls a conquering rebel who lives to an active old age. It did indicate, however, that Voltaire's rebelliousness was of limited scope and had become eminently respectable by the 1770's.

At any rate, neither Voltaire nor the other philosophes can be regarded as democratic, apart from their belief in equality before the law. Their view of the common people was condescending and skeptical even while sympathetic. Understandably, they were fearful of the uneducated masses, whose behavior was alien and threatening. Along with other well-to-do persons, they were appalled by the popular uprisings that periodically ran their violent course in European history. At best, most philosophes visualized a very long-term evolution in which education would eventually filter down to the masses and modify their behavior. Presently, they regarded the masses as ignorant, violent, superstitious, and irresponsible. Though they might object to certain privileges of the nobility, most philosophes were comfortable consorting in the salons and counting royal ministers and aristocrats as their friends, insisting merely on recognition for the talented of any social origin. They were, if one must label them, liberal elitists with a conscience.[6]

6 See Harry Payne, *The Philosophes and the People* (New Haven, Conn., 1976).

The Encyclopedia: *Landmark of an Age*

While Voltaire's correspondence created a communications network throughout Europe's enlightened circles, it was Diderot's *Encyclopedia* that became the philosophes' public landmark. Like Voltaire, Denis Diderot (1713–1784) was a professional writer who helped to create the role of intellectual-activist. Though the range of his writings was enormous—including novels and plays, mathematical treatises, muckraking pamphlets, and philosophical discourses—his main concern was summarized in the plaintive statement: "Force me to be silent on religion and government [i.e., contemporary issues], and I will have nothing more to say." The dread of being silenced was no flight of Diderot's fancy. As a young man, though not yet an atheist, he had published an outspoken criticism of religion. The book was seized by the authorities and its author arrested. Diderot spent over one hundred days in prison until he agreed to a humiliating public apology. The charge: authoring a book "contrary to religion, morals, and the state."

Only a work as sprawling as the twenty-eight-volume *Encyclopedia, or classified dictionary of the sciences, arts, and trades* (1751–1772), edited by Diderot and the mathematician Jean d'Alembert, could encompass the philosophes' full range of interests. The work had modest origins as a publisher's venture to translate an older five-volume British reference work. Eventually Diderot convinced the publisher to sponsor an entirely new work that would inventory all current fields of knowledge and set forth the most advanced ideas. It was not to be a mere reference work, but was designed (as the preface stated) "to change the general way of thinking." The articles were written by over a hundred specialists for contemplation by laymen. Almost four thousand subscribers paid large sums in advance of publication, so the extremely costly project could be undertaken without the sponsorship of any official agency—an unusual situation in a country where the arts were traditionally centralized under royal patronage. This independence was crucial to the editors' vision. "Our Encyclopedia is a work that could only be carried out in a philosophic century," they wrote. "All things must be examined without sparing anyone's sensibilities . . . we must return to the arts and sciences the liberty that is so precious to them."

Science was naturally one of the *Encyclopedia's* central concerns, but technology had an equally prominent place. Diderot felt that artisanal technology was a key to the progress of civilization. Many of the illustrations that filled eleven separate volumes of the work were detailed sketches and blueprints of machinery and manufacturing processes. The editors admired efficiency and ingenuity in production, though they recognized that drudgery was also involved. In devoting so much space to these subjects, Diderot was dignifying the hard work and skills of artisans, arguing that it was worthy of respect. He sought to establish a greater rapport between the science of scholars and the technological concerns of producers. By spurring interaction between them, he promoted the democratization of science.

The *Encyclopedia* was also a repository of contemporary moral philosophy and social science: theories concerning social organization, human nature, ethics, political economy, and government. In this fundamental area of eighteenth-century thought, the most systematic contributions came from a circle of Scottish philosophers headed by David Hume (1711–1776). The *Encyclopedia*'s viewpoint was in harmony with much of this "moral sense" school, as it was called, especially with Hume's influential *Treatise of Human Nature* (1739), which argued that a science of man was possible, based on observation and reflection, on "systematized common sense." Since laboratory experiments were not possible, experiences must be taken "as they appear in the common course of human life." One conclusion from such experience was the realization that man is on his own in framing the values by which he lives. Since there is no pre-

A typical illustration from the *Encyclopedia*, showing an industrial process.

David Hume. *A towering figure in the history of philosophy, as well as a pioneering social scientist, Hume (in Peter Gay's phrase) was a complete modern pagan, expounding an uncompromisingly secular world view with rigor and sophistication.*

ordained standard of behavior to refer to, man must contrive rules that prove to be as useful as possible. One yardstick of such values was that they produce "the greatest good for the greatest number," a utilitarian notion put forward elsewhere by such writers as Helvétius and Beccaria.

Of course, religion could scarcely be ignored in an encyclopedic work, though it could not be assaulted with the fervor of Voltaire's satire or Hume's critique in *The Natural History of Religion* (1755). Insofar as the claims of religion could be supported by critical reason, they were accepted; otherwise, they were subjected to searching discussion and even cautious satire. In the article on Lent, for example, the author did not attack what he clearly considered to be extravagant Lenten observances. Instead, he described the great variety of fasting customs found in church history, thus implying that Lent was merely a human practice subject to numerous mutations. Above all the Bible was never invoked as an authority in the *Encyclopedia,* while in such entries as "Man," the divine dimension was lacking—something a devout Christian might reasonably object to.

After the first three volumes appeared, criticism began to mount against the whole venture, and with the publication of the seventh volume in 1757, a storm of controversy erupted. The catalyst was d'Alembert's admiring article on Geneva (where he had visited the previous year), which was devoted almost entirely to the allegedly modern attitudes of the Genevan clergy.

> The clergy of Geneva have exemplary morals. . . . Several no longer believe in the divinity of Jesus Christ, a doctrine so zealously defended by Calvin, their leader and for which they burned Servetus. . . . Hell—one of the principal points of our belief—is no longer one today for several ministers of Geneva [who] maintain that we should never interpret literally in the Holy Books all those passages that seem to offend humanity and reason. . . . To put the matter briefly, several pastors of Geneva reject everything called a *mystery* and suppose that the first principle of a true religion is to propose nothing as a belief which runs counter to reason. Thus when they are pressed on the *necessity* of revelation, the dogma so essential to Christianity, several of them substitute here the term "usefulness," which seems more moderate and agreeable to them.[7]

Clearly d'Alembert had been imprudent. The description offended not only the Genevans but all upholders of orthodox religious values. Reacting against several of the philosophes' books that had appeared in the late 1750's as well as the *Encyclopedia*, the attorney general of France entered the fray declaring that "there is a project formed, a society organized to propagate materialism, destroy religion, inspire a spirit of independence, and nourish the corruption of morals." In 1759 he attacked the *Encyclopedia* before the Paris *Parlement*, seeking to have it banned: "According to its true purpose it should have been the book of all knowledge, but has become instead the book of all error." Both the court and the crown condemned the *Encyclopedia* and revoked its license to publish, asserting that it had done "irreparable damage to morality and religion," and demanding that the subscribers be reimbursed. The latter declined this offer and, despite the defection of d'Alembert and Voltaire, Diderot went underground and persevered in bringing the project to its conclusion without a license. By 1765 the storm had blown over, Diderot received unofficial authorization to continue, and gradually the remaining volumes appeared.

The epilogue to this story is revealing. By the 1770's opposition to the *Encyclopedia* had abated and the work was much sought after. To satisfy the demand, various publishers brought out an ambitious series of reprints. With each new edition the price came down and the number of sets in circulation increased. Altogether some sixteen thousand sets were printed in addition to the original edition of four thousand. While the latter had sold at between 1,000 and 1,500 livres a set, the smaller-format reprints were priced between 384 and 230 livres a set. The demand was

---

[7] *The Encyclopedia: Selections*, ed. by S. J. Gendzier (New York, 1967), pp. 115–17.

so great that a consortium of publishers, bankers, and printers was necessary to plan, finance, and execute the new editions. This massive undertaking severely strained the available supplies of paper, ink, type, and skilled printing labor. Costing something over 1 million livres to finance, the venture yielded an income of about 2.4 million, and thus cleared over 1 million livres in profit. Moreover, the political climate had changed so greatly in the intervening decade that the publishers, instead of working secretly to avoid government harassment, now relied on the government to protect their copyright against other publishers who sought to pirate even cheaper editions. Thus the *Encyclopedia* spread among Europe's elites, beyond the wealthy nobles, merchants, and officials who had subscribed to the expensive original edition, to doctors, lawyers, clergymen, teachers, and army officers who could now afford to purchase this landmark of the Enlightenment.[8]

While the *Encyclopedia* found a substantial market, another work of the 1770's proved to be an even more popular encapsulation of the Enlightenment's spirit. However, whereas virtually every book mentioned in this chapter is still being read with pleasure or at least being studied in the classroom, the best-seller of Abbé Raynal (1713–1796) is all but forgotten today. As celebrated in its time as the works of Montesquieu, Voltaire, and Rousseau—and like them, officially prohibited by the censorship—his work had little enduring literary merit or intellectual distinction. Eighteenth-century readers nonetheless devoured it. Guillaume Raynal's six-volume history of European expansion overseas, *The Philosophical and Political History of European Colonies and Commerce in the Two Indies* (1770), appeared in at least seventy versions (some licensed by the original publishers, others pirated), including a ten-volume set published in Geneva in 1780–1781, and an edition published as late as 1787. It was evidently *the* book of the Enlightenment's later phase.

Ostensibly a chronological and geographical survey of European trade and settlement in Asia, Africa, and the Americas, it fed the public's hunger for information about those exotic places. Like the *Encyclopedia*, *The History of the Two Indies* was the product of collaboration between its principal author Raynal and a number of other contributors, including Diderot. Known to his friends as "the inquisitive one," Raynal produced a book in which the reader could never be sure what surprising fact or argument would turn up on the next page. Its lack of specific focus is one reason why the *History* is so unreadable today. Yet, at the time it seemed to offer an awesomely learned and pointed critique of prevailing

[8] Robert Darnton, "The Encyclopedia Wars of Pre-revolutionary France," *American Historical Review*, Vol. LXXVIII (1973), pp. 1331–52.

institutions and values. For while it concentrated on the colonial world —exploring exotic native customs and religions, the topography of the Orient and the New World, the extermination of native populations by Europeans, and the whole issue of slavery—it was equally concerned with the conquering European civilizations themselves.

Raynal worked at three different levels in his prolix and rambling work. The most obvious and appealing was the level of emotional outrage. In many sections Raynal came across as an angry man, denouncing the tyranny, inhumanity, violence, and irrationality of Europe's ways, particularly in relation to slavery and the exploitation of the new world's populations. Then he would shift to a more abstract level, discussing the principles governing such things as government, trade, and morality. Yet principle did not necessarily dictate practice. Raynal finally shrank back from the implications of his own outrage and analysis and, pragmatically coming to terms with existing realities, offered only mild proposals for reforms. Thus, despite his animus against slavery, he did not call for its abolition; while clearly "anticolonialist" in sentiment, he acknowledged that it was too late to decolonize Europe's empires; despite his feeling that organized religion was a kind of myth, he did not call for a society without religion; and despite his vehement denunciations of despotism, he scarcely proposed any significant changes in France's government.[9] It is therefore not surprising to observe how Raynal, who survived most of the other philosophes, behaved during the French Revolution. At a loss to understand its dynamics of violence and democratization, he was very quickly left behind and ended up alienated from the revolutionary cause. In any case, his mixture of emotion, theoretical analysis, and mild reform proposals was a package well designed to please a large audience, and Raynal's now-forgotten *History of the Two Indies* can be seen as a final blooming of the Encyclopedist spirit.

Political Thought and "Enlightened Absolutism"

Enlightenment thought typically concerned moral and philosophical issues—the values by which a society should live—as well as practical matters such as penology, trade, or the powers of the Church. The propounding of political theory, on the other hand, posed certain problems. After all, in this age of monarchy and aristocracy the exercise of political authority was confined to very small and entrenched groups. Could political arrangements be subjected to the scrutiny of critical reason without appearing subversive? Still, there was room for disagreement in theory on

9 William Womack, "Eighteenth-Century Themes in the *Histoire Philosophique et politique des Deux Indes* of Guillaume Raynal," *Studies on Voltaire and the Eighteenth Century*, Vol. XCVI (Geneva, 1972), pp. 129–265.

priorities within the existing systems of power. Some writers emphasized the importance of liberty, and were most fearful of tyranny or despotism. Others were more concerned with effective government which, they believed, only a strong royal authority could insure.

The most renowned spokesman for the first position was Charles de Secondat, Baron de Montesquieu (1689–1755). A distinguished member of the Bordeaux *Parlement,* Montesquieu had made a great impact with his youthfully iconoclastic *Persian Letters* (1721). In what proved to be one of the first salvos of the Enlightenment, exotic characters and situations were used to satirize contemporary social practices. His second major work was very different and far more influential, despite its ponderous prose and inordinate length. *The Spirit of the Laws, or the Relation that the laws should have with the constitution of each government, the customs, climate, religion, commerce etc.* (1748) was, as its subtitle indicates, a pioneering work in political sociology in which the study of government was related to the geography, history, and customs of various peoples and countries. Despite this modern perspective of cultural relativism, Montesquieu's preference for the English form of mixed government was clear. So was his hope that in France too the monarchy might be effectively limited by other institutions, such as the thirteen *Parlements*

Montesquieu. *Portrayed here in the garb of a Roman statesman, Montesquieu was France's leading political theorist in the eighteenth century. Doubtless he cherished the image of republican virtue evoked by the ancient Roman historians, whose work was familiar to all well educated Europeans.*

in which the magistrates were independent because they held their positions as a form of property and were normally not removable by the crown. Montesquieu affirmed that a powerful upper class was the only force that could serve as a barrier against royal tyranny. Only such a class was independent and motivated enough to resist royal abuses of power. Thus for Montesquieu, freedom from tyranny would be defended by strengthening the nobility's political privilege. Perverse as it sounds, he was in effect arguing that "privilege is the ancestor of liberty." For the liberal elitists who admired Montesquieu, despotism was the main enemy, the despotism of an all-powerful crown—or of an unchecked populace.

Montesquieu's emphasis on the nobility was merely one application of his general belief in the balance of powers and the separation of powers. He defined liberty as the absence of any one dominating power in the state. Countervailing powers were clear in England: the Lords, the Commons, the Crown, the country gentry. In France, there were somewhat weaker countervailing powers that derived from the old corporate structure: the church, the *Parlements*, the provincial estates, the chartered cities, the guilds. In the thirteen former British colonies that were to form the United States, there was no question of a king or hereditary nobility, but the American constitution makers of 1787 had Montesquieu in mind as they established separate executive, legislative, and judicial branches of government, combined direct and indirect elections, and struck a careful balance between the federal government and the states.

Montesquieu's essentially defensive emphasis was not universally accepted in France or the United States. Others looked to the monarchy (or in the United States, to the federal executive) as a source of progressive initiative rather than as a threat of despotism. Voltaire, for example, judged the French nobility rather than the crown to be the chief source of tyranny historically and the principal obstacle to progress in his own day. Referring to the ancient struggles between the nobility and Louis XI in the fifteenth century, he quipped that the king's repressive policies made about fifty (noble) families unhappy, and gave more than five hundred thousand families cause to celebrate. Along with certain royal officials, Voltaire emphasized the monarchy's ability to effect reform, which was being held back by vested interest groups such as the *Parlements*, the very *Parlements* Montesquieu wished to strengthen. Only a strong monarchy could overcome the self-interest and obstructionism of these corporate groups. Unlike Montesquieu, Voltaire was not overly concerned with the forms of government, and pragmatically supported acts by authoritarian monarchs and ministers so long as they seemed to benefit the public interest. Except for the tenure of Turgot as finance minister (see Chapter 9), however, the philosophes had little influence on the course of political events in France one way or the other.

In Germany, it is true, Frederick II made it appear as if his style of ruling was related to the Enlightenment. While French kings never stooped to justify their power, Frederick furnished a new image of kingship. In contrast to Louis XIV, who regarded himself and the state as identical ("I am the state"), Frederick defined the state as a collectivity above the monarch: the king is merely "the first servant of the state." As an admirer of the philosophes, who invited Voltaire to live at his court for several years, as a deist who promoted religious toleration, and as the author of essays about the desirability of humane laws, Frederick appeared to create an alliance between enlightenment and monarchy. Indeed, nineteenth-century German historians believed that Frederick's Prussia (as well as Joseph II's Austria) represented a new type of monarchy, an "enlightened absolutism," which, they claimed, provided the best road to modern nationhood. In contrast, France, with its unenlightened kings and violent revolutions, had followed a far less desirable path to the same end.

"Enlightened absolutism" or "enlightened despotism" has stuck as a label for discussing monarchy in the later eighteenth century, and is useful provided its meaning is not exaggerated. For one thing, clerics committed to the interests of their church were having less and less influence

Voltaire and Frederick the Great. For three years the Prussian king offered the hospitality of his palace of Sans Souci in Potsdam to the self-exiled French philosopher. One could well argue that here were the two quintessential figures of the eighteenth century: the reflective man of action, and the intellectual who sought to change his society's values. The influence of each on the other, however, should not be exaggerated.

in the councils of government, as rulers increasingly relied on secular advisors. Since the baneful influence of religion was alleged by the philosophes to be holding back progress, this in itself would seem to represent a step toward enlightenment. Then too, self-conscious efforts were being made by rulers and prime ministers in several lesser European states— Baden, Portugal, Naples, Spain under Charles III, and Tuscany under Joseph's brother Leopold—to cultivate enlightened policies on religion, taxation, and economic development. The ruler of Baden abolished serfdom, while Portugal was the first to expel the Jesuits. Leopold even entertained the idea of granting a written constitution to his Tuscan subjects and sharing power with them. This, however, never came close to being carried out, nor did such a development occur in any other state without the intervention of revolution. As for the major states, Catherine of Russia as well as Frederick carried on public relations campaigns to cultivate their enlightened images, such as when Catherine offered to help Diderot financially by mortgaging his library. As far as their policies were concerned, however, they continued the work of state building begun by their decidedly traditional predecessors. Enlightenment always took second place to power when there was a problem or conflict. In the one case where a sovereign did initiate a genuinely bold break with past social policies, Joseph II's agrarian edicts, we have seen that he failed.

Still, the concept of "enlightened absolutism" remains useful for discussing the development of Austria and Prussia. Even if there was substantial continuity between Frederick William I and his son Frederick the Great, and between Maria Theresa and her son Joseph, the latters' reigns were unusually successful in consolidating the work of state building and putting the whole process of government on a more solid footing. Frederick and Joseph did more than impart a new tone to the governing process. They provided it with a new coherence. The state now loomed above the constituent elements of society, drawing them together and harnessing their energy, for better and for worse in the future. Out of this great push forward a governing tradition developed among royal officials—a "Frederickian" tradition in Prussia, a "Josephinian" tradition in the Habsburg Monarchy—which outlasted the two rulers themselves.[10]

Political theory in the "Frederickian" or "Josephinian" tradition contained no debate over power or sovereignty. It was taken for granted that this lay entirely with the monarch. The question was: how could he best administer his state? The answer was to be found in theories of enlightened administration. These compared the state to a machine, with the ruler as its mainspring. Any flaw in the machine's operation could be at-

[10] See Leonard Krieger, Kings and Philosophers, 1689–1789 (New York, 1970), chap. 8, and M. S. Anderson, Historians and Eighteenth-Century Europe, 1715–1789 (Oxford, 1979), chap. 3.

tributed to a lack of skill. To develop the necessary expertise, to learn how to work the machine, future officials would have to study its principles, just as a physician studied the fundaments of anatomy. Academic training for high government officials therefore became the practice in Germany. The resulting bureaucracy was organized on what we call civil-service principles: professionalism, merit promotions, and standardized procedures. This bureaucratic tradition may have been the most durable achievement attributable to "enlightened absolutism." Sovereign, civil servants, and subjects were bound together by reciprocal obligations. Officials obeyed the ruler, and expected obedience in turn from his subjects, because the ultimate purpose of the state was to promote the welfare of all. (Ironically this was best expressed by the British conservative Edmund Burke, a great opponent of the French Revolution, who wrote that the principal right of the people was the right to be well governed.) Even under a regime of absolute monarchy and aristocratic privilege, and without any participation in the governing process, German subjects could feel that they lived in a well-ordered, well-governed state. Here then, was one root of the German tradition of duty and obedience that was to clash so dramatically in the future with liberal and democratic values.

Economic Theory

One area where theory had a sharp impact on government policy was the economy. At the beginning of the century mercantilism still held sway. Trade was either regulated, taxed, or subsidized by the state to promote an influx of gold and silver, since bullion was considered the primary form of wealth. Also, as explained in the discussion of food riots (Chapter 5), a tradition of paternalism had led governments to regulate the trade and pricing of grain, flour, and bread, sometimes at the expense of the cultivator's or miller's freedom to sell their goods at the market price. While a considerable body of critical writing on these practices had accumulated, no author had yet offered a comprehensive analysis of the economic "laws" that governed human society. No one had systematically analyzed the nature of wealth or the factors that could increase a society's total wealth. This was to be the great contribution of eighteenth-century writers, working under the Enlightenment's influence. Two writers in particular offered comprehensive, antimercantilist studies of what they called the natural economic order, and stern views of what governments should and should not do in that domain.

The French physiocrats, most notably the court physician François Quesnay (1694–1774), derived their insights from an appreciation of English agriculture. They argued that agriculture was the only source of true economic "surplus." As against precious metals, luxury items, or manufactured goods, only the land's produce represented a *net* enrichment. Since agriculture produced society's most valuable commodities, its condition would determine society's level of prosperity. The key social group for the physiocrats was accordingly the landlords (*propriétaires*) who controlled the net surplus. If they used their position wisely and invested their capital effectively, they could enhance the soil's productivity and generate new wealth. The model landlord was one who encouraged large-scale farming and the use of progressive methods. It was essential that his efforts be rewarded with "good prices." Prosperity depended on a combination of abundance and of sufficiently high and therefore profitable agricultural prices. The farmer could then reinvest part of the profit in his land, pay decent wages to his workers, and pay substantial taxes to the state based on the land's value. In an article on "Grains" that he contributed to Diderot's *Encyclopedia*, Quesnay put the matter this way: "Agricultural abundance without value is not wealth. High prices with scarcity is utter poverty. [Only] Abundance with high prices is opulence." To assure this, the government would have to cease its manipulation and regulation of the grain trade, allowing a free market in grain. Quesnay believed that this would lead to a useful but not excessive rise in prices. With an incentive for profit, farmers could better respond to rising demand. A reliable national grain supply would gradually come to replace the fragmented, artificial, and fluctuating markets that made the lives of the consuming masses so insecure. In addition, the physiocrats advocated a single, rationalized tax on land values to replace the crazy quilt of inequitable taxes and privileges that currently existed.

Quesnay's ideas had great appeal but not everyone agreed with them. The first French attempt to implement free trade in grain in the 1760's unfortunately coincided with a period of scarcity in certain regions of France, with the predictable result of misery and widespread food riots. Certain royal officials and intellectuals (including Diderot, Simon Linguet, and the Neapolitan Abbé Galiani) concluded that practical considerations made an unregulated grain trade impossible, desirable as it mght be in theory. Nonetheless, the physiocrats' prescription for a free and prosperous agrarian economy made many converts, was implemented for a second time unsuccessfully in 1775, and became one influence in the French Revolution's liberal phase. Above all the physiocrats helped create the model of "economic man," according to which the absolute right of private property was seen as the fundamental human freedom, and individual self-interest as the motive force of economic growth.

The latter idea was brought into even greater prominence by the Scottish philosopher Adam Smith (1723–1790). Having visited with the physiocrats in the 1760's, Smith was at once impressed and critical. Sharing their hostility to the mercantilist system of privileges, restraints, and monopolies, he endorsed their slogan, "laissez-faire" (free the economy). His own

Adam Smith. *The Scottish philosopher's enormously influential book,* The Wealth of Nations, *laid the foundations for classical or free-market economic theory, which held sway for much of the nineteenth century in Britain and the United States.*

study of the economy's "natural laws," however, yielded a different prescription for prosperity. The result was a milestone of the Enlightenment, *An Inquiry into the Nature and Causes of the Wealth of Nations* (1776). Like the physiocrats, Smith rejected the bullionism of the mercantilist era as well as its preoccupation with fostering a favorable balance of trade. For Smith the true source of wealth was neither precious metals nor agriculture but manufacturing, which created value where none had existed before. Smith analyzed in detail how value was bestowed on commodities through labor—thus developing an early version of the labor theory of value that Karl Marx would turn to such different ends—but he also argued that only accumulated capital could give labor its opportunity to create wealth.

Perhaps Adam Smith's most accessible idea was his prophetic notion that the division of labor was the principal mechanism for increasing productivity. He extolled both specialization of labor within the manufacturing of each product, and specialization among different nations in different types of production. Division of tasks among workers in a particular industry would lead to increased dexterity and opportunities for introducing new technology. At the international level, Smith argued that each nation should pursue what it did best, on the basis of free competition, without the artificial barriers of tariffs and prohibitions.

With the physiocrats, Smith considered individual self-interest to be the fundamental motor of the economic order. He had earlier developed this concept in his moral philosophy, positing the idea of an "invisible hand" that harmonized individual interests. This metaphor he now extended to the economy, maintaining that the heavy, visible hand of interfering government must be removed in favor of competing individual interests. Yet this advocate of a free-market economy was no apologist for industrialists or merchants. Like most philosophes, he did not sacrifice his empirical sense of reality to the symmetry of theory, and his book is full of passages expressing skepticism about the ethics of capitalists. "People of the same trade seldom meet together, even for merriment and diversion," he asserted in a famous passage, "but the conversation ends in a conspiracy against the public, or in some contrivance to raise prices [or to lower wages]." While he felt that such behavior ought to be discouraged, he restricted the government's role to building the infrastructure of a free economy: roads, schools, police forces, and the like. In the end, notwithstanding his numerous insights into the liabilities of free competition and the division of labor, Smith regarded these as the only foundation for a prosperous economy. Accordingly, he was quickly embraced by the new class of industrialists in Britain, and his work invoked as a gospel to keep the government's hand off their enterprise.

Rousseau: The Moral Dimension

Voltaire's exile at Ferney was a matter of caution and convenience rather than a principled withdrawal from society's mainstream. Jean Jacques Rousseau (1712–1778) effected a different kind of exile, a self-conscious withdrawal from high society reflecting an alienation of spirit. The ambitious son of a Geneva watchmaker, Rousseau spent a wandering youth in several countries before heading for Paris to make his mark as a composer. He failed in that objective, but successfully fell in with the philosophes and their patrons of the Parisian salons. In 1744, however, he was abruptly dismissed from his post as secretary to an aristocrat for alleged insolence, and this crystallized his growing disillusion with the glittering world of the elites. Prone to quarreling both with potential patrons and his philosophe friends, Rousseau periodically withdrew into a self-imposed "solitude." Far from undermining his creative energies, however, his tempestuous personal life produced a flow of literary and philosophic writings in the 1760's that made him known to all of educated Europe, and also obliged him to flee France for a time. The posthumous publication of his autobiographical Confessions in 1782 capped his fame and raised Rousseau to the status of a culture-hero. For this book, while dis-

Jean Jacques Rousseau. *Despite his quarrelsome personality, Rousseau caught the fancy of his generation and became a veritable culture hero among men and women alike. It was not every writer whose image appeared on plates, snuffboxes, and playing cards, shown here.*

playing his persecution mania for all to see, transmuted his quarrelsome personality into an inspirational model of individual freedom and moral earnestness.

Rousseau's first recognition came with publication of a prize-winning essay submitted in 1749 to the provincial academy of Dijon on the following topic: "Has the revival of science and the arts contributed to the purification or the corruption of social morality?" This was followed in 1755 by his *Discourse on the Origin of Inequality*. In these essays Rousseau contrasted the corruption of contemporary society with the simplicity that he imagined to be characteristic of man's natural state. He argued that society's supposedly highest achievements—the arts and sciences—actually promoted conformity, idleness, and servility. Altogether they were a source of decadence, destroying the simple self-reliance that ought to characterize human existence. Similarly, he argued that the institution of private property was orginally a kind of usurpation that had engendered envy, gross inequality, and pervasive insecurity. Even on this purely speculative level, however, Rousseau did not make the mistake of idealizing primitive, unsocialized man. He recognized that the state of nature was also a state of anarchy ruled by two undesirable things: the brute force of the strong against the weak, and individual appetites to which no bounds were opposed. Rousseau did not wish to return to a primitive state of nature. Rather he wished to salvage the potential virtues of natural or uncorrupted man which society had smothered.

Rousseau's most popular works were two didactic novels published back to back in 1761–1762: *Julie, ou La Nouvelle Héloïse* and *Emile, or Education*. The first went through seventy editions between 1761 and 1789, probably surpassing a hundred thousand copies. The basic question in these novels was: what makes a human being human? Rousseau answered that it was moral sense or sensibility, whose source was feeling or conscience. He was not attempting to dismiss the role of reason or intellect, but he denied to reason the primacy that most philosophes tended to accord it. He was seeking to promote a balance between reason and feeling, between the head and the heart. Moral judgment—the most basic human attribute—depended on a conscience possessed alike by peasants and scholars, by the poor and the rich. Reason may show what is good, but only conscience impels a man to embrace it. "Conscience does not teach us right reasoning but right action." In contrast to the utilitarian calculation that was gaining ground among progressive thinkers, Rousseau was interested in the love of right. "Virtue, sublime science of simple minds," he proclaimed, "are not your principles graven on every heart? Need we do more, to learn your laws, than examine ourselves and listen to the voice of conscience?" In *Emile* Rousseau focused on the education of a morally autonomous individual, and brilliantly portrayed the notion of education as a process of self-development, more dependent on experience than book learning. Furthermore, to know oneself, Rousseau argued in *Emile*, a man must commune in solitude with the world of nature, which alone can sharpen his religious or spiritual sense. Again at variance with the materialism and atheism that a handful of philosophes were beginning to expound, Rousseau advocated a profound spirituality essentially deistic or pantheistic but far more emphatic than Voltaire's casual deism. Rousseau's spirituality, however, was not dependent on the Bible or the figure of Christ, so that Catholic and Protestant authorities alike found it subversive. Like Voltaire, Rousseau saw his work burned in his native Geneva as well as in Paris and Rome.

Rousseau's primary concern was the moral potential and dignity of individuals. Neither a social nor a political reformer, he nonetheless put his boldest and most original ideas into a work of political theory, *The Social Contract* (1762). Not nearly as popular as *Julie* or *Emile* in its time, the book gained celebrity in the wake of the French Revolution despite the fact that it had no direct connection with that momentous event. In his essays Rousseau had argued that society had corrupted a potentially good human nature, though only in society could it be morally regenerated. An individual's inner moral freedom could only develop within a properly constituted community. Rousseau felt that such societies had existed in the past, in Sparta, in the Roman Republic, and in an idealized version of his native Geneva. These were close-knit homogeneous communities (relatively speaking), where a rough kind of equality and independence were shared by their citizens. Of course, eighteenth-century republics such as Venice, Genoa, and even Geneva were oligarchies, but idealized republics of the past continued to provide inspiration. Their image conveyed the sense that something better than the pretensions and tyrannies of monarchies could be brought into being, that communities could exist where citizens shared an enthusiasm for promoting each others' well-being. French revolutionaries would later call this feeling "public spirit" or "civic virtue." During the enlightenment it was a subterranean stream of utopianism that occasionally surfaced in odd places, but it was Rousseau who articulated it dramatically in *The Social Contract.*

The book was neither a description of something that had existed in the past, nor a blueprint for an actual state of the future. Rather, it was normative, setting an ideal standard of community organization. At the very beginning of *The Social Contract* readers were jolted with the assertion that "Men are born free and everywhere they are in chains." Why? Because they are subject to governments entirely distinct from themselves. An individual is free only if he submits to an authority of which he is part. In that case, when he obeys the law he is obeying himself. The only legitimate "sovereign," Rousseau asserted, are the people themselves. Voluntary participation rather than the chance destiny of history or birth ought to be the foundation of society. Ideally, all people in a society should create that society by joining in a social contract, which in turn provides for a government.

Rousseau believed that there had to be a consensus that would provide the basis for community—an impersonal "general will," he called it, which subsumes individual interests. In the course of the book Rousseau tried to suggest certain mechanisms and principles by which the general will could be promoted. First, since consensus rather than mere majority rule was to be the basis of this society, the best way to establish its constitution would be to find a supremely wise "legislator" to draft the structure of government for the citizens' approval. Modeled on the ancient Greek lawgiver Solon, this legislator would have no subsequent role in the functioning of the government. Second, a rough equality among citizens was not simply a desirable goal but an operative necessity. The prototype of a citizen was to be found in the independent artisans that Rousseau had known in Geneva, small-scale, direct producers beholden to no one but themselves for their livelihood. At the least, the extremes of wealth and poverty must be avoided. "Everyone [must] have something, and nobody too much," he had written in one of his essays, for only that situation would assure the dignity of all. Constant vigilance and participation by citizens in the affairs of government were also necessary. The British, he declared, were free only when they voted. Citizenship is a full-time concern, and government is a revocable trust. Laws, drafted by the executive, must be approved by the people in referendums. Finally, there must be no intermediary corporations within the state that group and divide citizens from each other on arbitrary lines. Rousseau disagreed with Montesquieu's view that such constituted bodies or interest groups as *Parlements* or guilds were valuable buffers against tyranny.

In a community that followed the principles and practices he outlined, Rousseau believed that a citizen would be morally bound to obey the law even if it appeared to conflict with his personal interests. For, in obeying the laws of such a state, he would be doing what he *ought* to do, not merely what he *wanted* to do. That, to Rousseau, was the highest good. As he put it in a paradoxical phrase, sometimes the government—a properly constituted government—must "force a citizen to be free." In other words, the best interests of the community must be his own best interests as well. The political community became in Rousseau's thought not merely a set of convenient arrangements to protect life and property—the classic formulation of Locke—but an ethical imperative, the context for a moral life. The law in a justly constituted state would govern and educate simultaneously. The individual citizen would learn the meaning of moral freedom in a delicate balance of consent and participation on the one hand, and subordination and obedience on the other. To make this explicit, Rousseau further suggested that the ideal state needed a civil religion in which these values would be evoked ritualistically. Non-sectarian, recognizing God as creator, and even offering some sense of immortality for the soul, this civil religion would foster the sense that justly constituted laws were sacred.

Ever since the beginnings of the French Revolution, critics and scholars have interpreted Rousseau's political thought in conflicting ways. Some, citing his insistence that the *Social Contract* could apply only to a small cohesive state, used Rousseau as an authority for a conservative position. For the Jacobins in the French Revolution, on the contrary, Rousseau was the inspiration for a democratic politics in which the participation of citizens was pushed to its limits. Others have taken a dim view of Rousseau. Noting his impatience with any "intermediary corps," they feel that he missed a crucial underpinning of liberal democracy: the pluralism of diverse and even competing institutions. Some scholars, focusing on Rousseau's concept of a uniform, and ultimately coercive general will, see him as a harbinger of totalitarianism. Rousseau's writings certainly leave room for such disagreement. What is indisputable is Rousseau's insistence that the state's ultimate purpose was not simply the well-being of its citizens but their moral development.

DIFFUSION AND RESISTANCE

For both ideological and tactical reasons, the philosophes' foremost demand was freedom of expression. Only through the unimpeded circulation and discussion of ideas could reason prevail. In this respect England stood as something of a model. Along with its relatively open political life, the island kingdom enjoyed a wide degree of free expression, at least since 1695. The Restoration government of Charles II had sponsored a Licensing Act in 1662, which had required the precensorship of printed matter and had restricted the number of authorized printers. When this legislation lapsed in 1695, however, it was not renewed and the English press was thereafter largely free. Only the laws of libel, sedition, and obscenity limited expression through the printed word. True, some minor impediments remained and should be noted. Until the 1770's, for example, Parliament prohibited the direct reporting or transcription of its debates, holding such an act to be a breach of its privileges. Newspapers attempted to circumvent the ban by various stratagems and eventually, at the risk of incurring penalties, opposed it directly and succeeded in breaking it down. Parliament's taxing power could also be used to curb the press. By levying a stiff stamp tax on newsprint, Parliament could jeopardize the financial viability of certain newspapers. This power was used intermittently to harass opposition newspapers, especially early nineteenth-century radical and working-class editors who were therefore forced to publish "unstamped newspapers" illegally. Finally, the theater remained subject to a kind of censorship, for once a play opened it could be promptly shut down by order of the Lord Chamberlain if it were alleged to offend public morals or decency. Yet even with these qualifications, England remained a yardstick for measuring freedom of expression. The absence of precensorship meant that people could publish what they wished, and that no bureaucracy existed to keep watch over the printed word. In contrast, most other major states required the submission of manuscripts in advance for permission to publish, and maintained a "police-state" apparatus to search out unauthorized domestic or imported publications.

Censorship and Smuggling in France

All aspects of publishing were regulated and controlled in France. The number of authorized printers as well as the number of lawful booksellers were limited both by the government and by the guild structure. More important, a publisher was supposed to submit his manuscripts in advance to royal censors for permission to publish them. When granted, this permission (or "the king's privilege") certified that there was nothing in the book offensive to religion, morals, or the state. Over a thousand manuscripts were unable to pass muster and were forbidden to be published. Far from tapering off as the century progressed, the laws on censorship were renewed in 1757, including the stipulation of a possible death sentence for authors or publishers of unauthorized works. In keeping with the expansion of publishing, the royal censorship office more than doubled in size between 1740 and 1789, by which time it employed some 178 censors. Prosecutions for violations continued throughout the century, facilitated by paid informants of the lieutenant general of police in Paris who supervised the book trade. Occasionally, a harsh exemplary sentence such as a term in the galleys was meted out; more commonly the penalty was exile, a stay in the Bastille, or a hefty fine. Even if the royal censors cleared a book, it could subsequently be banned by the *Parlements* or censored by the theology faculty of the University of Paris. Moreover, the crown from time to time would prohibit altogether any publication on a currently controversial topic such as a religious dispute or tax policy.

At the same time, however, there was collusion within the royal government itself that allowed authors and publishers to circumvent precensorship. Heterodox works on morality or philosophy could not be stamped with the government's seal of approval, but publishers could be given tacit permission to publish their works without such approval: informal assurance that they need not fear prosecution. Under the keeper of the seals and chief censor Malesherbes, who held office from 1750 to 1763, this practice was institutionalized, and he thereby became one of the philosophes' chief patrons. Such important works as Montesquieu's *Spirit of the Laws*, Rousseau's *Nouvelle Héloïse*, and several volumes of the *Encyclopedia* appeared under tacit permission. Indeed, while there were only about thirty tacit permissions granted each year in the 1730's, over one hundred were granted annually by the 1750's, and after 1760 from three to four hundred. In the last decades of the old regime in France the number of unofficially tolerated books almost approached the number of authorized books being published "with the king's privilege."

A second strategy for circumventing the censorship, especially for outspoken or blasphemous works, was clandestine publication. Centers of illicit publishing could be found in the Low Countries, Switzerland, and other enclaves across the French border, from which the illegal and usually anonymous books were smuggled into France over back roads and mountain passes. Capitalizing on the appeal of illicit material, the publishers could command good prices that compensated for the risks.

The state's halfhearted attempt to control the expression of thought took its toll on the philosophes as well as other writers. Despite their prudence, few escaped seeing their works banned or confiscated, while several suffered short periods of imprisonment or long periods of exile. Claude Adrien Helvétius, a well-connected noble, for example, had great difficulty in securing permission to publish his learned utilitarian and materialistic treatise, *De l'Esprit* (1758). No sooner had it finally appeared when it was denounced by various religious and secular authorities. Despite his connections, Helvétius was obliged to make the most mortifying apology in order to avoid prosecution. Voltaire, who was brilliant at cultivating the protection of influential people, nonetheless only felt secure away from Paris at the court of Frederick the Great or on his estate at Ferney just across the Swiss border. Similarly, Diderot, who in his early days spent four months in prison as we have seen, left some of his most original manuscripts unpublished altogether. In sum, the censorship did cause the philosophes great anxiety, and occasionally intimidated them, though it was not nearly effective enough to silence them. On the contrary, harassment fed the fires of their critical zeal.

The clandestine circulation of books smuggled across the border from such places as Leiden, Neuchâtel, and Liège served the cause of philosophes such as Voltaire in the 1750's and 1760's. By the later decades of the old regime, however, the flow of "undesirable books" (as the authorities called them) greatly increased and became more volatile. Thanks to pioneering research by Robert Darnton into the records of one major Swiss publisher—the Typographical Society of Neuchâtel—the dimensions and characteristics of this illicit trade are now visible. One of Darnton's studies analyzes the transactions between the publisher and one of its clandestine dealers in France, a retailer who ordered approximately a thousand volumes of illegal books for his customers in the year 1783, in addition to a number of legal books. While the classification of these illegal titles poses certain difficulties, we can follow Darnton's categories.[11]

First, there were antireligious works—blasphemous satires, as well as serious treatises questioning the claims of organized religion under such titles as *Critical History of Jesus Christ* or *Christianity Unveiled*. These books sometimes professed an explicit atheism of the kind espoused by Baron d'Holbach in his Parisian salon, and were published anonymously in the context of a materialistic philosophy. What had once circulated in handwritten form among a narrow circle of skeptics in the 1730's now appeared publicly in the form of smuggled books from abroad. Another

---

[11] Robert Darnton, "The Trade in Taboo," in *The Widening Circle: Essays on the Circulation of Literature in Eighteenth Century Europe*, ed. by P. Korshin (Philadelphia, 1976).

type of prohibited literature was pornography. Most commonly, eighteenth-century pornography was set in the world of high-society courtesans and thus had an antiaristocratic edge; occasionally a monastic or religious setting was used to add spice. Whatever the setting, this material had no redeeming "social value," which perhaps made its appeal all the greater. Little better, in the censors' eyes, were the books designed to satisfy the public's hunger for information on the latest fads and gossip about what was going on in the fashionable drawing rooms of Paris and Versailles. Under such titles as *Scandalous Chronicles* or *The English Spy*, these newsletters pandered to curiosity about the modish and the outlandish. Certain serious books also enjoyed good sales, undoubtedly heightened by the fact that they were prohibited. These included such important works of the late Enlightenment as Sebastien Mercier's utopian tract *The Year 2400*; the same author's *Tableau of Paris*, a fascinating description of Parisian popular life; and of course Raynal's *History of the Two Indies*.

The leading type of banned literature in this clandestine dealer's inventory of 1783 was political in some fashion, though one has to stretch that rubric very far to make it apply. Most of these items were *libelles*— anonymous attacks on well-known individuals such as the king, the queen, and certain high aristocrats or government officials. Like the gutter press in the nineteenth century, the *libelle* traded in scandal and defamation. Still, it was arguably political because it drew an implicit (and occasionally explicit) indictment of France's rulers, suggesting that France had become a decadent society, and the monarchy a despotism. In Darnton's view, "by slandering eminent individuals they desecrated the whole regime"; the *libelles* were a kind of "hard-hitting underground journalism," which communicated images and allegations damaging to the regime. The image of despotism was unquestionably conveyed in sensational but more serious political tracts such as Simon Linguet's *Memoirs of the Bastille* and Count Honoré de Mirabeau's *Lettres de Cachet*, two signed works whose authors had suffered persecution firsthand. These widely read accounts attacking arbitrary imprisonment were available only in smuggled editions.

There was a curious point of agreement between the purveyors of illicit books and the authorities who tried doggedly to suppress them. Dealers and police alike lumped them all together. The publishers called them "philosophic books" (*livres philosophiques*) on their lists of offerings, while the police labeled them "undesirable books" in their reports. They certainly formed a curious amalgam: one part serious moral, religious, and political criticism for every two or three parts pornography, character assassination, and gossip. Much of the latter material was trash, and some of it, if not published anonymously, would probably have been actionable in court under the libel laws. For the booksellers, it was doubtless a marketing ploy to hide an array of scandal sheets, gossip, and pornography under the mantle of banned books by serious writers such as Raynal, d'Holbach, Rousseau, and Mercier. Yet the government played the same game, lumping them all together in its intolerance for outspokenly heterodox ideas, and trying to discredit serious criticism by equating it with *libelles* and pornography.

In the year under discussion (1783) the royal authorities in fact made an all-out effort to stop the smuggling of "undesirable books" by altering the methods under which imported books were inspected en route, methods which had been lax enough to permit complex patterns of bribery and smuggling. To a certain extent, one can sympathize with the authorities, since we now have a better idea of the mixed contents of these cartons of illicit books. In a sense the lieutenant general of police was in a position similar to that of the French Academy of Sciences. With the right, vested by royal charter, to certify what was good science and to disapprove work that did not meet its standards of judgment, the Academy sincerely believed that it was stemming the tide of charlatanism and pseudoscience. If unchecked, the latter would deluge good science and undermine its respectability and usefulness. However, figures such as Mesmer or Marat whose work was rejected did not accept such verdicts and were furious at being lumped together with cranks. To them, the Academy was a form of privilege and tyranny. The censorship could look much the same. Some of the officials involved were high-minded men who believed that the book trade should be supervised by the official guilds and controlled by the government in order to stem the tide of trash. Hack literature, they argued, pandered to the lowest public taste and debased literary standards, while subverting religion, morality, and authority. With Voltaire and other luminaries, the police despised the "literary rabble" that produced such trash. The trouble was that at one and the same time they were suppressing legitimate works of criticism whose value was widely recognized. Where, then, could the line be drawn?

That question still has no definite answer, but the censorship in eighteenth-century France was in any case fighting a losing battle. The clandestine book trade was lucrative and widespread—a smashingly successful end run around the censorship. True, many of the dealers were marginal operators who moved from one place to another often only one step ahead of their creditors, in a kind of unscrupulous, cutthroat literary underworld. But the respectable, licensed booksellers also dealt in clandestine books as a sideline to their normal business. The trade in "philosophic books"—from the treatises of the late Enlightenment to the stream of *libelles* and scandalous chronicles—could be halted temporarily by resolute measures, but it could not be stopped as long as substantial profit was to be made. There is reason to suppose that these books contributed to

264 / An Age of Enlightenment

the climate of discontent in the 1780's more perhaps than the works of the great philosophes, most of whom were dead by then. If the revolutionary mentality of 1789 had literary or cultural origins, the unsung writers who turned out trash were doubtless in the vanguard of alienated spirits, even if they turned up on all sides of the political spectrum after 1789. The nature of France's illicit book trade is also important in understanding why other countries were so adamant about censorship, and why they feared and despised the French influence even before the Revolution. French literature scandalized not only because of its radical moral philosophy and critical spirit, but because of the decadence of its hack writing.

Criticism and Repression in Other States

Despite the censorship, then, there was evidently no book that could not be obtained in France. In the privacy of their homes, "enlightened" aristocrats, officials, doctors, army officers, lawyers, merchants, and even clergymen read and discussed the century's most controversial ideas, while the French provincial academies openly disseminated the milder reformist and utilitarian attitudes of the Enlightenment. In contrast, much of the rest of Europe was intellectually torpid. Whether from the legacy of a repressive Catholic Reformation, geographical isolation, or the absence of an indigenous high culture, the educated elites of Spain, Austria, Prussia, and Russia did not experience the Enlightenment's full force. True, the rulers of these states were anxious to stimulate a measure of cultural development as a component of administrative and economic reform. Stirrings of critical intellectual activity and faint echoes of the Enlightenment can therefore be found almost everywhere. When such activity became threatening or controversial, however, the rulers were quick to cut it off. By 1789 censorship and repression were still very much the order of the day.

In Spain free thought was inhibited in two ways: by the royal government's rigorous precensorship, and by the Catholic Inquisition, which maintained an Index of Forbidden Books, foreign and domestic. Conducting its investigations in secret, the Inquisition operated through fourteen tribunals in Spain's leading cities, which relied on agents and advisors scattered about the country who reported on any activity or literature inimical to "the purity of the Catholic faith." Possession of or reading a prohibited book could bring excommunication, fines, and exile. Some writers, such as Calvin, Kepler, and Voltaire, were proscribed completely; more often individual books were banned, such as those two seminal works of the Enlightenment, Bayle's *Critical Dictionary* and Montesquieu's *Spirit of the Laws*. The Inquisition also sought to suppress heterodox Catholic theological works, all anonymous books, and pornography.

Charles III (ruled 1759–1786), whose religious policies will be discussed in the next chapter, took steps to make the Inquisition's procedures less arbitrary. He stipulated that its prohibitions had to be approved by the royal government, that the accused be given a proper hearing, and that punishments be moderated in most cases. Yet with Charles's blessing the Inquisition remained powerful and threatening. Like the censorship in France, it struck with occasional harshness in order to intimidate others. Thus in 1776, an otherwise auspicious year for liberty, the Inquisition began to investigate Pablo Olavide. This esteemed royal official happened to be an acquaintance of Voltaire's and a low-keyed admirer of French thought. As a royal intendant he had been especially effective in carrying out the monarchy's policies on religious and educational reform. If Olavide could be humbled, then no one in Spain was safe to entertain or propagate heterodox ideas. A lengthy trial was held with Charles's implicit consent, and in the end Olavide was convicted of heresy on such charges as his correspondence with Voltaire and his advocacy of Copernican ideas. Obliged to abjure his "errors," Olavide also suffered harsh punishment. His property was confiscated, he was exiled from his home, and he was forced to undergo religious indoctrination. Such a spectacular case indicated that the Inquisition could operate with harsh intolerance even under the relatively progressive reign of Charles III; under his benighted successors it would be even more formidable, as Spain tried to fend off "contagion" from France.

Yet the general history of the Inquisition in the eighteenth century also points to a different sort of conclusion. On the whole it perpetrated few such outrages, because there was very little dissent in Spain to combat in the first place. With very few exceptions, even the most progressive Spaniards mirrored Charles's moderation and were completely loyal to the Catholic Church and the existing social order. Such men were therefore permitted a certain latitude in expressing their mildly reformist views. With the king's support, for example, economic improvement associations (*Amigos del Pais*) were formed in many cities to encourage innovation in agriculture, commerce, and industry, and to found schools. Reformers could even express themselves in print, up to a point. From 1761 to 1767, for example, a Spanish periodical modeled on the *Spectator* appeared, sallying forth with mildly satirical articles critical of the idle, unproductive segments of the nobility, and the more ignorant, superstitious clergy. There followed an hiatus of several years when no periodical represented the "progressive" point of view; then in 1781 another single-essay periodical was started under the title *El Censor*. "All that departs in any way from reason hurts me," claimed its editor, who extolled the virtues of open-mindedness, while attacking his compatriots' complacent traditionalism. Without being very specific, *El Censor* was trying to extend the critical spirit south of the Pyrenees, deploring the fact that Spain's environment seemed hostile to lively, inquiring minds:

> Suppose that the wisest authors of modern times had been born in Spain; behold [they would be considered] so many impious heretics. Why? Because Dame Fortune had the whim to give us here a sense of smell so delicate that we smell these vices a hundred leagues away. . . . We discover impiety or heresy and catch it in the very place where the wisest and most pious men of other nations overlooked it.[12]

Yet even this mild irony eventually got the editor into trouble with the royal censorship. After several skirmishes he was forced to cease publication in 1787, at which time the Inquisition brought him to trial. Even before the French Revolution, Spain's flirtation with the progressive spirit was petering out.

Northern Germany had a reputation for high culture and learning in the eighteenth century, though not for the corrosive type of thought found in the French Enlightenment. There was a strong commitment to the education and moral formation (*Bildung*) of clergymen and officials, both of whom were university trained. The multiplicity of small states in the region was a blessing in cultural terms, since a number of the ruling princes were anxious to patronize gifted writers, who brought prestige to their small realms. The small duchy of Saxe-Weimar, for example, became known as a congenial environment for writers, including Johann Wolfgang von Goethe and Friedrich von Schiller.

Prussia, the largest state in the region, shared in this reputation for intellectual freedom, but it is arguable how deeply it ran. A small periodical press was free from precensorship, but its editors practiced self-censorship by refraining from any discussion of political issues. This was evidently the price that Frederick II insisted on. The intellectuals in his universities and academies could communicate without inhibition so long as they spoke only to each other; they were not permitted to create an open-ended public discourse that might challenge the status quo. Periodicals were correctly viewed as potential instruments in the formation of public opinion. The peculiar atmosphere in Prussia was scathingly depicted by the great German dramatist and critic Gotthold Lessing. About to depart from Berlin, he wrote to a friend in 1769:

> Don't talk to me about your Berlinese freedom of thought and writing. It only consists of the freedom to make as much fun as you like of religion.

[12] Quoted in Richard Herr, *The Eighteenth-Century Revolution in Spain* (Princeton, 1958), p. 186. My discussion of Spain relies heavily on this book.

. . . Let someone try to write about other things in Berlin as freely as Sonnenfels has written in Vienna; let him try to tell the gang at court the truth in the way he has done; let someone in Berlin stand up for the rights of the peasants, or protest against despotism and exploitation as they now do even in France and Denmark, and you will soon know by experience which country is to this day the most slavish in Europe.[13]

This was a doubly startling judgment, for no one would have considered Vienna as an intellectual beacon ten or twenty years earlier. On the contrary, Austria's intellectual life had been severely stifled by the Catholic Reformation. At mid-century there was scarcely a distinguished Austrian writer to be found (though a number were waiting in the wings) or any tradition of patronage for literary talent. The glimmerings of change had appeared under Maria Theresa, notably the founding of chairs in natural law and public administration at Austrian universities, and the transfer of censorship from the control of the Jesuits to a state bureau with a mixed lay and clerical membership. Like the censorship in France, however, Austria's remained an all-embracing mechanism to prohibit books deemed offensive to the true faith, good morals, or the state. Even some of the most notable German authors, such as Schiller, found their works banned —though not necessarily unread.

Under the coregency of Joseph and Maria Theresa, however, the pace of innovation accelerated, and soon Lessing could reasonably compare Vienna favorably with Berlin. For the first time, an enterprising bookseller (J. T. Trattner) created a Viennese publishing empire, ruthlessly pirating north German literature, but also offering commissions and outlets to Austrian writers. Then came the founding by Josef von Sonnenfels (1733–1817) of a new periodical, again similar to the *Spectator*. A recently ennobled and converted Jew, Sonnenfels, though something of an outsider, was held in high esteem by the two rulers who had appointed him to a university chair in public administration. In 1765 he started a weekly called *The Man Without Prejudice*, which survived for three tempestuous years. Operating at the edge of permissible criticism, Sonnenfels in fact extended that boundary as far as possible. Occasionally he was reprimanded for his daring, especially in his bolder essays on agrarian conditions. For example, using a literary convention of the period, he depicted the visit of a mystical Oriental traveler to Europe who called on Austrian peasants in their homes. This worthy visitor found that the peasants could scarcely feed their own families, let alone their guest, because their feudal obligations were excessive and their land was used unproductively. Eventually Sonnenfels was ordered to drop that line of criticism, but he soon found other

[13] Quoted in the *New Cambridge Modern History*, Vol. VIII (Cambridge, 1965), pp. 297–98.

issues such as religious toleration, judicial torture, and the death penalty. Operating from within the political establishment, Sonnenfels carefully limited his thrusts by a kind of self-censorship, and his periodical therefore survived long enough to breach the wall which traditionally separated the official elite from the general reading public.

The most fervid stage of development in Austrian intellectual life began when Joseph became sole ruler in 1780 and substantially relaxed the censorship. The number of censors dwindled to six, while the Directory of Forbidden Books shrank from about forty-five hundred titles in 1774 to about nine hundred a decade later. True, certain works of the Enlightenment, including books by Voltaire, Lessing, and Helvétius, remained among the banned titles, particularly those that seemed to attack Christianity outright; but the prohibited list also included many religious works that were deemed excessively superstitious, and pornography. Equally important, pamphleteering on public issues was now permitted with the government's blessing. As a contemporary observed, "books educate scholars, while pamphlets educate people." Hoping for support for his reforms, Joseph was initially willing to let the chips fall where they might, with the result that there was an outpouring of pamphlets. On the one hand, this stimulated serious discussion of important issues—so much so that the English ambassador to Vienna declared that freedom of debate in the capital's coffeehouses was almost as extensive as in England. On the other hand, the majority of pamphlets evidently pandered to low taste, for a great many were on trivial, modish subjects, while others were simply pornographic. Whether these pamphlets were serious or silly, Austria under Joseph was enjoying an unprecedented openness in its intellectual life.[14]

Ultimately, however, the free circulation of ideas in printed form proved to be a privilege rather than a right. As such, it could be withdrawn as suddenly as it had been granted. When Joseph encountered widespread opposition to his agrarian and church reforms, when direct criticism of his policies mounted, and when the French Revolution offered an unsettling example of disorder, Joseph reimposed censorship. Indeed, he actually exacerbated it by creating a new secret political police department to enforce it. Instead of consolidating the liberal cultural environment of the 1780's, Austria's government slipped back into its old authoritarian style in Joseph's last days. The monarchy would soon be ready to assume its place in the Holy Alliance of early nineteenth-century despots against French and English liberalism, an alliance inspired by Russia.

---

[14] See Ernst Wangermann, *The Austrian Achievement, 1700–1800* (London, 1973), chaps. 3 and 4, and Paul Bernard, *Jesuits and Jacobins: Enlightenment and Enlightened Despotism in Austria* (Urbana, Ill., 1971).

In its cultural and intellectual activity, Russia before 1760 approximated a desert. The cultural life of the nobility in Moscow and St. Petersburg was wholly imported, either German or French. Russian book publishing was virtually non-existent (fewer than twenty-five titles published annually), and the first university was founded only in 1755, staffed by German professors. Catherine II's accession in 1762, however, brought a breath of fresh air to the scene much as Joseph's would in Austria. The empress expressed a desire to nurture culture and to create "a new breed of people," a responsible body of educated opinion with forums for the discussion of new ideas. This, she hoped, would help sustain her efforts at reforming and strengthening the Russian state.[15] In an effort to coax this body of opinion into existence—to stimulate discussion of public issues and create some intellectual momentum in the provinces—she convened a Legislative Commission in 1767. With 560 delegates chosen by various constituencies, including even a handful of free peasants but few representatives of the state administration, she produced an unprecedented assemblage. In an elaborate document called "The Instruction," Catherine set forth her views about the need for legal reform, humanitarianism, and reason in public affairs; she then invited the delegates to submit their grievances and proposals. About fifteen hundred petitions and documents were drafted in response, many complaining about the neglect of the provinces and the draining of wealth from the country to the city. After much exciting discussion, nothing tangible came of this gathering, however, for Catherine grew disenchanted with the strains of such consultation. When a suitable excuse presented itself (the outbreak of war), she prorogued the Commission and never reconvened it. Even though the Legislative Commission produced no new policies, it did mark a modest step toward the growth of public opinion in Russia. As one historian has stated, it was "a legalized beginning of national self-examination."

Beyond that, Catherine supported the founding of new schools and the growth of the publishing industry, whose output during her reign grew until it reached about 350 titles a year by 1790. The empress also encouraged the birth of a periodical press, with journals (as we might expect by now) modeled on the *Spectator*. She herself contributed articles to these mildly satirical journals, which attacked the boorish ignorance of provincial life and advocated the refinement of manners.

Even more than Frederick II or Joseph II, however, Catherine's tolerance for criticism evaporated whenever she could not control it. A case in point was the prosecution of Nikolai Novikov (1744–1818), one of her most talented early protégés and a clerk at the Legislative Commission.

---

[15] See *The Eighteenth Century in Russia*, ed. by J. G. Garrad (Oxford, 1973), chaps. 1 and 6.

Under the influence of Freemasonry, Novikov had dedicated his life to good works and reformist activities, including the opening of schools for Moscow's poor. To raise money for these schools he founded a printing business, and published several journals that grew unusually independent and critical. Catherine responded by harassing him and finally threw him into jail in 1789. A similar fate befell Alexander Radishchev. His *Journey from St. Petersburg to Moscow* (1790), a pioneering work of social criticism depicting the miseries and injustices of life in the Russian countryside, was the most radical critique of serfdom to appear in print. For his pains, Catherine had him imprisoned under the harshest conditions.

The cases of Olavide, Sonnenfels, and Novikov are helpful in assessing the diffusion of the Enlightenment's critical spirit across Europe. This process required people of vision and intellect who were unwilling to accept the status quo; publishers who would print their books and articles; and a minimal freedom of expression in which to test and articulate their ideas. In Spain, Austria, and Russia, the tentative stirrings of critical thought that occurred during the later eighteenth century proved extremely fragile, and were ultimately stifled by the rulers' repressive measures. In Joseph's case this happened reluctantly, but in the end no less decisively than under the brusque dictates of Catherine or the Spanish Inquisition. What the rulers could not personally countenance or control, they were unwilling to tolerate. Only in England, the Dutch Netherlands, and France was there as yet an adequate social foundation for an independent "public opinion." Only there (despite the censorship in France) was the middle class sufficiently dynamic, and artisanal culture sufficiently advanced, to ensure that "public opinion" would extend beyond the circles of government and nobility to influence public life.

CHAPTER 8

Church and Religion

DESPITE THE PHILOSOPHES' assaults, Christianity still claimed the loyalty of most Europeans, while the established churches—Catholic, Protestant, or Eastern Orthodox—remained the most important institutions outside of government. For just that reason rulers attempted to assert authority over the churches in their domains. In some countries this was a long-standing policy while in others, especially in the Habsburg Monarchy, the process of "nationalization" was relatively abrupt and radical. The cause of religious toleration was likewise advanced by the state in several countries as a result of government's increasingly utilitarian outlook. With certain notable exceptions, however, change ought not to be the main theme in any discussion of eighteenth-century churches. The church was a conservative institution that reflected and reinforced social hierarchy, privilege, and tradition. State control over the church may have increased, but most churches themselves did not change dramatically. A sketch of the church as an institution and of the clergy as a profession in fact rounds out the earlier discussion of the old regime's social order.

A more difficult question is whether or not religious devotion itself was waning, either as a result of the rise of skepticism, or as a consequence of the churches' own ossification. The evidence is conflicting. There seems to have been a spectrum of religious mentalities within the body of Christian believers, with a worldly, moderate religious outlook at one extreme and the superstitious fervor of the popular classes at the other. Especially within Catholicism it sometimes appeared as if popular religious belief and practice thrived in disregard of the Church's official theology. Yet recent research in French history has also uncovered new evidence of a falling-off of religiosity in at least one large geographic region even before the French Revolution turned against the Church. Meanwhile, there is clear evidence that many Protestants hungered for more satisfactory ways to express their spirituality than those provided by the established churches of Germany or England. The eighteenth century witnessed a religious revival in Germany called Pietism, and a revival in England so strong as to spawn the new Protestant denomination of Methodism.

THE CHURCH AS AN INSTITUTION

Church and State in Catholic Europe

The situation of the Catholic churches changed considerably in the eighteenth century—though whether this was a renewal or decline remains an open question. At the period's start, almost everywhere in Catholic Europe (Spain, France, Italy, most of the Habsburg Monarchy, Poland, and parts of Germany) Catholicism was the only religious faith that could be exercised publicly, and its adherents the only people who could hold public office. Inquisitions in Spain and Italy suppressed all deviates, while in France and Austria Protestants had no civil rights. The papacy still wielded considerable influence; even in France, where Louis XIV had bullied and threatened the pontiff, he had usually come around to conciliating him. In the Society of Jesus, headquartered in Rome, the pope had a formidable international force, whose members were ensconced in the aforementioned countries, as well as in the Latin American colonies of Spain and Portugal, and in China. Much of the Church's wealth and personnel was to be found in the ranks of the regular clergy, the monks and nuns of the various religious orders. Spain, for example, had two thousand monasteries and one thousand convents with a total of a hundred thousand members, vast landholdings, and substantial investments. Although the rulers were usually involved in choosing bishops, the Church was either a self-governing corporation within the state (as in France), or it received considerable direction from Rome. In either case its immense wealth seemed largely beyond the direct grasp of the temporal regime, apart from contributions made by the churches voluntarily.

By the 1780's much of this had changed. Except in the Papal States, the papacy's power was markedly diminished. The Jesuits had been expelled from several major states, and then had been dissolved altogether by a reluctant Pope Clement XIV under pressure from the Catholic rulers. Monasticism had entered a period of decline, and several states (not including Spain) had attempted to force adjustments in the ways that it operated. Meanwhile, a number of Catholic governments had begun to advance the cause of toleration. All told, Catholic sovereigns were demanding more control, seeking to "nationalize" the churches within their domains. Louis XIV had already accomplished this in mastering his "Gallican" clergy. Now Charles III was moving in that direction in Spain, and, most dramatically of all, Joseph II (building on his mother's precedents) was about to launch a Habsburg revolution in church-state relations.

Spain was the most deeply Catholic (or what its critics would call the most fanatical) country outside of Italy. The Spanish Habsburg had been the standard-bearers of the Catholic Reformation, and their Bourbon successors were no less devoted to the faith. A pious Charles III (who ruled from 1759 to 1788), while promoting administrative and economic reforms to enhance the state's power, was inclined to accept the religious status quo. Yet even Charles entered the arena of church-state relations decisively. In the first place, he concluded a concordat with the papacy which gave the state essential control over appointments to the Spanish episcopate. Secondly, he insisted that royal permission would henceforth be required for the proclamation of papal bulls. In addition, he took in hand the Spanish Inquisition, an autonomous agency of censorship and repression that was responsive to Rome's direction. As we have seen, its mandate to deal with heresy was now more strictly defined, and its procedures modified to make it somewhat less arbitrary and punitive. These measures brought Spain no further than France had long since come in its control of the French Catholic church, but they nevertheless constituted a dramatic reversal of the balance of power between Rome and Madrid. Here the Spanish reforms stopped, however, since Charles III pledged to maintain and protect the church's traditions "from the odious discussion and degrading measures that have been employed in other lands." The only other change that occurred in Spain was the expulsion of the Jesuits, a fate the Society had already suffered in Portugal and France.

The Society of Jesus, that imposing arm of the Catholic Reformation, had in a sense succeeded too well. The Jesuits' overseas missionary and commercial activity in French, Spanish, and Portuguese colonies had created privileged enclaves that aroused resentment back home. Their brilliant success as educators of young lords made them appear to be allies of an aristocracy that was the main challenger to absolutist authority. Yet at the same time, individual Jesuits who were well established within the councils of government itself were perceived as rivals of other ambitious political figures. Then too, their moral theology, while well attuned to the easy-going moral atmosphere of the eighteenth century, was opposed by certain other clerics who deplored what they considered to be the Jesuits' laxity. Above all, their international network centering on Rome made them a target of the nationalizing tendencies at work within the leading Catholic states.

The first confrontation came in Portugal, a small, backward state with an enormous colonial empire in Brazil and Paraguay. Under the leadership of the ambitious statesman Sebastião Marquis de Pombal, the lethargic monarchy of Joseph I (ruled 1750–1777) was asserting its authority over the traditional power structure of high aristocrats and Catholic interests.

The Jesuits were well established among these groups and thus appeared as rivals, resisting Pombal's reforms. One of Pombal's top priorities was to increase the profitability of the empire, most of whose gold stuck to the fingers of British merchants or remained in the pockets of colonial settlers over whom the mother country had diminishing authority. Among these settlers the Jesuits formed a particularly important group. In the wake of their missionary activity, the Jesuits had established a virtually autonomous state-within-a-state in Paraguay, holding complete sway over the native Indians and the region's commerce. Pombal decided to break the Jesuit hold and he acted with remarkable force. Trumping up a charge of an assassination conspiracy against the royal house (and using certain Jesuit writings of the sixteenth century to show that the Society countenanced regicide), Pombal secured the expulsion of the Jesuits from Portugal and its colonies in 1759, and confiscated their property. No mere parochial power struggle, Pombal's attack was only the first of several blows, for the next round came in France.

Burying the Jesuits. *In this hostile allegory two figures mourn over the Jesuits' tomb: on the right,* Hypocrisy, *with its arm around the cross, a mask of piety in its lap, and a telltale snake nearby; on the left,* Murder, *with a sword and a human head under its foot—doubtless a reference to the Jesuits' alleged condoning of regicide.*

SOCIETATIS JESU CINERES ET EXUVIÆ .

In a eulogy to Louis XV, who died in 1774, Voltaire found one particular act for which to praise that unloved monarch: the suppression of the Jesuits that occurred during his reign. This cause célèbre at first glance appeared to be a triumph for the philosophes, but the Jesuits' staunchest foes had in fact come from within the Church itself and from influential political interests that had little sympathy for the philosophes. In short, the Jesuits had encountered a broad coalition of enemies.

Intrachurch conflict had begun back in the seventeenth century when the Catholic Church in France had seen a revival of Augustinianism, an austere emphasis on grace rather than merit or good works as the basis of salvation. This doctrine, soon referred to as Jansenism after one of its proponents, was opposed by Louis XIV's orthodox clergy, and in the vanguard of the attack were the Jesuits. Their efforts helped secure the bull *Unigenitus* from the Pope in 1713, which condemned one hundred allegedly Jansenist propositions. Thereafter, Jansenism became identifiable not only by its theological coloration, but by a strong hostility to papal or episcopal "despotism." Above all, Jansenists deplored the Jesuits as instruments of such tyranny, as well as advocates of a lax religious morality. The Jesuits, for their part, continued their crusade to extirpate the Jansenist heresy, in particular by obtaining a papal ruling that extreme unction could only be administered to a Catholic who had previously confessed to a priest who accepted *Unigenitus*. Proof of such a confession was to be in the form of a special certificate or bulletin of confession. Opposition to these certificates naturally became the focus of Jansenist polemics.

Now the *Parlements* entered the fray, objecting not only to the Jesuits' theology, but to the meddling of both Rome and the Jesuits in the rights of French Catholics. The *Parlements* intervened to block the issuance of bulletins of confession, and insisted that, on the contrary, no French priest could accord *Unigenitus* the authority of a rule of faith. In other words, the *Parlements*—taking up the Jansenist cause—were effectively trying to annual a papal bull, while stigmatizing the Jesuits as the papacy's principal agent in the affair. The philosophes joined the battle, since they considered the Jesuits a pillar of the clerical establishment. For a time the monarchy backed the Jesuits; then it sought (in typical fashion) to stifle the debate altogether by prohibiting any publication on the matter. None of this worked, for the *Parlements* were totally committed. Their opportunity for administering a deathblow to the Jesuits was provided by a curious case which arose from the Society's foreign commercial activities. Having amassed large debts in the colony of Martinique, a bankrupt Jesuit official was pursued in court by his creditors, who insisted on suing the entire Society of Jesus. This opened the door for judicial scrutiny of Jesuit affairs generally, and before long the hoary charge of condoning regicide was raised. But the pretexts were incidental, for by now the Jesuits had alienated too many important people. The attack was consummated in the wake of Portgual's example, and the Jesuits were expelled from France in 1763 by order of the king, their property being confiscated by the state.

Opposition to the Jesuits in Spain also reflected a power struggle within the government. In brief, the reformers who surrounded Charles III feared the Jesuits' entrenched interests, particularly their influence over the aristocratic grandees whose children they educated in their *collèges*. When violent street riots erupted in Madrid in 1766—primarily in response to rising food prices—opponents of the order mendaciously accused it of fomenting the riots in order to embarrass the government. After a long trial the following year, at which the Jesuits were accused of disloyalty, they were expelled from Spain and its colonies. The Bourbon regimes of Spain and France then pressed the attack further, demanding that the pope dissolve the Society altogether. In 1773 an extremely reluctant pope capitulated, giving dramatic indication of the new national emphasis within Catholicism and of the papacy's weakness.

Further blows to the papacy came in the Habsburg dominions, though the church reforms of Maria Theresa and Joseph II had more far-reaching objectives than merely altering the balance of power between Rome and Vienna. Again, it must be noted that both mother and son were good Catholics in their own way—the one traditionally pious and close to the clergy, the other a more "modern" Catholic, anxious to see the church operate more flexibly and effectively. Yet even for the traditional Maria Theresa, state building was an overriding preoccupation, and the church was not to be immune from its demands. In fact, it was during her reign that relations with Rome were first transformed, when she simply asserted that in any matter even remotely temporal, the state would dictate to the church. She then proceeded to try to negotiate certain financial and appointive matters with the papal curia, and when the latter proved obdurate, she proclaimed them unilaterally. These included taxation of the Austrian clergy without papal dispensation, and state control over the promulgation of papal bulls. New regulations cut down on the entry of young men and women into monastic institutions that were considered unproductive, and on the "dowries" that entering postulants could bring with them. In sum, Maria Theresa did two things: she asserted unequivocally the principle of Erastianism or state control of the church, and she instituted reforms to avail the state of the church's resources. When the Jesuits were suppressed in 1773, mother and son decided that the order's wealth should be seized and used to underwrite a state-supported system of primary education.

Upon his mother's death in 1780, Joseph II carried her policies to radical lengths, with a bold utilitarian spirit and an impatience for compromise. The linchpin of his program was the Edict on Idle Institutions, by which he unilaterally suppressed the contemplative monastic orders, closing down about seven hundred institutions out of a total of twenty-two hundred monastic houses. The number of monks in the Habsburg lands dropped from sixty-five thousand to twenty-seven thousand. Only houses that performed such social services as charity, education, or nursing were permitted to continue. The rest of the regular clergy were expected to become parish priests or teachers, or to retire on pensions. Meanwhile, the vast properties that now came under state control (amounting to one-fifth of the church's wealth) were used for benevolent purposes and to underwrite changes in church organization. Parish and diocesan lines were redrawn and new ones established where needed. Existing seminaries were suppressed and replaced by new "general seminaries" located in each provincial capital. Under direct state control, these seminaries were to insure that the Habsburg clergy pursued a modern course of study and was suitably trained to become effective public servants. Clerical salaries were modified to make them more equitable, and pluralism (the holding of more than one benefice at a time) was prohibited.[1] In his zeal to purify and modernize the church, Joseph carried his authority beyond plausible limits into the domain of daily religious practice. Irritated by the superstitious rituals and beliefs of the uneducated, he insisted that church liturgy be simplified, that pilgrimages and observances of saint's days be curtailed. Unfortunately (as we shall see later), saints, pilgrimages, and symbolic rituals—even if they seemed like hocus-pocus to the enlightened—were the heart of popular Catholic devotion, and the peasantry was bitter at this intrusion into its religious life. Consequently, Joseph was perceived at the grass roots as a meddlesome tyrant violating the true faith. This resentment rebounded against him, and helps to explain why he could not rally the peasantry to agrarian reforms that were directly in their interest.

The State of the Church in France

The traditions and abuses that Joseph attacked in Austria were to be found in the French Catholic Church as well. Having addressed the question of church-state relations in several states, we can now look more closely at the Catholic Church as an institution, using France as an example: at its wealth, organization, recruitment, and corporate identity.

The Church's wealth came from two sources: income from its extensive landholdings in the countryside, and income from the tithe. About one-tenth of France's arable land belonged to the Church, as much as 30

---

[1] Ernst Wangermann, *The Austrian Achievement, 1700–1800* (London, 1973), pp. 74–105.

percent in some northern regions. This property had come to the Church in bequests down through the centuries, and constituted in its view "an inalienable and sacred domain"—a view that the state was beginning to contest, especially since the land was exempt from taxation and was often used unproductively. As a result of its ownership of land, a monastery or cathedral was often the seigneurial lord of a peasant community, collecting rents and dues through the intermediary of agents and "farmers." In addition, the Church collected a proportion of the harvest on *all* land. The tithe averaged between 1/13 and 1/15 of the gross harvest, producing revenues of between 100 and 120 million livres annually.

The bulk of Church revenues went to the upper clergy—the bishops and the heads of monasteries, convents, and cathedral chapters, most of whom were nobles. Leading bishops enjoyed extravagant incomes, such as the Bishop of Strasbourg, with his annual income of 100,000 livres. The majority of priests, on the other hand, did not collect the tithe from the land within their parishes. Often as not, the tithe went to a monastery, cathedral, or bishopric, which paid the priests in its jurisdiction a stipend called the *portion congrue*. The "congruist" priests received only 300 livres a year until 1768, when their stipend was raised to 500 livres; in 1786 it went to 700 livres. (Their vicars or assistants received 150 livres, raised in 1786 to 350.) In some areas as many as 90 percent of the parish priests were congruists—a situation that created a double set of resentments. The priests were resentful toward the "prior-curés" who actually collected the tithe, pocketed most of it, and payed them a relative pittance. At the same time, peasants and landowners who paid the tithe were angry at seeing their money siphoned out of the parish to some distant place that had little if anything to do with their own spiritual life. Most Frenchmen were probably willing to pay a reasonable tithe, provided it went directly to support their parish church.

The distribution of church income underscores the hierarchical structure of the church, which in turn reflected the privilege and hierarchy of society at large. The same was true of the clergy's recruitment. Bishops, most abbots and abbesses who headed the monastic houses, and the heads of cathedral chapters were nominated by the crown. As in the military, with its near total separation between officers and men, clerical careers were rigidly divided between the upper and lower clergy. The aforementioned notables were generally not recruited from the rank-and-file of experienced priests, but were drawn from a distinct pool of well-connected noble families. In this way the church's resources were integrated into the system of royal patronage: lucrative positions in the church were bestowed by the king on individuals and families he wished to favor. Moreover, many of these positions were sinecures, and their aristocratic holders absentees who—to make matters worse—often accumulated several

Strasbourg Cathedral.

such positions. A parish priest, on the other hand, was obliged to reside in his parish and exercised an eminently functional role.

There was no uniform pattern for the appointment of priests. Some parishes were under the control of their bishops, but many priests—a majority in some dioceses—were nominated by cathedral chapters, the heads of monasteries, or lay patrons. The right of nomination, like so many aspects of old-regime society, reflected the crazy-quilt pattern of local variation. In addition, there was one other widely-used route to the priesthood: the practice of resignation *in favorem*. This occurred when an elderly priest decided to retire and exercised the prerogative of naming his own successor, often a nephew or cousin. In the diocese of Paris a third of the priests came to office in this way.

The road to appointment as a parish priest in France could be arduous. Basic requirements included the attainment of one's twenty-fourth birthday, an irrevocable oath of celibacy, two years of study in a seminary, and apprenticeship as a vicar. The post of parish priest was essentially permanent, but a man usually had to wait about ten years for the position. Priests rarely came from the ranks of the common people; rather they were the sons of merchants, middle-level officeholders, and well-to-do peasants. One reason for this—apart from unequal access to the necessary Latin education—was the requirement that a candidate for ordination be guaranteed an annual income of about a hundred livres by his family, which required a capital investment of about two thousand livres. This was to assure that the cleric would not be left without resources as he waited for a suitable post. In any case, contrary to a common assumption, most eighteenth-century French priests were not of peasant origin, for even the wealthy peasantry provided no more than perhaps 20 to 25 percent of the priesthood, though their share was increasing toward the end of the century. For example, in the important diocese of Reims in the 1770's, the social origins of parish curés were as follows: approximately 5 percent came from the families of nobles and rentiers; 20 percent, officeholders; 5 percent, teachers and surgeons; 33 percent, merchants; 16 percent, master artisans; and 19 percent, *laboureurs* (prosperous peasants). In the diocese of Gap, half of the families of new priests were in the upper 15 percent of local taxpayers.[2]

The parish priest had numerous functions aside from conducting religious services and administering the sacraments. He was supposed to preach submission to the laws and to the civil authorities, and was responsible for maintaining records of births, deaths, and marriages. Where the parish had a school, the priest supervised the schoolmaster if he did not actually teach himself; likewise, he was supposed to monitor the work of the parish midwife. He was expected to administer charitable contributions, using whatever meager funds his congregants provided as well as his personal funds, and to provide certificates for parishioners who left town so that they would not be arrested for vagrancy. Sometimes he was the village's spokesman to the outside world, charged with presenting protests against tax assessments and the like. While the priest associated with the prominent people of the area, he had to be on amicable terms with the common people as well.

Priests were expected to behave with propriety, avoiding taverns, gambling, or any intimation of sexual activity. They were not expected to be saintly, just proper; they were not supposed to be highly learned, but were expected to be articulate and knowledgeable about both religious and worldly matters. To this end, the Catholic hierarchy had taken pains in the late seventeenth century to raise the standards of education and moral formation in the training of the priesthood. The Enlightenment's anticlericalism was not in fact aimed at the typical parish priest but rather at the ignorant, hypocritical, or venal variety of the species and at the idle members of certain monastic orders. The *bon curé* (good parish priest), on the contrary, was considered by one and all as an asset to the

[2] Jean-Pierre Gutton, *La Sociabilité villageoise dans l'ancienne France* (Paris, 1979), chaps. 6–7, and Timothy Tackett, *Priest and Parish in Eighteenth Century France* (Princeton, N.J., 1977).

community and a man of moral stature. Nevertheless, this pillar of Catholicism had little say in the governance of his Church.

The Church in France was a self-governing corporation ruled, of course, from the top down. On the local level the Church was run by a diocesan bureau that was an oligarchy of cathedral canons and other Church notables and had few if any representatives from the ranks of the parish priests. If for no other reason, this was a grievance because of the way the clergy taxed itself. To pay its corporate expenses—notably its "free gift" to the crown paid in lieu of royal taxation—the Church taxed its own members who were otherwise tax-exempt. The diocesan bureaus carried out the assessments for this tax, with the result that parish priests were overtaxed (relative to their income), while monasteries and cathedral chapters were undertaxed. It was no wonder that some priests were beginning to complain in the 1770's about "episcopal despotism."

Inequitable distribution of resources; pluralism and absenteeism in the clergy's upper ranks; the relative penury of the parish clergy; oligarchy in Church governance; the control of vast properties by a declining monastic clergy—all this resulted in acute dysfunction. The Church's structures were ill-suited to the maximal fulfillment of its spiritual mission to the Catholic masses. Its organization groaned under the weight of privilege. These generalizations can be illustrated by taking a tour through one French city whose ecclesiastical history has been meticulously reconstructed. Angers was a fair-sized city in western France of about thirty-four thousand inhabitants and a notable Church center, where one out of every sixty adults depended directly on the Church for his or her livelihood —not counting the lawyers who battened on its litigation, or the artisans and merchants who provided it with goods and services.[3]

As the city had evolved in preceding centuries, seventeen parish churches had been established to serve it. Once established, however, a parish was almost impossible to relocate, and recent population shifts in the city had destroyed any semblance of balance among them. One parish served eleven thousand residents, mostly the poor, while others were all but deserted. Yet the priests' income did not vary according to the size of their task; the largest and neediest parishes were mong the most poorly funded.

In addition to the parish churches, there were twelve monasteries and fifteen convents in Angers, and of the latter, only three ran schools for girls. Altogether they housed one hundred monks or friars and three hundred nuns. The orders owned extensive urban properties, which Angers' middle class eyed enviously, feeling that the buildings could be put to

[3] John McManners, *French Ecclesiastical Society Under the Ancien Régime: a study of Angers in the Eighteenth Century* (Manchester, 1960).

better uses, both private and public. Most of the monastic establishments were underpopulated, since recruitment into the regular clergy had declined steeply since the seventeenth century. In the wealthiest—a Benedictine monastery—income from property totalled fifty thousand livres a year, from which the head abbot drew a salary of twenty thousand livres. The abbot held the job as a sinecure and did not reside in Angers. From this fact one can assume that the institution suffered from a lack of spiritual vitality. A few of the other monastic orders did perform a function: the Christian Brothers maintained schools, the Sisters of Charity were a nursing order, and the Oratorians ran a *collège*. Most, especially the female orders, were simply comfortable places for noble families of modest wealth to place their daughters and younger sons. Performing no useful spiritual or charitable duties, they diverted substantial wealth in the form of rents, properties, and tithes for the use of their upper-class members.

The parish churches, monasteries, and convents do not complete the picture, however, for at the summit of ecclesiastical society stood the cathedral chapter, which presided over Angers' wealthiest and most splendid church, and controlled most of the tithe in the surrounding agricultural hinterland. The thirty-odd canons who constituted the cathedral chapter had few useful functions, enjoyed substantial incomes (a minimum of three thousand livres annually), and monopolized most local sinecures as well, such as staffing private chapels and serving as confessors to the wealthy. Thus, while the parish curés were overworked and underpaid, trying desperately to minister to the spiritual and material needs of the popular classes, the cathedral canons enjoyed an exceedingly comfortable life with minimal responsibility. In part because of such maldistribution of resources and manpower, the church was unable to fulfill its educational, charitable, and spiritual roles adequately.

Little was done about this range of problems before the French Revolution opened up new options for their solution. The French Catholic Church, while significantly independent of Rome, was too powerful a corporate group to permit the kind of intervention that Joseph II initiated in Austria. Its legislative body, the Assembly of the Clergy, still held firm control over the Church's internal affairs. Its executive agents were perhaps the foremost lobbyists (to use a modern term) for a special interest group in all of France. With such corporate muscle, the Church was well positioned to head off any serious initiatives by the government. Thus, an attempt to levy the *vingtième* tax on church property in the 1750's was beaten back despite the resolute stand of the finance ministry. When a full-scale investigation of monastic wastefulness was launched by the crown, the Church's lobbying succeeded in blunting the results so that only a few hundred virtually abandoned institutions were closed or, more commonly, amalgamated with others. In short, Rome was not the principal obstacle to change. On the contrary, it was the French clergy's own corporate power that prevented the kind of reforms that Joseph had demanded in his realms. Only when the Revolution put an end to the very principle of corporate power within the state would the way be opened for such reform.

Toleration

The Enlightenment's plea for religious toleration struck a responsive chord among nonbelievers such as Frederick the Great. On simple utilitarian grounds, people of any religion who might contribute to the state's prosperity were welcomed. Frederick, it was said, "despised and tolerated" most religions equally, and continued the Hohenzollern tradition of accepting religious minorities who might augment Prussia's manpower or wealth. For devout rulers, however, the issue of toleration was more troublesome. Religion affected nothing less than eternal well-being, and for most orthodox believers there seemed only one road to salvation. Hence, it could be considered the ruler's duty to defend the claims of the one and only true religion, whatever it was. Toleration, as Maria Theresa put it, was the equivalent of indifference. Heterodox sects were a kind of poison in the state that had to be checked, if not altogether eliminated. Persecution—forced conversions, expulsions, massacres, and executions—still occurred from time to time in the age of enlightenment. In Spain and Italy, for example, Inquisitions continued to suppress all deviates—be they Protestants, freethinkers, heretical Catholics, or (in Spain) clandestine Jews; at times their proceedings ended in an auto-da-fé, the public burning of a heretic. Even as such persecution receded (the last burning took place in 1781), religious minorities continued to suffer from various disabilities almost everywhere. Voltaire had praised England for its tolerance of diverse religions, but this did not extend to according their members full civil or political rights. Dissenting Protestants were still excluded from most public posts and political rights, while English Catholics (not to mention Irish "papists") suffered an even greater degree of exclusion. Even in Amsterdam, a haven for persecuted minorities of all stripes, political rights were reserved to members of the official Dutch Reformed Church.

In the Holy Roman Empire all-out war between Protestants and Catholics had given way to a coexistence of the three major creeds: Lutheranism, Calvinism, and Catholicism. Peace had been restored in 1648 under the rule that "the prince's religion is the religion of his subjects"—which at least guaranteed the survival of each religion in Germany. On an official level, the proximity of the three major faiths produced a grudging toleration. Thus, the Habsburg Emperor, who was dedicated to eliminating

Protestantism in his own domains, routinely dealt with Protestant emissaries and even saw to it that religious balance was maintained in the imperial administrative organs and on the committees of the imperial Diet. The fate of minorities *within* Germany's various states, however, was still in question.

The major Catholic territories were the Habsburg Monarchy, Bavaria, and a number of ecclesiastical principalities such as the Archbishoprics of Mainz and Cologne. Lutheranism predominated in Saxony, Mecklenburg, Prussia, Württemberg, and many of the smaller states, each of which had its own "territorial church"—that is, a Lutheran church structured independently within the state and subject to the territory's ruler. Calvinism was primarily confined to the Palatinate and the neighboring lower Rhine region and to parts of Silesia. Problems with this arrangement had arisen in the preceding century when a ruling house changed religions, as when the Hohenzollerns converted to Calvinism in 1613, or the rulers of the Palatinate became Catholic under Louis XIV's influence. Nonetheless, the "official" religious map of Germany was more or less stable by the eighteenth century.

Theoretically, the Empire guaranteed liberty of conscience to all Germans. But this was not meant to entail freedom of public worship, a privilege that could be granted or withheld by the territorial ruler. Certain princes remained religious fanatics, persecuting and on occasion expelling religious minorities. Others, such as the Hohenzollerns, fostered peaceful coexistence—a sensible policy, since most of their subjects were Lutherans while the dynasty was Calvinist. In Austria, on the other hand, the Habsburgs were committed to religious uniformity. As Maria Theresa put it, "a fixed cult and subordination to the True Church" were fundamental to the Habsburg mission. This was a serious matter since Protestantism had taken deep root in many Habsburg lands during the Reformation. Indeed (to look ahead for a moment), when Joseph II introduced a bold new policy of toleration, he was dismayed to discover how many ostensible Catholics came out of the closet and registered as Protestants. In any case, before 1780 Maria Theresa and her predecessors had sought to promote Catholicism as actively as possible. In 1777, for example, when thousands of Moravian Catholics converted to Protestantism in a wave of religious revivalism, she attempted to reconvert them by arresting their leaders, forbidding them to meet, inducting males into the army or forced labor projects, and assigning youths to priests for indoctrination. Only under dogged criticism from Joseph and Count Kaunitz did she finally relent.

In France, smoldering anti-Protestant sentiments exploded in 1685 when Louis XIV revoked the Edict of Nantes, under which the two faiths had coexisted for almost a century. His motives were complex, but among them was the hope of attaining religious uniformity in his realm. The revocation intensified efforts at forcible conversion, which resulted in atrocities, emigration, and expulsions. Some of the more resolute Calvinists, or Huguenots, fled to Prussia, the Dutch Netherlands, England, and even America. Those who remained and resisted conversion sometimes perished in the *dragonnades* or roundups conducted by rampaging royal troops. Most Huguenots probably went "underground," secretly clinging to their religious beliefs while outwardly conforming to the state's requirements. The resentments of these "new converts" came to the surface during the War of the Spanish Succession. As France's armed forces were sent to the front, Huguenot peasants in the mountains of Languedoc (the area of southeastern France where Protestantism was strongest) launched a guerrilla war. Atrocities on both sides during this ill-fated Camisard Rebellion (1702–1705) deepened the legacy of hatred and distrust between adherents of the two faiths.

When the dust settled from this bloody episode, it was clear that the surviving Huguenot community was still substantial and diverse. It comprised not only peasants, but also an urban community of artisans, as well as prosperous and well-connected merchants and financiers. Such individuals—who might emigrate if pushed too hard—were a valuable asset to any state, and their influence served to moderate the government's hostile attitude as the eighteenth century wore on. Nevertheless, the Huguenots continued to live in a no-man's-land of de facto toleration that could give way to repression at any time. Determined to maintain their religion, they founded a seminary-in-exile at Lausanne, Switzerland in the 1730's, which assured an inflow of trained pastors who could hold the faithful together. Periodically, the Huguenots would surface by holding large public worship services, as if testing the authorities' resolve. Usually repression would result: dispersal, arrests, fines, and, in extreme cases, executions. Huguenots were still distrusted for their potentially subversive tendencies, and for their past record of flouting authority.[4]

This legacy of distrust, combined with a powerful current of religious bigotry, culminated in the Calas case—a notorious miscarriage of justice that occurred in Toulouse in 1761. When the son of Calvinist Jean Calas was found hung (in reality a depressive suicide), the father was accused of murdering his own son in order to prevent his rumored conversion to Catholicism. Not only did a credulous populace accept this astounding allegation, but the all-Catholic *Parlement* of Toulouse also adjudged Calas guilty and sentenced him to die an agonizing death on the wheel.

---

[4] See James Hood, "Protestant-Catholic Relations and the Roots of the First Popular Counterrevolutionary Movement in France," *Journal of Modern History*, Vol. XLIII (1971), pp. 245–75.

The verdict outraged enlightened opinion. Voltaire launched a successful crusade to rehabilitate Calas posthumously, denouncing the climate of fanaticism in which such barbarism could occur. In the wake of the Calas case and Voltaire's campaign, persecution more or less ceased. The Protestants had shown by several decades of tactful behavior that they no longer threatened national security. The authorities (though not the clergy or the Catholic masses) proved increasingly willing to meet the Calvinists half-way. As long as they kept a low profile, they could live in peace. This did not mean, of course, that full-scale toleration obtained. Protestants were not only barred from public worship (though they could worship quietly in private homes) and from certain professions and public offices; they also lacked civil rights. They remained, in effect, nonpersons. Specifically, their marriages were not recognized, if conducted by pastors rather than Catholic priests. Their children were therefore technically illegitimate and their wills subject to challenge in court. Around 1770 the courts began finding loopholes through which to uphold the Protestants' position and beat back challenges to their marriages and wills. In 1787 the crown finally moved to harmonize the law with such de facto recognition.[5] An edict on the rights of non-Catholics, while still barring Calvinists from public worship and from certain positions, granted them full civil rights. Baptisms and marriages performed by their pastors would henceforth be legally valid. Only the French Revolution, however, would bring full religious equality and political rights—much to the dismay of orthodox elements of the clergy, and of Catholics in the areas where Protestants were clustered.

Meanwhile, more extensive religious toleration had been granted in Austria by Joseph II in 1781. Free of Maria Theresa's inhibiting hand, Joseph could now implement his thoroughly utilitarian and liberal attitude toward religious minorities. He had long argued (in the manner of Frederick the Great) that it was to the state's advantage "to employ any persons, without distinction of religion, in purely temporal matters, allow them to own property, practice trades, be citizens if they were qualified and if this would be of advantage to the State and its industry." His Toleration Patent of 1781, like the French edict of 1787, stipulated that "the Catholic Religion alone shall continue to enjoy the prerogative of the public practice of its faith"—which is to say that the Lutherans, Calvinists, and Greek Orthodox were limited to unobtrusive worship. Apart from that reservation, equality was granted. "Non-Catholics are in future admitted under dispensation to buy houses and real property, to practice as master craftsmen, to take up academic appointments and posts

[5] David Bien, "Catholic Magistrates and Protestant Marriage in The French Enlightenment," *French Historical Studies*, Vol. XI (1962), pp. 3–23.

Toleration. *Writers and artists came to the support of Joseph II's Toleration Patent of 1781, invoking a liberal interpretation of the Christian spirit.* Engraving by J. H. Löschenkohl.

in public service, and are not to be required to take the oath in any form contrary to their religious tenets."[6]

Joseph's concept of toleration was so comprehensive that it extended to the Jews, a despised and persecuted minority in most of Europe. Though a pariah status clung to all Jews, they were in fact a diverse group, and some had won a grudging place in European society. The great majority of Jews (perhaps close to a million) were settled in Poland and Lithuania where they sought to live by biblical and rabbinic precepts. These Ashkenazic Jews were segregated from the rest of society, barred from owning land and participating in most occupations, subject to restrictions on their movements, and obliged to pay heavy and demeaning special taxes. They had no security apart from the guarantee of the prince or lord in a given area—a pledge that could be abruptly withdrawn. Their safety was doubly precarious since popular wrath might explode against them at any time. Whether out of ethnic and religious bigotry, or resentment against Jews as moneylenders and canny peddlers, the masses could "make policy" directly by attacking Jewish communities. Such episodes of systematic looting and massacre were known as pogroms. On occasion violence was stirred up by vicious propaganda, such as the "blood libels" alleging that

[6] C. A. Macartney, *The Habsburg and Hohenzollern Dynasties in the Seventeenth and Eighteenth Centuries* (New York, 1970), pp. 145–68 prints the texts of Joseph's church and religious decrees.

Jews engaged in the ritual slaughter of Christian children for their Passover ceremonies. While educated opinion tended to discount this kind of slur—Pope Clement XIII himself denounced "blood libels" in 1760—they were still credited by the popular masses. Even in England, where a small number of Jews enjoyed relative acceptance, the populace could make policy. When a bill passed Parliament in 1753 which permitted the naturalization of foreign-born Jews (specifically by allowing them to omit the phrase "on the true faith of a Christian" from the oath of allegiance), it had to be repealed in the face of popular protests. Abetted by financial interests wary of Jewish competitors, the protests were in the main products of bigotry.

Jews had become moneylenders in the Middle Ages since Catholics were theoretically prohibited from practicing usury, though in fact lending at interest was widely practiced among them. Jews were also peddlers, traders in imported good, and bankers of a sort. Some of the more successful businessmen had their roots among the educated and assimilated Sephardic Jews, families expelled from Spain in the fifteenth century who had settled in such places as Amsterdam, Venice, London, Bordeaux, and Frankfurt. Their international contacts gave them the same type of advantage enjoyed by the circles of Protestant merchants and bankers who operated out of Geneva and Amsterdam. These contacts made possible the rise of the "court Jews" in central Europe—Jews who had risen out of ghettos through their invaluable service to the princes in raising credit for the state, supplying its armies, and making profitable investments for the rulers. All in all, the position of the Jews in eighteenth-century Europe was anomalous. While a few performed important services at the pinnacle of the public sector, their religion set all Jews apart, and this religious separateness engendered social resentment. The successful urban businessmen were as easily reviled for their wealth as the impoverished rural majority were despised for their wretchedness.

A number of enlightened individuals proposed that Jews be accepted by society despite their differentness. From John Locke's *Letter Concerning Toleration* (1689) to Lessing's *Nathan the Wise* (1779), the argument was made that pagans, Jews, and Moslems were all equally human and worthy of citizenship regardless of their religion. On the other hand, certain leading philosophes were extremely hostile to the Jews, for various reasons. To Voltaire and d'Holbach they made a good target in the crusade against organized religion. Their superstitious and exotic customs, as well as the more dubious aspects of their biblical history, made the Jews fair (or unfair) game for their pens. No doubt both proponents and antagonists of the Jews saw the solution to the Jewish problem as the eventual assimilation of Jews into the mainstream of society. To good Christians that would ultimately have to include their conversion to

Religious persecution in the Habsburg Monarchy and Italy. *In 1745 an estimated seventy thousand Jews were expelled from Prague, presumably to appease anti-Semitic sentiment. Christian heretics continued to be burned at the stake in the eighteenth century by Inquisitions in Spain, Portugal, the Kingdom of Naples, and other Italian states. The engraving below shows an auto-da-fé in Palermo in 1724.*

Christianity. While certain upper-class Jews did convert, most Jews would not have welcomed liberation on such terms.

Joseph II's utilitarian Jewish policy steered something of a middle course between simple toleration and pressure to assimilate. "It is our purpose to make the Jews more useful and serviceable to the State, principally by according their children better instruction and enlightenment, and by employing them in the sciences, arts, and handicrafts." His Jewish decrees did not grant the Jews the same measure of equality that Protestants and Orthodox received, for certain restrictions remained. But they were granted more freedom of movement, the opportunity to engage in various trades, access to education, and (under certain circumstances) to public office. Customary disabilities such as the obligation to wear beards, being prohibited from appearing out-of-doors before noon on Sundays, or paying double fees for any judicial transaction were eliminated. Jews were encouraged to establish factories, to attend German schools, or, alternatively, to set up their own schools where German would be taught. Restrictions remained on their right to own land, to settle in Vienna and certain other areas, to acquire guild masterships, and of course, to worship in public. While still treating them as a distinct group, Joseph was encouraging them to enter the mainstream of Austrian life. He sought to liberate them not only from the state's most blatant restrictions, but from the self-imposed apartness that made them a suspect people. Accordingly, he also reduced the authority of the Jewish communities to regulate their own affairs, ordered Jewish children to learn German, and, characteristically, subjected Jews to the possibility of military service.

The French monarchy was considering similar moves when the Revolution took the matter out of its hands. Subsequently, the National Assembly successfully fought off an anti-Jewish coalition of conservative clergy and deputies from Alsace, where the main body of French Jews lived. This anti-Jewish block sought to exclude what they regarded as an alien and parasitic people from citizenship in the new nation. Instead, the Jews were granted virtually full civic and political rights. The reformers hoped that, once liberated from exclusion and persecution, the Jews would gradually alter their behavior, enter more edifying occupations, learn French and French values, and throw off the authority of the rabbis. That would happen eventually, but only over several generations. In any case the number of Jews in Austria or France was small compared to the masses who now lived under Russian jurisdiction after the partition of Poland in 1772. For these ghettoized, impoverished, and orthodox Jews, the debates in Paris, London, or Vienna had scant import.

RELIGIOSITY

Catholic Popular Piety

Having discussed church-state relations, the church as an institution, the clergy as a career, and policies toward religious minorities, we may now turn to the central issue of the people's religious attitudes and behavior. By most (but not all) evidence, the populace of Catholic Europe was devoutly religious. Even those whose faith was weak displayed their adherence at certain moments: the baptism of an infant, a Christian death and burial, and the annual outing to church for Easter Communion. The latter was considered the crucial contemporary occasion for measuring religious identification, and it is estimated that about 90 or even 95 percent of the people attended church on Easter Sunday. How many were weekly churchgoers, on the other hand, we do not really know. In the countryside, at least, the church was often the principal center of village life, the only tangible form of community available. Village hierarchies and rivalries might be reflected in the parish's lay vestry, selection to which was a local honor. The vestry had control over pew assignments, burial plots, certain charitable appeals and relilgious festivals, as well as collections and expenditures for church upkeep. The church building itself, as well as the adjoining cemetery, were unofficial gathering places for the exchange of news and views, while the church's bell was the village tocsin used not only for religious purposes, but for emergencies or notable events.

In the towns, Catholics expressed their religious faith not only by attending their parish church, but by joining confraternities, lay organizations devoted to piety and good works. Some were simply adjuncts of the parish church itself, organized and directed by the priest or by a nearby religious order. This was particularly true of women's groups, such as the Confraternity of the Rosary. Men tended to form their own autonomous groups, sometimes organized along class or craft lines, in which case membership might carry a certain social prestige. Confraternities usually centered around the veneration of a particular patron saint, and the members' proudest moment came when they marched together wearing their special robes in various religious processions. Also acting as burial societies, confraternities guaranteed their members an impressive funeral as well as remembrance afterwards. Generally the confraternities established their own chapels and hired their own chaplains. On occasion their brief services could rival rather than complement observances at the parish church. A priest in the diocese of Gap complained that "while the Penitents' chapel is filled with people, all hurrying to sing a few psalms and hear a low mass, the principal parish church is deserted."

In town and country alike, popular Catholic devotion was selective. The invaluable diary of a country priest in the impoverished parish of Sennely-en-Sologne, for example, complained of the selective and "undisciplined" faith of his devout parishoners. They were good about attending mass and responded well to the sacrament of the Eucharist, the central mystery of the Catholic liturgy, but they were extremely resistant to confession, seeming to fear or hate the confessional. Unwilling to take it seriously, they tried to fool themselves and the priest, when they did not avoid confession altogether. Also, while the faithful observed Lent scrupulously in Sennely, and were eager to give alms to the poor despite their own squalid condition, they talked and joked during church services. The testimony of Sennely's curé is supported by another remarkable eyewitness account: the chronicle of local events kept by a pious Lille textile artisan named Pierre Chavatte in the late seventeenth century. Both documents indicate that the Catholic populace preferred collective and symbolic forms of religious devotion which were marginal to official Catholic doctrine, and that it was extremely superstitious.[7] For one thing, French Catholics were fervent devotees of the cult of the Virgin Mary. While supported by some segments of the clergy (especially in Spain, Poland, and Italy), emphasis on this aspect of the faith was not considered wholesome by most elements of the Church hierarchy in France. As the bishop in charge of Lille wrote, supporters of the cult of the Virgin "try to persuade the people that the Holy Virgin will save from hell at the last minute those whose sins have already destined them to that fate." To the bishop, emphasis on the Virgin was merely playing on popular credulity. Yet, as Chavatte noted, "the whole city" rejected these admonitions and rallied to the support of the monks who backed the cult.

The cult of the Virgin was but one aspect of an enthusiastic, externalized style of worship that involved an intense devotion to saints, images, and relics. Each parish, each guild, each confraternity had its patron saint, who was repeatedly importuned to intervene against various kinds of afflictions. (For this practical reason, the groups were not above shifting their loyalty to another patron saint should the first one's interventions prove consistently ineffective.) Popular devotion to images and relics often went too far in the clergy's opinion. The bishop of Lille and the parish priest at Sennely both maintained that popular religion involved "a thousand superstitions." As the latter put it, his parishoners "are more superstitious than devout. . . . they sometimes appear as baptized idolators." Many of their superstitions seemed decidedly pagan and could find scant support in Catholic theology. For reasons best known to themselves, Senneley's peasants avoided weddings on Wednesdays, and hoped to avoid giving birth on Fridays. When they died, they tried to depart in a certain position to make it more difficult for the devil to secure their souls. They

[7] See Gérard Bouchard, *Le Village immobile: Sennely-en-Sologne au XVIIIe siècle* (Paris, 1973), and Alain Lottin, *Chavatte, ouvrier lillois: un contemporain de Louis XIV* (Paris, 1979).

thought that ringing the church bells could ward off evil, and since they still believed in witchcraft (though the judiciary had quietly ceased prosecuting such alleged offenses), the congregants at Sennely tolled the church bell through the night on St. John's Eve, the favored witching time in popular belief. The Catholic populace saw the hand of God—or of Satan and his evil minions—everywhere. On the one hand, this bred a kind of fatalism in the face of general or personal disasters, as reflected in Chavatte's chronicle. On the other hand, it made people alert to the presumed portents of evil in the stars or elsewhere, and heightened their reliance on the saving power of the Virgin Mary or their patron saint. This freewheeling, earthy, superstitious religiosity can be seen as a form of "baptized idolatry", and it certainly created a gap between the popular masses and more learned, moderate Catholics. Among the latter, there was a desire to curb excessive and allegedly "indecent" behavior in order to make Catholicism more reasonable, respectable, and orderly.

Popular religion was also recreational, however, and as such did not lend itself to the quest for decorum. The people were most enthusiastic about processions in which they could participate, especially pilgrimages to consecrated places. These events (as we have seen earlier) were usually

The hub of village life. *This engraving reflects the central place of the parish church in the communal life of rural Europe. Religious and harvest festivals were the social high points of the year, but all year round the cemetery could serve as a village green.*

mixtures of the sacred and profane: the adoration of a relic combined with a picnic, dancing, and drinking. Naturally the clergy looked askance at this, for they wished to purify religious observances. For the inhabitants of a desolate place like Sennely, such outings were the very essence of religious life.

In sum, then, saints, pilgrimages, and processions were the chief focus of popular Catholic religiosity, and were consistent with its superstitious and "practical" qualities. These externalized and collective practices were not necessarily antithetical to official Catholic doctrine, but neither did they coincide with the learned clergy's sense of order and propriety. Still, the Catholic Church was flexible enough to accommodate more than one religious style, and to offer a range of rituals and observances that could satisfy its more "superstitious" as well as its more moderate adherents. The established Protestant churches, on the other hand, were less adaptable in this regard.

The evidence for popular Catholic piety is thus very strong. Yet one must also be prepared to see massive hostility to the church during and after the French Revolution. The question is: was such widespread anti-Catholic sentiment born abruptly with the Revolution (as has generally been assumed), or did the old regime already witness a quiet decline of religiosity at the grass-roots that prepared the way for the great cleavage in French society after 1789? Some ingenious research by a French scholar, Michel Vovelle, supports the second hypothesis.[8] Vovelle has found a method for measuring the pattern of religious belief, and he has concluded that by the end of the old regime, France had already experienced a decline in religiosity. His sources are the last wills and testaments drawn up during the eighteenth century in Provence, a large region of southern France. In the first half of the century, he discovered, most wills in Provence provided for elaborate "baroque" funeral services for the testator when he or she died—a form of religious commemoration that signified an intense Catholic view of death and strategy for meeting it. "Baroque" funeral arrangements included the following: invocations in the will to the Virgin Mary, the Holy Ghost, and various saints; itineraries for the funeral procession, including arrangements for paupers to follow the bier and be rewarded with alms; legacies for religious orders, confraternities, and charities; the designation of clerics and nuns to participate in the funeral; and most important of all, the provision of funds for the saying of masses in honor of the deceased, usually specifying a large number of such masses.

All of this changed in the period from 1760 to 1790. The language of

---

[8] Michel Vovelle, *Piété baroque et déchristianisation en Provence au XVIIIᵉ siècle* (Paris, 1973).

wills became almost entirely secular, the number of legacies to religious groups diminished, and the involvement of religious confraternities in funerals declined. Public funeral processions fell off markedly, as did the number of clergy requested for the testator's entourage. Above all, the number of people requesting masses to be said for them after death declined to well below 50 percent, as opposed to the earlier figure of at least 80 percent. Moreover, those desiring masses asked for far fewer than used to be customary. Probing his figures further, Vovelle determined that middle-class merchants and professionals had substantially abandoned "baroque Catholicism" (from 80 percent down to 40 percent). In Provence's medium- and large-sized cities, artisans and shopkeepers had done so in similar proportions, while in Marseilles, the urban wage earners appear to have become almost completely secularized. Even in peasant communities this change was occurring. In one small town outside of Marseilles, where the bulk of the population of twenty-five hundred were peasants, 80 percent of all testators had requested masses in the 1700's; 100 percent did so in the 1750's (the height of baroque Catholicism in the whole region); but by the 1780's, the number had plummeted to 30 percent. In general, it seems, the more urbanized and market-oriented the location, the greater the "dechristianization." Finally, it appears that women remained more loyal to past religious practices than men, and nobles more than non-nobles. Interpreting these statistics is of course another matter. It could be argued that the decline in external practices signified an interiorization of religiosity, in place of ostentatious outward displays. But Catholicism was a religious system enmeshed in ritual, formal practices, institutions, and symbols. It seems likely that a secular outlook was gaining ground even before the French Revolution—at least in Provence.

Protestant Revivals: Pietism and Methodism

The impulse of Protestants to seek salvation on their own terms has frequently spawned new movements at the fringes of established denominations. This was true in two of Protestantism's eighteenth-century strongholds, Anglican England and Lutheran Germany, where Protestantism had passed its inspirational stage and was leaving many of its adherents dissatisfied.

In the numerous Protestant states of Germany, the princes not only determined the religion of their subjects but directed the temporal affairs of the established church. The clergy was an arm of the territorial state, and ministers were expected to serve as sources of local information and to preach submission to the laws. This connection with the state perhaps lent prestige to the profession for the men of relatively low social origins who sought out clerical careers. The church was a channel of upward mobility and dignity, but for that very reason it was an overcrowded profession in which conditions were hard. Clerics often had to wait decades in the lowly post of schoolteacher or tutor to a wealthy family until a parish became available, and then their appointment depended on the patronage of wealthy landowners, who enjoyed the right to nominate local ministers. Even when he secured an appointment, the pay was low and he was often obliged to supplement his salary by farming or teaching. As the great German intellectual Herder, himself a clergyman, acidly put it: "A minister is only entitled to exist now under state control and by authority of the prince as a moral teacher, a farmer, a list-maker, and a secret agent of police." Intellectually, Lutheranism had cohered around a rigid, formalistic theology in which future ministers were instructed at the universities. While the clergy had a deserved reputation for culture and learning, their theological disputations were remote from the spiritual concerns of the average worshiper. The ground was ripe for the development of a more appealing form of religion.

In the late seventeenth century a number of German clerics began to advocate a more intense personal devotion to God, a narrowing of the gap between clergy and laity, and the active practice of charity. Putting spiritual values at the center of existence—rather than relegating them to formal expression on Sunday mornings—they sought to turn religion into "a transforming way of life" by undertaking missionary work and organizing prayer meetings. Several decades later this movement, known as Pietism, intensified under the influence of Count Nikolaus Ludwig von Zinzendorf (1700–1760) who turned his estate of Herrnhut over to a sect called the Moravian Brethren. Zinzendorf's mystical brand of religion clashed with the rationalistic approach of the orthodox clergy. "He who wishes to comprehend God with his mind," declared Zinzendorf, "becomes an atheist." Pietism, in other words, was an emotional approach to religion that cultivated a simple faith in God by means of intense introspection. To prevent the individual from being carried away by his personal sense of God, however, the Moravian Brethren imposed upon themselves a collective discipline similar to monasticism.

Where the Brethren exemplified a mystical and separatist form of Pietism, a more widespread variant did not advocate separation from church and society, but sought to penetrate both with an idealistic Christian spirit, especially with good works, which were deemed the foremost expression of inner faith. This was the Pietist spirit that dominated the University of Halle, and was important in the civic culture of certain smaller German states. In Württemberg, for example, Pietist influence reinforced a traditional constitutionalism that stood in opposition to the occasional absolutist tendencies of the ruling dukes. Pietism taught that religion was relevant to public as well as private morality, that an ethical

Christian life involved civic idealism as well as charity. The emotionalism, individualism, and activism of the Pietist movement proved a multifaceted stimulus to German religious, cultural, and public ilfe. Pietism stoked the fires of religious faith that might otherwise have cooled within the confines of orthodox Lutheranism. Moreover, in a highly fragmented Germany, Pietism cut across political borders in a manner that inadvertently made it a carrier of nationalist sentiment.

English Protestantism, meanwhile, seemed to be in the same doldrums as Lutheranism. After the upheavals of the seventeenth century, in which religious conflict tore at the fabric of English society, religious calm prevailed and the Church of England enjoyed uncontested supremacy. Catholicism and Protestant Dissent had both been routed by an established church that was internally unified as it had not been before. This supremacy, however, soon lapsed into complacency. Anglican doctrine was now "latitudinarian"—easy-going and admirably accommodating, but also lacking in vitality. It was now so easy to be a good Anglican! Services were dignified, rituals undemanding, and spirituality subdued. All this was "reasonable" in the way John Locke had hoped Christianity might become, but it had little appeal to those men and women who still felt deep spiritual hunger.

Social respectability seemed to be the Church of England's strongpoint in the eighteenth century. Local rectors were under the patronage of wealthy individuals and reflected the latter's social prejudices, generally holding the populace in contempt. For their part, the common people seemed to regard the clergy with an unfriendly mockery. Positions in the clergy's lower ranks were socially respectable but financially unrewarding: over half of the parishes paid their rectors less than £50 a year. Hence the lower ranks attracted many of mediocre talent, while the more ambitious and well-connected clergymen sought multiple positions, thus creating a serious problem of pluralism and absenteeism. At the church's summit were twenty-six bishops whose appointments by the crown were heavily political. The bishops sat by right in the House of Lords and the crown required loyal party men in these posts. Their loyalty was cemented by the practice of rewarding faithful bishops with appointments to better dioceses (the values of which ranged from £400 to £7,000 annually, thus giving great latitude for such manipulation). As that devout Anglican Samuel Johnson was forced to admit, an Anglican cleric "could not be made a bishop for his learning and piety; his only chance for promotion is his being connected with somebody who has parliamentary interests."

Meanwhile the Dissenters—the Puritans of old, as well as Quakers and Baptists—had passed into a relatively tranquil period. Enjoying toleration for their form of worship, but excluded from full civil rights, most government posts, and admission to Oxford and Cambridge, some turned to arguing with each other over fine points of doctrine. Others grew increasingly liberal, turned their attention to matters of education at the excellent academies that they founded, and—at the extreme liberal fringe—embraced the splinter sect of Unitarianism that was not far removed from deism. Deism was making even greater inroads among educated Anglicans, and indeed, represented a challenge to organized Christianity everywhere. All in all, the English churches seemed uninspiring, entangled in class prejudice and political preferment, and out of contact with the populace. Especially in developing areas of textile manufacturing and mining, where the Church of England did not keep up with population shifts, England seemed ripe for secularization. Yet instead of abandoning religion, many English men and women responded enthusiastically to the revivalism of Wesley.

John Wesley (1703–1791) came from a clerical family that took its Anglican religion with uncommon seriousness. In fact, his ascetic intensity as a theology student at Oxford made him something of a laughingstock among his fellow students. After an ill-fated missionary venture to Georgia, Wesley returned to London and suffered a prolonged religious crisis, a despairing sense of unworthiness and sinfulness. With the spiritual guidance of a Moravian Pietist from Germany he weathered the crisis by undergoing a mystical experience. In his own words: "I felt I did trust in Christ alone for salvation; and an assurance was given me, that He had taken away my sins, even mine, and saved me from the law of sin and death. I felt my heart strangely warmed." Wesley experienced a feeling of direct contact with God, the gift of God's grace, and a consequent sense of salvation. This type of religious experience was scarcely congenial to Anglican practice, which had come to depend on formal rituals to assure salvation. Indeed ,the church vehemently criticized religious "enthusiasm" as a form of superstition. Though he remained within the Church of England that had ordained him, Wesley's enthusiasm could not be contained. His sense of personal, inner transformation by the direct experience of God's grace led him to take up an evangelical mission. An evangelist feels that something special has happened to him, and he hopes that, with his encouragement, it will happen to others. This was all the more urgent for Wesley, since he believed in the possibility of salvation for everyone. Unlike the Calvinist Puritans, who believed in grace by predestination for the "elect" only, Wesley subscribed to the Arminian tradition (named after a seventeenth-century Dutch theologian). "The glad tidings of salvation" could be universal. Everyone who wished to believe in God's grace and to prepare himself to receive it could be saved. Wesley set out to stimulate and encourage the mystical experience that would open sinners to God's grace.

Wesley preaching. *While the Methodist movement was aimed principally at working people who had grown alienated from the Church of England, it also appealed to "respectable" members of the middle classes. When the circumstances allowed it, Wesley preferred to segregate the sexes, as in this unusual two-tiered meetinghouse in Nottingham.*

Since the common people were not coming into the churches, Wesley brought the gospel to the people. In an almost unprecedented fashion (for one or two others had already tried it), he took to preaching in open fields, seeking out especially those usually ignored by the church, such as coal miners, weavers, and artisans. He sought (as he put it) "to lower religion to the level of the lowest people's capacities." In his preaching strategy and in his Arminian theology, Wesley was an egalitarian and as such evoked an enthusiastic response. After inspiring and rousing his listeners to a high pitch, helping them to "feel" God's grace, Wesley worked to harness their enthusiasm by organizing them into Methodist societies or classes, as they came to be called. At their meetings the members could watch over each other's morals and faith, and promote the upright behavior and good works that Wesley considered the final step in ensuring salvation. These groups functioned on a spiritual plane like small monastic cells, except that their members lived their everyday lives in the regular world. This activist, communal brand of religiosity evidently fulfilled deep spiritual needs in his followers. The Methodist societies gave people a sense of participation and responsibility. They also promoted the virtues of frugality, sobriety, and hard work that in fact helped many adherents acquire the self-discipline necessary for successful lives. The movement also gave people low on the social scale a sense of personal worth and dignity. In the bosom of their societies, Methodists not only prayed together and sang stirring hymns, but regarded themselves as "brothers" and "sisters."

While spiritually egalitarian, Wesley was extremely conservative on questions of social order and politics. He was accordingly intent on establishing authority over this movement. Instead of depending on a specially trained clergy to preach in the Methodist societies or chapels, Wesley and his assistants nominated lay preachers from among the chapel members. These preachers were rotated from chapel to chapel so they would be free of the local politics that tended to embroil ministers with their congregants. Instead, they followed circuits of chapels and remained under the control of a central supervisory council, the Central Methodist Conference, which was headed by Wesley himself until his death. This organizational stratagem gave the Conference ultimate control over the chapels. It also allowed the movement to spread quickly to places where people were most responsive.[9]

Wesley intended his activities to remain under the umbrella of Anglicanism, though his theology was unorthodox, and his organizing activities disruptive of the Church's established leadership. The issue of ordaining new ministers, however, ultimately caused a complete schism, and Methodism passed from being a "connection" to a full-fledged, autonomous denomination in 1791, after Wesley's death. At the same time, however, certain Anglicans bestirred themselves to recapture some of the ground that had been lost to Methodism. Launching a mildly evangelical revival of their own within the Anglican church, they proselytized the poor, established charity schools, encouraged Sabbath observance and temperance, and in some cases espoused antislavery.

The qualities that Methodism apparently promoted—a sense of belonging, of worthiness, of dedication—are qualities often found in modern revolutionary movements. It has been argued by the historian Elie Halévy that, as forged in Wesley's vision, Methodism indeed functioned as a "quiet revolution" in the lives of tens of thousands of English common people. Without resort to radical economic or political doctrines (for Wesley was a thoroughgoing Tory), Methodism effectively promoted a sense of spiritual equality and fraternity. Having satisfied that inner need, Halévy argues, Methodism may therefore have been a major reason why England did not experience a violent social or political upheaval during Europe's revolutionary era of the 1790's. While this theory is by no means universally accepted, there is no doubt that Methodism was a remarkably successful evangelical movement, and a sure sign that Christianity was still a vital force in the late eighteenth century.

[9] See Bernard Semmel, The Methodist Revolution (New York, 1973).

CHAPTER 9

The Road to Revolution

EUROPE'S UPPER CLASSES—its nobilities, landed gentries, and urban patriciates—shared power uneasily with kings and princes in the eighteenth century, but on the whole enjoyed an extended period of stability until the 1770's. In almost every state, the "political nation," those involved in government and its spoils, was extremely narrow. Aristocracies and oligarchies usually exerted their influence through constituted bodies: self-perpetuating or cooptive assemblies, diets, councils, and estates, sanctioned by long usage or written charters. Other citizens, no matter how reasonable their claims or serious their grievances, could not breach the walls of these institutions. They were simply excluded from any legitimate voice in public affairs. Pressure against this exclusion began to mount in the 1770's, producing cracks of various kinds in the old regime's facade. These movements revealed the inadequacies of Europe's political and social institutions almost everywhere, but nowhere were the pressures on the traditional framework of government stronger than in France. While the old order defended itself successfully against eruptions in England, the Low Countries, Poland and elsewhere—if need be by foreign military intervention—the crisis in France would prove impossible to contain.

CRACKS IN THE OLD ORDER
The Pugachev Rebellion
In a chapter that will deal primarily with forward-looking movements of reform and revolution, we must, to do justice to the events that shook Europe in the 1770's and 1780's, begin on an entirely different note. For the old order was also threatened, as it had been perennially, by peasant revolts. These violent uprisings or "furies" usually sought to undo some immediate burden or to restore an imagined golden age. Major revolts

had erupted in medieval England, in Germany at the time of the Reformation, and in several regions of France during the seventeenth century. If England, Germany, and France were essentially free of such jacqueries in the eighteenth century, that was not the case everywhere. In 1775 peasant rebellion struck Bohemia, for example, where Maria Theresa's government had been exploring the possibility of agrarian reform in the 1770's without implementing a satisfactory plan. Thousands of exasperated Bohemian peasants, claiming that a royal decree freeing them of labor services had been suppressed by the seigneurs—a common tactic of peasant rebels—rose in arms, fighting and plundering their way toward the capital of Prague. An army of no less than forty thousand men was mustered to stop them. Yet on the advice of the coregent, Joseph II, the ensuing repression was relatively lenient. On the contrary, plans for agrarian reform continued, and, as we have seen, were decisively set in motion by Joseph after he took the throne in 1780.

The Bohemian peasant revolt, however, was far less of a shock to the old order than the Pugachev rebellion in Russia that had been crushed a year earlier. On the surface, Russian society might have appeared fairly simple in its "backwardness": a tsarist autocracy allied with a nobility that controlled land and serfs. This picture was accurate but incomplete, since it reflected conditions only in the central dominions of Muscovite Russia, without conveying the ethnic and social diversity of the frontier areas to the east and south. In fact, the government wished to reduce these differences and forcibly integrate the various groups living in the distant provinces. Pugachev's rebellion originated as a reaction to these assimilationist policies on the frontier. It soon spread to the core provinces of the Volga Valley, however, where it ignited a bloody peasant war against the traditional oppression of lords and state.

The southeastern frontier region of the Volga Valley had been settled recently by free peasants—mainly escaped serfs and ex-soldiers—who had become homesteaders. Gradually Russian nobles began to acquire this land and assert control over the homesteading settlers, obliging them to perform the labor services they so detested and had sought to flee. Further south was another discontented group, the Cossacks. Tribal warriors who had voluntarily served the Russian state in its battles against the Turks, the Cossacks were an independent people who traditionally chose their own leaders, called elders. Tsarist autocracy was intent on eliminating this independence and absorbing the Cossacks into the Russian Empire's regular military establishment. The government took to bribing the Cossack elders, effectively transforming them into tsarist officials. The government also began to curb traditional Cossack privileges (such as fishing rights), levied new taxes on them (such as a salt tax), and introduced conscription. When Cossacks tried to object, they were punished with whippings and executions, which of course stoked the fires of resentment. To most Cossacks tsardom was no longer a legitimate authority but an oppressive tyranny.

The same resentment against Russian autocracy was growing among nomadic tribes in the south, for the government was seeking to assimilate these non-Russians as well. Muslim Tatars and pagan tribes were pressured to convert to Russian Orthodox Christianity, while new taxes were levied on them. In order to appropriate the vast tracts of land on which they grazed their cattle and lived their traditional wandering life, the government also sought to convert them from nomads into sedentary agriculturalists. As with the Cossacks, this plan was pursued in part by bribing their chiefs with money and other favors. To help control, tax, and eventually assimilate Cossacks and Tatar tribes, Empress Anna ordered the construction of a new city. The frontier capital of Orenburg rose in their midst, a tangible symbol of tsardom's intrusion and a focal point of their hostility.

To the north lay yet another area of potential unrest. For in the midst of agrarian Russia, a large industrial region of mines and factories had developed in the Ural Mountains, employing a labor force of about two hundred thousand workers by 1770. Most of the workers were serfs of some kind, conscripted as forced labor; some were peasants owned by the state, who were sent to the factories during lulls in the harvest cycle. Forced to live away from their families in harsh conditions for many months of the year, they wished simply to return to their homes. Other workers actually "belonged" to the factories, which were owned either by the state or by private entrepreneurs.[1]

Emelyan Pugachev was the obscure and unlikely leader of a movement that shook Russia to its foundations. An almost illiterate Cossack with a shady past that included desertion from the army, he nursed a burning resentment against the noble officers who had humiliated him during his military service. In 1773 Pugachev moved among the Cossacks claiming to be Tsar Peter III. The ruler of Russia briefly in 1762, Peter had been dethroned by his ambitious wife and successor Catherine II. During his truncated reign he had toyed with reforms for certain categories of state serfs and religious dissenters, and had created a mood of expectancy, in which many peasants believed that real emancipation would follow. Cut short by his death, these hopes still remained, causing unrest in the Moscow district in which thirty landlords were slain between 1764 and 1769, and feeding the myth of a "redeemer tsar." This enduring motif of Russian popular culture held out the hope that a benevolent tsar would appear

---

[1] Marc Raeff, "Pugachev's Rebellion," in *Preconditions of Revolution in Early-Modern Europe*, ed. by R. Forster and J. Greene (Baltimore, 1970).

304 / The Road to Revolution

one day to liberate his people from oppression. In popular mythology the "redeemer tsar" was portrayed as a martyr—killed or driven out by the mighty because of his love for his people—who would one day be resurrected or return from exile to save them. How deeply Pugachev's claim was believed we cannot say, but masses of the discontented rallied to his banner: Cossacks, nomads, religious dissenters who had been persecuted, homesteaders who were being reduced to serfdom. His first target was the hated provincial capital of Orenburg. Despite the rebels' failure to take the city, the countryside fell under Pugachev's control from the Urals to the Volga, as he attempted to improvise "a popular tsardom with extensive local autonomy."

Back in St. Petersburg an enraged Catherine considered Pugachev an ignorant barbarian who would destroy the foundations of civilization in Russia if he were not crushed. The full-sized army she sent against him chased Pugachev up and down the country but did not at first succeed in capturing him. On the contrary, the rebellion widened, spreading to the Urals where many industrial serfs took the opportunity to flee, and where Pugachev's men could find more weapons. The rebels then headed toward the provincial city of Kazan, which they occupied for a few days and sacked. Moving on from Kazan, Pugachev proclaimed the suspension of taxes and conscription, rallying peasants to his cause.

No prior popular uprising had ever reached as far as Moscow and neither would Pugachev's. Instead his plan was to head south, igniting the Volga Valley in his wake, and if necessary, seeking safety amongst the Cossacks where he had begun. In fact Pugachev's "withdrawal" was the rebellion's high point. For the first time in the course of the rebellion, peasants from private estates formed the bulk of his supporters, and they turned on their lords with unprecedented fury. In an attempt to consolidate his support, Pugachev issued a manifesto in July 1774 placing all peasants under the protection of his "state" and pledging them freedom from excessive taxes, conscription, and religious oppression. He also urged them to exterminate the nobility and seize their estates, with the result that over fifteen hundred estate owners and members of their families were slain.[2] When he reached the south, however, Pugachev was unable to rally the Don Cossacks, the most important and least discontented of the Cossack hosts. Moreover, the disruption of rural life had created near-famine conditions which had a souring effect on the rebellion. On its side, the government's pursuit became more resolute and the balance was finally tipped. Once this happened, Pugachev was betrayed by his subordinates who sought to save themselves by turning him in. Eventually he was brought back to Moscow in an iron cage, tortured, and executed.

[2] Paul Avrich, *Russian Rebels, 1600–1808* (New York, 1972), chap. 4.

The fact that his movement was able to attract such a wide variety of support—certain Cossack hosts, Tatars and other nomads, frontier homesteaders, industrial serfs, religious dissenters, and private serfs in the Russian heartland—suggests a profound discontent in Russian society. The common enemies of all the rebels were a despotic, centralizing government with its conscription, taxes, and religious orthodoxy, and an oppressive nobility that sought to monopolize land and labor. Against these forces Pugachev's supporters rebelled to recover the loss of traditional customs and rights. Posing as the "redeemer tsar," Pugachev offered the peasants a mythical ideal of the tsar as the father and protector of his people, whose rule could be personal and benevolent instead of being usurped by a self-interested bureaucracy or nobility. Not surprisingly, the backlash in St. Petersburg served precisely to strengthen the bureaucracy and nobility. Catherine reacted with a determined program of administra-

Pugachev.

tive change in which she sought to link the gentry (*dvorianstvo*) more effectively to the machine of state. Likewise, she reassured the nobility of its preeminent position and its control over the serfs, which were formally proclaimed in the Charter of the Nobility (1785). Even the discussion of agrarian reform seemed to be taboo. When Radischev published his indictment of serfdom in 1790, Catherine threw him into jail and denounced him as "more dangerous than Pugachev."

Colonial Rebellion in America

In its goals and tactics, the Pugachev rebellion did not signify anything really new in Europe's history. While its origins were related directly to the initiatives of centralizing absolutism in the later eighteenth century, the revolt must have struck the upper classes as being typical of the masses, whose violence had been recorded in blood through centuries of jacqueries. The next dramatic episode to shake the old order could not have been more different. Across the Atlantic, settlers in Britain's thirteen colonies—articulate lawyers, merchants, and plantation owners, along with independent farmers and artisans—were about to rewrite the rules of political sovereignty and nationhood in a manner that was bound to affect the consciousness if not the behavior of Europe's elites. The latter would read about these events, discuss them in their salons or coffeehouses, and, in a few notable instances, set off for the New World to share in them.

Ironically, the American rebellion can be considered a by-product of Britain's sweeping victory in the Seven Years' War, for there followed in its wake not only large war debts, but problems of integrating, managing, and policing vast dominions. In America, the crown decided to establish a line of demarcation in the west beyond which colonists would not be permitted to settle, so as to preclude conflict with the Indians. In addition a permanent garrison was now stationed in the colonies to deal with the Indians. To help defray the cost of past military commitments and to pay for those of the future, the British cabinet decided to tighten up enforcement of the mercantilist system, and to levy certain taxes on the colonists which their brethren in Britain already paid. The Sugar Act of 1764 (which taxed sugar and molasses imported from the West Indies for conversion into rum), and the Stamp Act of 1765 (which taxed newspapers, pamphlets, legal documents, and licenses) were two results of this policy. Colonial merchants had good reason to object to the Sugar Act, while all colonists denounced the Stamp Act on the grounds that it was an unprecedented and illegal extension of taxing powers. While the colonists acknowledged London's right to regulate and tax trade, they did not admit Parliament's right to tax them directly without their consent. Since they had no representatives in Parliament, and rejected the claim that they were "virtually represented" by all members of Parliament, the colonists had no means of consent.

There followed a ten-year struggle between colonial activists and the London government to define the bounds of sovereignty and the power to tax. It was a multifront, escalating conflict, in which a majority of the colonists came to view the British government as thoroughly corrupt and tyrannical. The customs service is a good example of the issues that divided the two sides. In order to enforce its trade regulations and discourage the smuggling that was a way of life for certain colonial merchants, the British not only expanded their customs service, but established new vice-admiralty courts that deliberated on smuggling cases without juries. The colonists reacted not merely with self-interested indignation, but with a genuine concern for liberty. Customs agents, or excisemen, were traditionally the bane of free citizens, empowered to make searches and seizures without normal due process and notoriously corruptible, while the use of vice-admiralty courts was obviously a serious departure from the system of jury trials which the colonists (as good Englishmen) prized.

The issue of taxation also flared up repeatedly. Prime Minister George Grenville repealed the Stamp Act in 1766 after violent rioting in the colonies in which tax collectors were assaulted, customs houses burned,

The Boston Massacre. *The clash between Boston's citizens and British redcoats in 1770 was a galvanizing incident in colonial resistance. The artist was the silversmith—and later minuteman—Paul Revere.*

and organizations formed to promote disobedience. But in the "Declaratory Act," passed immediately after the repeal of the Stamp Act, Parliament reserved its right to tax the colonists in the future. The following year, Lord Townshend—perhaps the most inept British leader of the period—proposed another series of duties, and the colonists responded with boycotts of British imports. Again Parliament backed down, though again it reserved the right to levy such taxes. Finally, in 1773, Parliament activated a tax on tea (the one tax imposed by the Townshend Acts that had not been repealed) while at the same time encouraging the East India Company to unload large amounts of its tea in the colonies under advantageous terms. To this a group of Boston residents reacted not simply by boycotting the tea, but by preventing it from landing altogether. Dressed as Indians they boarded the ships and dumped the offending cargo overboard. Britain then responded with a series of punitive "coercive acts": the port of Boston was closed until restitution was made, the "excessively democratical" government of Massachusetts was curbed by limiting the frequency of town meetings and by replacing an elected upper legislative house with an appointed one, and a royal garrison was sent to occupy Boston. It was not long before the garrison clashed with the population, which was arming itself and organizing militias, whose members were called "minutemen." At the same time, radicals in the various colonies began exchanging views through committees of correspondence, and by 1774 plans were being laid to convene an extralegal Continental Congress of delegates from all thirteen colonies.

Initially, these opposition leaders had expressed their anger as loyal British subjects being denied their just rights. Eventually, however, there was a complete disenchantment with British society and government, while the image of "America" began to emerge as the foundation for an ideology of independence. The development of these Americans—these new kinds of men in a new kind of society—is not the province of this book. Their disgust with the British motherland is very much a part of our story, however, since the colonists were saying in extreme form what dissenters and reformers in England felt themselves. Indeed, colonial resistance was applauded by many respectable Englishmen, who denounced George III and his ministers for their heavy-handed actions against his subjects in the New World.

As Bernard Bailyn has shown, the ideas of political opposition in the colonies after 1763 were traceable to opposition elements in England itself, and represented a critique of English society shared on both sides of the Atlantic. Its main point was the charge that England's political system was corrupt at its roots and prone to abridging liberty at home and abroad. Perhaps the most widely cited source in the colonial pamphlet and newspaper war against British tyranny was *Cato's Letters* (1720), an indictment of government corruption, standing armies, the national debt, and excise schemes—none of which seemed appropriate in a society of truly free men. While the Glorious Revolution of 1688 had more or less destroyed the arbitrary "prerogative power" of the crown, it had opened the way for corrupt bargains between crown and Parliament. In the colonies themselves, this situation was all the more dangerous since the colonial governors were royal appointees who had many powers, including a veto power over the enactments of colonial legislatures that the crown had already lost in Britain itself.

Sensitive colonists who traveled to England were shocked by the political corruption they discovered. "Whoever presides in the Treasury Department can command in Parliament," reported one observer, while another marveled at how widespread and obvious bribery was at election time. Why, the colonists began to ask, should they entrust their destinies to such a system? After 1765 these fears seemed to be confirmed. The spread of the customs administration meant the spread of placemen and corruption. The extension of taxation without consent could grow until government was financially independent of those it ruled. Vice-admiralty courts without juries, political appointments in the hands of royal governors, the use of general warrants (writs of assistance), the emplacement of permanent military garrisons, all exemplified the threat to liberty.[3] In the exaggerated imagery of colonial radicals, responsibility for all this was laid on a cabal of ministers and favorites of the king, such as Lord North, along with a handful of treacherous colonials like Governor Hutchinson of Massachusetts. Though George III and Lord North were the leading villains, the radicals realized that it was the whole British political system they opposed, including a docile Parliament kept in line by "influence," which allowed the crown and its ministers to rule arbitrarily. Consequently, the colonists had no place to turn. The logic of their resistance, met by intransigence in London, soon led to the Declaration of Independence from both king and Parliament. In 1776 the Continental Congress, which had started as a resistance lobby, became the government of a new nation based in theory on the sovereignty of its people, whose delegates were now free to frame their own constitution.

Crowds and Reformers in England

While confronting its restive colonials, the British government was not immune to agitation at home over comparable, if less portentous issues. Metropolitan London was an especially volatile arena, with its relatively broad parliamentary franchise and its institutions of local self-government. Traditionally, Londoners distrusted incumbent governments, or the so-called "court party," and were ever alert to oppose corruption or tyranny. The great Whig peers were not popular there, and the national figure who commanded most support among politically active Londoners was William Pitt the elder, the champion of British glory and maritime interests. Naturally, when young George III forced Pitt to resign in 1761, opinion in London turned against the king.

On the outer fringes of Pitt's circle was a man named John Wilkes (1727–1797), an ambitious member of Parliament and a sharp-tongued journalist of unsavory reputation. Wilkes was to find himself at the center of a decade of public agitation that caused some of the first cracks in the tranquil surface of eighteenth-century British public life. As a supporter of Pitt, he published an opposition newspaper that attacked George III's ministers and their policy of conciliation toward France. In No. 45 of his North Briton (23 April 1763), Wilkes penned a scathing

---

[3] Bernard Bailyn, *The Ideological Origins of the American Revolution* (Cambridge, Mass., 1967).

denunciation of the ministry, which the king considered a libelous insult. Instead of taking Wilkes to court, however, the government ordered his arrest on a general warrant (the equivalent of a French *lettre de cachet*). Wilkes in turn sued the crown, winning his release and compensatory damages, but Parliament reacted by voting 237 to 111 that *North Briton No. 45* was scandalous and seditious. Under threat of prosecution for sedition, Wilkes fled to France. Parliament then expelled him from his seat and declared him an outlaw. A few years later Wilkes slipped back into England, prepared now to stand trial, but also to vindicate himself publicly. In the election of 1768 he won the contest in the borough of Middlesex adjoining London, a relatively democratic constituency in which shopkeepers and craftsmen voted. Unimpressed by the results of this vote, Parliament denied Wilkes his seat. Twice new elections were held, twice more Wilkes was returned, and twice again he was excluded. Further, when Parliament banned him for the final time in 1769, it had the audacity to seat his opponent, who had lost the election. To many people, this suggested that as presently constituted, Parliament was an oligarchy which set its own rules regardless of the popular will.

What made the Wilkes episode especially significant was the support he was winning outside Parliament from two different social groups, each representing a new type of voice in politics. In the first place Wilkes drew support from the common people—"the mob" in the eyes of some, but whom historians such as George Rudé take more seriously. During the tumult of Wilkes's election campaign and trial there were numerous demonstrations on his behalf. People excluded from voting paid tribute to him in this fashion, and in one instance a dozen paid with their lives. On that day a crowd of over twenty thousand Londoners gathered in St. George's Field to salute the imprisoned Wilkes. Ordered to disperse by the authorities, the crowd was reluctant to do so, and without much provocation soldiers were called in and fired, killing twelve people. London was filled with working people shouting and chalking the slogan "Wilkes and Liberty" all over the city. Several times his supporters controlled the streets of London, obliging people to illuminate their windows in Wilkes's honor and breaking the windows of those who refused. Thus Wilkes was a symbol for Londoners without the vote, who seemed to have strong feelings about liberty.

The second element of Wilkes's support was the "middling element" of voting freeholders: small merchants, guild masters and the like, who belonged to the guilds in London and who voted in Middlesex, London, and Westminster. They returned Wilkes to Parliament repeatedly, as well as electing him sheriff of London (1771) and eventually lord mayor (1774). When Parliament kept excluding Wilkes it was a direct challenge to *their* liberty as voters and citizens. Forming a Society for the Protection of the

Wilkes's supporters. *In an early demonstration of support, a crowd of Wilkites tries to stop the burning of No. 45 of Wilkes's newspaper,* The North Briton.

Bill of Rights, they circulated petitions on Wilkes's behalf. Over thirty-eight thousand freeholders in fifteen counties, and another seventeen thousand voters in a dozen boroughs signed them—a total of perhaps one-quarter of all county voters and about one-fifth of all borough voters. Opposition factions within Parliament, such as the Rockingham Whigs, encouraged this petition campaign since championing Wilkes's cause had become a way of criticizing the incumbent government.[4]

Wilkes's more radical supporters, however, had further designs. The "Wilkes and Liberty" campaign became for them a movement to reform the British Parliament. Several Wilkite petitions demanded the election of Parliament every three years instead of every seven; the elimination of rotten boroughs; increased representation for the counties; and limitations on pensions and sinecures controlled by the crown. With the exception of the last point, the majority of Wilkes's voters do not seem to have rallied to these proposals, and the opposition Whigs certainly did not. Their chief interest was to embarrass George III's ministry, and their goal was the limited one of "economical reform," that is, reducing the influence of the crown in politics by curbing the places and pensions it controlled. This

[4] George Rudé, *Wilkes and Liberty: a social study of 1763–1774* (Oxford, 1962), pp. 132–35 and *passim*.

they eventually succeeded in doing to a modest extent, and thereafter the Whig opposition factions lost their enthusiasm for reform.

Whig oppositionists were always uneasy about the popular dimensions of the "Wilkes and Liberty" agitation. When the Gordon riots swept London in 1780, it amply confirmed their distaste for political activity outside the narrow channels of parliamentary politics. The Gordon riots originated in popular reaction to a bill of 1778 extending limited toleration to Catholics that had passed the House of Commons. Vehement opposition was headed by the anti-Catholic agitator Lord George Gordon. Initially Gordon mobilized "the better sort of tradesmen" to demonstrate before Parliament for repeal of the bill, and he collected forty-four thousand signatures on an anti-Catholic petition. But many people from "the inferior set"—as the working classes and the poor were referred to—joined in the demonstrations and raised their temperature. Before long a riot began that gripped London for seven days and nights, and as it developed, it took on overtones of class as well as religious conflict. Prisons were forced open, their poor inmates released; the houses of prominent officials and of wealthy Catholics were pulled down; arson was rampant. When the crowd threatened the Bank of England, sufficient troops were finally mustered to restore law and order. The scale of violence in the Gordon riots was awesome, with at least fifty buildings totally demolished, and almost 300 people killed in the fighting between rioters and troops. Another 450 were arrested of whom 160 were brought to trial, and 25 hanged. This shattering episode put a damper on popular agitation for years to come.

The issue of parliamentary reform persisted, however, in part through the efforts of the Yorkshire Freeholders Association founded in 1780 by the Reverend Christopher Wyvill. While initially petitioning Parliament for "economical reform," and thus gaining the support of the Whig opposition, the Association movement also began to petition for parliamentary reform. Political maneuvering came to a head in the general election of 1784, in which the supporters of young William Pitt (1759–1806), backed by the Yorkshire movement and the London radicals, outpolled a coalition of Whig factions. One by-product of this defeat was an attempt by the bested factions to forge a veritable opposition party in the future. They had scant success, however, since in young Pitt, George III had finally found the loyal, popular, yet independent prime minister with whom he could establish a durable working relationship. In the future, Pitt's name would become indelibly linked with England's stand against revolutionary France. At the start of his tenure, however, Pitt agreed to introduce a bill to abolish thirty-six rotten boroughs and to transfer their seats to populous counties and cities. Several times he tried to have it passed, but each time the bill was defeated, in 1785 by a vote of 248 to 174—at which point Pitt abandoned his effort.

Interestingly enough, among the bill's opponents was the Whig publicist Edmund Burke (1729–1797), destined to become one of Europe's leading ideological opponents of the French Revolution. In 1790 Burke would extol the virtues of peaceful evolution as compared with the radical transformation of institutions in France. Yet in 1784 Burke assaulted Pitt's modest proposal for parliamentary reapportionment with the same vehemence that he later directed against France, while making extravagant claims for the perfection of the existing British constitution. "You have an equal representation now," he claimed, "because you have men [in Parliament] equally interested in the prosperity of the whole." [5] Such thinking was typical of conservative opinion elsewhere, for example in the Low Countries where the existing political bodies were considered, by those privileged to sit in them, inherently representative of society as a whole.

Constitutional Conflicts in the Low Countries

In the last few years before the outbreak of the French Revolution, demands for constitutional reform were raised in the United (Dutch) Netherlands and in the Austrian Netherlands (Belgium), where they produced triangular struggles of princes, "aristocrats," and "democrats," and eventually precipitated armed conflicts.

The United Netherlands was a federation of seven Dutch provinces, Holland being the most important. Nowhere in Europe were local particularism and provincial autonomy more deeply rooted. Ostensibly the federation was ruled by a States-General, which drew its delegates from estates in the seven provinces, where sovereignty over most matters actually lay. Members of the provincial estates were in turn drawn from the municipal oligarchies that ruled the nation's numerous towns. The metropolis of Amsterdam, for example, was governed by a council of thirty-six regents who coopted new council members, and who, with the regents of other towns, controlled most government positions in the federation. So dominant had these "periwigged oligarchs" become that they had developed an informal system of "contracts of correspondence" by which they allotted the spoils among members of their families.

The executive branch of government was headed by the stadholder, a prince from the House of Orange-Nassau, which was closely linked to the English royal family after 1688. In the struggle for independence against Spain, the House of Orange had served admirably as a rallying point, but thereafter it was looked upon resentfully by the regents who objected to any taint of monarchism in their "republican" system of governance. The stadholder, however, had considerable influence in several of the lesser

---

[5] Quoted in Robert R. Palmer, *The Age of the Democratic Revolution*, Vol. I (Princeton, N.J., 1959), p. 315.

provinces and served as commander-in-chief or "captain-general" of the Dutch armed forces. The incumbent between 1751 and 1795 was William V who, in the most charitable assessment, was a vain and incompetent leader.

At the time of the American Revolution, the anti-Orangist regents hoped to stem the decline of Dutch power in Europe and abroad by declaring war on their maritime rival—and traditional ally—Britain, in 1780. Led by the regents of Holland, the ruling oligarchies began a series of maneuvers against the stadholder which intensified as the latter's half-hearted, inept leadership of the war effort terminated disastrously for the Dutch in 1784. The regents' objectives were to renegotiate and curtail the stadholder's prerogatives, to lower Holland's 60 percent quota of taxation in the federation, to spend more on naval preparedness rather than

The Dutch Regents. *While not technically a hereditary, privileged aristocracy, these patricians were as exclusive and powerful as any landed nobility in Europe, controlling both municipal and provincial affairs. Painting by Cornelis Troost.*

on the stadholder's army, and in general to conduct a foreign policy independent of Britain.

What started out as a struggle within the confines of the traditional political system broadened, however, into something quite different. Public opinion in this literate, middle-class society was galvanized first against the House of Orange, but soon against the regent oligarchies as well. Sympathetic to developments in America, Patriots (as they called themselves) began to hold meetings and frame pro-American petitions, while advocating moral and national regeneration at home—a desire that depended for its fulfillment on the responsiveness of the ruling groups. The movement passed from speech to action when Dutch burghers (artisans, professionals, merchants, shopkeepers) began to form urban militias called Free Corps. The regents initially believed that this would increase the weight of their own intrigues against the stadholder. In the city of Utrecht, however, they were disabused of this illusion when the Free Corps began to agitate for democratic reforms, demanding that the municipal oligarchy negotiate with their delegates about opening up the co-optive municipal council through electoral representation. After several inconclusive skirmishes, a massive demonstration of Patriots blockaded the regents in the town hall, vowing not to release them until they capitulated. In this determined but as yet bloodless show of force, the Patriot burghers had created and imposed their own concept of political liberty. The movement for "people's government by representation" now spread to other cities and effected changes in the composition of several provincial estates, while others remained immune to its influence. The Dutch States-General therefore ended up immobilized by division between regent conservatives, pro-Orangists, and Patriots from democratic strongholds.[6]

Internal resistance was the lesser of the Patriot's two problems, however, since the republic's destiny—like that of most minor European powers—was not entirely in its own hands. British, French, and Prussian interests were all at stake here, and the threat of intervention hung heavily over the incipient revolution. The British reasonably saw their interests as linked to the stadholder's, and their cause was forcefully defended by their ambassador, James Harris. He intrigued relentlessly to shore up Prince William, arousing orthodox religious support, disbursing British secret-service money, and winning over the more conservative regents. The lines of battle were drawn when Orangist forces were dispatched to drive out Patriots who had taken power in two small towns of the generally pro-Orangist province of Gelderland. This successful attack in the summer of 1787 was the conflict's first major bloodshed and seemed to the Patriots like a declaration of civil war. They now began to organize their defenses

---

[6] My account of the Dutch Revolution relies on Simon Schama, *Patriots and Liberators: Revolution in the Netherlands, 1780–1813* (New York, 1977), chaps. 2–3.

GRONINGEN

FRIESLAND

NORTH SEA

ZUIDER ZEE

Amsterdam

OVERIJSSEL

The Hague

Utrecht

HOLLAND

UTRECHT

GELDERLAND

ZEELAND

Cleves

HOLY

Bruges

Antwerp

Ghent

BRABANT

FLANDERS

Brussels

BISHOPRIC OF LIEGE

Cologne

ROMAN

Scheldt

Liege

Meuse R.

Rhine R.

FRANCE

LUXEMBOURG

EMPIRE

Luxembourg

Moselle R.

0   50 Miles

in earnest with a "military cordon" taking in the major cities of Amsterdam, Utrecht, and The Hague. At this juncture a municipal revolution finally occurred in Amsterdam, where sixteen thousand burghers signed a petition demanding the removal of the temporizing municipal regents. Following the ouster, rioting crowds pillaged the houses of leading regents and Orangists, though no organized repression against them was undertaken. Meanwhile, the Patriots began to consider the notion of creating a popularly-elected National Assembly to replace the deadlocked States-General.

It was too late, however, for the Patriots' fate had been sealed. Harris got the confrontation that he sought, even if inadvertently, when the spirited Princess Wilhelmina—the stadholder's wife and the sister of the new king of Prussia—traveled to The Hague to rally the Orangists. When she was arrested by Patriot militia, King Frederick William exploded in outrage and prepared to intervene, especially when it became clear that France, despite its bluffs to the contrary, would not risk the costs of a

war to protect the Dutch Patriots, whose democratic tendencies were in any
case unsettling the French monarchy. An army of twenty-six thousand
Prussians crossed the Dutch frontier in September, 1787, easily routed the
Patriot forces, and within a month had reinstalled William V in The
Hague. Sweeping purges of all government bodies followed, along with
the dissolution of the Patriot press and militia, and the looting of Patriot
homes by Orangist crowds. Several thousand Patriots fled to the Austrian
Netherlands and France.

   The Dutch refugees were not destined to find tranquility in either country. In the Austrian Netherlands there was a somewhat different con-
figuration of interests, but again an oligarchy massed in its constituent
bodies stood at the center of events. The ten estates of the provinces
that made up this realm were to a large extent autonomous and self-
governing, although the provinces had been bound together under Spanish
sovereignty until 1714, when they were ceded by Spain to Austria. The
estates were controlled by nobles, clerics, and municipal oligarchs, much
like the provincial estates in France. Conflict was predictable when a
reform-minded Joseph II, in typical autocratic fashion, unilaterally imposed judicial and administrative reorganization in 1787 that seriously
abridged the estates' prerogatives and privileges. Whatever his enlightened views, Joseph appeared to the Belgians as an enemy, since the customs and charters of their estates formed a kind of traditional constitution
and a network of "liberties." Shrouded in the rhetoric of liberty, the
estates' resistance to Joseph was really a conservative defense of privilege.
This became clear later when the Estates Party (as that wing of anti-
Austrian resistance was called), having temporarily driven the Austrians
out, refused to convene a new representative assembly that would have
involved the Belgium citizenry more actively in the struggle. Instead, it
simply converted the old estates of the major province of Brabant into
an Estates-General for all ten provinces.
   Just as happened in the Dutch Netherlands, a democratic movement
developed alongside the initial nationalist resistance to Habsburg "tyranny." A two-sided struggle became a triangular conflict. Led by a lawyer
named Jean François Vonck (1743–1792), Belgian burghers who had
helped oust the Austrians in 1789 sought to broaden the bounds of the
political nation, preferably by changing the Estates into a representative
assembly of some kind, but at the least by adding an additional chamber
to the Estates-General to be elected by the previously unrepresented
burghers. Though Vonck's proposal seems quite moderate, the Estates
Party would have none of it. They wished to establish independence from
Austria, but also to retain their independence from the people. Even more

rigid than their Dutch counterparts, they risked weakening their base of support by stirring up priests and peasants against the urban democrats, as the Vonckists called themselves, hounding many of them into exile in France. In these circumstances it became all the easier for Austrian armies to put down the independence movement the following year.[7]

As R. R. Palmer has argued, the intensity of these conflicts in the Low Countries stemmed not simply from the nature of the democrats' demands, but also from the intransigent defense of their interests and privileges by the oligarchies or "aristocrats." Democratic movements generally started in moderate fashion, as exemplified by the peaceful petitions of the Utrecht Free Corps to the regents, or by Vonck's compromise offer to reform the Estates' structure instead of sweeping it away. But the old constituted bodies offered not even a modicum of concession. After 1789, conservative writers would attack the French revolutionaries for resorting to violent, sweeping revolution instead of peaceful, gradual reform. Yet when conservatives held power in the Low Countries they would not admit the desirability or possibility of any change in their powers, despite their own struggles against their respective princes.

Revolution and Intervention in Poland

This discussion of political conflicts in the late eighteenth century will of course conclude with France. Yet these same years were as decisive, even if negatively, for Poland. As in the Dutch Netherlands, a revolution of sorts developed in the wake of a complex political dispute, lacking, to be sure, the democratic component of the Dutch revolt, but similar in its central thrust against the traditional constituted bodies of the aristocracy. What the Dutch and Polish revolutions had most in common, however, was the fate of being quashed by foreign military intervention.

After the partition of Poland in 1772 Russia had become the guarantor of Polish territorial integrity, provided that the Poles did not cause any trouble. The Russians were responsible enough to establish a body called the Permanent Council, which gave the country a somewhat more effective executive, even if nationalists regarded the Council as a Russian puppet. Otherwise, however, the Russians blocked reforms that might have enhanced Poland's ability to reclaim its true independence. In the years that followed there was a great deal of political factionalism, little political change, and considerable cultural and ideological ferment. Segments of the aristocratic elite began to think more critically about their traditions, shedding their "native" clothing and customs in order to adopt

[7] E. H. Kossmann, *The Low Countries, 1780–1940* (Oxford, 1978), pp. 47–64, and Palmer, *Age of the Democratic Revolution*, Vol. I, chap. 11.

Western styles. Publications multiplied, including political tracts and magazines modeled on the *Spectator*. Some nobles attempted to manage their estates more progressively, and to promote trade and industry. Townsmen grew more assertive about their lowly status and lack of any political voice.

King Stanislaus II (ruled 1764–1795), a modern man much taken with Western styles and notions of reform, played a waiting game, cooperating with the Russians who, he hoped, would support his efforts to strengthen the Polish state. Traditional Polish "republican" ideology, however, was too rigid to accept any growth in royal power, with or without the Russian connection. The situation grew more fluid when Russia was obliged to pull out of Poland in 1788 as it went to war against the Turks. In the Diet convened in that year (called by historians the Four Years' Diet), there ensued a brief period of exultation in which noble "Patriots" congratulated themselves on their triumph over the Russians. This soon gave way to protracted and fruitless wrangling over how to fashion a political structure that would protect this new-won independence. The Diet was all but immobilized by conflicts between traditionalist "libertarians," Patriot reformers, and supporters of the king. Some magnates eventually began to recognize that an aristocratic reaction based on traditional Polish liberties would simply perpetuate chaos and weakness. In the words of the magnate Ignacy Potocki, they reluctantly concluded that "for a certain time, royalist government will be most appropriate." Drawing closer to the king, whom they had previously distrusted or scorned, a number of Patriots connived at a bloodless coup. On May 3, 1791, they held a rump session of the Diet, during an Easter recess when the majority of members were away, at which they pushed through a new constitution.[8]

The May Constitution, along with several statutes passed in the same Diet, added up to a political revolution. It strengthened the executive, reformed the nation's representative institutions, and altered the position of several social classes. First, the monarchy was to become hereditary, no longer subject to the electoral bribery and influence of magnates or foreign powers. At the same time an executive cabinet was authorized, staffed by ministers to be appointed by the king though in some measure responsible to the Diet. Second, landless *szlachta* were excluded from voting in the local dietines. This meant that the magnates would no longer control these elections through their patronage, and that voting would be more representative of the landed gentry. Third, the free veto in the Diet was abolished; henceforth decisions would be made by plurality without the need for elaborate emergency confederations. Fourth, the towns would now send delegates to the Diet who could speak on all issues and vote on commercial and urban matters. Towns were to receive charters providing

[8] Daniel Stone, *Polish Politics and National Reform, 1775–1788* (New York, 1976).

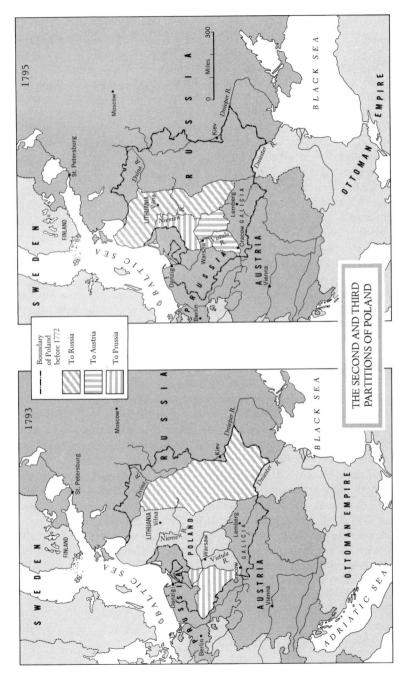

THE SECOND AND THIRD
PARTITIONS OF POLAND

for a restoration of self-government. All resident proprietors in the towns (though not the numerous Jews) now received formal "burgher rights": they could elect and serve on town councils, purchase "noble" land in the countryside, and be appointed to national offices. Provision was also made for ennobling a number of wealthy burghers each year. Thus the status of citizenship was defined more in terms of wealth and function than mere birth. The elites (landed nobles and wealthy burghers) would have a voice in public affairs, while the landless nobles, who had nothing but their arrogance and their titles, were shunted to the sidelines. The basic social order of separate classes was preserved, but the prerogatives of several classes were altered. This did not extend to the mass of peasant serfs, however, to whom the May Constitution offered no change, though it might conceivably have opened the way to eventual legislation in their favor.

Still, it was a dramatic change in Polish traditions, substituting a more modern conception of government for the ancient "republican liberties" of the *szlachta* and magnates. Some of the magnates predictably launched protests in several provinces and soon a number of nobles—both old-fashioned idealists and opportunists—began to negotiate with the foreign powers who hovered along Poland's vulnerable borders. Russia, previously willing to observe Polish territorial integrity, had become alienated in the wake of the Four Years' Diet's fierce anti-Russian nationalism. When the war with Turkey came to an end in January 1792, Russia could act. Catherine was now eager to appease and share in Prussian desires for territorial acquisition, in exchange for Prussia's agreement to intervene against France, whose revolution was even more offensive to her. Austria did not object since its temperate sovereign Leopold II had died in March 1792. Gathering together a group of anti-reform Poles as their cover, the Russians invaded Poland in May, setting in motion the destruction of the May 3 regime and a second partition in 1793. Poland was again humiliated, carved up by Russia and Prussia, and shorn completely of its reforms. However, the old order that survived in what was left of Poland was too distasteful to some of the surviving Patriots and in 1794 a rebellion broke out with the aim of liberating Poland from foreign occupation, restoring the reforms of 1791, and perhaps extending them further. This heroic but ill-fated effort, led by the legendary General Thaddeus Kosciuszko, was crushed in 1794–1795. In its aftermath a third and final partition obliterated the Polish state completely. Even more than the Dutch revolt, the Belgian struggle for independence, or the English parliamentary reform movement, the Polish revolution ended in complete failure.

THE CRISIS OF THE OLD REGIME IN FRANCE

Social Tensions

Though they did not directly cause the French Revolution, the tensions generated by France's social structure assured that the crisis of authority in France would have far more explosive consequences than other contemporaneous revolutions. Ironically, the first major event in the Revolution—the summoning of the Estates-General—was calculated to obscure the complexity of the social order by resurrecting the official but deceptive notion that France's population comprised three estates: the clergy, the nobility, and the rest of the people or the third estate. But where did such a classification situate the nation's elites? In a country at once "aristocratic" and "middle class," the French elites could of course be found both within the nobility and the third estate. One element of the old regime's crisis was precisely a growing contentiousness among the elites over their relationships and prerogatives. Marxist historians have emphasized the bourgeois versus noble element of this conflict, while recent "revisionist" historians have underscored intraelite rivalries that did not necessarily depend on that dividing line. The least that can be said is that a great deal of recrimination and resentment was mounting within the ranks of the elites before 1789.

No doubt the French nobility had once been a cohesive upper class holding a virtual monopoly on military leadership and landowning. By the eighteenth century the first of these monopolies had been eroded and the second was long since gone. The typical noble living in the countryside might still be a captain in the army and the owner of a seigneury or manor, but there were now other types of nobles as well. For one thing, old-line country nobles were not always wealthy. In Brittany (a province with an exclusive, haughty nobility), it is estimated that about 46 percent of the noble families were wealthy to comfortable, but that 54 percent were in circumstances ranging from moderate to poor. In either case, the typical country nobles had little in common with the two thousand or so opulent families who attended the royal court at Versailles. Likewise, there were few similarities between the country nobles and the nobility of the robe, the members of the thirteen *Parlements* who attained hereditary noble status starting in Louis XIV's reign. Not only were these judicial nobles immensely wealthy and highly intellectual, but they played an extremely important role in the state, and therefore had a greater sense of responsibility and self-importance than most nobles. To further complicate matters, the nobility was not a closed hereditary caste. Each year the crown recognized new nobles. A few were created by royal letters of nobility, but most were ennobled through the purchase of expensive venal offices. These sinecures, bearing a large price tag and little or no substantial function, allowed the elevation of over twenty-five hundred wealthy bourgeois into the nobility during the reign of Louis XVI between 1774 and 1789. The only trouble was that many old-line nobles—the *noblesse de race*, as they called themselves—did not accept these new men as genuine nobles. Resenting their pretensions, they tried to keep the new men in a social limbo. For example, the Ségur Law, pushed through the royal council under the prompting of the military aristocracy in 1781, restricted the sale of all future military commissions to men who could boast four generations of paternal nobility. Its goal was to limit the officer corps (aside from small numbers promoted to lieutenant after long service in the ranks) to men who came from old aristocratic families, where military service was a cherished tradition. The effect was to exclude not simply bourgeois but also ennobled commoners.[9]

Any notion of a unified upper class of nobles standing against the rest of society is thus misleading. Various nobles nursed substantial disdain for other types of nobles. Some wished to play an active, useful role in society but without having to compete for that prerogative. Others were content to live off their privileges and bask in the eminence of their ancient family names. The French nobility was too diverse to be a cohesive, self-confident ruling class, but at the same time it was too exclusive and powerful to permit sufficient upward mobility for a large, talented, and ambitious middle class.

It is true that wealthy men from the middle classes appeared quite similar to the nobility in some respects. Both tended to invest their money in land, the purchase of offices, or annuities—safe, secure types of investment that yielded a modest but steady return befitting a "gentlemanly" way of life. This pattern of investment tied both groups to the foundations of the old regime: to the prevailing system of landed property, and to the royal government on whose solvency the value of their annuities and offices depended.[10] While some bourgeois displayed an aggressive pride in their mercantile or professional achievements, and disdain for the pretensions and alleged vices of the aristocracy, others retired after making their fortunes in commerce, and pointed their children away from careers in business. Converting their capital into land, offices, or annuities, they "lived nobly" as gentlemen without having to work, thus resembling the English gentry who were not nobles either. They differed, however, in that the English gentry played a prominent role in parliamentary elections and local government, whereas the French middle classes did not. It was exactly this question of participation in public life that would ultimately force Frenchmen to confront the relationship of nobles and

[9] David Bien, "La Réaction aristocratique avant 1789: l'exemple de l'armée," *Annales*, Vol. XXIX (1974), pp. 23–48 and pp. 505–34.

[10] George Taylor, "Non-Capitalist Wealth and the Origins of the French Revolution," *American Historical Review*, Vol. LXXII (1967), pp. 469–96.

bourgeois. What would happen if absolutism weakened and new opportunities for participation in government were created? How would the various groups regard each other when it came to allocating new sources of political power?

Whatever their differences, the wealth and status of the elites set them apart from people who worked with their hands for a living: artisans, shopkeepers, journeymen, unskilled workers, and servants—not to mention the indigent. The elites were concerned with opportunities to acquire property, and with access to respectable positions for themselves or their children; in the security of their wealth and status they could also be interested in questions of liberty or political reform. Artisans and shopkeepers, who stood between the elites and the laboring poor, might well share these aspirations and interests, but generally they had more modest horizons. Indeed, they resented the large concentrations of economic resources which the elites considered necessary to economic growth. Along with the laboring poor, artisans and shopkeepers were most immediately concerned with subsistence questions during hard times. Then, the problem of putting food on the table eclipsed most others, and was the likeliest issue to mobilize popular opinion.

In the countryside, subsistence was certainly the peasantry's preoccupation as well, but it was directly related to the ownership and use of land. There was intense competition for land both among the peasants themselves (whose property tended to be subdivided with each generation), and between the peasants and the elites. On the eve of the Revolution, land ownership was distributed approximately as follows, these figures being rough national estimates that conceal great regional variation:

Nobility	20%
Urban Bourgeois	20–25%
The Church	10%
Peasantry	35–40%

Late eighteenth-century trends in the control and use of land threatened the peasantry's precarious existence even further. Wealthy urban bourgeois purchasing land in the countryside drove up the prices and made it harder than ever for peasants to increase their landholdings. In what is sometimes referred to as a "seigneurial reaction," some lords were now managing their estates with unprecedented harshness, finding every occasion to maximize their peasants' obligations. Sometimes they refused to renew leases, or foreclosed current leases for unpaid debts, so that a group of parcels could be leased to one large farmer. Similarly, some lords attempted to enclose their open fields or to divide village common lands, thus eliminating the open pasturage that poorer peasants depended on to graze their meager livestock. In sum, there seems to have been a struggle in some parts of France between two agrarian mentalities: the traditional peasant mentality, with its emphasis on small-scale land use, subsistence agriculture, and collective rights, as against a more capitalistic approach that sought to consolidate landholdings and orient production toward urban markets.[11] Whether "seigneurial" or "capitalist" in nature, innovations in estate management created tensions which fed the peasantry's centuries-old grievances.

The Failure of Reform

Though it was a prosperous decade of demographic and economic growth, the 1760's ushered in a period of governmental failure. In the Seven Years' War that ended in 1763 France had been soundly defeated on the continent and in the colonial world. What was worse, the war had been financed by loans that had created a large national debt. Administrative and financial reforms were incumbent, yet the outlook for such reform was dubious. Authority in France was weak and fragmented, contrary to the image of absolutism once projected by Louis XIV. There had been little advance in the monarchy's unifying mission since the Sun King's demise. Regional diversity continued to prevail in agricultural policy, civil law, taxation, and even administration. The use of intendants may have been emulated elsewhere in Europe, but it had not been brought to fulfillment at home. Several outlying provinces retained their own traditions, unwritten constitutions, and local constituted bodies, called provincial estates. Even at the center of decision making there was an absence of decisiveness. The crucial post of controller-general of finances, for example, was held by some nineteen men in a period of thirty-five years.

The monarchy seemed unable to complete the process of bureaucratizing its personnel and policies. The court at Versailles, the world of the grand aristocracy, intruded on the affairs of state. Under the same roof, the best minds of the realm competed for influence with the most parasitical special interests. New reforms and old abuses coexisted side by side in an uncertain balance. What is more, reform-minded men did not constitute one identifiable group. Instead they clustered into small, rival factions from which the king selected his ministers. Under such circumstances constant shifts of policy and personnel were inevitable, and unified, resolute ministries unlikely.[12]

[11] Emmanuel LeRoy Ladurie, "Rural Revolts and Protest Movements in France from 1675 to 1788," *Studies in Eighteenth Century Culture*, Vol. V (Madison, Wis., 1976), pp. 423–51.

[12] See Denis Richet, *La France Moderne: l'esprit des institutions* (Paris, 1973), pp. 151–78, and Pierre Goubert, *L'Ancien Régime*, Vol. II, *Les Pouvoirs* (Paris, 1973), chaps. 10–12.

Outside the framework of royal government stood the *Parlements*. These thirteen law courts, whose magistrates purchased their offices, were a unique French institution combining judicial and political functions with eminent social standing. As mentioned earlier, the *Parlements* were courts of record in which every royal decree had to be registered in order to be legally valid. From this minor clerical function the *Parlements* had developed real political power. By refusing to register an edict, and by protesting or "remonstrating" against it, they could block its implementation. True, the crown had ways of forcing the *Parlements* to register its acts, such as exiling the magistrates, and Louis XIV had used them all to intimidate the *Parlements* into submission. Yet in 1715 the *Parlements* had regained the right to remonstrance, having connived to break Louis XIV's will and install the Duke of Orléans as regent. Ever since then the *Parlements* had served as something of a brake on royal absolutism.

By the later eighteenth century, elite opinion looked favorably on the *Parlements'* self-assigned role as guardians of "liberty." A mood prevailed at this time which one historian has aptly called "the triumph of Montesquieu." Montesquieu's notion of privileged intermediary bodies as bulwarks against monarchy's arbitrary will was perfectly embodied in the *Parlements*. By the 1770's, the adulation of royalty that had prevailed under Louis XIV, when opposition was an isolated and usually private affair, had long since cooled. The basic idea that power must be limited, that the nation possessed an unwritten "constitution," was taken up by the *Parlements* in a series of challenges to royal authority, and for lack of any alternative check on absolutism, they found considerable public support. The *Parlements* should also be seen, however, as an example of Europe's constituted bodies or self-selecting oligarchies, which upheld the prerogatives of their own class and—in the case of the provincial *Parlements*—of their own region at the expense of the national interest as conceived by the monarchy. After the Seven Years' War, for example, the crown prepared to levy a new version of the *vingtième* or twentieth tax, a proportional tax on income which would have applied to nobles as well as commoners. The *Parlements* helped to block the new tax on the grounds that the monarchy should improve the administration of its finances, and that it should cut down on expenditures instead of levying new taxes—a point not without merit. Yet the new tax promised to be more equitable than existing taxes.

In the 1760's the *Parlements* and the crown were locked in combat several times on such matters without decisive results. Finally Louis XV appointed a chancellor named Maupeou who convinced him that a showdown with the *Parlements* was necessary to uphold royal authority. An edict reminiscent of Louis XIV was issued, curbing the *Parlements'* right to reject royal decrees or to issue political declarations. Naturally the

Parlements refused to accept this. And so one night in January 1771, every Parisian magistrate was awakened by two royal musketeers bearing a *lettre de cachet* ordering him to signify his obedience immediately. Most refused. Within two days 165 magistrates of the Paris *Parlement* were deprived of their posts and exiled to unpleasant parts of the country. Public opinion sided with the *Parlements* but Maupeou could not have cared less. The *Parlements* were replaced by new courts in which judges were appointed rather than venal, and in which the administration of justice was made more accessible and less costly. When the king died and Louis XVI assumed the throne in 1774, however, the issue immediately flared up again, and the monarch was advised that he should restore the magistrates to their rightful posts as an indication that he would not rule tyrannically. Wishing to be popular, the inexperienced sovereign agreed, and within two years it became evident that the Paris *Parlement* remained an obstacle to significant reforms in administration or finances.

Twenty years old in 1774, the new sovereign was a pious young man unprepared by temperament or training for the kingship. Lacking self-confidence, he was easily influenced by the courtiers around him. His court was a confusing milieu where reformist officials, aristocratic parasites, and pious men and women vied for influence. Initially the king installed an array of talented ministers, but his chief advisor remained Maurepas, a seventy-year-old courtier and intriguer whose guiding principle was to avoid excessive conflict.

Louis' first controller-general was Anne Robert Jacques Turgot (1727–1781), a contributor to the *Encyclopedia*, physiocrat, and experienced intendant. Believing that economic growth was the long-run solution to France's financial problems, since it would ultimately produce new revenues, Turgot proposed to stimulate the economy by freeing the grain trade from government regulation and by suppressing certain guilds, which would allow individuals to choose their trades freely. He also sought to cut back expenses at court, and to improve France's roads by converting the *corvée* (forced labor by peasants on the royal roads) into a small income tax payable by all landowners. Each proposal had merits and defects, and each obviously affected special interests adversely. The *corvée* issue was especially sensitive, reminiscent as it was of the proposed *vingtième* tax. The *Parlements* opposed Turgot's plans "because," as the British ambassador reported, "of the injustice of laying part of the new tax, which is to be substituted in the place of the *corvées*, upon the gentlemen of the country who were not subject to the former burden. . . . The next ground of opposition is the danger of this tax being diverted hereafter to a different purpose for which it was given [i.e., road building]. . . ." As for the guilds, he observed, the *Parlements* naturally supported "old establishments," and in addition, the magistrates had a personal stake in the litigation created by the guilds' existence. In a vehement attack on Turgot's edicts, which clearly displayed its class bias, the Paris *Parlement* blasted his tax proposal as a menace to "the prerogatives of birth and station." "Any system which, in the name of humanity and public good, tends to establish among men equality of duties, and to destroy fundamental [social] distinctions will soon lead to disorder." What the *Parlement* started, intrigue by various courtiers and rivals of Turgot completed. Two years after his promising appointment he was dismissed by a king who sought tranquility even if it meant retreat.[13]

The Turgot episode revealed an impasse over reform in the old regime. Reform impulses were amply present at Versailles, but they were usually blocked by the opposition of powerful interests. A weak king was caught in the middle, but the blame cannot be laid simply upon him. It was a structural problem. Reformers themselves formed shifting coteries divided by personal rivalries and varying priorities, and thus their initiatives were uncoordinated. Vested interests opposed innovations for combinations of popular and self-interested motives. In the end each abortive reform effort weakened the monarchy's authority without enhancing anyone else's as an alternative. This structural impasse stemmed from the clash between a centralizing, authoritarian monarchy that would not willingly share its power, and the traditions of aristocracy, provincial liberties, and constituted bodies that stood opposed to absolutism. Nor was a "Prussian" or "Russian" solution possible, in which the crown simply struck a bargain of sorts with the aristocracy. France's aristocracy was too complex and fragmented, and its middle classes too large and articulate to accept such an arrangement. Yet it was impossible to do nothing, because the deteriorating state of royal finances demanded action.

Royal Finances: Taxation and Borrowing

A close discussion of royal finances is necessary at this point since it was *the* problem over which authority in the old regime ultimately unraveled. Taxation and borrowing had been pressed to the limit, but the more the state borrowed the more it needed to tax. Direct taxes (taxes on property or income) constituted about two-fifths of France's tax revenues and were notoriously inequitable. The *taille* or land tax was the principal tax; its amount was determined not by the ability of people to pay but by the needs of the crown. Each of the thirty-odd generalities into which France was divided administratively was periodically assigned a lump-sum amount. In the *pays d'état* (see map on p. 7) the provincial estates were able to bargain with the crown to reduce their share. These

---

[13] The quotes are from Douglas Dakin, *Turgot and the Ancien Régime in France* (New York, 1939), pp. 232 and 249. See in general chaps. 15–16.

favored areas constituted about one-quarter of the realm but payed only one-sixth of the *taille*. In those considerable parts of France where the *taille* was levied on the owner of the land, the nobility as well as most city dwellers were generally exempt. The *vingtième* that was sometimes added to the *taille* was supposed to be a universal and proportional tax on income, but it was only levied during wartime and its renewal invariably provoked successful efforts to create loopholes and exemptions.

The greater part of the state's revenue came from indirect taxes of three kinds: the *gabelle* or salt tax, excise or sales taxes, and internal customs duties. The *gabelle* was probably the most detested tax of all because of the manner in which it was levied. Monopolizing the mining and sale of salt, the state required its subjects to purchase a stipulated amount at a fixed price. The price varied by region, some areas being subject to an extremely high rate, while others paid only nominal amounts, with a spread of as much as thirty-five times between the extremes. Such a system naturally invited smuggling, and in response the administrators of the *gabelle* employed a veritable private army of inspectors with wide repressive powers. The *aides* or excise taxes virtually doubled the price of wine for the consumer, and also raised the price of soap, oil, tobacco, paper, and meat. Consumer prices were likewise driven up by internal customs duties—tolls on the transport of goods within France, which were collected like the *gabelle* by a tough private force of inspectors.

Taxes on landed property, on salt, wine, or the transport of goods might have been justifiable, but there was no mechanism for consultation with the taxpayers, other than their right to appeal a land-tax assessment after it was made. Moreover, the one exception to this rule, the special-interest bargaining of the *pays d'état*, made the burden all the greater on other regions. The incidence of almost every tax varied according to where one lived, and in many instances according to one's social class. Most taxes were regressive in that they applied in the same proportion to rich and poor alike. What is more, the *gabelle* and customs duties were farmed out, that is, contracted by the government to a private syndicate of financiers, which advanced lump sums to the government in exchange for the right to collect the taxes and to pocket the difference as profit. This syndicate—called the Royal General Farms—was drawn from a group of about a hundred wealthy families; in the 1750's it is estimated that it cleared about a 16 percent profit on its transactions.

As city dwellers generally exempt from the *taille*, most bourgeois escaped their fair share of taxation. They did contribute to the crown's finances, however, by making loans and by purchasing government annuities. Since tax revenues did not nearly suffice to meet expenses, the crown was locked into a cycle of ever escalating borrowing. Small investors as well as large-scale speculators sought the government's bonds and annuities, which usually carried high interest rates or other inducements. The Royal General Farms was another source of loans. Using their profits from tax collection, the tax farmers loaned money to the very government that had contracted for their services—money that would have been flowing directly into the royal coffers had the crown not required large advances from the tax farmers. Truly this was a vicious circle. The government's need for ready cash and credit obliged it to turn to these financiers at the cost of yet more indebtedness.

A further characteristic of royal finances was the absence of any central treasury to disburse the funds. Instead the government's money was managed by several hundred private accountants under orders of the controller-general and subject to periodic audits by a special court. There were several justifications for this extraordinary system. First, private responsibility, with a profit incentive for the accountants, was supposed to maximize their diligence and thrift. It was thought that they would have a greater stake in efficiency than mere salaried bureaucrats. Second, it was easier to audit several hundred individual sets of accounts than one massive series. Third, the accountants could provide short-term credit by making advances from their personal capital. Moreover, because of the accountants' personal wealth and connections with the crown, their private clients trusted them to make short-term loans to the government with their funds as well. The disadvantages of this system were that it encouraged chronic borrowing, and that it made it impossible to know in advance the balance of disbursements and income. Instead, as expenses came up, they were assigned to one accountant or another, who often had to borrow to cover the bill. "Deficits, like budgets, were not a contemporary notion," a historian of royal finances has observed. "The debt trickled into the system, as did the revenues, posing only such problems as government and nation chose to see in it." [14]

The obstacles to reforming this system were formidable. In the area of taxation, exemptions and regional privileges were regarded as sacred "liberties," even though they stood in the way of an equitable, rationalized allocation of the burden. The government's cash-flow or liquidity problem, meanwhile, made it extremely difficult to tinker with the system's other features, for by the 1770's the crown and its financiers were totally interdependent. Those who handled the crown's money (the tax farmers and the accountants) assured it of credit, yet at the same time they skimmed off a great deal of its potential income in the form of fees and interest. Moreover, the monarchy's attitude toward money was similar to the heedless way that certain aristocrats managed their personal finances. As Col-

[14] John Bosher, *French Finances 1770–1795: from business to bureaucracy* (Cambridge, 1970), and François Hincker, *Les Français devant l'impôt sous l'ancien régime* (Paris, 1971).

bert, Louis XIV's controller-general had once put it, "the king never consults his finances [i.e., revenues] in order to determine his expenditures." The monarchy spent lavishly on its personal expenses and military establishment, leaving its finance ministers to worry about paying the bills.

This situation grew untenable after France's exorbitant commitment to the independence of the Thirteen Colonies. A vast French naval undertaking as well as an expeditionary force had been financed entirely by loans. Controller-general Jacques Necker boasted of not having raised taxes to carry this off, but he left a legacy of burdensome interest payments. By the 1780's his successors had pieced together an approximate rendering of the total budget in which expenditures were startlingly weighted toward servicing an accumulated national debt of about four billion livres. Annual expenditures were divided approximately as follows:

> 165,000,000 livres (about 27%) on the military
> 145,000,000 livres (about 23%) on civil expenditures
> 310,000,000 livres (just under 50%) on debt service, most of it in
>   interest payments

Not only did debt service account for half of the annual expenditures, but it contributed to an annual deficit of about a hundred million livres, which necessitated even more loans and even greater interest payments.

Breakdown, 1787–1789

As the French monarchy entered the 1780's—its reputation tarnished by previous political conflicts and false starts toward reform—it was too strong to surrender authority willingly, but too hemmed in by the constituted bodies and special interests to exercise sovereignty effectively. There seemed to be no way to forge a consensus, no mechanisms or institutions to harmonize diverse viewpoints. But the financial crisis would not solve itself. The monarchy was obliged to search for new remedies and launch out in new directions.

A new finance minister, Charles de Calonne (1734–1802), revealed just how serious the debt problem was, though interestingly his gloomy picture was not universally believed. Unlike Necker he recommended a new tax. The "territorial subvention" was to be a proportional tax on the income of landed property, payable by all landowners regardless of their social class or region. To obtain cooperation in administering the tax, and to build the kind of consensus that reform required, Calonne proposed establishing new *provincial assemblies* of a purely advisory nature, to be elected by large landowners regardless of social class. These modest proposals to treat the landed elites equally in this matter did not threaten the nobility's other privileges. However, they did point the way toward

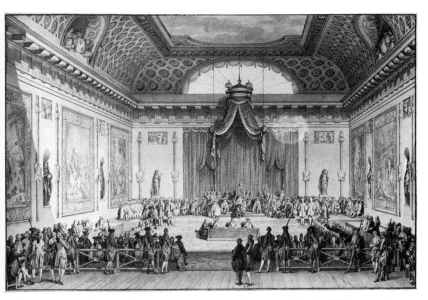

The Assembly of Notables. *The attempt by the monarchy in 1787 to enlist the elites' support for Calonne's reforms backfired completely. One contemporary cartoon depicted the notables as geese who, when asked with what sauce they wished to be eaten, replied that they did not wish to be eaten at all. Musée de Versailles.*

a social system emphasizing equal rights and duties, and they seemed to breach the privileged position of certain provinces and their constituted bodies.

Calonne sought to allay the inevitable opposition by convincing a selected group of important persons to accept the proposals in advance. Louis XVI therefore convened 150 dignitaries from such groups as the magistracy, titled nobility, episcopacy, and municipal oligarchies in an Assembly of Notables. This august body met in February 1787 and immediately expressed its total distrust of Calonne. His plan was denounced for bypassing the traditional liberties of the realm, and for proposing yet another new tax. While Calonne attacked privilege, the notables replied by attacking despotism. Meanwhile, several royal accountants had declared bankruptcy and fear was mounting that the state might actually become insolvent.

Calonne was forced to resign and his plan for a new tax was shelved while his successor, Archbishop Lomenie de Brienne, sought to negotiate additional emergency loans. Now the Paris *Parlement* used its leverage and threatened to block any loans unless the crown promised to convene the

Estates-General—the nationwide representative institution that had not met since 1614, and which had seemed incompatible with the absolutism of the seventeenth and eighteenth centuries. Going farther than it ever had before, the *Parlement* issued a manifesto on the "fundamental laws of the realm," in which it proclaimed itself the guardian of these laws. In effect it asserted that the monarchy must share its sovereignty with the nobility of the robe, which in turn would use its powers to protect the rights and privileges of all subjects. This assault by the *Parlement* was a mixture of liberal principles and aristocratic pretensions. Claiming almost revolutionary powers for its own class, the *Parlement* was spearheading an aristocratic revolt. As the British traveler Arthur Young commented, "France is on the verge of revolution, but one likely to add to the scale of the nobility and clergy."

The monarchy moved to counter this revolt, as it had in 1770, by dissolving the *Parlement*, exiling its leaders, and creating new courts. The May Edicts of 1788, however, only seemed to prove the charge that the crown was tyrannical. Clergy, provincial *Parlements*, and elite opinion in general raised a fierce outcry. Meanwhile, a second front in the aristocratic offensive had opened outside the capital as some of the provincial estates tried to reorganize themselves and increase their bargaining power. Like its Belgian counterpart, the nobility in most cases asserted and sought to strengthen its traditional position of eminence in these bodies. Except in Dauphiné, where an accord was reached, the second estate had no intention of amalgamating itself with the middle classes in the manner that Calonne's provincial assemblies had visualized. It was in these local battles (especially in Brittany) that the middle classes first began to develop their own point of view. While they were united with the nobility in the struggle against royal absolutism, middle-class leaders were beginning to recognize that the organized nobility was not necessarily a benign ally.

Immobilized by conflict, faced with unprecedented hostility to its initiatives, especially to the May Edicts, and still on the verge of bankruptcy, the crown capitulated. In July 1788, Brienne agreed to convene the Estates-General in Versailles the following May, and to reinstate the *Parlement*. The question was then immediately posed: how would the Estates-General be organized? *Parlement* took this under advisement and in September issued its opinion that the Estates-General should meet as it last had in 1614. There should be three separate chambers: clergy, nobility, third estate, each having one cumulative vote. With a single stroke *Parlement* thus altered the alignment of forces, making it clear that the middle classes would be relegated to an inferior position as against the powerful corporate interests of the clergy and nobility. Instead of reducing the barrier between noble and non-noble elites, an Estates-General that voted by order would solidify it. Instead of facilitating a fusion of noble and non-noble elites, an Estates-General meeting this way signified to the middle classes that they were being socially demoted, lumped together with the common people.[15]

Middle-class opinion now shifted decisively, encouraged by an outpouring of pamphlets such as Abbé Sieyès's *What is the Third Estate?* Protesting the *Parlement's* ruling, and attacking the aristocracy in an unprecedented manner, Sieyès asked: "What is the Third Estate? Everything! What has it been in the political order up to the present? Nothing!" The aristocracy monopolizes all lucrative positions, he claimed with exaggeration, while doing none of the "truly laborious" work of society. Free competition among all individuals should be possible; talent must be recognized and service rewarded, regardless of birth. Specifically, Sieyès and other patriots (as they called themselves) demanded that the deputation of the third estate be doubled, so that it would equal the other two combined, and that voting on major issues take place by head rather than by order. What had begun as a two-sided struggle between crown and aristocracy had turned into a triangular conflict. The enemy was not simply royal despotism but also aristocratic pretension. Middle-class publicists having come to life most unexpectedly, the nobility gradually made its peace with the crown so that both could stand against the escalating demands of the middle classes for a share of political power.

Early in 1789 assemblies of citizens from each estate met all across France to choose electors and to draw up grievance petitions (*cahiers*) which the king had invited. Most of the third estate's *cahiers* were concerned with local issues, and with the excesses of the tax and seigneurial burdens. They did not remotely foretell a radical overturn of the established political and social order. The electors chosen in these primary assemblies subsequently met in regional assemblies to choose deputies to the Estates-General and to draft consolidated petitions or general *cahiers*. In the nobility's *cahiers*, equality in taxation had by now been accepted in principle, and there was also general agreement on the need for individual rights, legal reform, and periodic meetings of the Estates-General. On the issue of social status and political power, however, the second estate demanded such things as the vote by order in the Estates-General as a guarantee of its position. The more radical general *cahiers* of the third estate, meanwhile, called for a reorganization of the Estates General, with the boldest among them going so far as to advocate the drafting of a constitution to replace traditional liberties and privileges, though at this point such demands were not widely voiced.

The electoral process itself was sharpening the state of public opinion, and identifying potential leaders. The elections in Paris, for example,

[15] Colin Lucas, "Nobles, Bourgeois, and the Origins of the French Revolution," *Past and Present*, No. 60 (August, 1973), pp. 84–126.

Prerevolutionary propaganda, 1788-1789. "This won't last forever." Engravings and cartoons emphasized the same point: the productivity of the third estate and the idleness of the privileged orders. The monkey symbolized the royal government. "Let's hope this ends soon." This typical cartoon of a stooped peasant illustrated in the most graphic way how the third estate was forced to carry the clergy and nobility on its back. The slip of paper in the peasant's pocket reads "salt and tobacco, land tax, corvée, tithe, militia," while the rabbits and birds nibbling at his feet represent the depredations caused by the lords' hunting rights.

indicate the nature of the emerging middle-class leadership. In the first place, out of thirty-thousand eligible tax-paying third-estate voters, only about twelve thousand appeared at the capital's sixty primary assemblies. The petty bourgeois—the mass of Parisian artisans and shopkeepers— was evidently not yet self-confident enough to stake out its political claims. Lawyers, and to a lesser extent wholesale merchants, intellectuals, and officeholders controlled the primary assemblies and dominated the assembly of four hundred Parisian electors who chose the city's deputies to the Estates-General and drafted its general *cahier*. On the drafting commission of thirty-six, and on the twenty-man deputation there was scarcely an artisan or shopkeeper. The third-estate leadership was solidly bourgeois. But these were bourgeois of the old regime itself, self-assured, accomplished men who had made their careers and attained considerable standing within the world of the old regime's law courts, academies, corporate groups, and government bureaus. "Success in the old regime clearly determined the choice of the founders of the new regime." [16] Without a single artisan or peasant from anywhere in France, the third estate's deputies at Versailles did not remotely reflect the social composition or attitudes of the populace. They were well equipped, however, to confront one of Europe's strongest aristocracies and to press the claim of the third estate for power.

By the time the Estates-General convened in May 1789 a consensus existed among reformist nobles and commoners for the limitation of absolute monarchy, equality in taxation, rationalization of government, and individual liberties. There was profound disagreement, however, over the terms and extent of reform. Most of the nobility was drawing closer to the crown now that they faced an aroused middle class. For their part, the "patriots" of the middle class, along with their liberal noble allies, claimed to speak in the name of the entire third estate, though they were largely strangers to the aspirations of peasants, urban artisans, and the laboring poor. Yet as 1789 began, the expectations of the peasants and urban popular classes had been aroused by the deluge of propaganda, the drafting of *cahiers*, and the elections. More important, the winter and spring of 1788–1789 had been a time of severe economic difficulties, with crop failures and grain shortages more than doubling the price of bread, while unemployment and stagnating trade from an earlier depression had not yet been overcome. Vagrants and beggars filled the roads, grain convoys and marketplaces were besieged by angry consumers, and relations between town and country were strained. This short-term conjuncture would have

[16] François Furet, "Les Elections de 1789 à Paris: le tiers état et la naissance d'une classe dirigeante," in *Von Ancien Régime zur Französischen Revolution*, ed. by E. Hinrichs *et al.* (Göttingen, 1978).

profound importance for the course of events. The triangular struggle among patriots, aristocrats, and monarchy in the Estates-General would be played out against a vast panorama of popular mobilization over subsistence issues. Normally such popular protest and rioting would have been contained and eventually suppressed by the military. In 1789, however, the fabric of royal authority had unraveled so completely that the outcome would be different. Struggles among the elites and disturbances among the common people would merge, making the third estate invincible and 1789 a year of revolution.

Suggestions for Further Reading

(Books marked * are available in paperback.)

HISTORIOGRAPHY AND BIBLIOGRAPHY

Recent approaches to the study of European history are described in *Historical Studies Today*, ed. by Felix Gilbert and Stephen Graubard (New York, 1975) (Norton) and in George Iggers, *New Directions in European Historiography* (New York, 1975). For the "Annales School" of French historiography specifically, see Triran Stoianovich, *French Historical Method: the Annales Paradigm* (New Brunswick, N.J., 1976); *Faire l'Histoire*, ed. by J. LeGoff and P. Nora (3 vols.: Paris, 1974); and Emmanuel LeRoy Ladurie, *The Territory of the Historian* (Chicago, 1979). On the eighteenth century there is a useful volume by M. S. Anderson, *Historians and Eighteenth-Century Europe, 1715–1789* (Oxford, 1979). General guides to bibliography include the American Historical Association's *Guide to Historical Literature* (Washington, 1961), and *A Select List of Works on Europe and Europe Oversees, 1715–1815*, ed. by J. S. Bromley and A. Goodwin (London, 1956). As an example of more specialized bibliographies see, for England, S. Pargellis and D. Medley, *Bibliography of British History, 1714–89* (Oxford, 1951) and Judith B. Williams, *Guide to the Printed Materials for English Social and Economic History, 1750–1850* (2 vols.: New York, 1966).

GENERAL WORKS

Among the many one-volume surveys of the eighteenth century the most comprehensive is M. S. Anderson, *Europe in the Eighteenth Century, 1713–1783* (London, 1976) (Longman). Leonard Krieger, *Kings and Philosophers, 1689–1789* (New York, 1970) (Norton) is outstanding on political history, thought, and the relation between the two, while the strength of George Rudé's *Europe in the Eighteenth Century: Aristocracy and the Bourgeois Challenge* (New York, 1972) is in social history. Both volumes are perhaps more useful to someone already acquainted with the period, which is also true of Pierre Chaunu, *La Civilisation de l'Europe des lumières* (Paris, 1971). *The Eighteenth Century: Europe in the Age of the Enlightenment*, ed. by Alfred Cobban (New York, 1969), a collection of chapters by experts, and C. B. E. Behrens's suggestive interpretive essay, *The Ancien Régime* (London, 1967) (Harcourt), are both lavishly illustrated.

Two standard multivolume series on European history in English treat political, diplomatic, and cultural history in detail, but the short time span of each volume virtually precludes an adequate discussion of social history. Nonetheless, these are very useful reference works. In the *New Cambridge Modern History* (Cambridge), see Vol. VII, *The Old Regime, 1713–1763*, ed. by J. O. Lindsay (1957), and Vol. VIII, *The American and French Revolutions, 1763–1793*, ed. by Albert Goodwin (1965) (Cambridge). In *The Rise of Modern Europe* (New York), known as the Langer series, the three relevant volumes are lively though dated, and contain extensive scholarly bibliographies: Penfield Roberts, *The Quest for Security, 1715–40* (1947); Walter Dorn, *The Competition for Empire, 1740–63* (1940); and Leo Gershoy, *From Despotism to Revolution, 1763–89* (1944).

For histories of particular countries the best served is England, starting with the older "Oxford History of England" volumes: Basil Williams, *The Whig Supremacy, 1715–60* (1939), and J. Steven Watson, *The Reign of George III, 1760–1815* (1960). In Harvard's new series there is W. A. Speck, **Stability and Strife: England, 1714–60* (Cambridge, Mass., 1977) (Harvard), whose companion volume has not yet appeared. John B. Owens's dry and detailed *The Eighteenth Century, 1714–1815* (London, 1975) is in the Nelson "History of England" series. There are remarkably few general books in English on France, the best being Alfred Cobban, **History of Modern France*, Vol. I, 1715–1799 (Baltimore, 1966) (Pelican). John Lough's *An Introduction to Eighteenth-Century France* (New York, 1960) is not as useful as the same author's fine volume on the seventeenth century. In French, there are several brief volumes on the old-regime period by Hubert Méthivier in the "Que Sais-Je?" series. Hajo Holborn's *A History of Modern Germany*, Vol. II, 1648–1840 (New York, 1964) is written with a master's hand, but a decidedly old-fashioned one. For the Habsburg Monarchy there is a brief but brilliant overview in Ernst Wangermann, **The Austrian Achievement, 1700–1800* (London, 1973) (Harcourt). Richard Herr's **The Eighteenth-Century Revolution in Spain* (Princeton, 1958) (Princeton), though not meant as a general introduction, can nonetheless fill that role in the absence of any alternatives. For Italy there is likewise a paucity of synthesis, with the best introduction being Jean Delumeau, *L'Italie de Botticelli à Bonaparte* (Paris, 1974). On Sweden consult *Essays in Swedish History*, ed. by Michael Roberts (Minneapolis, 1968) and B. J. Hovde, *The Scandinavian Countries, 1720–1865: The Rise of Middle Classes* (2 vols.: Boston, 1944). For Belgium and the Netherlands see the opening chapters of E. H. Kossman, *The Low Countries, 1780–1940* (Oxford, 1978).

THE STATE

Overviews of eighteenth-century political history are provided in Max Beloff, *The Age of Absolutism, 1660–1815* (New York, 1962) and E. N. Williams, *The Ancien Régime in Europe: Government and Society in the Major States, 1648–1789* (New York, 1970). On the later or "enlightened" phase of absolutism see, for example, John Gagliardo, **Enlightened Despotism* (New York, 1967) (AHM), T. C. W. Blanning, *Joseph II and Enlightened Despotism* (London, 1970), and, with an emphasis on theory, Leonard Krieger, *An Essay on the Theory of Enlightened Despotism* (Chicago, 1975). A collection of topical essays is provided in *The Formation of National States in Western Europe*, ed. by Charles Tilly (Princeton, 1975). Other useful thematic treatments are Georges Durand, *Etats et Institutions, XVIᵉ–XVIIIᵉ siècle* (Paris, 1969), Ernest Barker, *The Development of Public Services in Western Europe, 1660–1930* (Oxford, 1944), and A. R. Myers, **Parliaments and Estates in Europe to 1789* (London, 1975) (Harcourt).

There is of course a large literature on the era of Louis XIV, whose importance as a background for eighteenth-century development is apparent.

For an introduction see Pierre Goubert, *Louis XIV and Twenty Million Frenchmen* (New York, 1970) (Random), John B. Wolf's biography, *Louis XIV* (New York, 1968), and *Louis XIV and the Craft of Kingship*, ed. by John Rule (Columbus, Ohio, 1970). On France's political institutions there is no better introduction than Pierre Goubert, *L'Ancien Régime*, Vol. II, *Les Pouvoirs* (Paris, 1973), which also provides a reliable guide to work in French. For a superficial survey of Louis XV's long reign see G. P. Gooch, *Louis XV, the Monarchy in Decline* (London, 1956). The two major centers of power in France were the intendants and the *Parlements*, treated in Vivian Gruder, *The Royal Provincial Intendants: a governing elite in eighteenth-century France* (Ithaca, N.Y., 1968); James Shennan, *The Parlement of Paris* (Ithaca, N.Y., 1968); James D. Hardy Jr., *Judicial Politics in the Old Regime: the Parlement of Paris during the Regency* (Baton Rouge, La., 1968); and Jean Egret, *Louis XV et l'Opposition parlementaire, 1715–1774* (Paris, 1970).

Sidney B. Fay, *The Rise of Brandenburg-Prussia to 1786* (New York, 1964) is a dry but useful introduction. Robert Ergang, *The Potsdam Führer: Frederick William I, father of Prussian militarism* (New York, 1941) is a fine biography despite its World-War-II-inspired title. See also R. A. Dorwart, *The Administrative Reforms of Frederick William I of Prussia* (Cambridge, Mass., 1953). On his successor consult *Frederick the Great: a profile*, ed. by Peter Paret (Englewood Cliffs, N.J., 1972); Gerhard Ritter, **Frederick the Great: a historical profile* (Berkeley, 1968) (University of California); and Hubert C. Johnson, *Frederick the Great and His Officials* (New Haven, 1975). For an interpretation of Prussian state building see Hans Rosenburg, **Bureaucracy, Aristocracy, and Autocracy: the Prussian Experience, 1660–1815* (Boston, 1958) (Beacon).

In addition to Wangermann's superb volume, useful books on the Habsburg realm include Robert Pick, *Empress Maria Theresa: the earlier years, 1717–1757* (New York, 1966); Saul K. Padover's enthusiastic *The Revolutionary Emperor, Joseph II* (New York, 1934); Paul Bernard, *Joseph II* (New York, 1968); Daniel Klang, *Tax Reform in Eighteenth-Century Lombardy* (New York, 1977); and Robert Kerner, *Bohemia in the Eighteenth Century* (New York, 1932), devoted primarily to the brief reign of Leopold II (1790–1792). Leopold's full-scale biography in German is by Adam Wandruszka, who has also written *The House of Habsburg: six hundred years of a European dynasty* (New York, 1964). An excellent collection of primary documents has been edited by C. A. Macartney, *The Habsburg and Hohenzollern Dynasties in the Seventeenth and Eighteenth Centuries* (New York, 1970).

For developments elsewhere in the Holy Roman Empire see F. L. Carsten, *Princes and Parliaments in Germany* (New York, 1959); Helen Leibel, *Enlightened Bureauracy versus Enlightened Despotism in Baden, 1750–92* (Philadelphia, 1965); T. C. W. Blanning, *Reform and Revolution in Mainz, 1743–1803* (London, 1974); and John Gagliardo, *Reich and Nation: The Holy Roman Empire as Idea and Reality, 1763–1806* (Bloomington, Ind., 1980). On Russia see B. H. Sumner, **Peter the Great and the Emergence of Russia* (New York, 1951) (Macmillan); *Russia in the Era of Peter the Great*, ed. by L. Jay Oliva, (Englewood Cliffs, N.J., 1969); *Catherine the Great: a profile*, ed. by Marc Raeff (Englewood Cliffs, N.J., 1972); Gladys Thompson, *Catherine the Great and the Expansion of Russia* (New York, 1962); Paul Dukes, *Catherine the Great and the Russian Nobility*

(Cambridge, 1967); John T. Alexander, *Autocratic Politics in a National Crisis: the Imperial Russian government and Pugachev's revolt, 1773–1775* (Bloomington, Indiana, 1969); and Paul Avrich, **Russian Rebels, 1600–1800* (New York, 1972) (Norton). On Spain, consult W. N. Hargreaves-Mawdsley, *Eighteenth-Century Spain, 1700–1788: A Political, Diplomatic, and Institutional History* (London, 1978).

Introductions to eighteenth-century English politics are provided by J. H. Plumb, *The Origins of Political Stability in England, 1675–1725* (Boston, 1967), and Betty Kemp, *Kings and Commons, 1660–1832* (New York, 1957). The first part of the century is treated brilliantly in J. H. Plumb's two-volume biography *Sir Robert Walpole* (Boston, 1956–61). Our view of the system at mid-century was dramatically altered by Lewis Namier, *The Structure of Politics at the Accession of George III* (London, 1929) and his **England in the Age of the American Revolution* (London, 1930) (St. Martin's). For a critical evaluation of Namier see, among other works, Herbert Butterfield's *George III and the Historians* (London, 1957). Namier's influence may be seen in such works as John Brooke, *The House of Commons, 1754–90*. For perhaps the most widely respected view of English politics see Richard Pares, *King George III and the Politicians* (Oxford, 1953). There are numerous studies of particular ministries (see the bibliography in John B. Owens's book cited above), and of various opposition factions; for an overview of the latter see Archibald Foord, *His Majesty's Opposition* (Oxford, 1964). Other references to French and English politics will be found in the bibliography for Chapter 9, "The Road to Revolution," below.

INTERNATIONAL RIVALRY

To place the eighteenth century in perspective see chapter 3 of Ludwig Dehio, *The Precarious Balance: four centuries of the European power struggle* (New York, 1962). For concise treatments of the preceding era see R. N. Hatton, **Europe in the Age of Louis XIV* (London, 1969) (Norton) and, on Britain's growing involvement in European affairs, J. R. Jones, **Britain and Europe in the Seventeenth Century* (New York, 1966) (Norton). In the introductory volume to his monumental history of diplomacy in the revolutionary era, Albert Sorel offered a cynical view of old regime diplomacy, which volume is available in several editions, including *Europe and the French Revolution: the political tradition of the old regime* (New York, 1971). For an entirely different, Germanic approach to the question of old-regime statecraft see Friedrich Meinecke, *Machiavellism: The doctrine of raison d'état and its place in modern history* (New Haven, 1957). On the development of diplomacy as a career see D. B. Horn, *The British Diplomatic Service* (Oxford, 1961). That author is honored in a useful collection of essays, *Studies in Diplomatic History: essays in honor of D. B. Horn*, ed. by R. Hatton and M. S. Anderson (London, 1970).

The details of diplomatic history are extensively treated in the *Rise of Modern Europe* series and in the *New Cambridge Modern History* volumes. For a sampling of monographs see Arthur Wilson, *French Foreign Policy during the Administration of Cardinal Fleury* (Cambridge, Mass., 1936); Herbert Butterfield, *The Reconstruction of an Historical Episode* (Glasgow, 1951), on the outbreak of the Seven Years' War; L. Jay Oliva, *Misalliance: French Policy in Russia during the Seven Years' War* (New York, 1964); and Herbert Kaplan, *The First Partition of Poland* (New York, 1962). On

European interests in the New World see Vol. I of the *Cambridge History of the British Empire* (Cambridge, 1929); H. I. Priestly, *France Overseas through the Old Regime*(New York, 1939); Richard Pares, *War and Trade in the West Indies, 1739–1763* (Oxford, 1936); C. R. Boxer, **The Dutch Seaborne Empire, 1600–1800* (New York, 1965) (Humanities) and *The Portuguese Seaborne Empire, 1415–1825* (New York, 1969); and J. H. Parry, *The Spanish Seaborne Empire* (New York, 1966).

André Corvisier provides a good history of armies (especially France's) as social and political institutions in *Armies and Societies in Europe, 1494–1789* (Bloomington, Ind., 1979), while the relevant chapters of **Makers of Modern Strategy*, ed. by E. M. Earle (Princeton, 1944) (Princeton) discuss their use. Alfred Vagts, **A History of Militarism* (London, 1938) (Free) is still stimulating. The most concise history of a particular army is Christopher Duffy's *The Army of Frederick the Great* (London, 1974). The same author has also written on the Habsburg army, while Lee Kennett, *The French Armies in the Seven Years' War* (Durham, N.C., 1967) treats an army that suffered unexpected defeat.

THE SOCIAL ORDER

Probably the best introduction to eighteenth-century social history is Pierre Goubert's synthesis on France, **The Ancien Régime*, Vol. I (New York, 1973) (Harper & Row). A more idiosyncratic approach is Roland Mousnier, *The Institutions of France under the Absolute Monarchy*, Vol. I *Society and the state* (Chicago, 1979). Pre-World War II works in social history tend to be unsatisfying today but one exception that has stood up well is W. H. Bruford, **Germany in the Eighteenth Century: The Social Background of the Literary Revival* (Cambridge, 1935) (Cambridge). In comparison, Eda Sagarra, *A Social History of Germany, 1648–1914* (New York, 1977) is an unsatisfying patchwork.

An introductory overview of rural society is provided by Frank Huggett, **The Land Question and European Society Since 1650* (London, 1975) (Harcourt), while Jerome Blum, **The End of the Old Order in Rural Europe* (Princeton, 1978) (Princeton), covering the eighteenth and nineteenth centuries, is an invaluable mine of information. Blum has also given us **Lord and Peasant in Russia from the Ninth to the Nineteenth Century* (Princeton, 1961) (Princeton), with a great deal of attention to our period, while in French the works of Michel Confino on Russia are fundamental. French historians have studied other agrarian societies as well (such as Pierre Vilar's work on Catalonia in Spain), but most have been drawn to regional studies of the French peasantry. These works are used in Goubert's synthesis, in the *Histoire de la France rurale*, ed. by G. Duby and A. Wallon, Vol. II, *L'Age classique, 1340–1789* (Paris, 1975), and in *Histoire économique et sociale de la France*, Vol. II: *1660–1789*, ed. by F. Braudel and E. Labrousse (Paris, 1970). For a critical discussion of this landmark volume see I. Woloch, "French Economic and Social History," *Journal of Interdisciplinary History*, Vol. IV (Winter 1974), and for an introduction to rural studies in France see **The Peasantry in the Old Regime: conditions and protests*, ed. by I. Woloch (New York, 1970) (Krieger). The great theses on French rural history include G. Lefebvre on the Nord, A. Poitrineau on Auvergne, P. Goubert on the Beauvaisis, P. Saint Jacob on Burgundy, G. Frêche on the Toulouse region, and Emmanuel LeRoy Ladurie on Languedoc. The latter is the only one thus far available in English: *The Peasants of Languedoc*(Urbana, Ill., 1974) (University of Illinois). There are also studies of individual villages including Thomas Sheppard, *Lourmarin in the Eighteenth Century* (Baltimore, 1971), and Patrice Higonnet, *Pont-de-Montvert: Social Structure and Politics in a French Village 1700–1914* (Cambridge, Mass., 1971). Studies of rural society in the Habsburg Monarchy have focused on the problem of agrarian reform: Edith M. Link, *The Emancipation of the Austrian Peasantry, 1740–1789* (New York, 1949), and William E. Wright, *Serf, Seigneur and Sovereign: agarian reform in eighteenth-century Bohemia* (Minneapolis, 1966). Informative studies of rural society across Europe are collected in the volume *L'Abolition de la féodalité dans le monde occidental* (Paris, 1971), while the question of "feudal" conditions in France is considered in Sidney Herbert, *The Fall of Feudalism in France* (New York, 1921).

   The European Nobility in the Eighteenth Century, ed. by Albert Goodwin (London, 1953) is a useful but uneven comparative introduction to the elites. On France see the collection edited by Guy Chaussinand-Nogaret, *Une histoire des élites, 1700–1848* (Paris, 1975); the same author's bold synthesis, *La Noblesse au XVIIIe siècle: de la féodalité aux lumières* (Paris, 1976); and the pioneering work of François Bluche and Jean Meyer. In English there is Franklin Ford, *Robe and Sword: the regrouping of the French aristocracy after Louis XIV* (Cambridge, Mass., 1953), and two outstanding studies by Robert Forster: *The Nobility of Toulouse in the Eighteenth Century* (Baltimore, 1960), and *The House of Saulx-Tavanes: Versailles and Burgundy, 1700–1830* (Baltimore, 1971). On Russia see Marc Raeff's highly original *The Origins of the Russian Intelligentsia: the eighteenth-century nobility* (New York, 1966) (Harcourt), and Robert E. Jones, *The Emancipation of the Russian Nobility, 1762–1785* (Princeton, 1973). The powerful Hungarian nobility is portrayed in Béla Kiraly, *Hungary in the Late Eighteenth Century* (New York, 1969). For the landed elites in England see G. E. Mingay, *English Landed Society in the Eighteenth Century* (Toronto, 1963), and *Aristocratic Government and Society in Eighteenth-Century England*, ed. by Daniel Baugh (New York, 1975). There have been at least three efforts to deal analytically with the bourgeoisie, all unsuccessful but at least suggestive: Bernard Groethuysen, *The Bourgeois: Catholicism vs. Capitalism in the Eighteenth Century* (New York, 1927); Charles Morazé, *The Triumph of the Middle Classes* (New York, 1968); and Elinor Barber, *The Bourgeoisie in Eighteenth-Century France* (Princeton, 1955) (Princeton).

   Eighteenth-century urban society and its working classes have been far less extensively studied than the peasantry. Maurice Garden, *Lyon et les lyonnais au XVIIIe siècle* (Paris, 1975) was one of the first to apply French methods to the urban scene, with superb results. Jean-Claude Perrot's *Genèse d'une ville moderne: Caen au XVIIIe siècle* (Paris, 1975) is more concerned with economic processes than Garden's book. Both volumes are heavily quantitative, in the manner of French theses on rural regions. Other studies of urban society in France include Franklin L. Ford, *Strasbourg in Transition, 1648–1789* (Cambridge, Mass., 1958) (Norton); Olwen Hufton, *Bayeux in the Late Eighteenth Century: a social study* (Oxford, 1968); Jeffry Kaplow, *Elbeuf During the Revolutionary Period: history and social structure* (Baltimore, 1964); and P. Butel and J.-P. Poussou, *La Vie Quoti-*

dienne à Bordeaux au XVIIIᵉ siècle (Paris, 1980). On Germany see Mack Walker's original *German Home Towns: community, state, and general estate, 1648–1871* (Ithaca, N.Y., 1971). Among the urban studies of England see M. Dorothy George, *London Life in the Eighteenth Century* (New York, 1925); George Rudé, *Hanoverian London, 1714–1808* (Berkeley, Calif. 1971); and Gordon Jackson, *Hull in the Eighteenth Century, 1750–1789* (Oxford, 1972).

Most history touching on eighteenth-century working people seems to be leading up to the nineteenth century and industrialization, as in Louise Tilly and Joan Scott's excellent *Women, Work and Family* (New York, 1978) (Holt). Exceptions include Jeffry Kaplow, *The Names of Kings: the Parisian Laboring poor in the eighteenth century* (New York, 1972), and Louis Trénard, "The Social Crisis in Lyons on the Eve of the French Revolution," in *New Perspectives on the French Revolution*, ed. by J. Kaplow (New York, 1965), and, on English labor disputes, C. R. Dobson, *Masters and Journeymen* (London, 1979). On servants, an important segment of the working classes, see Jean Hecht, *The Domestic Servant in Eighteenth-Century England* (London, 1956), and Cissie Fairchilds, "Masters and Servants in Eighteenth-Century Toulouse," *Journal of Social History*, Vol. XII (1979).

POPULATION

T. H. Hollingsworth, *Historical Demography* (London, 1969) is a convenient introduction to the methodology. Two of the leading English practitioners of the field have written general works: Edward A. Wrigley, *Population and History* (New York, 1969) (McGraw), and Peter Laslett, *The World We have Lost* (London, 1965) (Scribner). Among the numerous collections of articles the following are especially useful: *Population in History*, ed. by D. V. Glass and D. E. C. Eversley (London, 1964); the Spring 1968 issue of *Daedalus*, devoted to historical population studies; and *Family and Society: selections from the "Annales"*, ed. by R. Forster and O. Ranum (Baltimore, 1976) (Johns Hopkins). For a concise introduction to the work of French historical demographers see Pierre Goubert, "Historical Demography and the Reinterpretation of Early Modern French History," *Journal of Interdisciplinary History*, Vol. I (1970), and Jacques Dupaquier, "French Population in the 17th and 18th Centuries," in *Essays in French Economic History*, ed. by R. Cameron (Homewood, Ill., 1970). The best general history of population is M. Reinhard, A. Armengaud and J. Dupaquier, *Histoire générale de la population mondiale* (Paris, 1968).

In the 1970's historical demography moved beyond quantitative studies of births, marriages and deaths to address the qualitative issues of family life, sexuality, and attitudes towards life and death. The following are among the best works: François Lebrun, *Les Hommes et la mort en Anjou aux 17ᵉ et 18ᵉ siècles: essai de démographie et de psychologie historique* (Paris, 1971); *Family and Inheritance: Rural Society in Western Europe, 1200–1800*, ed. by J. Goody, J. Thirsk, and E. P. Thompson (Cambridge, 1976) (Cambridge); Jean-Louis Flandrin, *Families in Former Times: kinship, household, and sexuality* (Cambridge, 1979) (Cambridge); François Lebrun, *La Vie conjugale sous l'ancien régime* (Paris, 1975); and Lawrence Stone, *The Family, Sex, and Marriage in England, 1500–1800* (New York,

1977) (Harper Torchbook). Though it has been superceded by further research, mention should also be made of Philippe Ariès' pioneering, *Centuries of Childhood: a social history of family life (New York, 1965) (Random).

THE ECONOMY

Various aspects of economic history are treated in two standard multivolume series: The Cambridge Economic History of Europe, and the *Fontana Economic History of Europe, edited by Carlo Cipolla (see Vols. 3 and 4) (Watts). For a superb synthesis of the period before the great spurt of economic growth see Jan deVries, *The Economy of Europe in an Age of Crisis, 1600–1750 (Cambridge, 1976) (Cambridge), while Pierre Léon, Economies et sociétés préindustrielles, Vol. II, 1650–1789 (Paris, 1970) covers the later years as well. On England see Charles Wilson, England's Apprenticeship, 1603–1767 (New York, 1965), and T. S. Ashton, *An Economic History of England: the Eighteenth Century (London, 1961) (Methuen). France's economic growth is traced in Roger Price, The Economic Modernisation of France, 1730–1800 (New York, 1975), and of course in the Histoire économique et sociale de la France, Vol. II, while Spain is treated in Jaime Vincens Vives, An Economic History of Spain (Princeton, 1969). For particular topics the following are representative: B. H. Slicher van Bath, The Agrarian History of Western Europe, A.D. 500–1850 (New York, 1962); Eli Heckscher, Mercantilism (2 vols.: New York, 1935) and *Revisions in Mercantilism, ed. by D. C. Coleman (London, 1969) (Methuen); Pierre Vilar, A History of Gold and Money, 1450–1920 (London, 1976); P. G. M. Dickson, The Financial Revolution in England: a study in the development of public credit, 1688–1756 (London, 1967); and David Ringrose, Transportation and Economic Stagnation in Spain, 1750–1850 (Durham, N.C., 1970). Economic history is considered from a novel perspective in Fernand Braudel, *Capitalism and Material Life, 1400–1800 (New York, 1973) (Harper & Row).

On maritime and colonial trade, in addition to the works cited above, under the heading "International Rivalry," there are comprehensive overviews by J. H. Parry, Trade and Dominion: European Overseas Empires in the Eighteenth Century (London, 1971) and Frédéric Mauro, L'expansion européenne, 1600–1870 (Paris, 1967). Ralph Davis's *The Rise of the Atlantic Economies (Ithaca, N.Y., 1973) (Cornell) is more interpretive. The most recent monograph is James Lang, Portuguese Brazil (New York, 1979). For a thorough case study of the trade in one commodity, tobacco, see Jacob Price, France and the Chesapeake (2 vols.: Ann Arbor, Mich., 1973). An excellent introduction to the whole issue of slavery is Michael Craton, *Sinews of Empire: a short history of British slavery (New York, 1974). Among the studies of plantation slavery, the most relevant are Richard S. Dunn, *Sugar and Slaves: the rise of the planter class in the English West Indies, 1624–1713 (Chapel Hill, N.C., 1972) (Norton) and Richard B. Sheridan, Sugar and Slavery: an economic history of the British West Indies, 1623–1755 (Baltimore, 1974). For European attitudes toward slavery see David B. Davis, *The Problem of Slavery in Western Culture (Ithaca, N.Y., 1966) (Cornell).

England's agricultural revolution is explained in J. D. Chambers and G. E. Mingay, *The Agricultural Revolution, 1750–1880 (London, 1966)

(David & Charles), but see also *Agriculture and Economic Growth in England, 1650–1815*, ed. by Eric L. Jones (London, 1967). For a comparison with the situation on the other side of the channel see M. Morineau, "Was There an Agricultural Revolution in 18th Century France?" in *Essays in French Economic History*, ed. by R. Cameron; Robert Forster, "Obstacles to Agricultural Growth in 18th Century France," *American Historical Review*, Vol. LXXV (1970); and A. J. Bourde, *The Influence of England on the French Agronomes, 1750–89* (Cambridge, 1953). For the beginnings of industrialization one should start with Franklin Mendels, "Protoindustrialization, the First Stage of Industrialization," *Journal of Economic History*, Vol. XXXII (1972). A detailed older account is Paul Mantoux, *The Industrial Revolution in the Eighteenth Century* (New York, 1928), while two highly regarded syntheses are T. S. Ashton, *The Industrial Revolution, 1760–1830* (Oxford, 1962) (Oxford), and Phyllis Deane, *The First Industrial Revolution* (Cambridge, 1965) (Cambridge). For the full sweep of the industrial revolution see the early chapters of the following: E. J. Hobsbawm, *Industry and Empire* (London, 1969) (Penguin); Peter Mathias, *The First Industrial Nation: an economic history of Britain, 1700–1914* (New York, 1969); David Landes, *The Unbound Prometheus: technological change and industrial development in Western Europe from 1750 to the present* (New York, 1969) (Cambridge); and W. O. Henderson, *Britain and Industrial Europe, 1750–1850* (Manchester, 1966). On the inventions see also the relevant chapters in *Technology in Western Civilization*, Vol. I, ed. by M. Kranzberg and C. W. Pursell (New York, 1967).

POVERTY AND PUBLIC ORDER

It would be hard to overstate the value of Olwen Hufton's *The Poor of Eighteenth Century France* (Oxford, 1974) (Oxford). Along with Jean-Pierre Gutton, *La Société et les pauvres en Europe, XVIᵉ–XVIIIᵉ siècles* (Paris, 1974) and Cissie Fairchilds, *Poverty and Charity in Aix-en-Provence, 1640–1789* (Baltimore, 1976), it has dramatically enlarged our perspective on the nature of poverty and the responses of the old regime. These books may be supplemented by Hufton's "Women and the Family Economy in Eighteenth Century France," *French Historical Studies*, Vol. IX (1975), and older works by Shelby McCloy, *Government Assistance in Eighteenth-Century France* (Durham, N.C. 1946) and *The Humanitarian Movement in Eighteenth-Century France* (Lexington, Ky., 1957).

Two early views of the English scene may be found in J. L. and B. Hammand, "Poverty, Crime, and Philanthropy" in *Johnson's England*, ed. by A. S. Turberville (2 vols., Oxford, 1933), and Dorothy Marshall, *The English Poor in the Eighteenth Century* (New York, 1926). On poor relief see G. W. Oxley, *Poor Relief in England and Wales, 1601–1834* (London, 1974); E. M. Hampson, *The Treatment of Poverty in Cambridgeshire, 1597–1834* (Cambridge, 1934); and Norman Longmate, *The Workhouse* (New York, 1974), chaps. 1–3. On the treatment of mental illness see Michel Foucault, *Madness and Civilization* (New York, 1973) (Random) and Kathleen Jones, *Lunacy, Law, and Conscience, 1744–1845* (London, 1955).

Within the past decade the subject of crime and punishment has drawn an increasing amount of attention from historians. The results may be assessed in four collections of articles: Douglas Hay *et. al.*, *Albion's Fatal Tree: Crime and Society in Eighteenth-Century England* (New York, 1975) (Pantheon); *Crime in England, 1550–1800*, ed. by J. S. Cockburn (Princeton, 1977); *Crimes et Criminalité en France 17ᵉ–18ᵉ siècles, Cahiers des Annales* No. 33 (Paris, 1971); and *Deviants and the Abandoned in French Society: selections from the "Annales,"* ed. by R. Forster and O. Ranum (Baltimore, 1978) (Johns Hopkins). The Cockburn volume has an exhaustive critical bibliography prepared by L. A. Knafla. Other work on France includes Michel Foucault's influential *Discipline and Punish: the birth of the prison* (New York, 1977) (Random) and Arlete Farge, *Le Vol d'aliments à Paris au XVIIIᵉ Siècle* (Paris, 1975). On England see E. P. Thompson, *Whigs and Hunters: the origin of the Black Act* (New York, 1975) (Pantheon); Michael Ignatieff, *A Just Measure of Pain: the Penitentiary in the Industrial Revolution, 1750–1850* (New York, 1980) (Columbia); and L. Radzinowicz, *A History of English Criminal Law and its Administration from 1750* (London, 1948), Vols. I–II—a work that has been criticized by historians such as Hay and Thompson. On penal theory in Europe see *Eighteenth-Century Penal Theory*, ed. by J. Heath (Oxford, 1963), a collection of sources, and John Langbein, *Torture and the Law of Proof* (Chicago, 1977).

The pioneering work of George Rudé on crowds and popular rights is conveniently available in two of his books: *The Crowd in History: a study of popular disturbances in France and England, 1730–1848* (New York, 1964) and *Paris and London in the Eighteenth Century: studies in popular protest* (New York, 1973). All sides of the subsistence controversy in France are illuminated in Steven Kaplan's exhaustive *Bread, Politics, and Political Economy in the Reign of Louis XV* (2 vols.: The Hague, 1976). On England the starting place is E. P. Thompson's seminal article "The Moral Economy of the English Crowd in the Eighteenth Century," *Past and Present*, No. 50 (1971). See also R. B. Rose, "Eighteenth Century Price Riots and Public Policy in England," *International Review of Social History*, Vol. VI (1961), and W. J. Shelton, *English Hunger and Industrial Disorders: a study of social conflicts during the first decade of George III's reign* (London, 1973).

THE VARIETIES OF CULTURE

From the vast array of scholarship on cultural and literary life some of the most useful volumes are: W. H. Bruford, *Culture and Society in Classical Weimar, 1775–1806* (Cambridge, 1962); A. Ward, *Book Production, Fiction, and the German Reading Public, 1740–1800* (Oxford, 1974); A. S. Collins, *Authorship in the Days of Johnson: being a study of the relation between author, patron, publisher and public, 1726–1780* (London, 1927); *Man Versus Society in Eighteenth-Century Britain*, ed. by J. L. Clifford (Cambridge, 1968), with articles on artists, composers, and writers; Daniel Mornet's pioneering and wide-ranging survey, *Les Origines Intellectuels de la Révolution française, 1715–1787* (Paris, 1947); A. Dupront *et. al.*, *Livre et Société dans la France du XVIIIᵉ siècle* (2 vols.: Paris, 1965, 1970); Ian Watt, *The Rise of the Novel: studies in Defoe, Richardson, and Fielding* (Berkeley, Calif. 1957) (University of California); Ronald Paulson, *Hogarth: His Life, Art and Times* (Abridged edn., New Haven, 1974); and Walter Jackson Bate, *Samuel Johnson* (New York, 1977) (Harcourt). Though not on the same level of scholarship, Marcia Davenport's breezy *Mozart* (New York,

1932) (Avon) situates its subject readably in his times. On the question of neoclassical taste in the period see Walter Jackson Bate, *From Classic to Romantic: premises of taste in eighteenth-century England* (Cambridge, Mass., 1949), and James Sutherland, *A Preface to Eighteenth–Century Poetry* (Oxford, 1948). From the literature on Freemasonry, J. M. Roberts, *The Mythology of the Secret Societies* (London, 1972), is one of the more interesting contributions.

The best introduction to the issue of education is Lawrence Stone, "Literacy and Education in England, 1640–1900," *Past and Present*, No. 42 (1969). Stone has led study groups on various aspects of education whose results he has edited in two publications: *The University in Society* (2 vols.: Princeton, 1974), with important essays by Richard Kagan on Spain and by Stone himself on Oxford, and *Schooling and Society* (Baltimore, 1976), about primary education. As usual the French are very active too, and have already published an excellent work of synthesis: R. Chartier and D. Julia, *L'Education en France de XVIe au XVIIIe siècle* (Paris, 1976). For England the early chapters of Brian Simon, *Studies in the History of Education, 1780–1870* (London, 1969) are highly recommended. In addition see N. Hans, *New Trends in Education in the Eighteenth Century* (London, 1951); M. G. Jones, *The Charity School Movement* (London, 1964); Charles Bailey, **French Secondary Education, 1763–90: the secularization of Ex-Jesuit colleges* (Philadelphia, 1978) (American Philosophical Society); and Charles McClelland, *State, Society and University in Germany, 1700–1914* (Cambridge, 1980). As indicated in the text, Daniel Roche's thesis *Le Siècle des lumières en Province: académies et académiciens provinciaux, 1680–1789* (2 vols.: Paris and The Hague, 1978) is a landmark in social and cultural history. Two other excellent books on the academies are Roger Hahn, *The Anatomy of a Scientific Instition: the Paris Academy of Sciences, 1666–1803* (Berkeley, Calif., 1971), and Eric Cochrane. *Tradition and Enlightenment in the Tuscan Academies, 1690–1800* (Chicago, 1961). For the world of science in general see Herbert Butterfield, **The Origins of Modern Science* (New York, 1957) (Free), and Charles C. Gillispie, **The Edge of Objectivity* (Princeton, 1966) (Princeton).

As an approach to the professions W. J. Reader, *Professional Men: the rise of the professional classes in nineteenth century England* (London, 1966) is suggestive for our period as well. The exemplary monograph in this area is Lenard Berlanstein, *The Barristers of Toulouse in the Eighteenth Century* (Baltimore, 1975). Other valuable studies of the legal profession include Robert Robson, *The Attorney in Eighteenth Century England* (Cambridge, 1959); Paul Lucas, "A Collective Biography of Students and Barristers of Lincoln's Inn, 1680–1804," *Journal of Modern History*, Vol. XLVI (1974); Richard Kagan, "Law Students and Legal Careers in Eighteenth-Century France," *Past and Present*, No. 69 (1975); and Philip Dawson, "The Bourgeoisie de Robe in 1789," *French Historical Studies*, Vol. IV (1965). On the medical profession see Lester King, *The Medical World of the Eighteenth Century* (Chicago, 1958); Michel Foucault, **The Birth of the Clinic* (New York, 1975) (Random); the Summer 1977 issue of the *Journal of Social History* devoted to medicine; and **Medicine and Society in France: Selections from the "Annales"*, ed. by R. Forster and O. Ranum (Baltimore, 1980) (Johns Hopkins).

Popular culture has been more extensively studied for earlier and later periods than for the eighteenth century. A great deal of the research for the entire early modern period, however, is summarized and forcefully interpreted in Peter Burke's splendid *Popular Culture in Early Modern Europe* (New York, 1978 (Harper & Row). William Beik's review article, "Searching for Popular Culture in Early Modern France," *Journal of Modern History*, Vol. XLIX (1977), constitutes a useful introduction as do several essays in *The Wolf and the Lamb: Popular Culture in France from the Old Regime to the Twentieth Century*, ed. by J. Beauroy, M. Bertrand, and E. Gargan (Stanford, Calif., 1976) (Anma Library). The best charted area so far is popular literature: Geneviève Bollème, *La Bibliothèque bleue* (Paris, 1971) provides a collection of excerpts as well as a reliable interpretation. With Bernard Capp's painstaking *English Almanacs, 1500–1800: astrology and the popular press* (Ithaca, N.Y., 1979) the field has taken a big stride forward. Festivals and other forms of collective behavior have also received a good deal of attention recently, as in Yves-Marie Bercé, *Fête et révolte: des mentalités populaires de XVIe au XVIIIe siècle* (Paris, 1976). On popular sociability we have the landmark of Maurice Agulhon, covering both elites and popular classes, *Pénitents et Francs-Maçons de l'ancienne Provence: essai sur la sociabilité méridionale* (Paris, 1968), while for sport and recreation there is Robert Malcolmson, *Popular Recreation in English Society, 1700–1850* (Cambridge, 1973).

THE ENLIGHTENMENT

Most of the major works of the Enlightenment are available in English, particularly the writings of Voltaire, Montesquieu, and Rousseau. The best short introduction to the Enlightenment is Norman Hampson, *A Cultural History of the Enlightenment* (New York, 1968). Peter Gay's *The Enlightenment: an interpretation* (2 vols.: New York, 1966–69) (Norton) is the most comprehensive and lively synthesis, and is also notable for its exhaustive bibliographical essay. Paul Hazard has written extensively on intellectual history, though his first volume,* *The European Mind, 1680–1715* (New Haven, 1935) (New American Library) is of more fundamental importance than the sequel, *European Thought in the Eighteenth Century: from Montesquieu to Lessing* (New Haven, 1946). Among the books that deal with the thought of the Enlightenment in a more abstract way are Ernst Cassirer, *The Philosophy of the Enlightenment* (Boston, 1955) (Princeton); Alfred Cobban, *In Search of Humanity* (London, 1960); and Lester Crocker, *An Age of Crisis: man and world in eighteenth-century thought* (Baltimore, 1959), whose critical views may be compared to Gay's more favorable treatment. Books treating particular national cultures include Leslie Stephen's classic *History of English Thought in the Eighteenth Century* (London, 1876); Gladys Bryson, *Man and Society: the Scottish inquiry of the eighteenth century* (New York, 1945); Kingsley Martin, *The Rise of French Liberal Thought* (New York, 1954); Leonard Krieger, *The German Idea of Freedom* (Boston, 1957) (University of Chicago); F. Hertz, *The Development of the German Public Mind; a social history of German political sentiments, aspirations, and ideas* (London, 1957); Part I of Klaus Esptein, *The Genesis of German Conservatism* (Princeton, 1966) (Princeton); Robert A. Kann, *A Study in Austrian Intellectual History: late Baroque to Romanticism* (London, 1960); and Franco Venturi, *Italy and the Enlightenment: studies in a cosmopolitan century* (London, 1972).

Of the plentiful studies of individuals or small groups, the following constitute some of the notable contributions: Robert Schackleton, *Montesquieu, a critical biography* (London, 1961); Ira O. Wade, *The Intellectual Development of Voltaire* (Princeton, 1969); Peter Gay, *Voltaire's Politics: the poet as realist* (Princeton, 1959); René Pomeau, *La Religion de Voltaire* (Paris, 1956); Ronald Grimsely, *Jean D'Alembert, 1717–83* (Oxford, 1963); Arthur Wilson's definitive *Diderot* (New York, 1972); Jacques Proust, *Diderot et l'Encyclopédie* (Paris, 1962); John Lough, *The Encyclopédie* (New York, 1971); Raymond Birn, *Pierre Rousseau and the Philosophes of Bouillon* (Geneva, 1964); David W. Smith, *Helvétius, a Study in Persecution* (Oxford, 1965); Alan Kors, *D'Holbach's Coterie: an Enlightenment in Paris* (Princeton, 1976); Keith Baker, *Condorcet, from Natural Philosophy to Social Mathematics* (Chicago, 1975); Ernst Cassirer, **The Question of Jean-Jacques Rousseau* (New York, 1954) (Indiana); Judith Shklar, *Men and Citizens: a study of Rousseau's social theory* (London, 1969). For two anti-philosophes see Alfred Cobban, *Edmund Burke and the Revolt against the Eighteenth Century* (New York, 1960), and Darlene Levy, *The Ideas and Careers of Simon-Nicolas-Henri-Linguet* (Urbana, Ill., 1980).

Among thematic studies, the following are of particular interest: Franco Venturi, *Utopia and Reform in the Enlightenment* (Cambridge, 1971); Henry Vyverberg, *Historical Pessimism in the French Enlightenment* (Cambridge, Mass., 1958); Frank Manuel, *The Eighteenth Century Confronts the Gods* (New York, 1967); *The Economics of Physiocracy: essays and translations*, ed. by Ronald Meek (Cambridge, Mass., 1963); Elizabeth Fox-Genovese, *The Origins of Physiocracy* (Ithaca, N.Y., 1976); J. Mackrell, *The Attack on "Feudalism" in Eighteenth Century France* (London, 1973); Harry Payne, *The Philosophes and the People* (New Haven, 1976); Harvey Chisick, *The Limits of Reform in the Enlightenment: attitudes toward the education of the lower classes in Eighteenth-Century France* (Princeton, 1980).

On the circulation of books, censorship, and smuggling, the work of Robert Darnton has opened up broad new vistas: "Reading, Writing, and Publishing in Eighteenth-Century France," *Daedalus* (Winter 1971); "The Trade in Taboo," in *The Widening Circle: the diffusion of literature in the 18th century*, ed. by P. Korshin (Philadelphia, 1976); "The World of the Underground Booksellers in the Old Regime," in E. Hinrichs *et. al.*, *Von Ancien Régime zur Französischen Revolution* (Göttingen, 1978); and *The Business of Enlightenment: a publishing history of the Encyclopedia* (Cambridge, Mass., 1979). See also David Pottinger, *The French Book Trade in the Ancien Régime, 1500–1789* (Cambridge, Mass., 1958). On Austria see Wangermann, and Paul Bernard, *Jesuits and Jacobins: Enlightenment and Enlightened Despotism in Austria* (Urbana, Ill., 1971).

There are several studies of the petering-out of the Enlightenment, including Henri Brunschwig, *Enlightenment and Romanticism in Eighteenth-Century Prussia* (Chicago, 1974); Ernst Wangermann, *From Joseph II to the Jacobin Trials* (Oxford, 1959); Louis Trénard, *Lyon, de l'Encyclopédia au Pré-romantisme* (2 vols.: Lyon, 1958); Robert Darnton, **Mesmerism: the end of the enlightenment in France* (Cambridge, Mass., 1968) (Schocken) and his important article, "The High Enlightenment and the Low Life of Literature in Pre-revolutionary France," *Past and Present*, No. 51 (May 1971). For an up-to-date review of scholarship on the Enlightenment see

Part II of M. S. Anderson's *Historians and Eighteenth Century Europe, 1715–1789* (Oxford, 1979).

CHURCH AND RELIGION

Gerald R. Cragg, *The Church and the Age of Reason, 1648–1789* (London, 1966) (Penguin) is the ideal introduction to its subject, along with Jean Delumeau, *Le Catholicisme entre Luther et Voltaire* (Paris, 1971). For France the early chapters of André Latreille, *L'Eglise Catholique et la Révolution française*, Vol. I (Paris, 1946) offer a balanced overview. As indicated in the text, John McManners, *French Ecclesiastical Society under the Ancien Régime: a study of Angers in the Eighteenth Century* (Manchester, 1960) is a model case study. Other valuable works include Timothy Tackett, *Priest and Parish in Eighteenth-Century France . . . in a diocese of Dauphiné, 1750–1791* (Princeton, 1977); Louis Greenbaum, *Talleyrand, Statesman-Priest: the agent-general of the clergy and the Church of France at the end of the Old Regime* (Washington, 1970); and Dale VanKley, *The Jansenists and the Expulsion of the Jesuits from France, 1757–1765* (New Haven, 1975). On the inroads of secularism see R. R. Palmer's excellent study in intellectual history: *Catholics and Unbelievers in Eighteenth Century France* (Princeton, 1939), and Michel Vovelle's pioneering work on changing religious mentalities: *Piété baroque et dechristianisation en Provence au XVIIIᵉ siècle* (Paris, 1973).

On German Protestantism see A. L. Drummond, *German Protestantism since Luther* (London, 1951) and Koppel Pinson, *Pietism as a Factor in the Rise of German Nationalism* (New York, 1934), and on the Orthodox Church in Russia see Gregory Freeze, *The Russian Levites: Parish Clergy in the Eighteenth Century* (Cambridge, Mass., 1977). The standard work on religion in England is Norman Sykes, *Church and State in England in the Eighteenth Century* (Hamden, Conn., 1934). My own understanding of Methodism and other evangelical movements has profited greatly from R. A. Knox, *Enthusiasm* (Oxford, 1950), along with Bernard Semmel, *The Methodist Revolution* (New York, 1973). See also F. Baker, *John Wesley and the Church of England* (London, 1970), and for the "Halévy thesis," Elie Halévy, *The Birth of Methodism in England* (Chicago, 1971). There are several first-rate studies of religious minorities and the issue of toleration: David Bien, *The Calas Affair* (Princeton, 1960); Burdette C. Poland, *French Protestantism and the French Revolution, 1685–1815* (Princeton, 1953); C. H. O'Brien, *Ideas of Religious Toleration at the time of Joseph II* (Philadelphia, 1969) (American Philosophical Society); Arthur Hertzberg, *The French Enlightenment and the Jews* (New York, 1968); and the early chapters of Jacob Katz, *Out of the Ghetto: the social background of Jewish Emancipation, 1770–1870* (Cambridge, Mass., 1973) (Schocken).

THE ROAD TO REVOLUTION

The towering work on political conflict in late eighteenth-century Europe is R. R. Palmer's *The Age of the Democratic Revolution: a political history of Europe and America, 1760–1800*, Vol. I: *The Challenge* (Princeton, 1959). More than a comparative study, it is a convincing interpretation of the period. Since the appearance of this work there have been a few specialized studies which supplement its findings, including Simon Schama's masterful *Patriots and Liberators: Revolution in the Netherlands, 1780–1813* (New York, 1977); Daniel Stone, *Polish Politics and National Reform 1775–1788* (New York, 1976); Béla Kiraly, *Hungary in the late Eighteenth Century* (New York, 1969); T. C. W. Blanning, *Reform and Revolution in Mainz, 1743–1803* (Cambridge, 1974).

Two concise introductions to the American colonial rebellion are Ian R. Christie, *Crisis of Empire: Great Britain and the American Colonies, 1754–1783* (New York, 1966) (Norton) and Edmund Morgan, *The Birth of the Republic, 1763–1789* (Chicago, 1956) (University of Chicago). Some of the books that have particular relevance to the argument presented here are Edmund Morgan, *The Stamp Act Crisis* (Chapel Hill, N.C., 1963) (Macmillan); Bernhard Knollenberg, *Origin of the American Revolution, 1759–1766* (New York, 1960); John Shy, *Toward Lexington: the role of the British Army in the coming of the American Revolution* (Princeton, 1965); and Bernard Bailyn, *The Ordeal of Thomas Hutchinson* (Cambridge, Mass., 1974). On the ideological origins of the rebellion see Bailyn's *The Ideological Origins of the American Revolution* (Cambridge, Mass., 1967) (Harvard University), and Gary Wills, *Inventing America: Jefferson's Declaration of Independence* (New York, 1978) (Random). Reform and radicalism back in Britain are surveyed in Ian Christie, *Wilkes, Wyvill, and Reform: the parliamentary reform movement in British politics, 1760–1785* (London, 1962). See also Herbert Butterfield, *George III, Lord North, and the People* (London, 1949); George Rudé, *Wilkes and Liberty* (Oxford, 1962); and Eugene C. Black, *The Association: British extraparliamentary political organization, 1769–1793* (Cambridge, Mass., 1963). The period has recently been reevaluated in John Brewer's *Party Ideology and Popular Politics at the Accession of George III* (London, 1976).

Though it will someday have to be replaced in the light of accumulating research, Georges Lefebvre's *The Coming of the French Revolution* (New York, 1957) (Princeton), written in 1939, remains a classic introduction to the origins and onset of the Revolution. Much of this subsequent research is discussed in Michel Vovelle, *La Chute de la Monarchie, 1787–92* (Paris, 1972), while a number of contributions are collected in the following volumes: *New Perspectives on the French Revolution*, ed. by Jeffry Kaplow (New York, 1965); *French Society and the Revolution: essays from Past and Present*, ed. by D. Johnson (Cambridge, 1976); and E. Hinrichs et. al., *Von Ancien Régime zur Französischen Revolution* (Göttingen, 1978). Among the books that help to illuminate the crisis are Douglas Dakin, *Turgot and the Ancien Régime in France* (New York, 1939); William Doyle, *The Parlement of Bordeaux and the end of the Old Regime* (New York, 1974); John Bosher, *French Finances 1770–1795: from business to bureaucracy* (Cambridge, 1971); Robert Harris, *Necker, Reform Statesman of the Ancien Regime* (Berkeley, 1979); and Jean Egret, *The French Pre-Revolution, 1787–1788* (Chicago, 1978), which meticulously analyzes the precipitating events. An important computer analysis of the *cahiers* is the basis of George Taylor's "Revolutionary and Nonrevolutionary content in the cahiers of 1789," *French Historical Studies*, Vol. VII (Fall 1972), while Beatrice Hyslop's *A guide to the General Cahiers of 1789, with the texts of unedited cahiers* (New York, 1936) is an introduction to that unique historical source. For the stirrings of popular unrest in Paris consult the works of George Rudé mentioned earlier, while for the countryside reference should be made to a second classic account by Georges Lefebvre, *The Great Fear of 1789* (New York, 1973) (Random).

For interpretation of the Revolution's origins one should start with Alexis de Tocqueville's classic work of 1856, *The Old Regime and the French Revolution* (New York, 1955) (Cambridge, also Doubleday). A convenient review of the historiography is provided by John McManners, "The Historiography of the Revolution," *New Cambridge Modern History*, Vol. VIII. Recently there has been considerable dispute in this area. For a Marxist view see Albert Soboul, *A Short History of the French Revolution* (Berkeley, Calif. 1977) (University of California); for an Anglo-Saxon revisionist see Alfred Cobban, *The Social Interpretation of the French Revolution* (Cambridge, 1964) (Cambridge); for a French revisionist see François Furet, *Penser la Révolution française* (Paris, 1978). A collection of these and other conflicting viewpoints has been edited by Ralph Greenlaw in *The Social Origins of the French Revolution* (New York, 1975) (Heath). J. M. Roberts's short interpretive synthesis, *The French Revolution* (Oxford, 1978) (Oxford) navigates nicely through this debate, but is far from being the last word.

Index

absolutism:
  aristocracy and, 5, 8, 28–30, 74, 86–91, 248, 273, 306
  armies needed for, 4, 15, 36, 37–39, 59, 316
  Church and, 4–6, 271, 276–77
  enlightened, 249–51, 267–70
  taxation power and, 4, 10, 14
academies, 203–8
  national, 11, 203–5, 263
  provincial, 205–8
Addison, Joseph, 190–91
Africa, see slavery, slave trade
Angers, 281–82
Age of Louis XIV, The (Voltaire), 237
agrarian ecosystems, 67–71, 135–39, 326
agrarian reform, 73–79, 277, 302
Aix-la-Chapelle, Treaty of, 45
Alembert, Jean Le Rond d', 241, 243–44
Alexis Petrovich, son of Peter the Great, 25
almanacs, 223–24
American Revolution, 306–10, 316, 332
Amsterdam, 283, 314, 317
Anglicans, see Church of England
Anna Ivanovna, empress of Russia, 25, 303
Anti-Machiavel (Frederick II), 17
apothecaries, 213–14
apprenticeship system, 99, 210
architecture, royal patronage of, 11
aristocracy, 38, 39, 79–91, 117, 220, 240, 278, 295
  absolutism and, 5, 8, 28–30, 74, 86–91, 248, 273, 305
  additions to, 10–11, 85, 94, 95, 322, 323–24
  in army, 54–55, 59, 81–82, 90, 323, 324
  arts supported by, 92, 184
  commercial activity of, 82, 85, 91, 93
  commoners' perception of, 7–8, 334–37
  education of, 200–201, 226
  intellectuals in, 206–7, 231
  land ownership of, 60–61, 65, 75, 80, 83–84, 91
  nobility of the robe as, 93, 323, 334
  patriciate as, 93, 315

  privileges of, 61, 65–66, 71, 81, 89, 91, 175–77
  taxation of, 10, 62, 75, 77, 80, 85, 88, 89, 91, 327
  types of, 79–81, 92, 93, 323–24
  urban, 92–94
  "Westernization" of, 23–24, 319–20
Aristotle, 198
Arkwright, Sir Richard, 142, 144
armies, 51–59
  absolutism sustained by, 4, 15, 36, 37–39, 59, 316
  aristocracy in, 54–55, 59, 81–82, 90, 323, 324
  commoners in, 52, 53, 54, 55, 59, 324
  desertion from, 53, 57
  infantry in, 56–57
  recruitment for, 24, 52–55, 62
  siege warfare and, 58–59
  standing, 51, 52–53
  technology in, 56–57
Arminianism, 298, 299
artillery, 59
artisans, 98–102, 140, 226, 241–42, 325
asiento agreements, 127
Assembly of Notables, 333
atheism, 233, 234, 235
attorneys, 210–11
Australia, penal colonies in, 167
Austria, 2, 4, 18–23, 39, 177, 188, 189, 227, 318–19
  agrarian reform in, 75–78, 277
  Enlightenment in, 267–68
  Poland partitioned by, 49, 321–22
  religious differences in, 18, 276–77, 283–84
  in Seven Years' War, 41–44
autos-da-fé, 283, 288

Babeuf, François Noël, 207
Bach, Johann Sebastian, 188
Baden, Treaty of, 39
Bailyn, Bernard, 309
balance of power, 37, 38, 40–41, 50
banking, 122–23
Barbados, 132
barristers, 210–11
Bastille, 164, 165
Bavaria, 4, 20

Gustavus III, king of Sweden, 27
Gutton, Jean-Pierre, 151n, 156

Habsburg Monarchy, *see* Austria
Habsburgs, Spanish, 2, 18, 39
Haiti (Saint Domingue), 132, 134, 135
Halévy, Elie, 300
Halle, University of, 202, 296
Hammond, J. L. and Barbara, 138
Hanoverian monarchy, 30, 33–35, 40, 42
Harris, James, Lord, 316, 317
Hay, Douglas, 168, 177
Haydn, Franz Joseph, 188, 189
Helvétius, Claude Adrien, 243, 261
Henry, Louis, 113
Herder, Johann Gottfried von, 221, 296
historians, 323
    nineteenth-century, 34–35, 36–37
Historical and Critical Dictionary
    (Bayle), 232, 264
History of the Two Indies, The (Raynal),
    245–46, 262
Hogarth, William, 97, 170, 220
Hohenzollerns, 13–15, 283, 284
Holbach, Paul Henri Dietrich, baron d',
    187, 234, 288
Holy Roman Empire, 2–4, 13, 37, 283–
    84
"hometowns," 97–98, 99
hôpitals généraux, 152–53, 154, 158
Hôtel des Invalides, 53, 54
House of Commons, 31–33
House of Lords, 83, 297
Hufton, Olwen, 150n, 151, 162
Huguenots, 232, 284–86
Hume, David, 242–43
Hungary, 5, 18–21, 80–81

illegitimacy, 113, 114, 115, 159–62
India, 44, 46, 48, 125
indigence, 150–59
    criminality and, 153–54, 172, 173
    defined, 150
    religious institutions for, 151–53, 154,
    156
    state institutions for, 153–59
infanticide, 162–63
"influence," 31, 310
Inquisition, 264–66, 272, 273, 283, 289
intendants, 8–10, 21, 326
"intermediary corps," 6, 8
international congresses, 40
international rivalry, 1, 36–50
    for colonies, 40, 41, 44–47
    state building influenced by, 36–39
Ireland, 112
Italy, 189
    Inquisition in, 272, 283, 289
    weakness of, 4, 40, 41
    see also individual Italian states

Jacobites, 34
James I, king of England, 83

Jansenism, 275
Jenner, Edward, III
Jesuits (Society of Jesus), 18, 197, 235
    abolition of order, 276
    expulsions of, 273–76
Jews:
    Ashkenazic, 287
    occupations permitted to, 28, 288
    popular image of, 222, 288
    Sephardic, 288
    toleration of, 287–90, 322
Johnson, Samuel, 191, 192–93, 195, 297
Joseph II, Holy Roman emperor:
    agrarian reform of, 76–78, 302
    as enlightened despot, 21–23, 91, 156,
    227, 267–68, 318–19
    religious reforms of, 276–77, 284,
    286–87, 290
Joseph Andrews (Fielding), 196
Journey from St. Petersburg to Moscow
    (Radischev), 270
journeymen, 99–102
judicial system, 163–65, 178
    constabulary in, 154, 155, 163, 164–
    65
    judges in, 164, 165
    juries in, 165–66, 307, 310
    manorial, 62, 63, 66, 77, 163
    prisons in, 164, 170–71
    vice-admiralty courts in, 307, 310
    see also censorship; *Parlements*
Junkers, 13

Kant, Immanuel, 202, 231
Kaunitz, Count Wenzel Anton von, 41–
    44, 284
Kay, John, 141, 144
Kosciuszko, Thaddeus, 322
Kuchuk Kainarji, Treaty of, 38

Labrousse, Ernest, 120
Landau, Battle of, 58
Länder, 18
Landräte, 14–15, 21
Latin language, 183, 184, 198
Lavoisier, Antoine, 204
law, 37, 166
    game laws, 66, 175–77, 336
    philosophes' views on, 247–48, 257–
    58
    practitioners of, 209–11, 337
    state control of, 4, 177–78
    study of, 200–201, 210–11
    see also crime; judicial system; pun-
    ishment
Law, John, 122, 123
Lebrun, Charles, 11
Leopold I, Holy Roman emperor, 19
Leopold II, Holy Roman emperor, 22, 23,
    78, 156, 250, 321
Lessing, Gotthold, 266–67, 288
Letter Concerning Toleration (Locke),
    288

90 04